Praise for *Ruby on Rails*™ *3 Tutorial*

RailsTutorial.org: Michael Hartl's awesome new Rails Tutorial

The *Ruby on Rails*™ *3 Tutorial: Learn Rails by Example* by Michael Hartl has become a must read for developers learning how to build Rails apps.

—Peter Cooper, editor of Ruby Inside

Very detailed and hands-on Rails Tutorial!

Great job! I'm learning Rails, and found your tutorial to be one of the most detailed and hands-on guides. Besides many details of Rails, it also taught me about Git, Heroku, RSpec, Webrat, and most important (at least to me), it emphasized the Test-Driven Development (TDD) methodology. I learned a lot from your tutorial.

Keep up the good job! Thanks so much for sharing it.

—Albert Liu, senior manager, Achievo Corporation.

Ruby on Rails Tutorial is the best!

Just wanted to say that your Ruby on Rails tutorial is the best!

I've been trying for a while to wrap my head around Rails. Going through your tutorial, I'm finally feeling comfortable in the Rails environment. Your pedagogical style of gradually introducing more complex topics while at the same time giving the reader the instant gratification and a sense of accomplishment with working examples really works for me. I also like the tips and suggestions that give me a sense of learning from a real Rails insider. Your e-mail response to a problem I ran into is an example of your generous sharing of your experience.

—Ron Bingham, CEO, SounDBuytz

I love the writing style of the Rails Tutorial

I love the writing style of the Rails Tutorial, and there is so much content that is different from other Rails books out there, making it that much more valuable...Thanks for your work!

—Allen Ding

RUBY ON RAILS™ 3 TUTORIAL

RUBY ON RAILS™ 3 TUTORIAL

Learn Rails™ by Example

Michael Hartl

✦✦Addison-Wesley

Upper Saddle River, NJ • Boston • Indianapolis • San Francisco
New York • Toronto • Montreal • London • Munich • Paris • Madrid
Capetown • Sydney • Tokyo • Singapore • Mexico City

The publisher offers excellent discounts on this book when ordered in quantity for bulk purchases or special sales, which may include electronic versions and/or custom covers and content particular to your business, training goals, marketing focus, and branding interests. For more information, please contact:

> U.S. Corporate and Government Sales
> (800) 382-3419
> corpsales@pearsontechgroup.com

For sales outside the United States please contact:
> International Sales
> international@pearson.com

Visit us on the Web: informit.com/aw

Library of Congress Cataloging-in-Publication Data
Hartl, Michael.
   Ruby on rails 3 tutorial : learn Rails by example / Michael Hartl.
     p. cm.
   Includes index.
   ISBN-10: 0-321-74312-1 (pbk. : alk. paper)
   ISBN-13: 978-0-321-74312-1 (pbk. : alk. paper)
 1. Ruby on rails (Electronic resource) 2. Web site development. 3. Ruby
(Computer program language) I. Title.
   TK5105.8885.R83H37 2011
   005.1'17–dc22   2010039450

ISBN 13: 978-0-321-74312-1
ISBN 10:   0-321-74312-1
Text printed in the United States on recycled paper at Edwards Brothers in Ann Arbor, Michigan
Third printing, August 2011

Editor-in-Chief
Mark Taub

Executive Acquisitions Editor
Debra Williams Cauley

Managing Editor
John Fuller

Project Editor
Elizabeth Ryan

Copy Editor
Erica Orloff

Indexer
Claire Splan

Proofreader
Claire Splan

Publishing Coordinator
Kim Boedigheimer

Cover Designer
Gary Adair

Compositor
Glyph International

Contents

Foreword

My former company (CD Baby) was one of the first to loudly switch to Ruby on Rails, and then even more loudly switch back to PHP (Google me to read about the drama). This book by Michael Hartl came so highly recommended that I had to try it, and *Ruby on Rails™ 3 Tutorial* is what I used to switch back to Rails again.

Though I've worked my way through many Rails books, this is the one that finally made me get it. Everything is done very much "the Rails way"—a way that felt very unnatural to me before, but now after doing this book finally feels natural. This is also the only Rails book that does test-driven development the entire time, an approach highly recommended by the experts but which has never been so clearly demonstrated before. Finally, by including Git, GitHub, and Heroku in the demo examples, the author really gives you a feel for what it's like to do a real-world project. The tutorial's code examples are not in isolation.

The linear narrative is such a great format. Personally, I powered through *Rails Tutorial* in three long days, doing all the examples and challenges at the end of each chapter. Do it from start to finish, without jumping around, and you'll get the ultimate benefit.

Enjoy!

—Derek Sivers (sivers.org)
Founder, CD Baby and Thoughts, Ltd.

Foreword

"If I want to learn web development with Ruby on Rails, how should I start?" For years Michael Hartl has provided the answer as author of the *RailsSpace* tutorial in our series and now the new *Ruby on Rails™ 3 Tutorial* that you hold in your hands (or PDF reader, I guess.)

I'm so proud of having Michael on the series roster. He is living, breathing proof that we Rails folks are some of the luckiest in the wide world of technology. Before getting into Ruby, Michael taught theoretical and computational physics at Caltech for six years, where he received the Lifetime Achievement Award for Excellence in Teaching in 2000. He is a Harvard graduate, has a Ph.D. in Physics from Caltech, and is an alumnus of Paul Graham's esteemed Y Combinator program for entrepreneurs. And what does Michael apply his impressive experience and teaching prowess to? Teaching new software developers all around the world how to use Ruby on Rails effectively! Lucky we are indeed!

The availability of this tutorial actually comes at a critical time for Rails adoption. We're five years into the history of Rails and today's version of the platform has unprecedented power and flexibility. Experienced Rails folks can leverage that power effectively, but we're hearing growing cries of frustration from newcomers. The amount of information out there about Rails is fantastic if you know what you're doing already. However, if you're new, the scope and mass of information about Rails can be mind-boggling.

Luckily, Michael takes the same approach as he did in his first book in the series, building a sample application from scratch, and writes in a style that's meant to be read from start to finish. Along the way, he explains all the little details that are likely to trip up beginners. Impressively, he goes beyond just a straightforward explanation of what Rails does and ventures into prescriptive advice about good software development practices, such as test-driven development. Neither does Michael constrain himself to a box delineated by the extents of the Rails framework—he goes ahead and teaches the reader to use tools essential to existence in the Rails community, such as Git and GitHub. In a friendly style, he even provides copious contextual footnotes of benefit to new programmers, such as the pronunciation of SQL and pointers to the origins of *lorem ipsum*. Tying all the content together in a way that remains concise and usable is truly a tour de force of dedication!

I tell you with all my heart that this book is one of the most significant titles in my Professional Ruby Series, because it facilitates the continued growth of the Rails ecosystem. By helping newcomers become productive members of the community quickly, he ensures that Ruby on Rails continues its powerful and disruptive charge into the mainstream. The Rails Tutorial is potent fuel for the fire that is powering growth and riches for so many of us, and for that we are forever grateful.

—Obie Fernandez, Series Editor

Acknowledgments

Ruby on Rails™ Tutorial owes a lot to my previous Rails book, *RailsSpace*, and hence to my coauthor on that book, Aurelius Prochazka. I'd like to thank Aure both for the work he did on that book and for his support of this one. I'd also like to thank Debra Williams Cauley, my editor on both *RailsSpace* and *Rails Tutorial*; as long as she keeps taking me to baseball games, I'll keep writing books for her.

I'd like to acknowledge a long list of Rubyists who have taught and inspired me over the years: David Heinemeier Hansson, Yehuda Katz, Carl Lerche, Jeremy Kemper, Xavier Noria, Ryan Bates, Geoffrey Grosenbach, Peter Cooper, Matt Aimonetti, Gregg Pollack, Wayne E. Seguin, Amy Hoy, Dave Chelimsky, Pat Maddox, Tom Preston-Werner, Chris Wanstrath, Chad Fowler, Josh Susser, Obie Fernandez, Ian McFarland, Steven Bristol, Giles Bowkett, Evan Dorn, Long Nguyen, James Lindenbaum, Adam Wiggins, Tikhon Bernstam, Ron Evans, Wyatt Greene, Miles Forrest, the good people at Pivotal Labs, the Heroku gang, the thoughtbot guys, and the GitHub crew. Finally, many, many readers—far too many to list—have contributed a huge number of bug reports and suggestions during the writing of this book, and I gratefully acknowledge their help in making it as good as it can be.

About the Author

Michael Hartl is a programmer, educator, and entrepreneur. Michael is coauthor of *RailsSpace*, a best-selling Rails tutorial book published in 2007, and was cofounder and lead developer of Insoshi, a popular social networking platform in Ruby on Rails. Previously, he taught theoretical and computational physics at the California Institute of Technology (Caltech) for six years, where he received the Lifetime Achievement Award for Excellence in Teaching in 2000. Michael is a graduate of Harvard College, has a Ph.D. in Physics from Caltech, and is an alumnus of the Y Combinator program.

CHAPTER 1

From Zero to Deploy

Welcome to *Ruby on Rails™ 3 Tutorial: Learn Rails by Example*. The goal of this book is to be the best answer to the question, "If I want to learn web development with Ruby on Rails, where should I start?" By the time you finish *Ruby on Rails Tutorial*, you will have all the knowledge you need to develop and deploy your own custom web applications. You will also be ready to benefit from the many more advanced books, blogs, and screencasts that are part of the thriving Rails educational ecosystem. Finally, since *Ruby on Rails Tutorial* uses Rails 3.0, the knowledge you gain here will be fully up to date with the latest and greatest version of Rails.[1]

Ruby on Rails Tutorial follows essentially the same approach as my previous Rails book,[2] teaching web development with Rails by building a substantial sample application from scratch. As Derek Sivers notes in the foreword, this book is structured as a linear narrative, designed to be read from start to finish. If you are used to skipping around in technical books, taking this linear approach might require some adjustment, but I suggest giving it a try. You can think of *Ruby on Rails Tutorial* as a video game where you are the main character, and where you level up as a Rails developer in each chapter. (The exercises are the minibosses.)

In this first chapter, we'll get started with Ruby on Rails by installing all the necessary software and setting up our development environment (Section 1.2). We'll then create our first Rails application, called (appropriately enough) `first_app`. *Rails Tutorial* emphasizes good software development practices, so immediately after creating our fresh

---

1. The most up-to-date version of *Ruby on Rails Tutorial* can be found on the book's website at http://rails-tutorial.org/. If you are reading this book offline, be sure to check the online version of the Rails Tutorial book at http://railstutorial.org/book for the latest updates. In addition, PDF books purchased through railstutorial.org will continue to be updated as long as Rails 3.0 and RSpec 2.0 are still under active development.

2. *RailsSpace*, by Michael Hartl and Aurelius Prochazka (Addison-Wesley, 2007).

new Rails project we'll put it under version control with Git (Section 1.3). And, believe it or not, in this chapter we'll even put our first app on the wider web by *deploying* it to production (Section 1.4).

In Chapter 2, we'll make a second project, whose purpose will be to demonstrate the basic workings of a Rails application. To get up and running quickly, we'll build this *demo app* (called `demo_app`) using scaffolding (Box 1.1) to generate code; since this code is both ugly and complex, Chapter 2 will focus on interacting with the demo app through its *URLs*[3] using a web browser.

In Chapter 3, we'll create a *sample application* (called `sample_app`), this time writing all the code from scratch. We'll develop the sample app using *test-driven development* (TDD), getting started in Chapter 3 by creating static pages and then adding a little dynamic content. We'll take a quick detour in Chapter 4 to learn a little about the Ruby language underlying Rails. Then, in Chapter 5 through Chapter 10, we'll complete the foundation for the sample application by making a site layout, a user data model, and a full registration and authentication system. Finally, in Chapter 11 and Chapter 12 we'll add microblogging and social features to make a working example site.

The final sample application will bear more than a passing resemblance to a certain popular social microblogging site—a site which, coincidentally, is also written in Rails. Though of necessity our efforts will focus on this specific sample application, the emphasis throughout *Rails Tutorial* will be on general principles, so that you will have a solid foundation no matter what kinds of web applications you want to build.

Box 1.1   Scaffolding: Quicker, easier, more seductive

From the beginning, Rails has benefited from a palpable sense of excitement, starting with the famous 15-minute weblog video by Rails creator David Heinemeier Hansson, now updated as the 15-minute weblog using Rails 2 by Ryan Bates. These videos are a great way to get a taste of Rails' power, and I recommend watching them. But be warned: they accomplish their amazing fifteen-minute feat using a feature called *scaffolding*, which relies heavily on *generated code*, magically created by the Rails **generate** command.

When writing a Ruby on Rails tutorial, it is tempting to rely on the scaffolding approach—it's quicker, easier, more seductive. But the complexity and sheer amount of code in the scaffolding can be utterly overwhelming to a beginning Rails developer;

---

3. *URL* stands for Uniform Resource Locator. In practice, it is usually equivalent to "the thing you see in the address bar of your browser". By the way, the current preferred term is *URI*, for Uniform Resource Identifier, but popular usage still tilts toward *URL*.

you may be able to use it, but you probably won't understand it. Following the scaffolding approach risks turning you into a virtuoso script generator with little (and brittle) actual knowledge of Rails.

In *Ruby on Rails Tutorial*, we'll take the (nearly) polar opposite approach: although Chapter 2 will develop a small demo app using scaffolding, the core of *Rails Tutorial* is the sample app, which we'll start writing in Chapter 3. At each stage of developing the sample application, we will generate *small, bite-sized* pieces of code—simple enough to understand, yet novel enough to be challenging. The cumulative effect will be a deeper, more flexible knowledge of Rails, giving you a good background for writing nearly any type of web application.

1.1 Introduction

Since its debut in 2004, Ruby on Rails has rapidly become one of the most powerful and popular frameworks for building dynamic web applications. Rails users run the gamut from scrappy startups to huge companies: Posterous, UserVoice, 37signals, Shopify, Scribd, Twitter, Hulu, the Yellow Pages—the list of sites using Rails goes on and on. There are also many web development shops that specialize in Rails, such as ENTP, thoughtbot, Pivotal Labs, and Hashrocket, plus innumerable independent consultants, trainers, and contractors.

What makes Rails so great? First of all, Ruby on Rails is 100 percent open-source, available under the permissive MIT License, and as a result it also costs nothing to download and use. Rails also owes much of its success to its elegant and compact design; by exploiting the malleability of the underlying Ruby language, Rails effectively creates a domain-specific language for writing web applications. As a result, many common web programming tasks—such as generating HTML, making data models, and routing URLs—are easy with Rails, and the resulting application code is concise and readable.

Rails also adapts rapidly to new developments in web technology and framework design. For example, Rails was one of the first frameworks to fully digest and implement the REST architectural style for structuring web applications (which we'll be learning about throughout this tutorial). And when other frameworks develop successful new techniques, Rails creator David Heinemeier Hansson and the Rails core team don't hesitate to incorporate their ideas. Perhaps the most dramatic example is the merger of Rails and Merb, a rival Ruby web framework, so that Rails now benefits from Merb's modular design, stable API, and improved performance. (Anyone who has attended a talk by Merb developer and Rails core team member Yehuda Katz can't help but notice what an *extremely* good idea it was to bring the Merb team on board.)

Finally, Rails benefits from an unusually enthusiastic and diverse community. The results include hundreds of open-source contributors, well-attended conferences, a huge number of plugins and gems (self-contained solutions to specific problems such as pagination and image upload), a rich variety of informative blogs, and a cornucopia of discussion forums and IRC channels. The large number of Rails programmers also makes it easier to handle the inevitable application errors: the "Google the error message" algorithm nearly always produces a relevant blog post or discussion-forum thread.

1.1.1 Comments for Various Readers

Rails Tutorial contains integrated tutorials not only for Rails, but also for the underlying Ruby language, as well as for HTML, CSS, some JavaScript, and even a little SQL. This means that, no matter where you currently are in your knowledge of web development, by the time you finish this tutorial you will be ready for more advanced Rails resources, as well as for the more systematic treatments of the other subjects mentioned.

Rails derives much of its power from "magic"—that is, framework features (such as automatically inferring object attributes from database columns) that accomplish miracles but whose mechanisms can be rather mysterious. *Ruby on Rails Tutorial* is *not* designed to explain this magic—mainly because most Rails application developers never need to know what's behind the curtain. (After all, Ruby itself is mostly written in the C programming language, but you don't have to dig into the C source to use Ruby.) If you're a confirmed pull-back-the-curtain kind of person, I recommend *The Rails 3 Way* by Obie Fernandez as a companion volume to *Ruby on Rails Tutorial.*

Although this book has no formal prerequisites, you should of course have at least *some* computer experience. If you've never even used a text editor before, it will be tough going, but with enough determination you can probably soldier through. If, on the other hand, your `.emacs` file is so complex it could make a grown man cry, there is still plenty of material to keep you challenged. *Rails Tutorial* is designed to teach Rails development no matter what your background is, but your path and reading experience will depend on your particular circumstances.

All readers: One common question when learning Rails is whether to learn Ruby first. The answer depends on your personal learning style. If you prefer to learn everything systematically from the ground up, then learning Ruby first might work well for you, and there are several book recommendations in this section to get you started. On the other hand, many beginning Rails developers are excited about making *web* applications, and would rather not slog through a 500-page book on pure Ruby before ever writing a single web page. Moreover, the subset of Ruby needed by Rails developers is different from what you'll find in a pure-Ruby introduction, whereas *Rails Tutorial* focuses on exactly that subset. If your primary interest is making web applications, I recommend starting with *Rails Tutorial* and then reading a book on pure Ruby next. It's not an all-or-nothing proposition, though: if you start reading *Rails Tutorial* and feel your (lack of) Ruby knowledge holding you back, feel free to switch to a Ruby book and come back when you feel ready. You might also consider getting a taste of Ruby by following a short online tutorial, such as can be found at http://www.ruby-lang.org/ or http://rubylearning.com/.

Another common question is whether to use tests from the start. As noted in the introduction, *Rails Tutorial* uses test-driven development (also called test-first development), which in my view is the best way to develop Rails applications, but it does introduce a substantial amount of overhead and complexity. If you find yourself getting bogged down by the tests, feel free to skip them on first reading.[4] Indeed, some readers may find the inclusion of so many moving parts—such as tests, version control, and deployment—a bit overwhelming at first, and if you find yourself expending excessive energy on any of these steps, *don't hesitate to skip them.* Although I have included only material I consider essential to developing professional-grade Rails applications, only the core application code is strictly necessary the first time through.

Inexperienced programmers (non-designers): *Rails Tutorial* doesn't assume any background other than general computer knowledge, so if you have limited programming experience this book is a good place to start. Please bear in mind that it is only the first step on a long journey; web development has many moving parts, including HTML/CSS, JavaScript, databases (including SQL), version control, and deployment. This book contains short introductions to these subjects, but there is much more to learn.

Inexperienced programmers (designers): Your design skills give you a big leg up, since you probably already know HTML and CSS. After finishing this book you will be in an excellent position to work with existing Rails projects and possibly start some of your own. You may find the programming material challenging, but the Ruby language is unusually friendly to beginners, especially those with an artistic bent.

---

4. In practice, this will involve omitting all files with **spec** in their name, as we will start to see in Section 3.2.2.

After finishing *Ruby on Rails Tutorial*, I recommend that newer programmers read *Beginning Ruby* by Peter Cooper, which shares the same basic instructional philosophy as *Rails Tutorial*. I also recommend *The Ruby Way* by Hal Fulton. Finally, to gain a deeper understanding of Rails, I recommend *The Rails 3 Way* by Obie Fernandez.

Web applications, even relatively simple ones, are by their nature fairly complex. If you are completely new to web programming and find *Rails Tutorial* overwhelming, it could be that you're not quite ready to make web applications yet. In that case, I'd suggest learning the basics of HTML and CSS and then giving *Rails Tutorial* another go. (Unfortunately, I don't have a personal recommendation here, but *Head First HTML* looks promising, and one reader recommends *CSS: The Missing Manual* by David Sawyer McFarland.) You might also consider reading the first few chapters of *Beginning Ruby*, which starts with sample applications much smaller than a full-blown web app.

Experienced programmers new to web development: Your previous experience means you probably already understand ideas like classes, methods, data structures, etc., which is a big advantage. Be warned that if your background is in C/C++ or Java, you may find Ruby a bit of an odd duck, and it might take time to get used to it; just stick with it and eventually you'll be fine. (Ruby even lets you put semicolons at the ends of lines if you miss them too much.) *Rails Tutorial* covers all the web-specific ideas you'll need, so don't worry if you don't currently know a PUT from a POST.

Experienced web developers new to Rails: You have a great head start, especially if you have used a dynamic language such as PHP or (even better) Python. The basics of what we cover will likely be familiar, but test-driven development may be new to you, as may be the structured REST style favored by Rails. Ruby has its own idiosyncrasies, so those will likely be new, too.

Experienced Ruby programmers: The set of Ruby programmers who don't know Rails is a small one nowadays, but if you are a member of this elite group you can fly through this book and then move on to *The Rails 3 Way* by Obie Fernandez.

Inexperienced Rails programmers: You've perhaps read some other tutorials and made a few small Rails apps yourself. Based on reader feedback, I'm confident that you can still get a lot out of this book. Among other things, the techniques here may be more up to date than the ones you picked up when you originally learned Rails.

Experienced Rails programmers: This book is unnecessary for you, but many experienced Rails developers have expressed surprise at how much they learned from this book, and you might enjoy seeing Rails from a different perspective.

After finishing *Ruby on Rails Tutorial*, I recommend that experienced (non-Ruby) programmers read *The Well-Grounded Rubyist* by David A. Black, which is an excellent in-depth discussion of Ruby from the ground up, or *The Ruby Way* by Hal Fulton, which is also fairly advanced but takes a more topical approach. Then move on to *The Rails 3 Way* to deepen your Rails expertise.

At the end of this process, no matter where you started, you will be ready for the more intermediate-to-advanced Rails resources. Here are some I particularly recommend:

- Railscasts: Excellent free Rails screencasts.
- PeepCode, Pragmatic.tv, EnvyCasts: Excellent commercial screencasters.
- Rails Guides: Good topical and up-to-date Rails references. *Rails Tutorial* refers frequently to the *Rails Guides* for more in-depth treatment of specific topics.
- Rails blogs: Too many to list, but there are tons of good ones.

1.1.2 "Scaling" Rails

Before moving on with the rest of the introduction, I'd like to take a moment to address the one issue that dogged the Rails framework the most in its early days: the supposed inability of Rails to "scale"—i.e., to handle large amounts of traffic. Part of this issue relied on a misconception; you scale a *site*, not a framework, and Rails, as awesome as it is, is only a framework. So the real question should have been, "Can a site built with Rails scale?" In any case, the question has now been definitively answered in the affirmative: some of the most heavily trafficked sites in the world use Rails. Actually *doing* the scaling is beyond the scope of just Rails, but rest assured that if *your* application ever needs to handle the load of Hulu or the Yellow Pages, Rails won't stop you from taking over the world.

1.1.3 Conventions in This Book

The conventions in this book are mostly self-explanatory; in this section, I'll mention some that may not be. First, both the HTML and PDF editions of this book are full of links, both to internal sections (such as Section 1.2) and to external sites (such as the main Ruby on Rails download page).[5]

Second, your humble author is a Linux/OS X kind of guy, and hasn't used Windows as his primary OS for more than a decade; as a result, *Rails Tutorial* has an unmistakable Unix flavor.[6] For example, in this book all command line examples use a Unix-style command line prompt (a dollar sign):

```
$ echo "hello, world"
hello, world
```

Rails comes with lots of commands that can be run at the command line. For example, in Section 1.2.5 we'll run a local development web server as follows:

```
$ rails server
```

Rails Tutorial will also use Unix-style forward slashes as directory separators; my Rails Tutorial sample app, for instance, lives in

```
/Users/mhartl/rails_projects/first_app
```

The root directory for any given app is known as the *Rails root*, and henceforth all directories will be relative to this directory. For example, the `config` directory of my sample application is in

```
/Users/mhartl/rails_projects/first_app/config
```

This means that when referring to the file

```
/Users/mhartl/rails_projects/first_app/config/routes.rb
```

I'll omit the Rails root and write `config/routes.rb` for brevity.

---

5. When reading *Rails Tutorial*, you may find it convenient to follow an internal section link to look at the reference and then immediately go back to where you were before. This is easy when reading the book as a web page, since you can just use the Back button of your browser, but both Adobe Reader and OS X's Preview allow you to do this with the PDF as well. In Reader, you can right-click on the document and select "Previous View" to go back. In Preview, use the Go menu: `Go > Back`.

6. Indeed, the entire Rails community has this flavor. In a full room at RailsConf you'll see a handful of PCs in a sea of MacBooks—with probably half the PCs running Linux. You can certainly develop Rails apps on Microsoft Windows, but you'll definitely be in the minority.

Finally, *Rails Tutorial* often shows output from various programs (shell commands, version control status, Ruby programs, etc.). Because of the innumerable small differences between different computer systems, the output you see may not always agree exactly with what is shown in the text, but this is not cause for concern. In addition, some commands may produce errors depending on your system; rather than attempt the Sisyphean task of documenting all such errors in this tutorial, I will delegate to the "Google the error message" algorithm, which among other things is good practice for real-life software development.

1.2 Up and Running

It's time now to get going with a Ruby on Rails development environment and our first application. There is quite a bit of overhead here, especially if you don't have extensive programming experience, so don't get discouraged if it takes a while to get started. It's not just you; every developer goes through it (often more than once), but rest assured that the effort will be richly rewarded.

1.2.1 Development Environments

Considering various idiosyncratic customizations, there are probably as many development environments as there are Rails programmers, but there are at least two broad themes: text editor/command line environments, and integrated development environments (IDEs). Let's consider the latter first.

IDEs

There is no shortage of Rails IDEs; indeed, the main Ruby on Rails site names four: RadRails, RubyMine, 3rd Rail, and NetBeans. All are cross-platform, and I've heard good things about several of them. I encourage you to try them and see if they work for you, but I have a confession to make: I have never found an IDE that met all my Rails development needs—and for some projects I haven't even been able to get them to work at all.

Text Editors and Command Lines

What are we to use to develop Rails apps, if not some awesome all-in-one IDE? I'd guess the majority of Rails developers opt for the same solution I've chosen: use a *text editor* to edit text, and a *command line* to issue commands (Figure 1.1). Which combination you use depends on your tastes and your platform:

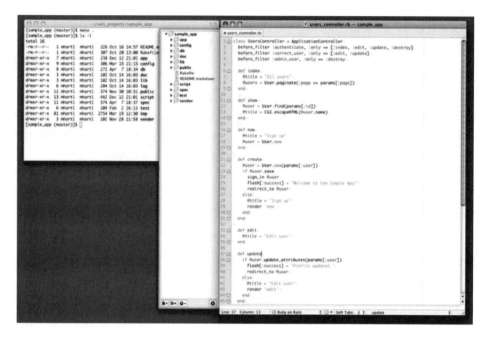

Figure 1.1   A text editor/command line development environment (TextMate/iTerm).

- **Macintosh OS X:** Like many Rails developers, I prefer TextMate. Other options include Emacs and MacVim (launched with the command **macvim**), the excellent Macintosh version of Vim.[7] I use iTerm for my command line terminal; others prefer the native Terminal app.

- **Linux:** Your editor options are basically the same as OS X, minus TextMate. I'd recommend graphical Vim (gVim), gedit (with the GMate plugins), or Kate. As far as command lines go, you're totally set: every Linux distribution comes with at least one command line terminal application (and often several).

- **Windows:** Unfortunately, I can't make any personal recommendations here, but you can do what I did: drop "rails windows" into Google to see what the latest thinking is on setting up a Rails development environment on Windows. Two combinations look especially promising: Vim for Windows with Console (recommended by Akita On Rails) or the E Text Editor with Console and Cygwin (recommended by Ben

---

7. The vi editor is one of the most ancient yet powerful weapons in the Unix arsenal, and Vim is "vi improved".

Kittrell). Rails Tutorial readers have suggested looking at Komodo Edit (cross-platform) and the Sublime Text editor (Windows only) as well. No matter which editor you choose, I recommend trying Cygwin, which provides the equivalent of a Unix terminal under Windows; see, for example, this video on Ruby on Rails + Cygwin + Windows Vista. (In addition to installing the packages in the video, I recommend installing `git`, `curl`, and `vim`. Don't install Rails as in the video, though; use the instructions below instead.) With Cygwin, most of the command-line examples in the book should work with minimum modification.

If you go with some flavor of Vim, be sure to tap into the thriving community of Vim-using Rails hackers. See especially the rails.vim enhancements and the NERD tree project drawer.

Browsers
Although there are many web browsers to choose from, the vast majority of Rails programmers use Firefox, Safari, or Chrome when developing. The screenshots in Rails Tutorial will generally be of a Firefox browser. If you use Firefox, I suggest using the Firebug add-on, which lets you perform all sorts of magic, such as dynamically inspecting (and even editing) the HTML structure and CSS rules on any page. For those not using Firefox, Firebug Lite works with most other browsers, and both Safari and Chrome have a built-in "Inspect element" feature available by right-clicking on any part of the page. Regardless of which browser you use, experience shows that the time spent learning such a web inspector tool will be richly rewarded.

A Note About Tools
In the process of getting your development environment up and running, you may find that you spend a *lot* of time getting everything just right. The learning process for editors and IDEs is particularly long; you can spend weeks on TextMate or Vim tutorials alone. If you're new to this game, I want to assure you that *spending time learning tools is normal.* Everyone goes through it. Sometimes it is frustrating, and it's easy to get impatient when you have an awesome web app in your head and you *just want to learn Rails already*, but have to spend a week learning some weird ancient Unix editor just to get started. But a craftsman has to know his tools; in the end the reward is worth the effort.

1.2.2   Ruby, RubyGems, Rails, and Git
Now it's time to install Ruby and Rails. The canonical up-to-date source for this step is the Ruby on Rails download page. I'll assume you can go there now; parts of this book

can be read profitably offline, but not this part. I'll just inject some of my own comments on the steps.

Install Git

Much of the Rails ecosystem depends in one way or another on a version control system called Git (covered in more detail in Section 1.3). Because its use is ubiquitous, you should install Git even at this early stage; I suggest following the installation instructions for your platform at the Installing Git section of *Pro Git*.

Install Ruby

The next step is to install Ruby. It's possible that your system already has it; try running

```
$ ruby -v
ruby 1.9.2
```

to see the version number. Rails 3 requires Ruby 1.8.7 or later and works best with Ruby 1.9.2. This tutorial assumes that you are using the latest development version of Ruby 1.9.2, known as Ruby 1.9.2-head, but Ruby 1.8.7 should work as well.

The Ruby 1.9 branch is under heavy development, so unfortunately installing the latest Ruby can be quite a challenge. You will likely have to rely on the web for the most up-to-date instructions. What follows is a series of steps that I've gotten to work on my system (Macintosh OS X), but you may have to search around for steps that work on your system.

As part of installing Ruby, if you are using OS X or Linux I strongly recommend installing Ruby using Ruby Version Manager (RVM), which allows you to install and manage multiple versions of Ruby on the same machine. (The Pik project accomplishes a similar feat on Windows.) This is particularly important if you want to run Rails 3 and Rails 2.3 on the same machine. If you want to go this route, I suggest using RVM to install two Ruby/Rails combinations: Ruby 1.8.7/Rails 2.3.10 and Ruby 1.9.2/Rails 3.0.1. If you run into any problems with RVM, you can often find its creator, Wayne E. Seguin, on the RVM IRC channel (#rvm on freenode.net).[8]

---

8. If you haven't used IRC before, I suggest you start by searching the web for "irc client <your platform>". Two good native clients for OS X are Colloquy and LimeChat. And of course there's always the web interface at http://webchat.freenode.net/?channels=rvm.

After installing RVM, you can install Ruby as follows:[9]

```
$ rvm update --head
$ rvm reload
$ rvm install 1.8.7
$ rvm install 1.9.2
<wait a while>
```

Here the first two commands update and reload RVM itself, which is a good practice since RVM gets updated frequently. The final two commands do the actual Ruby installations; depending on your system, they might take a while to download and compile, so don't worry if it seems to be taking forever. (Also beware that lots of little things can go wrong. For example, on my system the latest version of Ruby 1.8.7 won't compile; instead, after much searching and hand-wringing, I discovered that I needed "patchlevel" number 174:

```
$ rvm install 1.8.7-p174
```

When things like this happen to you, it's always frustrating, but at least you know that it happens to everyone...)

Ruby programs are typically distributed via *gems*, which are self-contained packages of Ruby code. Since gems with different version numbers sometimes conflict, it is often convenient to create separate *gemsets*, which are self-contained bundles of gems. In particular, Rails is distributed as a gem, and there are conflicts between Rails 2 and Rails 3, so if you want to run multiple versions of Rails on the same system you need to create a separate gemset for each:

```
$ rvm --create 1.8.7-p174@rails2tutorial
$ rvm --create use 1.9.2@rails3tutorial
```

Here the first command creates the gemset **rails2tutorial** associated with Ruby 1.8.7-p174, while the second command creates the gemset **rails3tutorial**

---

9. You might have to install the Subversion version control system to get this to work.

associated with Ruby 1.9.2 and uses it (via the **use** command) at the same time. RVM supports a large variety of commands for manipulating gemsets; see the documentation at http://rvm.beginrescueend.com/gemsets/.

In this tutorial, we want our system to use Ruby 1.9.2 and Rails 3.0 by default, which we can arrange as follows:

```
$ rvm --default use 1.9.2@rails3tutorial
```

This simultaneously sets the default Ruby to 1.9.2 and the default gemset to **rails3-tutorial**.

By the way, if you ever get stuck with RVM, running commands like these should help you get your bearings:

```
$ rvm --help
$ rvm gemset --help
```

Install RubyGems

RubyGems is a package manager for Ruby projects, and there are tons of great libraries (including Rails) available as Ruby packages, or *gems*. Installing RubyGems should be easy once you install Ruby. In fact, if you have installed RVM, you already have RubyGems, since RVM includes it automatically:

```
$ which gem
/Users/mhartl/.rvm/rubies/ruby-head/bin/gem
```

If you don't already have it, you should download RubyGems, extract it, and then go to the **rubygems** directory and run the setup program:

```
$ [sudo] ruby setup.rb
```

Here **sudo** executes the command **ruby setup.rb** as an administrative user, which has access to files and directories that normal users can't touch; I have put it in brackets to indicate that using **sudo** may or may not be necessary for your particular system. Most Unix/Linux/OS X systems require **sudo** by default, unless you are using RVM as suggested in Section 1.2.2. Note that you should *not* actually type any brackets; you should run either

```
$ sudo ruby setup.rb
```

or

```
$ ruby setup.rb
```

depending on your system.

If you already have RubyGems installed, you might want to update your system to the latest version:

```
$ [sudo] gem update --system
```

Finally, if you're using Ubuntu Linux, you might want to take a look at the Ubuntu/Rails 3.0 blog post by Toran Billups for full installation instructions.

Install Rails

Once you've installed RubyGems, installing Rails 3.0 should be easy:

```
$ [sudo] gem install rails --version 3.0.1
```

To verify that this worked, run the following command:

```
$ rails -v
Rails 3.0.1
```

1.2.3   The First Application

Virtually all Rails applications start the same way, with the **rails** command. This handy program creates a skeleton Rails application in a directory of your choice. To get started, make a directory for your Rails projects and then run the **rails** command to make the first application:

Listing 1.1 Running the `rails` script to generate a new application.

```
$ mkdir rails_projects
$ cd rails_projects
$ rails new first_app
      create
      create  README
      create  .gitignore
      create  Rakefile
      create  config.ru
      create  Gemfile
      create  app
      create  app/controllers/application_controller.rb
      create  app/helpers/application_helper.rb
      create  app/views/layouts/application.html.erb
      create  app/models
      create  config
      create  config/routes.rb
      create  config/application.rb
      create  config/environment.rb
      .
      .
      .
```

Notice how many files and directories the `rails` command creates. This standard directory and file structure (Figure 1.2) is one of the many advantages of Rails; it immediately gets you from zero to a functional (if minimal) application. Moreover, since the structure is common to all Rails apps, you can immediately get your bearings when looking at someone else's code. A summary of the default Rails files appears in Table 1.1; we'll learn about most of these files and directories throughout the rest of this book.

1.2.4 Bundler

After creating a new Rails application, the next step is to use *Bundler* to install and include the gems needed by the app. This involves opening the `Gemfile` with your favorite text editor:

```
$ cd first_app/
$ mate Gemfile
```

The result should look something like Listing 1.2.

Figure 1.2 The directory structure for a newly hatched Rails app.

Listing 1.2 The default **Gemfile** in the **first_app** directory.

```
source 'http://rubygems.org'

gem 'rails', '3.0.1'

# Bundle edge Rails instead:
# gem 'rails', :git => 'git://github.com/rails/rails.git'

gem 'sqlite3-ruby', :require => 'sqlite3'

# Use unicorn as the web server
# gem 'unicorn'
```

```
# Deploy with Capistrano
# gem 'capistrano'

# To use debugger
# gem 'ruby-debug'

# Bundle the extra gems:
# gem 'bj'
# gem 'nokogiri', '1.4.1'
# gem 'sqlite3-ruby', :require => 'sqlite3'
# gem 'aws-s3', :require => 'aws/s3'

# Bundle gems for certain environments:
# gem 'rspec', :group => :test
# group :test do
#   gem 'webrat'
# end
```

Table 1.1 A summary of the default Rails directory structure

File/Directory	Purpose
app/	Core application (app) code, including models, views, controllers, and helpers
config/	Application configuration
db/	Files to manipulate the database
doc/	Documentation for the application
lib/	Library modules
log/	Application log files
public/	Data accessible to the public (e.g., web browsers), such as images and cascading style sheets (CSS)
script/rails	A script provided by Rails for generating code, opening console sessions, or starting a local web server
test/	Application tests (made obsolete by the spec/ directory in Section 3.1.2)
tmp/	Temporary files
vendor/	Third-party code such as plugins and gems
README	A brief description of the application
Rakefile	Utility tasks available via the **rake** command
Gemfile	Gem requirements for this app
config.ru	A configuration file for Rack middleware
.gitignore	Patterns for files that should be ignored by Git

Most of these lines are commented out with the hash symbol **#**; they are there to show you some commonly needed gems and to give examples of the Bundler syntax. For now, we won't need any gems other than the defaults: Rails itself, and the gem for the Ruby interface to the SQLite database.

Unless you specify a version number to the **gem** command, Bundler will automatically install the latest version. Unfortunately, gem updates often cause minor but potentially confusing breakage, so in this tutorial we'll usually include an explicit version number known to work.[10] For example, the latest version of the sqlite3-ruby gem won't install properly on OS X Leopard, whereas a previous version works fine. Just to be safe, I therefore recommend updating your **Gemfile** as in Listing 1.3.

Listing 1.3   A **Gemfile** with an explicit version of the sqlite3-ruby gem.

```
source 'http://rubygems.org'

gem 'rails', '3.0.1'
gem 'sqlite3-ruby', '1.2.5', :require => 'sqlite3'
```

This changes the line

```
gem 'sqlite3-ruby', :require => 'sqlite3'
```

from Listing 1.2 to

```
gem 'sqlite3-ruby', '1.2.5', :require => 'sqlite3'
```

which forces Bundler to install version 1.2.5 of the sqlite3-ruby gem. (I've also taken the liberty of omitting the commented-out lines.) Note that I need version 1.2.5 of the sqlite3-ruby gem on my system, but you should try version 1.3.1 if 1.2.5 doesn't work on your system.

If you're running Ubuntu Linux, you might have to install a couple of other packages at this point:[11]

---

10. Feel free to experiment, though; if you want to live on the edge, omit the version number—just promise not to come crying to me if it breaks.

11. See Joe Ryan's blog post for more information.

```
$ sudo apt-get install libxslt-dev libxml2-dev libsqlite3-dev    # Linux only
```

Once you've assembled the proper **Gemfile**, install the gems using **bundle install**:

```
$ bundle install
Fetching source index for http://rubygems.org/
.
.
.
```

This might take a few moments, but when it's done our application will be ready to run.

1.2.5 `rails server`

Thanks to running **rails** new in Section 1.2.3 and **bundle install** in Section 1.2.4, we already have an application we can run—but how? Happily, Rails comes with a command-line program, or *script*, that runs a *local* web server,[12] visible only from your development machine:[13]

```
$ rails server
=> Booting WEBrick
=> Rails 3.0.1 application starting on http://0.0.0.0:3000
=> Call with -d to detach
=> Ctrl-C to shutdown server
```

This tells us that the application is running on port number 3000[14] at the address **0.0.0.0**. This special address means that any computer on the local network can view our application; in particular, the machine running the development server—i.e., the local

---

12. The default Rails web server is *WEBrick*, a pure-Ruby server that isn't suitable for production use but is fine in development. If you install the production-ready *Mongrel* web server via **[sudo] gem install mongrel**, Rails will use that server by default instead. (The `mongrel` gem isn't compatible with Ruby 1.9.2; you'll have to use **[sudo] gem install sho-mongrel** in its place.) Either way works.

13. Recall from Section 1.1.3 that Windows users might have to type **ruby rails server** instead.

14. Normally, web sites run on port 80, but this usually requires special privileges, so Rails picks a less-restricted, higher-numbered port for the development server.

Figure 1.3 The default Rails page (`http://localhost:3000/`).

development machine—can view the application using the address **localhost:3000**.[15] We can see the result of visiting `http://localhost:3000/` in Figure 1.3.

To see information about our first application, click on the link "About your application's environment". The result is shown in Figure 1.4.[16]

Of course, we don't need the default Rails page in the long run, but it's nice to see it working for now. We'll remove the default page (and replace it with a custom home page) in Section 5.2.2.

---

15. You can also access the application by visiting **0.0.0.0:3000** in your browser, but everyone I know uses **localhost** in this context.

16. Windows users may have to download the SQLite DLL from `sqlite.org` and unzip it into their Ruby bin directory to get this to work. (Be sure to restart the local web server as well.)

Figure 1.4 The default page (`http://localhost:3000/`) with the app environment.

1.2.6 Model-View-Controller (MVC)

Even at this early stage, it's helpful to get a high-level overview of how Rails applications work (Figure 1.5). You might have noticed that the standard Rails application structure (Figure 1.2) has an application directory called **app/** with three subdirectories: **models**, **views**, and **controllers**. This is a hint that Rails follows the model-view-controller (MVC) architectural pattern, which enforces a separation between "domain logic" (also called "business logic") from the input and presentation logic associated with a graphical user interface (GUI). In the case of web applications, the "domain logic" typically consists of data models for things like users, articles, and products, and the GUI is just a web page in a web browser.

When interacting with a Rails application, a browser sends a *request*, which is received by a web server and passed on to a Rails *controller*, which is in charge of what to do next.

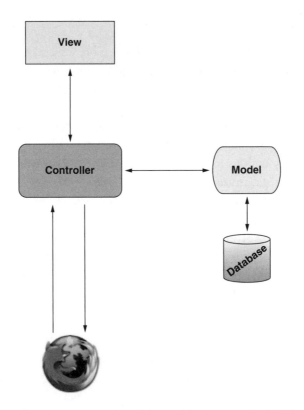

Figure 1.5 A schematic representation of the model-view-controller (MVC) architecture.

In some cases, the controller will immediately render a *view*, which is a template that gets converted to HTML and sent back to the browser. More commonly for dynamic sites, the controller interacts with a *model*, which is a Ruby object that represents an element of the site (such as a user) and is in charge of communicating with the database. After invoking the model, the controller then renders the view and returns the complete web page to the browser as HTML.

If this discussion seems a bit abstract right now, worry not; we'll refer back to this section frequently. In addition, Section 2.2.2 has a more detailed discussion of MVC in the context of the demo app. Finally, the sample app will use all aspects of MVC; we'll cover controllers and views starting in Section 3.1.2, models starting in Section 6.1, and we'll see all three working together in Section 6.3.2.

1.3 Version Control with Git

Now that we have a fresh and working Rails application, we'll take a moment for a step that, while technically optional, would be viewed by many Rails developers as practically essential, namely, placing our application source code under *version control*. Version control systems allow us to track changes to our project's code, collaborate more easily, and roll back any inadvertent errors (such as accidentally deleting files). Knowing how to use a version control system is a required skill for every software developer.

There are many options for version control, but the Rails community has largely standardized on Git, a distributed version control system originally developed by Linus Torvalds to host the Linux kernel. Git is a large subject, and we'll only be scratching the surface in this book, but there are many good free resources online; I especially recommend *Pro Git* by Scott Chacon (Apress, 2009). Putting your source code under version control with Git is *strongly* recommended, not only because it's nearly a universal practice in the Rails world, but also because it will allow you to share your code more easily (Section 1.3.4) and deploy your application right here in the first chapter (Section 1.4).

1.3.1 Installation and Setup

The first step is to install Git if you haven't yet followed the steps in Section 1.2.2. (As noted in that section, this involves following the instructions in the Installing Git section of *Pro Git*.)

First-Time System Setup

After installing Git, you should perform a set of one-time setup steps. These are *system* setups, meaning you only have to do them once per computer:

```
$ git config --global user.name "Your Name"
$ git config --global user.email youremail@example.com
```

I also like to use **co** in place of the more verbose **checkout** command, which we can arrange as follows:

```
$ git config --global alias.co checkout
```

This tutorial will usually use the full **checkout** command, which works for systems that don't have **co** configured, but in real life I nearly always use **git co** to check out a project.

As a final setup step, you can optionally set the editor Git will use for commit messages. If you use a graphical editor such as TextMate, gVim, or MacVim, you need to use a flag to make sure that the editor stays attached to the shell instead of detaching immediately:[17]

```
$ git config --global core.editor "mate -w"
```

Replace **"mate -w"** with **"gvim -f"** for gVim or **"mvim -f"** for MacVim.

First-Time Repository Setup

Now we come to some steps that are necessary each time you create a new *repository* (which only happens once in this book, but is likely to happen again some day). First navigate to the root directory of the first app and initialize a new repository:

```
$ git init
Initialized empty Git repository in /Users/mhartl/rails_projects/first_app/.git/
```

The next step is to add the project files to the repository. There's a minor complication, though: by default Git tracks the changes of *all* the files, but there are some files we don't want to track. For example, Rails creates log files to record the behavior of the application; these files change frequently, and we don't want our version control system to have to update them constantly. Git has a simple mechanism to ignore such files: simply include a file called **.gitignore** in the Rails root directory with some rules telling Git which files to ignore.

Looking again at Table 1.1, we see that the **rails** command creates a default **.gitignore** file in the Rails root directory, as shown in Listing 1.4.

Listing 1.4 The default **.gitignore** created by the **rails** command.

```
.bundle
db/*.sqlite3
log/*.log
tmp/**/*
```

---

17. Normally this is a feature, since it lets you continue to use the command line after launching your editor, but Git interprets the detachment as closing the file with an empty commit message, which prevents the commit from going through. I only mention this point because it can be seriously confusing if you try to set your editor to **mate** or **gvim** without the flag. If you find this note confusing, feel free to ignore it.

Listing 1.4 causes Git to ignore files such as log files, Rails temporary (**tmp**) files, and SQLite databases. (For example, to ignore log files, which live in the **log/** directory, we use **log/*.log** to ignore all files that end in **.log**.) Most of these ignored files change frequently and automatically, so including them under version control is inconvenient; moreover, when collaborating with others they can cause frustrating and irrelevant conflicts.

The **.gitignore** file in Listing 1.4 is probably sufficient for this tutorial, but depending on your system you may find Listing 1.5 more convenient. This augmented **.gitignore** arranges to ignore Rails documentation files, Vim and Emacs swap files, and (for OS X users) the weird **.DS_Store** directories created by the Mac Finder application. If you want to use this broader set of ignored files, open up **.gitignore** in your favorite text editor and fill it with the contents of Listing 1.5.

Listing 1.5 An augmented **.gitignore** file.

```
.bundle
db/*.sqlite3*
log/*.log
*.log
tmp/**/*
tmp/*
doc/api
doc/app
*.swp
*~
.DS_Store
```

1.3.2 Adding and Committing

Finally, we'll add the files in your new Rails project to Git and then commit the results. You can add all the files (apart from those that match the ignore patterns in **.gitignore**) as follows:[18]

```
$ git add .
```

---

18. Windows users may get the message **warning: CRLF will be replaced by LF in .gitignore**. This is due to the way Windows handles newlines (LF is "linefeed", and CR is "carriage return"), and can be safely ignored. If the message bothers you, try running **git config --global core.autocrlf false** at the command line to turn it off.

Here the dot '.' represents the current directory, and Git is smart enough to add the files *recursively*, so it automatically includes all the subdirectories. This command adds the project files to a *staging area*, which contains pending changes to your project; you can see which files are in the staging area using the **status** command:[19]

```
$ git status
# On branch master
#
# Initial commit
#
# Changes to be committed:
#   (use "git rm --cached <file>..." to unstage)
#
#       new file:   README
#       new file:   Rakefile
  .
  .
  .
```

(The results are long, so I've used vertical dots to indicate omitted output.)

To tell Git you want to keep the changes, use the **commit** command:

```
$ git commit -m "Initial commit"
[master (root-commit) df0a62f] Initial commit
42 files changed, 8461 insertions(+), 0 deletions(-)
create mode 100644 README
create mode 100644 Rakefile
  .
  .
  .
```

The **-m** flag lets you add a message for the commit; if you omit **-m**, Git will open the editor you set in Section 1.3.1 and have you enter the message there.

It is important to note that Git commits are *local*, recorded only on the machine on which the commits occur. This is in contrast to the popular open-source version control system called Subversion, in which a commit necessarily makes changes on a remote repository. Git divides a Subversion-style commit into its two logical pieces: a

---

19. If in the future any unwanted files start showing up when you type **git status**, just add them to your **.gitignore** file from Listing 1.5.

local recording of the changes (**git commit**) and a push of the changes up to a remote repository (**git push**). We'll see an example of the push step in Section 1.3.5.

By the way, you can see a list of your commit messages using the **log** command:

```
$ git log
commit df0a62f3f091e53ffa799309b3e32c27b0b38eb4
Author: Michael Hartl <michael@michaelhartl.com>
Date:   Thu Oct 15 11:36:21 2009 -0700

    Initial commit
```

To exit **git log**, you may have to type **q** to quit.

1.3.3 What Good Does Git Do You?

It's probably not entirely clear at this point why putting your source under version control does you any good, so let me give just one example. (We'll see many others in the chapters ahead.) Suppose you've made some accidental changes, such as (D'oh!) deleting the critical **app/controllers/** directory:

```
$ ls app/controllers/
application_controller.rb
$ rm -rf app/controllers/
$ ls app/controllers/
ls: app/controllers/: No such file or directory
```

Here we're using the Unix **ls** command to list the contents of the **app/controllers/** directory and the **rm** command to remove it. The **-rf** flag means "recursive force", which recursively removes all files, directories, subdirectories, and so on, without asking for explicit confirmation of each deletion.

Let's check the status to see what's up:

```
$ git status
# On branch master
# Changed but not updated:
#   (use "git add/rm <file>..." to update what will be committed)
#   (use "git checkout -- <file>..." to discard changes in working directory)
#
#       deleted:    app/controllers/application_controller.rb
#
no changes added to commit (use "git add" and/or "git commit -a")
```

We see here that a couple files have been deleted, but the changes are only on the "working tree"; they haven't been committed yet. This means we can still undo the changes easily by having Git check out the previous commit with the **checkout** command (and a **-f** flag to force overwriting the current changes):

```
$ git checkout -f
$ git status
# On branch master
nothing to commit (working directory clean)
$ ls app/controllers/
application_controller.rb
```

The missing directory and file are back. That's a relief!

1.3.4   GitHub

Now that you've put your project under version control with Git, it's time to push your code up to GitHub, a social code site optimized for hosting and sharing Git repositories. Putting a copy of your Git repository at GitHub serves two purposes: it's a full backup of your code (including the full history of commits), and it makes any future collaboration much easier. This step is optional, but being a GitHub member will open the door to participating in a wide variety of Ruby and Rails projects (GitHub has high adoption rates in the Ruby and Rails communities, and in fact is itself written in Rails).

GitHub has a variety of paid plans, but for open source code their services are free, so sign up for a free GitHub account if you don't have one already. (You might have to read about SSH keys first.) After signing up, you'll see a page like the one in Figure 1.6. Click on create a repository and fill in the information as in Figure 1.7. After submitting the form, push up your first application as follows:

```
$ git remote add origin git@github.com:<username>/first_app.git
$ git push origin master
```

These commands tell Git that you want to add GitHub as the origin for your main (*master*) branch and then push your repository up to GitHub. Of course, you should replace <username> with your actual username. For example, the command I ran for the **railstutorial** user was

```
$ git remote add origin git@github.com:railstutorial/first_app.git
```

Figure 1.6 The first GitHub page after account creation.

Create a New Repository

Create a new empty repository into which you can push your local git repo.

NOTE: If you intend to push a copy of a repository that is already hosted on GitHub, please fork it instead.

Project Name

first_app

Description

The first app for Ruby on Rails Tutorial

Homepage URL

Who has access to this repository? (You can change this later)
- ○ **Anyone** (learn more about public repos)
- ○ Upgrade your plan to create more private repositories!

Create Repository

Figure 1.7 Creating the first app repository at GitHub.

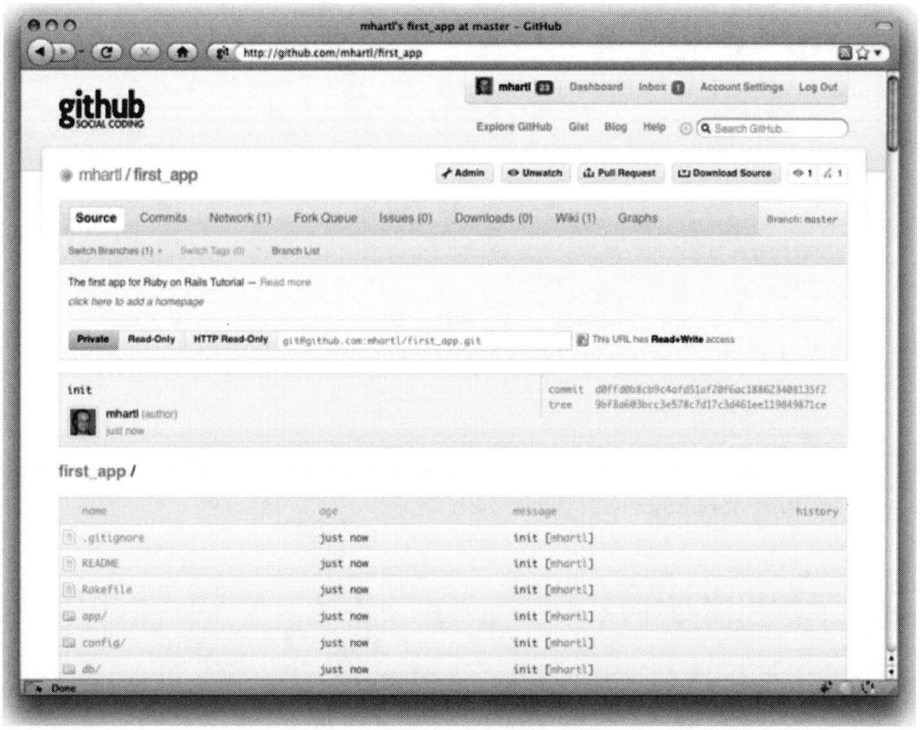

Figure 1.8   A GitHub repository page.

The result is a page at GitHub for the first application repository, with file browsing, full commit history, and lots of other goodies (Figure 1.8).

1.3.5 Branch, Edit, Commit, Merge

If you've followed the steps in Section 1.3.4, you might notice that GitHub automatically shows the contents of the **README** file on the main repository page. In our case, since the project is a Rails application generated using the **rails** command, the **README** file is the one that comes with Rails (Figure 1.9). This isn't very helpful, so in this section we'll make our first edit by changing the **README** to describe our project rather than the Rails framework itself. In the process, we'll see a first example of the branch, edit, commit, merge workflow that I recommend using with Git.

Branch

Git is incredibly good at making *branches*, which are effectively copies of a repository where we can make (possibly experimental) changes without modifying the parent files.

| script/ | 1 day ago | Init for Rails 2.3.4 [mhartl] |
| test/ | 1 day ago | Init for Rails 2.3.4 [mhartl] |

README

```
== Welcome to Rails

Rails is a web-application framework that includes everything needed to create
database-backed web applications according to the Model-View-Control pattern.

This pattern splits the view (also called the presentation) into "dumb" templates
that are primarily responsible for inserting pre-built data in between HTML tags.
The model contains the "smart" domain objects (such as Account, Product, Person,
Post) that holds all the business logic and knows how to persist themselves to
a database. The controller handles the incoming requests (such as Save New Account,
Update Product, Show Post) by manipulating the model and directing data to the view.
```

Figure 1.9   The initial (rather useless) **README** file for our project at GitHub. (full size)

In most cases, the parent repository is the *master* branch, and we can create a new topic branch by using **checkout** with the **-b** flag:

```
$ git checkout -b modify-README
Switched to a new branch 'modify-README'
$ git branch
master
* modify-README
```

Here the second command, **git branch**, just lists all the local branches, and the asterisk * identifies which branch we're currently on. Note that **git checkout -b modify-README** both creates a new branch and switches to it, as indicated by the asterisk in front of the **modify-README** branch. (If you set up the **co** alias in Section 1.3, you can use **git co -b modify-README** instead.)

The full value of branching only becomes clear when working on a project with multiple developers,[20] but branches are helpful even for a single-developer tutorial such as this one. In particular, the master branch is insulated from any changes we make to the topic branch, so even if we *really* screw things up we can always abandon the changes by checking out the master branch and deleting the topic branch. We'll see how to do this at the end of the section.

By the way, for a change as small as this one I wouldn't normally bother with a new branch, but it's never too early to start practicing good habits.

---

20. See the chapter Git Branching in *Pro Git* for details.

Edit

After creating the topic branch, we'll edit it to make it a little more descriptive. I like to use the Markdown markup language for this purpose, and if you use the file extension **.markdown** then GitHub will automatically format it nicely for you. So, first we'll use Git's version of the Unix **mv** ("move") command to change the name, and then fill it in with the contents of Listing 1.6:

```
$ git mv README README.markdown
$ mate README.markdown
```

Listing 1.6   The new **README** file, **README.markdown**.

```
# Ruby on Rails Tutorial: first application

This is the first application for
[*Ruby on Rails Tutorial: Learn Rails by Example*](http://railstutorial.org/)
by [Michael Hartl](http://michaelhartl.com/).
```

Commit

With the changes made, we can take a look at the status of our branch:

```
$ git status
# On branch modify-README
# Changes to be committed:
#   (use "git reset HEAD <file>..." to unstage)
#
#       renamed:    README -> README.markdown
#
# Changed but not updated:
#   (use "git add <file>..." to update what will be committed)
#   (use "git checkout -- <file>..." to discard changes in working directory)
#
#       modified:   README.markdown
#
```

At this point, we could use **git add .** as in Section 1.3.2, but Git provides the **-a** flag as a shortcut for the (very common) case of committing all modifications to existing files (or files created using **git mv**, which don't count as new files to Git):

```
$ git commit -a -m "Improved the README file"
2 files changed, 5 insertions(+), 243 deletions(-)
delete mode 100644 README
create mode 100644 README.markdown
```

Be careful about using the **-a** flag improperly; if you have added any new files to the project since the last commit, you still have to tell Git about them using **git add** first.

Merge

Now that we've finished making our changes, we're ready to *merge* the results back into our master branch:[21]

```
$ git checkout master
Switched to branch 'master'
$ git merge modify-README
Updating 34f06b7..2c92bef
Fast forward
 README           |  243 --------------------------------------------------------
 README.markdown  |    5 +
 2 files changed, 5 insertions(+), 243 deletions(-)
 delete mode 100644 README
 create mode 100644 README.markdown
```

Note that the Git output frequently includes things like **34f06b7**, which are related to Git's internal representation of repositories. Your exact results will differ in these details, but otherwise should essentially match the output shown above.

After you've merged in the changes, you can tidy up your branches by deleting the topic branch using **git branch -d** if you're done with it:

```
$ git branch -d modify-README
Deleted branch modify-README (was 2c92bef).
```

This step is optional, and in fact it's quite common to leave the topic branch intact. This way you can switch back and forth between the topic and master branches, merging in changes every time you reach a natural stopping point.

---

21. Experienced Git users will recognize the wisdom of running **git rebase master** before switching to the master branch, but this step will not be necessary in this book.

README.markdown

Ruby on Rails Tutorial: first application

This is the first application for *Ruby on Rails Tutorial: Learn Rails by Example* **by** Michael Hartl.

Figure 1.10 The improved **README** file formatted with Markdown. (full size)

As mentioned above, it's also possible to abandon your topic branch changes, in this case with `git branch -D`:

```
# For illustration only; don't do this unless you mess up a branch
$ git checkout -b topic-branch
$ <really screw up the branch>
$ git add .
$ git commit -a -m "Screwed up"
$ git checkout master
$ git branch -D topic-branch
```

Unlike the **-d** flag, the **-D** flag will delete the branch even though we haven't merged in the changes.

Push

Now that we've updated the **README**, we can push the changes up to GitHub to see the result:[22]

```
$ git push
```

As promised, GitHub nicely formats the new file using Markdown (Figure 1.10).

1.4 Deploying

Even at this early stage, we're already going to deploy our (still-empty) Rails application to production. This step is optional, but deploying early and often allows us to catch any deployment problems early in our development cycle. The alternative—deploying

---

22. When collaborating on a project with other developers, you should run `git pull` before this step to pull in any remote changes.

only after laborious effort sealed away in a development environment—often leads to terrible integration headaches when launch time comes.[23]

Deploying Rails applications used to be a pain, but the Rails deployment ecosystem has matured rapidly in the past few years, and now there are several great options. These include shared hosts or virtual private servers running Phusion Passenger (a module for the Apache and Nginx[24] web servers), full-service deployment companies such as Engine Yard and Rails Machine, and cloud deployment services such as Engine Yard Cloud and Heroku.

My favorite Rails deployment option is Heroku, which is a hosted platform built specifically for deploying Rails and other Ruby web applications.[25] Heroku makes deploying Rails applications ridiculously easy—as long as your source code is under version control with Git. (This is yet another reason to follow the Git setup steps in Section 1.3 if you haven't already.) The rest of this section is dedicated to deploying our first application to Heroku.

1.4.1 Heroku Setup

After signing up for a Heroku account, install the Heroku gem:

```
$ [sudo] gem install heroku
```

As with GitHub (Section 1.3.4), when using Heroku you will need to create SSH keys if you haven't already, and then tell Heroku your public key so that you can use Git to push the sample application repository up to their servers:

```
$ heroku keys:add
```

Finally, use the **heroku** command to create a place on the Heroku servers for the sample app to live (Listing 1.7).

---

23. Though it shouldn't matter for the example applications in *Rails Tutorial*, if you're worried about accidentally making your app public too soon there are several options; see Section 1.4.4 for one.

24. Pronounced "Engine X".

25. Heroku works with any Ruby web platform that uses Rack middleware, which provides a standard interface between web frameworks and web servers. Adoption of the Rack interface has been extraordinarily strong in the Ruby community, including frameworks as varied as Sinatra, Ramaze, Camping, and Rails, which means that Heroku basically supports any Ruby web app.

Listing 1.7 Creating a new application at Heroku.

```
$ heroku create
Created http://severe-fire-61.heroku.com/ | git@heroku.com:severe-fire-61.git
Git remote heroku added
```

Yes, that's it. The **heroku** command creates a new subdomain just for our application, available for immediate viewing. There's nothing there yet, though, so let's get busy deploying.

1.4.2 Heroku Deployment, Step One

To deploy to Heroku, the first step is to use Git to push the application to Heroku:

```
$ git push heroku master
```

(*Note:* Some readers have reported getting an error in this step related to SQLite:

```
rake aborted! no such file to load -- sqlite3
```

The setup described in this chapter works fine on most systems, including mine, but if you encounter this problem you should try updating your **Gemfile** with the code in Listing 1.8, which prevents Heroku from trying to load the sqlite3-ruby gem.)

Listing 1.8 A **Gemfile** with a Heroku fix needed on some systems.

```
source 'http://rubygems.org'

gem 'rails', '3.0.1'

gem 'sqlite3-ruby', '1.2.5', :group => :development
```

1.4.3 Heroku Deployment, Step Two

There is no step two! We're already done (Figure 1.11). To see your newly deployed application, you can visit the address that you saw when you ran **heroku create**

Figure 1.11   The first Rails Tutorial application running on Heroku.

(i.e., Listing 1.7, but with the address for your app, not the address for mine).[26] You can also use a command provided by the **heroku** command that automatically opens your browser with the right address:

```
$ heroku open
```

Once you've deployed successfully, Heroku provides a beautiful interface for administering and configuring your application (Figure 1.12).

---

26. Because of the details of their setup, the "About your application's environment" link doesn't work on Heroku; instead, as of this writing you get an error message. Don't worry; this is normal. The error will go away when we remove the default Rails page in Section 5.2.2.

Figure 1.12 The beautiful interface at Heroku.

1.4.4 Heroku Commands

There are tons of Heroku commands, and we'll barely scratch the surface in this book. Let's take a minute to show just one of them by renaming the application as follows:

```
$ heroku rename railstutorial
```

Don't use this name yourself; it's already taken by me! In fact, you probably shouldn't bother with this step right now; using the default address supplied by Heroku is fine. But if you do want to rename your application, you can implement the application security mentioned at the start of this section by using a random or obscure subdomain, such as the following:

```
hwpcbmze.heroku.com
seyjhflo.heroku.com
jhyicevg.heroku.com
```

With a random subdomain like this, someone could visit your site only if you gave them the address. (By the way, as a preview of Ruby's compact awesomeness, here's the code I used to generate the random subdomains:

```
('a'..'z').to_a.shuffle[0..7].join
```

Pretty sweet.)

In addition to supporting subdomains, Heroku also supports custom domains. (In fact, the Ruby on Rails Tutorial site lives at Heroku; if you're reading this book online, you're looking at a Heroku-hosted site right now!) See the Heroku documentation for more information about custom domains and other Heroku topics.

1.5 Conclusion

We've come a long way in this chapter: installation, development environment setup, version control, and deployment. If you want to share your progress at this point, feel free to send a tweet or Facebook status update with something like this:

> I'm learning Ruby on Rails with @railstutorial! http://railstutorial.org/

All that's left is to, you know, actually start learning Rails. Let's get to it!

CHAPTER 2

A Demo App

In this chapter, we'll develop a simple demonstration application to show off some of the power of Rails. The purpose is to get a high-level overview of Ruby on Rails programming (and web development in general) by rapidly generating an application using *scaffold generators*.[1] As discussed in Box 1.1, the rest of the book will take the opposite approach, developing a full application incrementally and explaining each new concepts as it arises, but for a quick overview (and some instant gratification) there is no substitute for scaffolding. The resulting demo app will allow us to interact with it through its URLs, giving us insight into the structure of a Rails application, including a first example of the *REST architecture* favored by Rails.

As with the forthcoming sample application, the demo app will consist of *users* and their associated *microposts* (thus constituting a minimalist Twitter-style app). The functionality will be utterly under-developed, and many of the steps will seem like magic, but worry not: the full sample app will develop a similar application from the ground up starting in Chapter 3, and I will provide plentiful forward-references to later material. In the mean time, have patience and a little faith—the whole point of this tutorial is to take you *beyond* this superficial, scaffold-driven approach to achieve a deeper understanding of Rails.

2.1 Planning the Application

In this section, we'll outline our plans for the demo application. As in Section 1.2.3, we'll start by generating the application skeleton using the **rails** command:

---

1. I urge you not to look too closely at the generated code; at this stage, it will only serve to confuse you.

41

```
$ cd ~/rails_projects
$ rails new demo_app
$ cd demo_app
```

Next, we'll use a text editor to update the **Gemfile** needed by Bundler with the contents of Listing 2.1.

Listing 2.1 A **Gemfile** for the demo app.

```
source 'http://rubygems.org'

gem 'rails', '3.0.0'
gem 'sqlite3-ruby', '1.2.5', :require => 'sqlite3'
```

(Recall that I need version 1.2.5 of the sqlite3-ruby gem on my system, but you should try version 1.3.1 if 1.2.5 doesn't work on your system.) We then install and include the gems using **bundle**:

```
$ bundle install
```

Finally, we'll initialize a Git repository and make the first commit:[2]

```
$ git init
$ git add .
$ git commit -m "Initial commit"
```

You can also optionally create a new repository (Figure 2.1) and push it up to GitHub:

```
$ git remote add origin git@github.com:<username>/demo_app.git
$ git push origin master
```

---

2. Recall that the **rails** command generates a default **.gitignore** file, but depending on your system you may find the augmented file from Listing 1.5 to be more convenient.

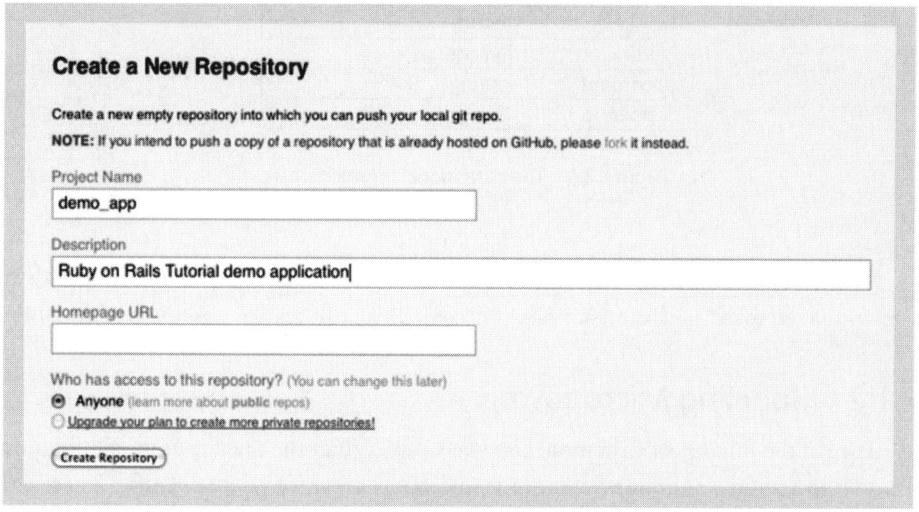

Figure 2.1 Creating a demo app repository at GitHub.

Now we're ready to start making the app itself. The typical first step when making a web application is to create a *data model*, which is a representation of the structures needed by our application. In our case, the demo app will be a stripped-down microblog, with only users and short (micro) posts. Thus, we'll begin with a model for *users* of the app (Section 2.1.1), and then we'll add a model for *microposts* (Section 2.1.2).

2.1.1 Modeling Users

There are as many choices for a user data model as there are different registration forms on the web; we'll go with a distinctly minimalist approach. Users of our demo app will have a unique `integer` identifier called `id`, a publicly viewable `name` (of type `string`), and an `email` address (also a `string`) that will double as a username. A summary of the data model for users appears in Figure 2.2.

users	
id	integer
name	string
email	string

Figure 2.2 The data model for users.

microposts	
id	integer
content	string
user_id	integer

Figure 2.3   The data model for microposts.

As we'll see starting in Section 6.1.1, the label **users** in Figure 2.2 corresponds to a *table* in a database, and the **id**, **name**, and **email** attributes are *columns* in that table.

2.1.2 Modeling Microposts

The core of the micropost data model is even simpler than the one for users: a micropost has only an **id** and a **content** field for the micropost's text (of type **string**).[3] There's an additional complication, though: we want to *associate* each micropost with a particular user; we'll accomplish this by recording the **user_id** of the owner of the post. The results are shown in Figure 2.3.

We'll see in Section 2.3.3 (and more fully in Chapter 11) how this **user_id** attribute allows us to succinctly express the notion that a user potentially has many associated microposts.

2.2 The Users Resource

In this section, we'll implement the users data model in Section 2.1.1, along with a web interface to that model. The combination will constitute a *Users resource*, which will allow us to think of users as objects that can be created, read, updated, and deleted through the web via the HTTP protocol.

As promised in the introduction, our Users resource will be created by a scaffold generator program, which comes standard with each Rails project. The argument of the **scaffold** command is the singular version of the resource name (in this case, **User**), together with optional parameters for the data model's attributes:[4]

---

3. When modeling longer posts, such as those for a normal (non-micro) blog, you should use the **text** type in place of **string**.

4. The name of the scaffold follows the convention of *models*, which are singular, rather than resources and controllers, which are plural. Thus, we have **User** instead **Users**.

```
$ rails generate scaffold User name:string email:string
      invoke  active_record
      create    db/migrate/20100615004000_create_users.rb
      create    app/models/user.rb
      invoke    test_unit
      create      test/unit/user_test.rb
      create      test/fixtures/users.yml
       route  resources :users
      invoke  scaffold_controller
      create    app/controllers/users_controller.rb
      invoke    erb
      create      app/views/users
      create      app/views/users/index.html.erb
      create      app/views/users/edit.html.erb
      create      app/views/users/show.html.erb
      create      app/views/users/new.html.erb
      create      app/views/users/_form.html.erb
      invoke    test_unit
      create      test/functional/users_controller_test.rb
      invoke    helper
      create      app/helpers/users_helper.rb
      invoke      test_unit
      create        test/unit/helpers/users_helper_test.rb
      invoke  stylesheets
      create    public/stylesheets/scaffold.css
```

By including **name:string** and **email:string**, we have arranged for the User model
to have the form shown in Figure 2.2. (Note that there is no need to include a parameter
for **id**; it is created automatically by Rails.[5])

   To proceed with the demo application, we first need to *migrate* the database using
Rake (Box 2.1):

```
$ rake db:migrate
==  CreateUsers: migrating =====================================================
-- create_table(:users)
   -> 0.0017s
==  CreateUsers: migrated (0.0018s) ============================================
```

This simply updates the database with our new **users** data model. We'll learn more
about database migrations starting in Section 6.1.1.

_____

5. The user id is needed as the *primary key* in the database.

Box 2.1 Rake

In the Unix tradition, the *make* utility has played an important role in building executable programs from source code; many a computer hacker has committed to muscle memory the line

```
$ ./configure && make && sudo make install
```

commonly used to compile code on Unix systems (including Linux and Mac OS X).

Rake is *Ruby make*, a make-like language written in Ruby. Rails uses Rake extensively, especially for the innumerable little administrative tasks necessary when developing database-backed web applications. The **rake db:migrate** command is probably the most common, but there are many others; you can see a list of database tasks using **-T db**:

```
$ rake -T db
```

To see all the Rake tasks available, run

```
$ rake -T
```

The list is likely to be overwhelming, but don't worry, you don't have to know all (or even most) of these commands. By the end of *Rails Tutorial*, you'll know all the most important ones.

With that, we can run the local web server using **rails s**, which is a shortcut for **rails server**:

```
$ rails s
```

With that, the demo application should be ready to go at `http://localhost:3000/`.

2.2.1 A User Tour

Visiting the root url `http://localhost:3000/` shows the same default Rails page shown in Figure 1.3, but in generating the Users resource scaffolding we have also created a large number of pages for manipulating users. For example, the page for listing all users is at /users, and the page for making a new user is at /users/new.[6] The rest of this

---

[6]. Since the `http://localhost:3000` part of the address is implicit whenever we are developing locally, I'll usually omit it from now on.

Table 2.1 The correspondence between pages and URLs for the Users resource

URL	Action	Purpose
/users	**index**	page to list all users
/users/1	**show**	page to show user with id **1**
/users/new	**new**	page to make a new user
/users/1/edit	**edit**	page to edit user with id **1**

section is dedicated to taking a whirlwind tour through these user pages. As we proceed, it may help to refer to Table 2.1, which shows the correspondence between pages and URLs.

We start with the page to show all the users in our application, called index; as you might expect, initially there are no users at all (Figure 2.4).

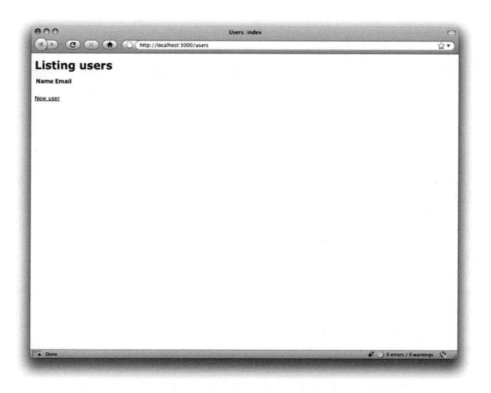

Figure 2.4   The initial index page for the Users resource (/users).

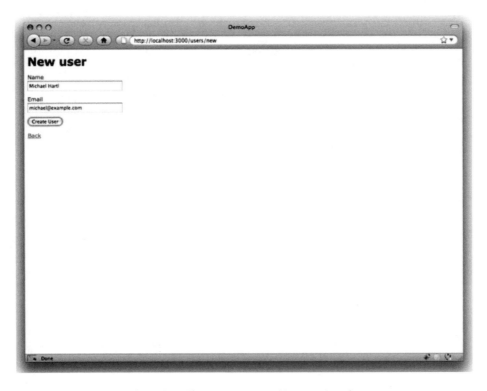

Figure 2.5   The new user page (/users/new).

To make a new user, we visit the new page, as shown in Figure 2.5. (In Chapter 8, this will become the user signup page.)

We can create a user by entering name and email values in the text fields and then clicking the Create button. The result is the user show page, as seen in Figure 2.6. (The green welcome message is accomplished using the *flash*, which we'll learn about in Section 8.3.3.) Note that the URL is /users/1; as you might suspect, the number **1** is simply the user's **id** attribute from Figure 2.2. In Section 7.3, this page will become the user's profile.

To change a user's information, we visit the edit page (Figure 2.7). By modifying the user information and clicking the Update button, we arrange to change the information for the user in the demo application (Figure 2.8). (As we'll see in detail starting in Chapter 6, this user data is stored in a database back-end.) We'll add user edit/update functionality to the sample application in Section 10.1.

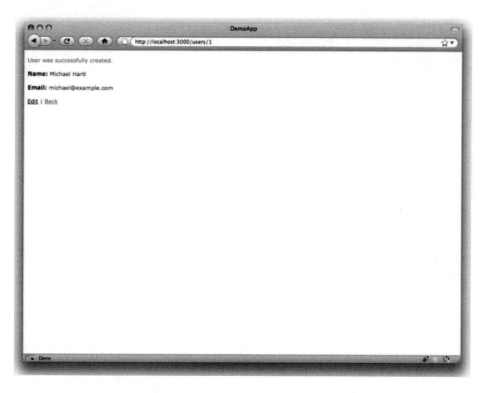

Figure 2.6 The page to show a user (/users/1).

Now we'll create a second user by revisiting the new page and submitting a second set of user information; the resulting user index is shown in Figure 2.9. Section 10.3 will develop the user index into a more polished page for showing all users.

Having shown how to create, show, and edit users, we come finally to destroying them (Figure 2.10, page 54). You should verify that clicking on the link in Figure 2.10 destroys the second user, yielding an index page with only one user. (If it doesn't work, be sure that JavaScript is enabled in your browser; Rails uses JavaScript to issue the request needed to destroy a user.) Section 10.4 adds user deletion to the sample app, taking care to restrict its use to a special class of administrative users.

2.2.2 MVC in Action

Now that we've completed a quick overview of the Users resource, let's examine one particular part of it in the context of the Model-View-Controller (MVC) pattern introduced

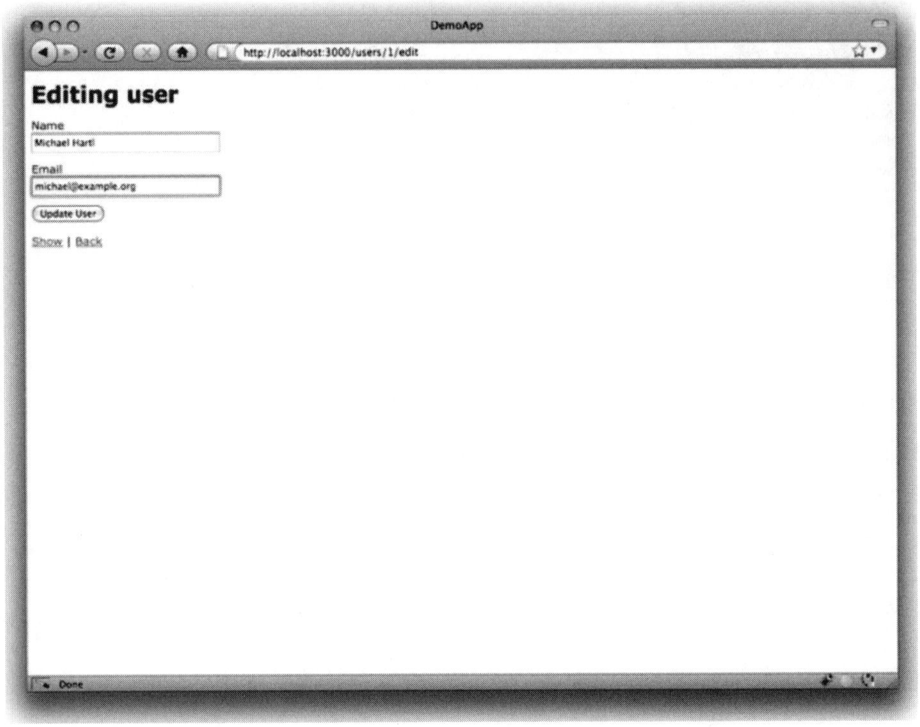

Figure 2.7   The user edit page (`/users/1/edit`).

in Section 1.2.6. Our strategy will be to describe the results of a typical browser hit—a visit to the user index page at /users—in terms of MVC (Figure 2.11, page 55).

The steps in Figure 2.11:

1. The browser issues a request for the /users URL.
2. Rails routes /users to the **index** action in the Users controller.
3. The **index** action asks the User model to retrieve all users (**User.all**).
4. The User model pulls all the users from the database.
5. The User model returns the list of users to the controller.
6. The controller captures the users in the **@users** variable, which is passed to the **index** view.

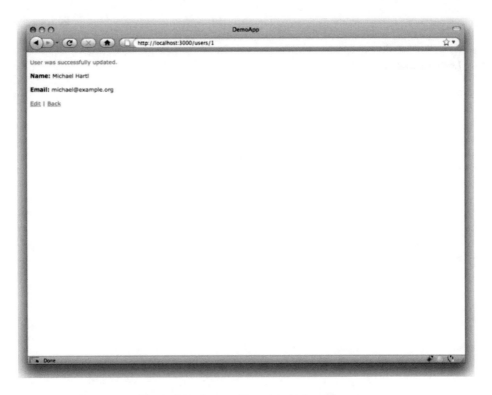

Figure 2.8   A user with updated information.

7. The view uses Embedded Ruby to render the page as HTML.
8. The controller passes the HTML back to the browser.[7]

We start with a request issued from the browser—i.e., the result of typing a URL in the address bar or clicking on a link (Step 1 in Figure 2.11). This request hits the *Rails router* (Step 2), which dispatches to the proper *controller action* based on the URL (and, as we'll see in Box 3.1, the type of request). The code to create the mapping of user URLs to controller actions for the Users resource appears in Listing 2.2;[8] this code effectively sets up the table of URL/action pairs seen in Table 2.1.

---

7. Some references indicate that the view returns the HTML directly to the browser (via a web server such as Apache or Nginx). Regardless of the implementation details, I prefer to think of the controller as a central hub through which all the application's information flows.

8. The strange notation `:users` is a *symbol*, which we'll learn about in Section 4.3.3.

Figure 2.9   The user index page (`/users`) with a second user.

Listing 2.2   The Rails routes, with a rule for the Users resource.
`config/routes.rb`

```
DemoApp::Application.routes.draw do
  resources :users
  .
  .
  .
end
```

The pages from the tour in Section 2.2.1 correspond to *actions* in the Users *controller*, which is a collection of related actions; the controller generated by the scaffolding is shown schematically in Listing 2.3. Note the notation **`class UsersController <`** **`ApplicationController`**; this is an example of a Ruby *class* with *inheritance*. (We'll discuss inheritance briefly in Section 2.3.4 and cover both subjects in more detail in Section 4.4.)

Listing 2.3 The Users controller in schematic form.
app/controllers/users_controller.rb

```ruby
class UsersController < ApplicationController

  def index
    .
    .
    .
  end

  def show
    .
    .
    .
  end

  def new
    .
    .
    .
  end

  def create
    .
    .
    .
  end

  def edit
    .
    .
    .
  end

  def update
    .
    .
    .
  end

  def destroy
    .
    .
    .
  end
end
```

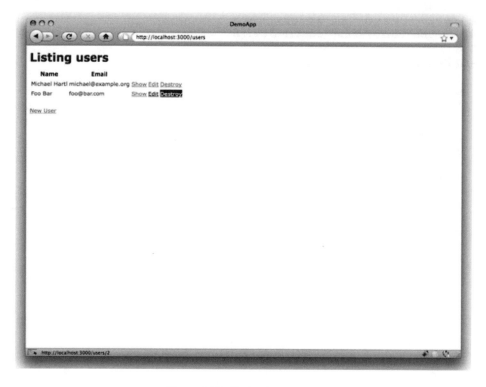

Figure 2.10 Destroying a user.

You may notice that there are more actions than there are pages; the **index**, **show**, **new**, and **edit** actions all correspond to pages from Section 2.2.1, but there are additional **create**, **update**, and **destroy** actions as well. These actions don't typically render pages (although they sometimes do); instead, their main purpose is to modify information about users in the database. This full suite of controller actions, summarized in Table 2.2, represents the implementation of the REST architecture in Rails (Box 2.2). Note from Table 2.2 that there is some overlap in the URLs; for example, both the user **show** action and the **update** action correspond to the URL /users/1. The difference between them is the HTTP request method they respond to. We'll learn more about HTTP request methods starting in Section 3.2.2.

Box 2.2   REpresentational State Transfer (REST)

If you read much about Ruby on Rails web development, you'll see a lot of references to "REST", which is an acronym for REpresentational State Transfer. REST is an

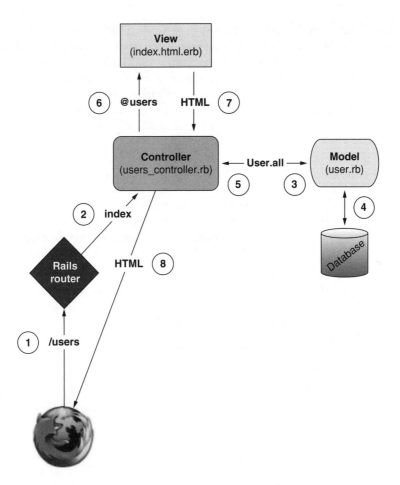

Figure 2.11 A detailed diagram of MVC in Rails.

Table 2.2 RESTful routes provided by the Users resource in Listing 2.2

HTTP request	URL	Action	Purpose
GET	/users	**index**	page to list all users
GET	/users/1	**show**	page to show user with id **1**
GET	/users/new	**new**	page to make a new user
POST	/users	**create**	create a new user
GET	/users/1/edit	**edit**	page to edit user with id **1**
PUT	/users/1	**update**	update user with id **1**
DELETE	/users/1	**destroy**	delete user with id **1**

architectural style for developing distributed, networked systems and software applications such as the World Wide Web and web applications. Although REST theory is
rather abstract, in the context of Rails applications REST means that most application components (such as users and microposts) are modeled as *resources* that can be
created, read, updated, and deleted—operations that correspond both to the CRUD
operations of relational databases and the four fundamental HTTP request methods:
POST, GET, PUT, and DELETE. (We'll learn more about HTTP requests in Section 3.2.2
and especially Box 3.1.)

The RESTful style of development helps you as a Rails application developer make
choices about which controllers and actions to write: you simply structure the application using resources that get created, read, updated, and deleted. In the case of users
and microposts, this process is straightforward, since they are naturally resources in
their own right. In Chapter 12, we'll see an example where REST principles allow us
to model a subtler problem, "following users", in a natural and convenient way.

To examine the relationship between the Users controller and the User model, let's
focus on a simplified version of the **index** action, shown in Listing 2.4.[9]

Listing 2.4 The simplified user **index** action for the demo application.
app/controllers/users_controller.rb

```ruby
class UsersController < ApplicationController

  def index
    @users = User.all
  end
  .
  .
  .
end
```

This **index** action has the line **@users = User.all** (Step 3), which asks the User
model to retrieve a list of all the users from the database (Step 4), and then places them
in the variable **@users** (pronounced "at-users") (Step 5). The User model itself appears
in Listing 2.5; although it is rather plain, it comes equipped with a large amount of
functionality because of inheritance (Section 2.3.4 and Section 4.4). In particular, by
using the Rails library called *Active Record*, the code in Listing 2.5 arranges for **User.all**
to return all the users.

---

9. The scaffold code is ugly and confusing, so I've suppressed it.

Listing 2.5   The User model for the demo application.
`app/models/user.rb`

```
class User < ActiveRecord::Base
end
```

Once the **@users** variable is defined, the controller calls the *view* (Step 6), shown in Listing 2.6. Variables that start with the **@** sign, called *instance variables*, are automatically available in the view; in this case, the **index.html.erb** view in Listing 2.6 iterates through the **@users** list and outputs a line of HTML for each one.[10]

Listing 2.6   The view for the user index. (You are not expected to understand it now.)
`app/views/users/index.html.erb`

```
<h1>Listing users</h1>

<table>
  <tr>
    <th>Name</th>
    <th>Email</th>
    <th></th>
    <th></th>
    <th></th>
  </tr>

<% @users.each do |user| %>
  <tr>
    <td><%= user.name %></td>
    <td><%= user.email %></td>
    <td><%= link_to 'Show', user %></td>
    <td><%= link_to 'Edit', edit_user_path(user) %></td>
    <td><%= link_to 'Destroy', user, :confirm => 'Are you sure?',
:method => :delete %></td>
  </tr>
<% end %>
</table>

<br />

<%= link_to 'New User', new_user_path %>
```

---

10. Remember, you aren't supposed to understand this code right now. It is shown only for purposes of illustration.

The view converts its contents to HTML (Step 7), which is then returned by the controller to the browser for display (Step 8).

2.2.3 Weaknesses of This Users Resource

Though good for getting a general overview of Rails, the scaffold Users resource suffers from a number of severe weaknesses.

- **No data validations.** Our User model accepts data such as blank names and invalid email addresses without complaint.

- **No authentication.** We have no notion signing in or out, and no way to prevent any user from performing any operation.

- **No tests.** This isn't technically true—the scaffolding includes rudimentary tests—but the generated tests are ugly and inflexible, and they don't test for data validation, authentication, or any other custom requirements.

- **No layout.** There is no consistent site styling or navigation.

- **No real understanding.** If you understand the scaffold code, you probably shouldn't be reading this book.

2.3 The Microposts Resource

Having generated and explored the Users resource, we turn now to the associated Microposts resource. Throughout this section, I recommend comparing the elements of the Microposts resource with the analogous user elements from Section 2.2; you should see that the two resources parallel each other in many ways. The RESTful structure of Rails applications is best absorbed by this sort of repetition of form; indeed, seeing the parallel structure of Users and Microposts even at this early stage is one of the prime motivations for this chapter. (As we'll see, writing applications more robust than the toy example in this chapter takes considerable effort—we won't see the Microposts resource again until Chapter 11—and I didn't want to defer its first appearance quite that far.)

2.3.1 A Micropost Microtour

As with the Users resource, we'll generate scaffold code for the Microposts resource using **`rails generate scaffold`**, in this case implementing the data model from Figure 2.3:[11]

---

11. As with the User scaffold, the scaffold generator for microposts follows the singular convention of Rails models; thus, we have **`generate Micropost`**.

```
$ rails generate scaffold Micropost content:string user_id:integer
     invoke  active_record
     create    db/migrate/20100615004429_create_microposts.rb
     create    app/models/micropost.rb
     invoke    test_unit
     create      test/unit/micropost_test.rb
     create      test/fixtures/microposts.yml
      route  resources :microposts
     invoke  scaffold_controller
     create    app/controllers/microposts_controller.rb
     invoke    erb
     create      app/views/microposts
     create      app/views/microposts/index.html.erb
     create      app/views/microposts/edit.html.erb
     create      app/views/microposts/show.html.erb
     create      app/views/microposts/new.html.erb
     create      app/views/microposts/_form.html.erb
     invoke    test_unit
     create      test/functional/microposts_controller_test.rb
     invoke    helper
     create      app/helpers/microposts_helper.rb
     invoke      test_unit
     create        test/unit/helpers/microposts_helper_test.rb
     invoke    stylesheets
  identical    public/stylesheets/scaffold.css
```

To update our database with the new data model, we need to run a migration as in Section 2.2:

```
$ rake db:migrate
==  CreateMicroposts: migrating ===============================================
-- create_table(:microposts)
   -> 0.0023s
==  CreateMicroposts: migrated (0.0026s) ======================================
```

Now we are in a position to create microposts in the same way we created users in Section 2.2.1. As you might guess, the scaffold generator has updated the Rails routes file with a rule for Microposts resource, as seen in Listing 11.21.[12] As with users, the **resources :microposts** routing rule maps a micropost URLs to actions in the Microposts controller, as seen in Table 2.3.

---

12. The scaffold code may have extra newlines compared to Listing 11.21; this is not a cause for concern, as Ruby ignores extra newlines.

Table 2.3 RESTful routes provided by the Microposts resource in Listing 2.7

HTTP request	URL	Action	Purpose
GET	/microposts	**index**	page to list all microposts
GET	/microposts/1	**show**	page to show micropost with id **1**
GET	/microposts/new	**new**	page to make a new micropost
POST	/microposts	**create**	create a new micropost
GET	/microposts/1/edit	**edit**	page to edit micropost with id **1**
PUT	/microposts/1	**update**	update micropost with id **1**
DELETE	/microposts/1	**destroy**	delete micropost with id **1**

Listing 2.7 The Rails routes, with a new rule for Microposts resources.
`config/routes.rb`

```
DemoApp::Application.routes.draw do
  resources :microposts
  resources :users
  .
  .
  .
end
```

The Microposts controller itself appears in schematic form in Listing 2.8. Note that, apart from having **MicropostsController** in place of **UsersController**, Listing 2.8 is *identical* to the code in Listing 2.3. This is a reflection of the REST architecture common to both resources.

Listing 2.8 The Microposts controller in schematic form.
`app/controllers/microposts_controller.rb`

```
class MicropostsController < ApplicationController

  def index
    .
    .
    .
  end

  def show
    .
    .
    .
```

```
  end

  def new
    .
    .
    .
  end

  def create
    .
    .
    .
  end

  def edit
    .
    .
    .
  end

  def update
    .
    .
    .
  end

  def destroy
    .
    .
    .
  end
end
```

To make some actual microposts, we enter information at the new microposts page, /microposts/new, as seen in Figure 2.12.

At this point, go ahead and create a micropost or two, taking care to make sure that at least one has a **user_id** of **1** to match the id of the first user created in Section 2.2.1. The result should look something like Figure 2.13.

2.3.2 Putting the *Micro* in Microposts

Any *micro*post worthy of the name should have some means of enforcing the length of the post. Implementing this constraint in Rails is easy with *validations*; to accept microposts with at most 140 characters (à la Twitter), we use a *length* validation. At this point, you

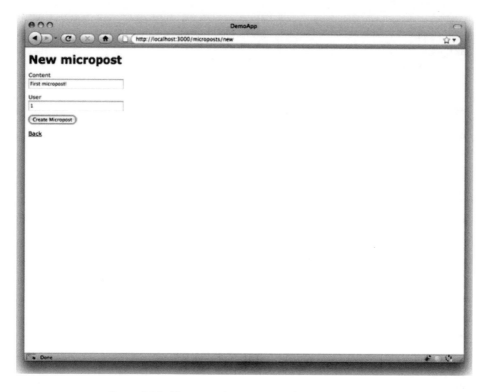

Figure 2.12   The new micropost page (/microposts/new).

should open the file **app/models/micropost.rb** in your text editor or IDE and fill it
with the contents of Listing 2.9. (The use of **validates** in Listing 2.9 is characteristic
of Rails 3; if you've previously worked with Rails 2.3, you should compare this to the
use of **validates_length_of**.)

Listing 2.9   Constraining microposts to at most 140 characters with a length validation.
app/models/micropost.rb

```
class Micropost < ActiveRecord::Base
  validates :content, :length => { :maximum => 140 }
end
```

The code in Listing 2.9 may look rather mysterious—we'll cover validations more
thoroughly starting in Section 6.2—but its effects are readily apparent if we go to the

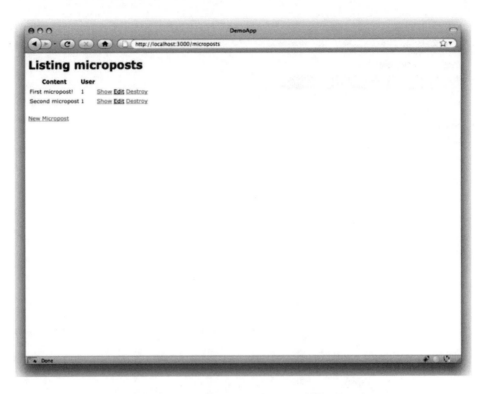

Figure 2.13 The micropost index page (/microposts).

new micropost page and enter more than 140 characters for the content of the post. As seen in Figure 2.14, Rails renders *error messages* indicating that the micropost's content is too long.[13] (We'll learn more about error messages in Section 8.2.3.)

2.3.3 A User `has_many` Microposts

One of the most powerful features of Rails is the ability to form *associations* between different data models. In the case of our User model, each user potentially has many microposts. We can express this in code by updating the User and Micropost models as in Listing 2.10 and Listing 2.11.

---

13. You might notice that the HTML Validator indicates an error; annoyingly, the default Rails error messages are not valid HTML.

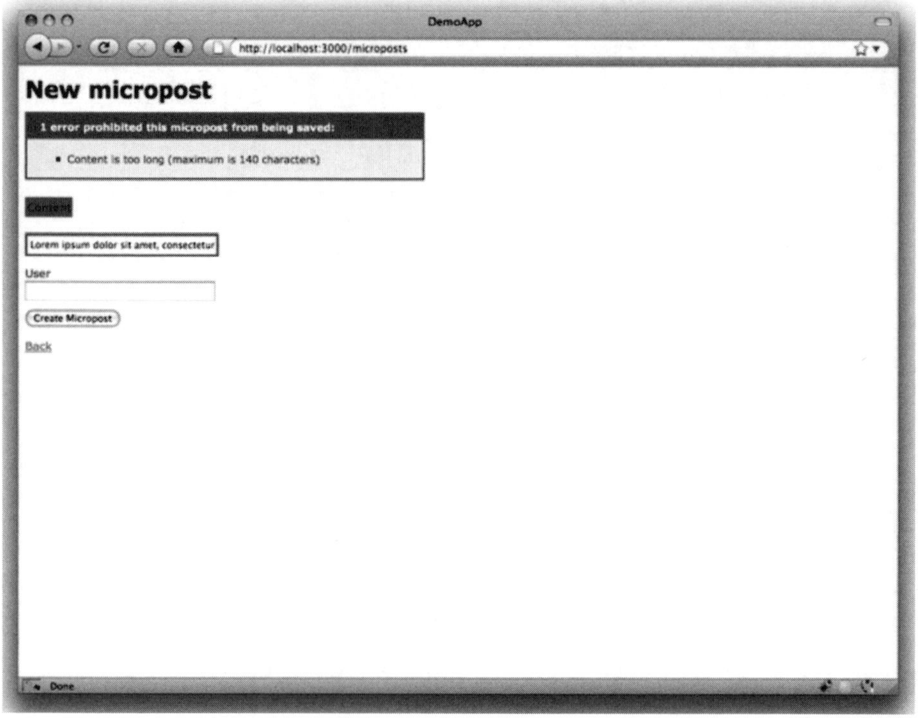

Figure 2.14   Error messages for a failed micropost creation.

Listing 2.10   A user has many microposts.
app/models/user.rb

```
class User < ActiveRecord::Base
  has_many :microposts
end
```

Listing 2.11   A micropost belongs to a user.
app/models/micropost.rb

```
class Micropost < ActiveRecord::Base
  belongs_to :user

  validates :content, :length => { :maximum => 140 }
end
```

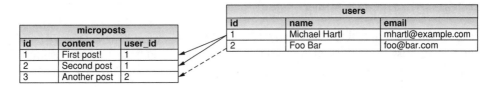

Figure 2.15 The association between microposts and users.

We can visualize the result of this association in Figure 2.15. Because of the **user_id** column in the **microposts** table, Rails (using Active Record) can infer the microposts associated with each user.

In Chapter 11 and Chapter 12, we will use the association of users and microposts both to display all a user's microposts and to construct a Twitter-like micropost feed. For now, we can examine the implications of the user-micropost association by using the *console*, which is a useful tool for interacting with Rails applications. We first invoke the console with **rails console** at the command line, and then retrieve the first user from the database using **User.first** (putting the results in the variable **first_user**):[14]

```
$ rails console
>> first_user = User.first
=> #<User id: 1, name: "Michael Hartl", email: "michael@example.org",
created_at: "2010-04-03 02:01:31", updated_at: "2010-04-03 02:01:31">
>> first_user.microposts
=> [#<Micropost id: 1, content: "First micropost!", user_id: 1, created_at:
"2010-04-03 02:37:37", updated_at: "2010-04-03 02:37:37">, #<Micropost id: 2,
content: "Second micropost", user_id: 1, created_at: "2010-04-03 02:38:54",
updated_at: "2010-04-03 02:38:54">]
```

Here we have accessed the user's microposts using the code **first_user.microposts**; with this code, Active Record automatically returns all the microposts with **user_id** equal to the id of **first_user** (in this case, **1**). We'll learn much more about the association facilities in Active Record in Chapter 11 and Chapter 12.

---

14. Your console prompt will probably be something like **ruby-1.9.2-head >**, but I'll use **>>** so that the prompt isn't tied to a specific Ruby version.

2.3.4 Inheritance Hierarchies

We end our discussion of the demo application with a brief description of the controller and model class hierarchies in Rails. This discussion will only make much sense if you have some experience with object-oriented programming (OOP); if you haven't studied OOP, feel free to skip this section. In particular, if you are unfamiliar with *classes* (discussed in Section 4.4), I suggest looping back to this section at a later time.

We start with the inheritance structure for models. Comparing Listing 2.12 and Listing 2.13, we see that both the User model and the Micropost model inherit (via the left angle bracket **<**) from **ActiveRecord::Base**, which is the base class for models provided by ActiveRecord; a diagram summarizing this relationship appears in Figure 2.16. It is by inheriting from **ActiveRecord::Base** that our model objects gain the ability to communicate with the database, treat the database columns as Ruby attributes, and so on.

Listing 2.12 The **User** class, with inheritance.
app/models/user.rb

```
class User < ActiveRecord::Base
  .
  .
  .
end
```

Listing 2.13 The **Micropost** class, with inheritance.
app/models/micropost.rb

```
class Micropost < ActiveRecord::Base
  .
  .
  .
end
```

The inheritance structure for controllers is only slightly more complicated. Comparing Listing 2.14 and Listing 2.15, we see that both the Users controller and the Microposts controller inherit from the Application controller. Examining Listing 2.16, we see that **ApplicationController** itself inherits from **ActionController::Base**; this is the base class for controllers provided by the Rails library Action Pack. The relationships between these classes is illustrated in Figure 2.17.

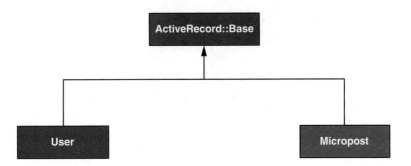

Figure 2.16 The inheritance hierarchy for the User and Micropost models.

Listing 2.14 The **UsersController** class, with inheritance.
`app/controllers/users_controller.rb`

```ruby
class UsersController < ApplicationController
  .
  .
  .
end
```

Listing 2.15 The **MicropostsController** class, with inheritance.
`app/controllers/microposts_controller.rb`

```ruby
class MicropostsController < ApplicationController
  .
  .
  .
end
```

Listing 2.16 The **ApplicationController** class, with inheritance.
`app/controllers/application_controller.rb`

```ruby
class ApplicationController < ActionController::Base
  .
  .
  .
end
```

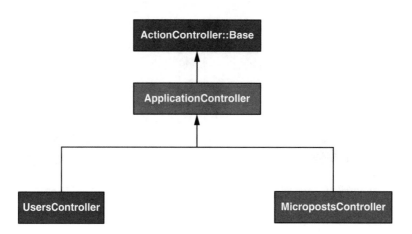

Figure 2.17   The inheritance hierarchy for the Users and Microposts controllers.

As with model inheritance, by inheriting ultimately from **ActionController::Base** both the Users and Microposts controllers gain a large amount of functionality, such as the ability to manipulate model objects, filter inbound HTTP requests, and render views as HTML. Since all Rails controllers inherit from **ApplicationController**, rules defined in the Application controller automatically apply to every action in the application. For example, in Section 8.2.4 we'll see how defining a rule in the Application controller allows us to filter passwords from all the Rails log files, thereby avoiding a serious potential security breach.

2.3.5 Deploying the Demo App

With the completion of the Microposts resource, now is a good time to push the repository up to GitHub:[15]

```
$ git add .
$ git commit -a -m "Done with the demo app"
$ git push
```

---

15. Ordinarily, you should make smaller, more frequent commits, but for the purposes of this chapter a single big commit at the end is just fine.

You can also deploy the demo app to Heroku:

```
$ heroku create
$ git push heroku master
$ heroku rake db:migrate
```

(If this doesn't work for you, see the note just above Listing 1.8 for a possible fix.) Note the final line here, which runs the database migrations on the Heroku server. This updates the database at Heroku with the necessary user/micropost data model. If you want to push the *data* up, too, you can do so using the taps gem and **db:push**:

```
$ [sudo] gem install taps
$ heroku db:push
```

2.4 Conclusion

We've come now to the end of the 30,000-foot view of a Rails application. The demo app developed in this chapter has several strengths and a host of weaknesses.

Strengths

- High-level overview of Rails
- Introduction to MVC
- First taste of the REST architecture
- Beginning data modeling
- A live, database-backed web application in production[16]

Weaknesses

- No custom layout or styling
- No static pages (like "Home" or "About")
- No user passwords

---

16. If you deployed to Heroku in Section 2.3.5.

- No user images
- No signing in
- No security
- No automatic user/micropost association
- No notion of "following" or "followed"
- No micropost feed
- No test-driven development
- **No real understanding**

The rest of this tutorial is dedicated to building on the strengths and eliminating the weaknesses.

CHAPTER 3
Mostly Static Pages

In this chapter, we will begin developing the sample application that will serve as our example throughout the rest of this tutorial. Although the sample app will eventually have users, microposts, and a full login and authentication framework, we will begin with a seemingly limited topic: the creation of static pages. Despite its seeming simplicity, making static pages is a highly instructive exercise, rich in implications—a perfect start for our nascent application.

Although Rails is designed for making database-backed dynamic websites, it also excels at making the kind of static pages we might make with raw HTML files. In fact, using Rails even for static pages yields a distinct advantage: we can easily add just a *small* amount of dynamic content. In this chapter we'll learn how. Along the way, we'll get our first taste of *automated testing*, which will help us be more confident that our code is correct. Moreover, having a good test suite will allow us to *refactor* our code with confidence, changing its form without changing its function.

As in Chapter 2, before getting started we need to create a new Rails project, this time called sample_app:

```
$ cd ~/rails_projects
$ rails new sample_app -T
$ cd sample_app
```

Here the **-T** option to the **rails** command tells Rails not to generate a **test** directory associated with the default Test::Unit framework. This is not because we won't be writing tests; on the contrary, starting in Section 3.2 we will be using an alternate testing framework called *RSpec* to write a thorough test suite.

As in Section 2.1, our next step is to use a text editor to update the **Gemfile** with the gems needed by our application. As in the case of the first application, note that the sqlite3-ruby gem is version 1.2.5, which as before we'll need for developing the application locally. (Recall that I need version 1.2.5 of the sqlite3-ruby gem on my system, but you should try version 1.3.1 if 1.2.5 doesn't work on your system.) On the other hand, for the sample application we'll also need two gems we didn't need before: the gem for RSpec and the gem for the RSpec library specific to Rails. The code to include them is shown in Listing 3.1. (*Note*: If you would like to install *all* the gems needed for the sample application, you should use the code in Listing 10.42 at this time.)

Listing 3.1 A **Gemfile** for the sample app.

```
source 'http://rubygems.org'

gem 'rails', '3.0.0'
gem 'sqlite3-ruby', '1.2.5', :require => 'sqlite3'

group :development do
  gem 'rspec-rails', '2.0.1'
end

group :test do
  gem 'rspec', '2.0.1'
  gem 'webrat', '0.7.1'
end
```

This includes rspec-rails in development mode so that we have access to RSpec-specific generators, and it includes rspec in test mode in order to run the tests. (We also include a gem for Webrat, a testing utility which used to be installed automatically as a dependency but now needs to be included explicitly.) To install and include the RSpec gems, we use **bundle install** as usual:

```
$ bundle install
```

In order to get Rails to use RSpec in place of Test::Unit, we need to install the files needed by RSpec. This can be accomplished with **rails generate**:

```
$ rails generate rspec:install
```

With that, all we have left is to initialize the Git repository:[1]

```
$ git init
$ git add .
$ git commit -m "Initial commit"
```

As with the first application, I suggest updating the **README** file (located in the root directory of the application) to be more helpful and descriptive, as shown in Listing 3.2.

Listing 3.2 An improved **README** file for the sample app.

```
# Ruby on Rails Tutorial: sample application

This is the sample application for
[*Ruby on Rails Tutorial: Learn Rails by Example*](http://railstutorial.org/)
by [Michael Hartl](http://michaelhartl.com/).
```

Then change it to use the **markdown** extension and commit the changes:

```
$ git mv README README.markdown
$ git commit -a -m "Improved the README"
```

Since we'll be using this sample app throughout the rest of the book, it's a good idea to make a repository at GitHub (Figure 3.1) and push it up:

```
$ git remote add origin git@github.com:<username>/sample_app.git
$ git push origin master
```

(Note that, as a result of this step, the repository at http://github.com/railstutorial/ sample app has the source code for the full sample application. You are welcome to consult it for reference, with two caveats: (1) You will learn a lot more if you type in the source code samples yourself, rather than relying on the completed version; (2) there may be minor differences between the GitHub repository and the code in the book. This is due both to the incorporation of some of the book's exercises and to the repository's use in the Rails Tutorial screencasts, which includes a few more tests.)

---

1. As before, you may find the augmented file from Listing 1.5 to be more convenient depending on your system.

Create a New Repository

Create a new empty repository into which you can push your local git repo.

NOTE: If you intend to push a copy of a repository that is already hosted on GitHub, please fork it instead.

Project Name

```
sample_app
```

Description

```
Ruby on Rails Tutorial sample application
```

Homepage URL

```
http://www.railstutorial.org/
```

Who has access to this repository? (You can change this later)

◉ **Anyone** (learn more about public repos)

○ Upgrade your plan to create more private repositories!

(Create Repository)

Figure 3.1   Creating the sample app repository at GitHub.

Of course, we can optionally deploy the app to Heroku even at this early stage:

```
$ heroku create
$ git push heroku master
```

(If this doesn't work for you, see the note just above Listing 1.8 for a possible fix.) As you proceed through the rest of the book, I recommend pushing and deploying the application regularly:

```
$ git push
$ git push heroku
```

With that, we're ready to get started developing the sample application.

3.1 Static Pages

Rails has two main ways of making static web pages. First, Rails can handle *truly* static pages consisting of raw HTML files. Second, Rails allows us to define *views* containing raw HTML, which Rails can *render* so that the web server can send it to the browser.

In order to get our bearings, it's helpful to recall the Rails directory structure from Section 1.2.3 (Figure 1.2). In this section, we'll be working mainly in the **app/controllers** and **app/views** directories. (In Section 3.2, we'll even add a new directory of our own.)

3.1.1   Truly Static Pages

We start with truly static pages. Recall from Section 1.2.5 that every Rails application comes with a minimal working application thanks to the **rails** script, with a default welcome page at the address http://localhost:3000/ (Figure 1.3).

To learn where this page comes from, take a look at the file **public/index.html** (Figure 3.2). Because the file contains its own stylesheet information, it's a little messy, but it gets the job done: by default, Rails serves any files in the **public** directory directly

```html
1  <!DOCTYPE html>
2  <html>
3    <head>
4      <title>Ruby on Rails: Welcome aboard</title>
5      <style type="text/css" media="screen">
6        body {
7          margin: 0;
8          margin-bottom: 25px;
9          padding: 0;
10         background-color: #f0f0f0;
11         font-family: "Lucida Grande", "Bitstream Vera Sans", "Verdana";
12         font-size: 13px;
13         color: #333;
14       }
15
16       h1 {
17         font-size: 28px;
18         color: #000;
19       }
20
21       a   {color: #03c}
22       a:hover {
23         background-color: #03c;
24         color: white;
25         text-decoration: none;
26       }
27
28
29       #page {
30         background-color: #f0f0f0;
31         width: 750px;
32         margin: 0;
33         margin-left: auto;
34         margin-right: auto;
35       }
36
37       #content {
38         float: left;
39         background-color: white;
40         border: 3px solid #aaa;
41         border-top: none;
42         padding: 25px;
```

Figure 3.2   The **public/index.html** file.

to the browser.[2] In the case of the special **index.html** file, you don't even have to indicate the file in the URL, as **index.html** is the default. You can include it if you want, though; the addresses

```
http://localhost:3000/
```

and

```
http://localhost:3000/index.html
```

are equivalent.

As you might expect, if we want we can make our own static HTML files and put them in the same **public** directory as **index.html**. For example, let's create a file with a friendly greeting (Listing 3.3):[3]

```
$ mate public/hello.html
```

Listing 3.3 A typical HTML file, with a friendly greeting.
public/hello.html

```
<!DOCTYPE html>
<html>
  <head>
    <title>Greeting</title>
  </head>
  <body>
    <p>Hello, world!</p>
  </body>
</html>
```

We see in Listing 3.3 the typical structure of an HTML document: a *document type*, or doctype, declaration at the top to tell browsers which version of HTML we're using (in this case, HTML5);[4] a **head** section, in this case with "Greeting" inside a **title** tag;

---

2. In fact, Rails ensures that requests for such files never hit the main Rails stack; they are delivered directly from the filesystem. (See *The Rails 3 Way* for more details.)

3. As usual, replace **mate** with the command for your text editor.

4. HTML changes with time; by explicitly making a doctype declaration we make it likelier that browsers will render our pages properly in the future. The extremely simple doctype **<!DOCTYPE html>** is characteristic of the latest HTML standard, HTML5.

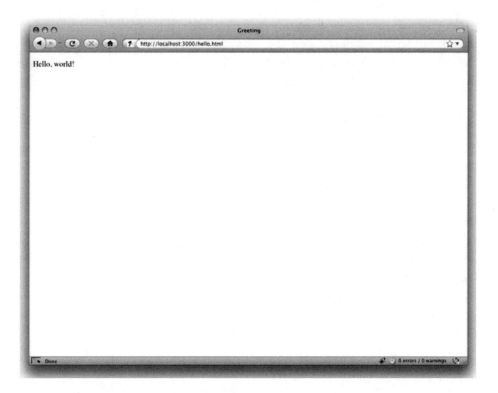

Figure 3.3 Our very own static HTML file (`http://localhost:3000/hello.html`).

and a **body** section, in this case with "Hello, world!" inside a **p** (paragraph) tag. (The indentation is optional—HTML is not sensitive to whitespace, and ignores both tabs and spaces—but it makes the document's structure easier to see.) As promised, when visiting the address `http://localhost:3000/hello.html`, Rails renders it straight-away (Figure 3.3). Note that the title displayed at the top of the browser window in Figure 3.3 is just the contents inside the **title** tag, namely, "Greeting".

Since this file is just for demonstration purposes, we don't really want it to be part of our sample application, so it's probably best to remove it once the thrill of creating it has worn off:

```
$ rm public/hello.html
```

We'll leave the **index.html** file alone for now, but of course eventually we should remove it: we don't want the root of our application to be the Rails default page shown in Figure 1.3. We'll see in Section 5.2 how to change the address http://localhost:3000/ to point to something other than **public/index.html**.

3.1.2 Static Pages with Rails

The ability to return static HTML files is nice, but it's not particularly useful for making dynamic web applications. In this section, we'll take a first step toward making dynamic pages by creating a set of Rails *actions*, which are a more powerful way to define URLs than static files.[5] Rails actions come bundled together inside *controllers* (the C in MVC from Section 1.2.6), which contain sets of actions related by a common purpose. We got a glimpse of controllers in Chapter 2, and will come to a deeper understanding once we explore the REST architecture more fully (starting in Chapter 6); in essence, a controller is a container for a group of (possibly dynamic) web pages.

To get started, recall from Section 1.3.5 that, when using Git, it's a good practice to do our work on a separate topic branch rather than the master branch. If you're using Git for version control, you should run the following command:

```
$ git checkout -b static-pages
```

Rails comes with a script for making controllers called **generate**; all it needs to work its magic is the controller's name. Since we're making this controller to handle (mostly) static pages, we'll just call it the Pages controller, and plan to make actions for a Home page, a Contact page, and an About page. The **generate** script takes an optional list of actions, so we'll include some of our initial actions directly on the command line:

Listing 3.4 Generating a Pages controller.

```
$ rails generate controller Pages home contact
      create  app/controllers/pages_controller.rb
       route  get "pages/contact"
       route  get "pages/home"
```

---

5. Our method for making static pages is probably the simplest, but it's not the only way. The optimal method really depends on your needs; if you expect a *large* number of static pages, using a Pages controller can get quite cumbersome, but in our sample app we'll only need a few. See this blog post on simple pages at has_many :through for a survey of techniques for making static pages with Rails. *Warning:* the discussion is fairly advanced, so you might want to wait a while before trying to understand it.

```
invoke   erb
create     app/views/pages
create     app/views/pages/home.html.erb
create     app/views/pages/contact.html.erb
invoke   rspec
create     spec/controllers/pages_controller_spec.rb
create     spec/views/pages
create     spec/views/pages/home.html.erb_spec.rb
create     spec/views/pages/contact.html.erb_spec.rb
invoke   helper
create     app/helpers/pages_helper.rb
invoke     rspec
```

(Note that, because we installed RSpec with **rails generate rspec:install**, the controller generation automatically creates RSpec test files in the **spec/** directory.) Here, I've intentionally "forgotten" the **about** page so that we can see how to add it in by hand (Section 3.2).

The Pages controller generation in Listing 3.4 automatically updates the *routes* file, called **config/routes.rb**, which Rails uses to find the correspondence between URLs and web pages. This is our first encounter with the **config** directory, so it's helpful to take a quick look at it (Figure 3.4). The **config** directory is where Rails collects files needed for the application configuration—hence the name.

Since we generated **home** and **contact** actions, the routes file already has a rule for each one, as seen in Listing 3.5.

Listing 3.5 The routes for the **home** and **contact** actions in the Pages controller. **config/routes.rb**

```
SampleApp::Application.routes.draw do
  get "pages/home"
  get "pages/contact"
  .
  .
  .
end
```

Here the rule

```
get "pages/home"
```

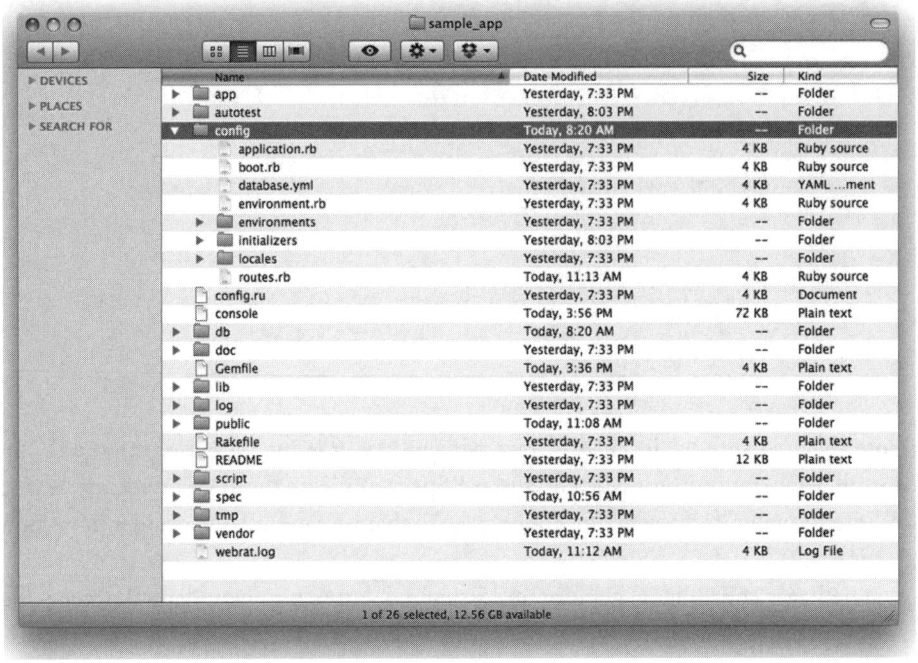

Figure 3.4   Contents of the sample app's `config` directory.

maps requests for the URL /pages/home to the **home** action in the Pages controller. Moreover, by using **get** we arrange for the route to respond to a GET request, which is one of the fundamental *HTTP verbs* supported by the hypertext transfer protocol (Box 3.1). In our case, this means that when we generate a **home** action inside the Pages controller we automatically get a page at the address /pages/home. To see the results, kill the server by hitting Ctrl-C, run **rails server**, and then navigate to /pages/home (Figure 3.5).

Box 3.1   GET, et cet.

The hypertext transfer protocol (HTTP) defines four basic operations, corresponding to the four verbs *get*, *post*, *put*, and *delete*. These refer to operations between a *client* computer (typically running a web browser such as Firefox or Safari) and a *server* (typically running a web server such as Apache or Nginx). (It's important to understand that, when developing Rails applications on a local computer, the client and server are the same physical machine, but in general they are different.) An emphasis on HTTP verbs is typical of web frameworks (including Rails) influenced by the *REST architecture*, which we'll start learning about in Chapter 8.

GET is the most common HTTP operation, used for *reading* data on the web; it just means "get a page", and every time you visit a site like google.com or craigslist.org your browser is submitting a GET request. POST is the next most common operation; it is the request sent by your browser when you submit a form. In Rails applications, POST requests are typically used for *creating* things (although HTTP also allows POST to perform updates); for example, the POST request sent when you submit a registration form creates a new user on the remote site. The other two verbs, PUT and DELETE, are designed for *updating* and *destroying* things on the remote server. These requests are less common than GET and POST since browsers are incapable of sending them natively, but some web frameworks (including Ruby on Rails) have clever ways of making it *seem* like browsers are issuing such requests.

To understand where this page comes from, let's start by taking a look at the Pages controller in a text editor; you should see something like Listing 3.6. (You may note that,

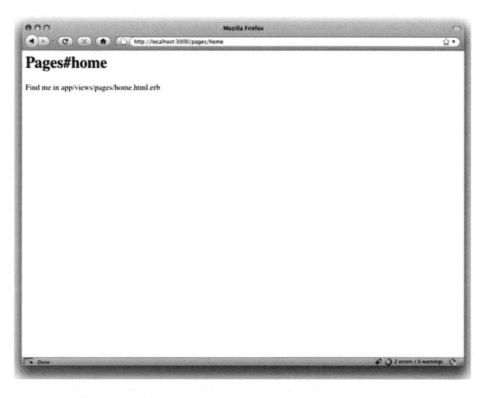

Figure 3.5   The raw home view (/pages/home) generated by Rails.

unlike the demo Users and Microposts controllers from Chapter 2, the Pages controller does not follow the REST conventions.)

Listing 3.6 The Pages controller made by Listing 3.4.
`app/controllers/pages_controller.rb`

```ruby
class PagesController < ApplicationController

  def home
  end

  def contact
  end
end
```

We see here that `pages_controller.rb` defines a *class* called `PagesController`. Classes are simply a convenient way to organize *functions* (also called *methods*) like the `home` and `contact` actions, which are defined using the `def` keyword. The angle bracket `<` indicates that `PagesController` *inherits* from the Rails class `Application-Controller`; as we'll see momentarily, this means that our pages come equipped with a large amount of Rails-specific functionality. (We'll learn more about both classes and inheritance in Section 4.4.)

In the case of the Pages controller, both its methods are initially empty:

```ruby
def home
end

def contact
end
```

In plain Ruby, these methods would simply do nothing. In Rails, the situation is different; `PagesController` is a Ruby class, but because it inherits from `Application-Controller` the behavior of its methods is specific to Rails: when visiting the URL `/pages/home`, Rails looks in the Pages controller and executes the code in the `home` action, and then renders the *view* (the V in MVC from Section 1.2.6) corresponding to the action. In the present case, the `home` action is empty, so all hitting `/pages/home` does is render the view. So, what does a view look like, and how do we find it?

If you take another look at the output in Listing 3.4, you might be able to guess the correspondence between actions and views: an action like `home` has a corresponding view called **home.html.erb**. We'll learn in Section 3.3 what the **.erb** part means; from the **.html** part you probably won't be surprised that it basically looks like HTML (Listing 3.7).

Listing 3.7 The generated view for the Home page.
app/views/pages/home.html.erb

```
<h1>Pages#home</h1>
<p>Find me in app/views/pages/home.html.erb</p>
```

The view for the **contact** action is analogous (Listing 3.8).

Listing 3.8 The generated view for the Contact page.
app/views/pages/contact.html.erb

```
<h1>Pages#contact</h1>
<p>Find me in app/views/pages/contact.html.erb</p>
```

Both of these views are just placeholders: they have a top-level heading (inside the **h1** tag) and a paragraph (**p** tag) with the full path to the relevant file. We'll add some (very slightly) dynamic content starting in Section 3.3, but as they stand these views underscore an important point: Rails views can simply contain static HTML. As far as the browser is concerned, the raw HTML files from Section 3.1.1 and the controller/action method of delivering pages are indistinguishable: all the browser ever sees is HTML.

In the remainder of this chapter, we'll first add the **about** action we "forgot" in Section 3.1.2, add a very small amount of dynamic content, and then take the first steps toward styling the pages with CSS. Before moving on, if you're using Git it's a good idea to add the files for the Pages controller to the repository at this time:

```
$ git add .
$ git commit -am "Added a Pages controller"
```

You may recall from Section 1.3.5 that we used the Git command **git commit -a -m "Message"**, with flags for "all changes" (**-a**) and a message (**-m**); Git also lets us roll the two flags into one as **-am**, and I'll stick with this more compact formulation throughout the rest of this book.

3.2 Our First Tests

If you ask five Rails developers how to test any given piece of code, you'll get about fifteen different answers—but they'll all agree that you should definitely be writing tests. It's in this spirit that we'll approach testing our sample application, writing solid tests without worrying too much about making them perfect. You shouldn't take the tests in *Rails Tutorial* as gospel; they are based on the style I have developed during my own work and from reading the code of others. As you gain experience as a Rails developer, you will no doubt form your own preferences and develop your own testing style.

In addition to writing tests throughout the development of the sample application, we will also make the increasingly common choice about *when* to write tests by writing them *before* the application code—an approach known as *test-driven development*, or TDD.[6] Our specific example will be to add an About page to our sample site. Fortunately, adding the extra page is not hard—you might even be able to guess the answer based on the examples in the previous section—which means that we can focus on testing, which contains quite a few new ideas.

At first, testing for the existence of a page might seem like overkill, but experience shows that it is not. So many things can go wrong when writing software that having a good test suite is invaluable to assure quality. Moreover, it is common for computer programs—and especially web applications—to be constantly extended, and any time you make a change you risk introducing errors. Writing tests doesn't guarantee that these bugs won't happen, but it makes them much more likely to be caught (and fixed) when they occur. Furthermore, by writing tests for bugs that *do* happen, we can make them much less likely to recur.

(As noted in Section 1.1.1, if you find the tests overwhelming, go ahead and skip them on first reading. Once you have a stronger grasp of Rails and Ruby, you can loop back and learn testing on a second pass.)

3.2.1 Testing Tools

To write tests for our sample application, our main tool is a framework called RSpec, which is a *domain-specific language* for describing the behavior of code, together with a program (called **rspec**) to verify the desired behavior. Designed for testing any Ruby

---

6. In the context of RSpec, TDD is also known as Behavior Driven Development, or BDD. (Frankly, I'm not convinced there's much of a difference.)

program, RSpec has gained significant traction in the Rails community. Obie Fernandez, author of *The Rails 3 Way*, has called RSpec "the Rails Way", and I agree.[7] If you followed the steps in the introduction, RSpec has already been installed via the Bundler **Gemfile** (Listing 3.1) and **bundle install**.

Autotest

Autotest is a tool that continuously runs your test suite in the background based on the specific file changes you make. For example, if you change a controller file, Autotest runs the tests for that controller. The result is instant feedback on the status of your tests. We'll learn more about Autotest when we see it in action (Section 3.2.2).

Installing Autotest is optional, and configuring it can be a bit tricky, but if you can get it to work on your system I'm sure you'll find it as useful as I do. To install Autotest, install the autotest and autotest-rails-pure[8] gems as follows:[9]

```
$ [sudo] gem install autotest -v 4.3.2
$ [sudo] gem install autotest-rails-pure -v 4.1.0
```

The next steps depend on your platform. I'll go through the steps for OS X, since that's what I use, and then give references to blog posts that discuss Autotest on Linux and Windows. On OS X, you should install Growl (if you don't have it already) and then install the autotest-fsevent and autotest-growl gems:[10]

```
$ [sudo] gem install autotest-fsevent -v 0.2.2
$ [sudo] gem install autotest-growl -v 0.2.4
```

If FSEvent won't install properly, double-check that Xcode is installed on your system.

---

7. The Shoulda testing framework is a good alternate choice (and in fact can be used with RSpec). It's the Other Rails Way, so to speak.

8. This used to be just autotest-rails, but it depends on the full ZenTest suite, which caused problems on some systems. The autotest-rails-pure gem avoids this dependency.

9. If you're running OS X Snow Leopard, you might have to use different versions. Simply omit the -v ... flag to get the latest version of the gem.

10. The Autotest Growl gem causes the test results to be automatically displayed to the monitor, whereas the FSEvent gem causes Autotest to use OS X filesystem events to trigger the test suite, rather than continuously polling the filesystem. Also note that with both gems you might need to use an updated version if you're running OS X Snow Leopard.

To use the Growl and FSEvent gems, make an Autotest configuration file in your Rails root directory and fill it with the contents of Listing 3.9:

```
$ mate .autotest
```

Listing 3.9 The **.autotest** configuration file for Autotest on OS X.

```
require 'autotest/growl'
require 'autotest/fsevent'
```

(Note: this will create an Autotest configuration for the sample application only; if you want to share this Autotest configuration with other Rails or Ruby projects, you should create the **.autotest** file in your *home* directory instead:

```
$ mate ~/.autotest
```

where ~ (tilde) is the Unix symbol for "home directory".)

If you're running Linux with the Gnome desktop, you should try the steps at Automate Everything, which sets up on Linux a system similar to Growl notifications on OS X. Windows users should try installing Growl for Windows and then follow the instructions at the GitHub page for **autotest-growl**. Both Linux and Windows users might want to take a look at autotest-notification; *Rails Tutorial* reader Fred Schoeneman has a write-up about Autotest notification on his blog.[11]

3.2.2 TDD: Red, Green, Refactor

In test-driven development, we first write a *failing* test: in our case, a piece of code that expresses the idea that there "should be an **about**" page. Then we get the test to pass, in our case by adding the **about** action and corresponding view. The reason we don't typically do the reverse—implement first, then test—is to make sure that we actually test for the feature we're adding. Before I started using TDD, I was amazed to discover how often my "tests" actually tested the wrong thing, or even tested nothing at all. By

---

11. http://fredschoeneman.posterous.com/pimp-your-autotest-notification

making sure that the test fails first and *then* passes, we can be more confident that the test is doing the right thing.

It's important to understand that TDD is not always the right tool for the job. In particular, when you aren't at all sure how to solve a given programming problem, it's often useful to skip the tests and write only application code, just to get a sense of what the solution will look like. (In the language of Extreme Programming (XP), this exploratory step is called a *spike*.) Once you see the general shape of the solution, you can then use TDD to implement a more polished version.

One way to proceed in test-driven development is a cycle known as "Red, Green, Refactor". The first step, Red, refers to writing a failing test, which many test tools indicate with the color red. The next step, Green, refers to a passing test, indicated with the color (wait for it) green. Once we have a passing test (or set of tests), we are free to *refactor* our code, changing the form (eliminating duplication, for example) without changing the function.

We don't have any colors yet, so let's get started toward Red. RSpec (and testing in general) can be a little intimidating at first, so we'll use the tests generated by **rails generate controller Pages** in Listing 3.4 to get us started. Since I'm not partial to separate tests for views or helpers, which I've found to be either brittle or redundant, our first step is to remove them. If you're using Git, you can do this as follows:

```
$ git rm -r spec/views
$ git rm -r spec/helpers
```

Otherwise, remove them directly:

```
$ rm -rf spec/views
$ rm -rf spec/helpers
```

We'll handle tests for views and helpers directly in the controller tests starting in Section 3.3.

To get started with RSpec, take a look at the Pages controller spec[12] we just generated (Listing 3.10).

---

12. In the context of RSpec, tests are often called *specs*, but for simplicity I'll usually stick to the term "test"— *except* when referring to a file such as **pages_controller_spec**, in which case I'll write "Pages controller spec".

Listing 3.10 The generated Pages controller spec.
`spec/controllers/pages_controller_spec.rb`

```ruby
require 'spec_helper'

describe PagesController do

  describe "GET 'home'" do
    it "should be successful" do
      get 'home'
      response.should be_success
    end
  end

  describe "GET 'contact'" do
    it "should be successful" do
      get 'contact'
      response.should be_success
    end
  end
end
```

This code is pure Ruby, but even if you've studied Ruby before it probably won't look very familiar. This is because RSpec uses the general malleability of Ruby to define a *domain-specific language* (DSL) built just for testing. The important point is that *you do not need to understand RSpec's syntax to be able to use RSpec.* It may seem like magic at first, but RSpec is designed to read more or less like English, and if you follow the examples from the **generate** script and the other examples in this tutorial you'll pick it up fairly quickly.

Listing 3.10 contains two **describe** blocks, each with one *example* (i.e., a block starting with **it "..." do**). Let's focus on the first one to get a sense of what it does:

```ruby
describe "GET 'home'" do
  it "should be successful" do
    get 'home'
    response.should be_success
  end
end
```

The first line indicates that we are describing a GET operation for the **home** action. This is just a description, and it can be anything you want; RSpec doesn't care, but you and other human readers probably do. In this case, **"GET 'home'"** indicates that the test corresponds to an HTTP GET request, as discussed in Box 3.1. Then the spec says that when you visit the home page, it should be successful. As with the first line, what goes inside the quote marks is irrelevant to RSpec, and is intended to be descriptive to human readers. The third line, **get 'home'**, is the first line that really does something. Inside of RSpec, this line *actually submits a GET request*; in other words, it acts like a browser and hits a page, in this case /pages/home. (It knows to hit the Pages controller automatically because this is a Pages controller test; it knows to hit the home page because we tell it to explicitly.) Finally, the fourth line says that the *response* of our application should indicate success (i.e., it should return a *status code* of 200; see Box 3.2).

Box 3.2   HTTP response codes

After a client (such as a web browser) sends a request corresponding to one of the HTTP verbs (Box 3.1), the web server *responds* with a numerical code indicating the HTTP status of the response. For example, a status code of 200 means "success", and a status code of 301 means "permanent redirect". If you install curl, a command-line client that can issue HTTP requests, you can see this directly at, e.g., www.google.com (where the --head flag prevents **curl** from returning the whole page):

```
$ curl --head www.google.com
HTTP/1.1 200 OK
.
.
.
```

Here Google indicates that the request was successful by returning the status 200 OK. In contrast, google.com is permanently redirected (to www.google.com, naturally), indicated by status code 301 (a "301 redirect"):

```
$ curl --head google.com
HTTP/1.1 301 Moved Permanently
Location: http://www.google.com/
.
.
.
```

(*Note:* The above results may vary by country.)

When we write **response.should be_success** in an RSpec test, RSpec verifies that our application's response to the request is status code 200.

Now it's time to run our tests. There are several different and mostly equivalent ways to do this.[13] One way to run all the tests is to use the **rspec** script at the command line as follows:[14]

```
$ rspec spec/
....

Finished in 0.07252 seconds

2 examples, 0 failures
```

(Unfortunately, lots of things can go wrong at this point. If any test fails, be sure that you've migrated the database with **rake db:migrate** as described in Section 1.2.5. If RSpec doesn't work at all, try running **bundle exec rspec spec/** instead of just **rspec spec/**. If that fails, try uninstalling and reinstalling it:

```
$ gem uninstall rspec rspec-rails
$ bundle install
```

If it still doesn't work and you're using RVM, try removing the Rails Tutorial gemset and reinstalling the gems:

```
$ rvm gemset delete rails3tutorial
$ rvm --create use 1.9.2@rails3tutorial
$ rvm --default 1.9.2@rails3tutorial
$ gem install rails -v 3.0.1
$ bundle install
```

If it still doesn't work, I'm out of ideas.)

When running **rspec spec/**, **rspec** is a program provided by RSpec, while **spec/** is the *directory* whose specs you want to run. You can also run only the specs in a particular subdirectory. For example, this command runs only the controller specs:

---

13. Most IDEs also have an interface to testing, but as noted in Section 1.2.1 I have limited experience with those tools.

14. You can also run **rake spec**, which is basically equivalent. (Annoyingly, if you want to run **rake spec** here you have to run **rake db:migrate** first, even though the tests in this chapter don't require a database.) When something goes wrong, **rspec spec/** will show the stack trace, whereas **rake spec** doesn't show the stack trace by default. Since the stack trace is often useful in debugging, **rspec spec/** is a prudent default.

```
$ rspec spec/controllers/
....
Finished in 0.07502 seconds

2 examples, 0 failures
```

You can also run a single file:

```
$ rspec spec/controllers/pages_controller_spec.rb
...
Finished in 0.07253 seconds

2 examples, 0 failures
```

The results of all three commands are the same since the Pages controller spec is currently our only test file. Throughout the rest of this book, I won't usually show the output of running the tests, but you should run **rspec spec/** (or one of its variants) regularly as you follow along—or, better yet, use Autotest to run the test suite automatically. Speaking of which. . .

If you've installed Autotest, you can run it on your RSpec tests using the **autotest** command:

```
$ autotest
```

If you're using a Mac with Growl notifications enabled, you should be able to replicate my setup, shown in Figure 3.6. With Autotest running in the background and Growl notifications telling you the status of your tests, TDD can be positively addictive.

Spork

You may have noticed that the overhead involved in running a test suite can be considerable. This is because each time RSpec runs the tests it has to reload the entire Rails environment. The Spork test server[15] aims to solve this problem. Spork loads the environment *once*, and then maintains a pool of processes for running future tests. Spork is particularly useful when combined with Autotest.

---

15. A *spork* is a combination spoon-fork. My guess is that the project's name is a pun on Spork's use of POSIX forks.

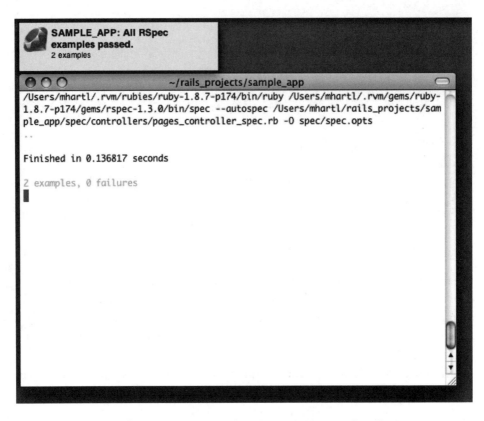

Figure 3.6   Autotest (via **autotest**) in action, with a Growl notification.

Configuring Spork and getting it to work can be difficult, and this is a rather advanced topic; in particular, as of this writing Spork doesn't officially support Rails 3, so this section is really just a collection of hacks. Nevertheless, the performance boost due to Spork is considerable, so I recommend giving it a shot at some point. (You'll have to rely on the Spork website and Google searches if these directions don't work for you.) **If you get stuck, don't hesitate to skip this section for now.**

The first step is to add the spork gem dependency to the **Gemfile** (Listing 3.11).

Listing 3.11   A **Gemfile** for the demo app.

```
source 'http://rubygems.org'

gem 'rails', '3.0.0'
gem 'sqlite3-ruby', '1.2.5', :require => 'sqlite3'
```

```
group :development do
  gem 'rspec-rails', '2.0.1'
end

group :test do
  gem 'rspec', '2.0.1'
  .
  .
  .
  gem 'spork', '0.8.4'
end
```

Then install it:

```
$ bundle install
```

Next, bootstrap the Spork configuration:

```
$ spork --bootstrap
```

Now we need to edit the RSpec configuration file, **spec/spec_helper.rb**, so that the environment gets loaded in a *prefork* block, which arranges for it to be loaded only once (Listing 3.12). *Note:* Only use this code if you are also using Spork. If you try to use Listing 3.12 without Spork, your application test suite will not run.

Listing 3.12 Adding environment loading to the **Spork.prefork** block.
spec/spec_helper.rb

```
require 'rubygems'
require 'spork'

Spork.prefork do
  # Loading more in this block will cause your tests to run faster. However,
  # if you change any configuration or code from libraries loaded here, you'll
  # need to restart spork for it take effect.
  ENV["RAILS_ENV"] ||= 'test'
  unless defined?(Rails)
    require File.dirname(__FILE__) + "/../config/environment"
  end
```

```
require 'rspec/rails'

# Requires supporting files with custom matchers and macros, etc,
# in ./support/ and its subdirectories.
Dir["#{File.dirname(__FILE__)}/support/**/*.rb"].each {|f| require f}

Rspec.configure do |config|
  # == Mock Framework
  #
  # If you prefer to use mocha, flexmock or RR, uncomment the appropriate line:
  #
  # config.mock_with :mocha
  # config.mock_with :flexmock
  # config.mock_with :rr
  config.mock_with :rspec

  config.fixture_path = "#{::Rails.root}/spec/fixtures"

  # If you're not using ActiveRecord, or you'd prefer not to run each of your
  # examples within a transaction, comment the following line or assign false
  # instead of true.
  config.use_transactional_fixtures = true

  ### Part of a Spork hack. See http://bit.ly/arY19y
  # Emulate initializer set_clear_dependencies_hook in
  # railties/lib/rails/application/bootstrap.rb
  ActiveSupport::Dependencies.clear
  end
end

Spork.each_run do
end
```

Note that we've also added the line

```
ActiveSupport::Dependencies.clear
```

at the end of the **Rspec.configure** block. This is to work around the current lack
of Rails 3 support in Spork. (As of this writing, Spork doesn't reload the application
files when using Autotest, leading to the absurd situation of not being able to get, say,
a failing Users controller spec example to pass by editing the Users controller. This
undermines TDD just a bit.) To complete the workaround, we also need to add a few

lines to **config/application.rb** (Listing 3.13). *Note:* As in the case of Listing 3.12, only use this code if you are also using Spork.

Listing 3.13 The last part of the hack needed to get Spork to run with Rails 3.
config/application.rb

```
require File.expand_path('../boot', __FILE__)

require 'rails/all'

# If you have a Gemfile, require the gems listed there, including any gems
# you've limited to :test, :development, or :production.
Bundler.require(:default, Rails.env) if defined?(Bundler)

module SampleApp
  class Application < Rails::Application
    .
    .
    .
    ### Part of a Spork hack. See http://bit.ly/arY19y
    if Rails.env.test?
      initializer :after => :initialize_dependency_mechanism do
        # Work around initializer in railties/lib/rails/application/bootstrap.rb
        ActiveSupport::Dependencies.mechanism = :load
      end
    end
  end
end
```

Before running Spork, we can get a baseline for the testing overhead by timing our test suite as follows:

```
$ time rspec spec/
..


Finished in 0.09606 seconds
2 examples, 0 failures

real    0m7.445s
user    0m5.248s
sys     0m1.475s
```

Here the test suite takes more than seven seconds to run even though the actual tests run in under a tenth of a second. To speed this up, we can open a dedicated terminal window, navigate to the Rails root directory, and then start a Spork server:

```
$ spork
Using RSpec
Loading Spork.prefork block...
Spork is ready and listening on 8989!
```

In another terminal window, we can now run our test suite with the --drb option[16] and verify that the environment-loading overhead is greatly reduced:

```
$ time rspec --drb spec/
..


Finished in 0.10519 seconds
2 examples, 0 failures

real    0m0.803s
user    0m0.354s
sys     0m0.171s
```

As expected, the overhead has been dramatically reduced.

To run RSpec and Spork with Autotest, we need to configure RSpec to use the --drb option by default, which we can arrange by adding it to the **.rspec** configuration file in the Rails root directory (Listing 3.14).

Listing 3.14 Adding the --drb option to the **.rspec** file.

```
--colour
--drb
```

With this updated **.rspec** file, the test suite should run as quickly as before, even without the explicit --drb option:

---

16. DRb stands for "Distributed Ruby".

```
$ time rspec spec/
..


Finished in 0.10926 seconds
2 examples, 0 failures

real    0m0.803s
user    0m0.355s
sys     0m0.171s
```

Of course, running **time** here is just for purposes of illustration; normally, you just run

```
$ rspec spec/
```

or

```
$ autotest
```

without the **time** command.

One word of advice when using Spork: if your tests are failing when you think they should be passing, the problem might be the Spork prefork loading, which can sometimes prevent necessary files from being re-loaded. When in doubt, quit the Spork server with Control-C and restart it:

```
$ spork
Using RSpec
Loading Spork.prefork block...
Spork is ready and listening on 8989!
^C
$ spork
```

Red

Now let's get to the Red part of the Red-Green cycle by writing a failing test for the **about** page. Following the models from Listing 3.10, you can probably guess the right test (Listing 3.15).

Listing 3.15 The Pages controller spec with a failing test for the About page.
`spec/controllers/pages_controller_spec.rb`

```
require 'spec_helper'

describe PagesController do
  render_views

  describe "GET 'home'" do
    it "should be successful" do
      get 'home'
      response.should be_success
    end
  end

  describe "GET 'contact'" do
    it "should be successful" do
      get 'contact'
      response.should be_success
    end
  end

  describe "GET 'about'" do
    it "should be successful" do
      get 'about'
      response.should be_success
    end
  end
end
```

Note that we've added a line to tell RSpec to *render the views* inside the controller tests. In other words, by default RSpec just tests actions inside a controller test; if we want it also to render the views, we have to tell it explicitly via the second line:

```
describe PagesController do
  render_views
  .
  .
  .
```

This ensures that if the test passes, the page is really there.

Figure 3.7 Failing spec for the About page using `rspec spec/`.

The new test attempts to **get** the **about** action, and indicates that the resulting response should be a success. By design, it fails (with a red error message), as seen in Figure 3.7 (**rspec spec/**) and Figure 3.8 (**autotest**). (If you test the views in the controllers as recommended in this tutorial, it's worth noting that changing the view file won't prompt Autotest to run the corresponding controller test. There's probably a way to configure Autotest to do this automatically, but usually I just just switch to the controller and press "space-backspace" so that the file gets marked as modified. Saving the controller then causes Autotest to run the tests as desired.)

This is Red. Now let's get to Green.

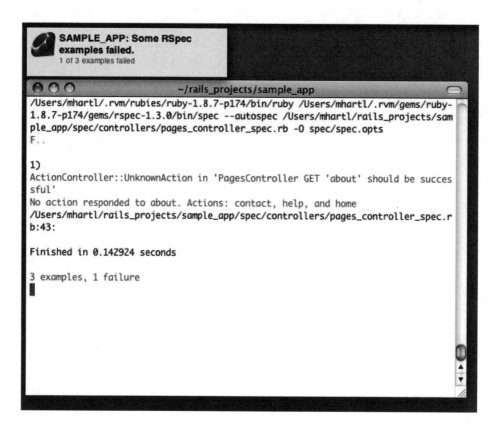

Figure 3.8   Failing spec for the About page using Autotest.

Green

Recall from Section 3.1.2 that we can generate a static page in Rails by creating an action and corresponding view with the page's name. In our case, the About page will first need an action called **about** in the Pages controller. Having written a failing test, we can now be confident that, in getting it to pass, we will actually have created a working **about** page.

Following the models provided by **home** and **contact** from Listing 3.6, let's first add an **about** action in the Pages controller (Listing 3.16).

Listing 3.16   The Pages controller with added **about** action.
`app/controllers/pages_controller.rb`

```
class PagesController < ApplicationController

  def home
```

```
  end

  def contact
  end

  def about
  end
end
```

Next, we'll add the **about** action to the routes file (Listing 3.17).

Listing 3.17 Adding the **about** route.
config/routes.rb

```
SampleApp::Application.routes.draw do
  get "pages/home"
  get "pages/contact"
  get "pages/about"
  .
  .
  .
end
```

Finally, we'll add the **about** view. Eventually we'll fill it with something more informative, but for now we'll just mimic the content from the generated views (Listing 3.7
and Listing 3.8) for the **about** view (Listing 3.18).

Listing 3.18 A stub About page.
app/views/pages/about.html.erb

```
<h1>Pages#about</h1>
<p>Find me in app/views/pages/about.html.erb</p>
```

Running the specs or watching the update from Autotest (Figure 3.9) should get us
back to Green:

```
$ rspec spec/
```

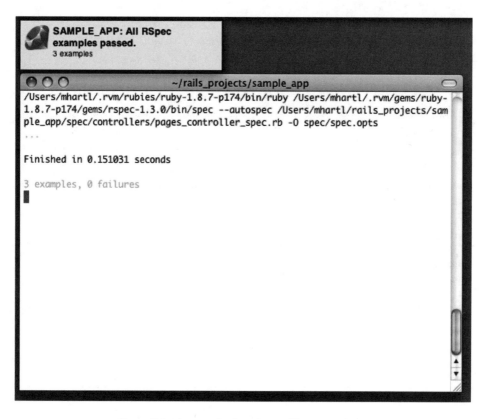

Figure 3.9   Autotest back to Green: All tests passing.

Of course, it's never a bad idea to take a look at the page in a browser to make sure our tests aren't completely crazy (Figure 3.10).

Refactor

Now that we're at Green, we are free to *refactor* our code by changing its form without changing its function. Oftentimes code will start to "smell", meaning that it gets ugly, bloated, or filled with repetition. The computer doesn't care, of course, but humans do, so it is important to keep the code base clean by refactoring frequently. Having a good (passing!) test suite is an invaluable tool in this regard, as it dramatically lowers the probability of introducing bugs while refactoring.

Our sample app is a little too small to refactor right now, but code smell seeps in at every crack, so we won't have to wait long: we'll already get busy refactoring in Section 3.3.3 of this chapter.

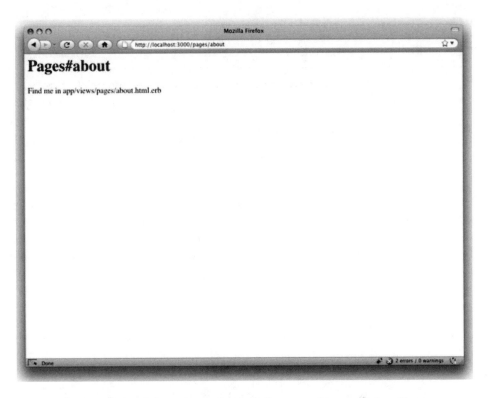

Figure 3.10   The new (and rather raw) About page (`/pages/about`).

3.3 Slightly Dynamic Pages

Now that we've created the actions and views for some static pages, we'll make them *very slightly* dynamic by adding some content that changes on a per-page basis: we'll have the title of each page change to reflect its content. Whether this represents *truly* dynamic content is debatable, but in any case it lays the necessary foundation for unambiguously dynamic content in Chapter 8.

(If you skipped the TDD material in Section 3.2, be sure to create an About page at this point using the code from Listing 3.16, Listing 3.17, and Listing 3.18.)

3.3.1 Testing a Title Change

Our plan is to edit the Home, Contact, and About pages to add the kind of HTML structure we saw in Listing 3.3, including titles that change on each page. It's a delicate matter to decide just which of these changes to test, and in general testing HTML can

Table 3.1 The (mostly) static pages for the sample app

Page	URL	Base title	Variable title
Home	/pages/home	`"Ruby on Rails Tutorial Sample App" "`	`| Home"`
Contact	/pages /contact	`"Ruby on Rails Tutorial Sample App" "`	`| Contact"`
About	/pages/about	`"Ruby on Rails Tutorial Sample App" "`	`| About"`

be quite fragile since content tends to change frequently. We'll keep our tests simple by just testing for the page titles.

By the end of this section, all three of our static pages will have titles of the form "Ruby on Rails Tutorial Sample App | Home", where the last part of the title will vary depending on the page (Table 3.1). We'll build on the tests in Listing 3.15, adding title tests following the model in Listing 3.19.

Listing 3.19 A title test.

```
it "should have the right title" do
  get 'home'
  response.should have_selector("title",
                   :content => "Ruby on Rails Tutorial Sample App | Home")
end
```

This uses the **have_selector** method inside RSpec; the documentation for **have_selector** is surprisingly sparse, but what it does is to check for an HTML element (the "selector") with the given content. In other words, the code

```
response.should have_selector("title",
                 :content => "Ruby on Rails Tutorial Sample App | Home")
```

checks to see that the content inside the `<title></title>` tags is **"Ruby on Rails Tutorial Sample App | Home"**.[17] It's worth mentioning that the content need not be an exact match; any substring works as well, so that

---

17. We'll learn in Section 4.3.3 that the **:content => "..."** syntax is a *hash* using a *symbol* as the key.

```
response.should have_selector("title", :content => " | Home")
```

will also match the full title.[18]

Note that in Listing 3.19 I've broken the material inside **have_selector** into two lines; this tells you something important about Ruby syntax: Ruby doesn't care about newlines.[19] The *reason* I chose to break the code into pieces is that I prefer to keep lines of source code under 80 characters for legibility.[20] As it stands, I still find this code formatting rather ugly; Section 3.5 has a refactoring exercise that makes them much prettier.[21]

Adding new tests for each of our three static pages following the model of Listing 3.19 gives us our new Pages controller spec (Listing 3.20).

Listing 3.20 The Pages controller spec with title tests.
spec/controllers/pages_controller_spec.rb

```
require 'spec_helper'

describe PagesController do
  render_views

  describe "GET 'home'" do
    it "should be successful" do
      get 'home'
      response.should be_success
    end

    it "should have the right title" do
      get 'home'
      response.should have_selector("title",
                        :content => "Ruby on Rails Tutorial Sample App | Home")
    end
  end
```

---

18. I consider this a step back from RSpec 1.3, which used **have_tag** in this context, which could be used to require an exact match. Unfortunately, as of this writing **have_tag** is not available in RSpec 2.

19. A newline is what comes at the end of a line, starting a, well, new line. In code, it is represented by the character \n.

20. Actually *counting* columns could drive you crazy, which is why many text editors have a visual aid to help you. Consider TextMate, for example; if you take a look back at Figure 1.1, you'll see a small vertical line on the right to help keep code under 80 characters. (It's actually at 78 columns, which gives you a little margin for error.) If you use TextMate, you can find this feature under View > Wrap Column > 78.

21. Rails 2.3/RSpec 1.3 used the shorter **have_tag** instead of **have_selector**, and the **:content** argument wasn't necessary either. Newer isn't always better...

```
describe "GET 'contact'" do
  it "should be successful" do
    get 'contact'
    response.should be_success
  end

  it "should have the right title" do
    get 'contact'
    response.should have_selector("title",
                    :content =>
                        "Ruby on Rails Tutorial Sample App | Contact")
  end
end

describe "GET 'about'" do
  it "should be successful" do
    get 'about'
    response.should be_success
  end

  it "should have the right title" do
    get 'about'
    response.should have_selector("title",
                    :content =>
                        "Ruby on Rails Tutorial Sample App | About")
  end
end
end
```

Note that the **render_views** line introduced in Listing 3.15 is necessary for the title tests to work.

With these tests in place, you should run

```
$ rspec spec/
```

or use Autotest to verify that our code is now Red (failing tests).

3.3.2 Passing Title Tests

Now we'll get our title tests to pass, and at the same time add the full HTML structure needed to make valid web pages. Let's start with the Home page (Listing 3.21), using the same basic HTML skeleton as in the "hello" page from Listing 3.3.

Note: In Rails 3, the controller generator creates a *layout* file, whose purpose we will explain shortly, but which for now you should remove before proceeding:

```
$ rm app/views/layouts/application.html.erb
```

Listing 3.21 The view for the Home page with full HTML structure.
app/views/pages/home.html.erb

```
<!DOCTYPE html>
<html>
  <head>
    <title>Ruby on Rails Tutorial Sample App | Home</title>
  </head>
  <body>
    <h1>Sample App</h1>
    <p>
      This is the home page for the
      <a href="http://railstutorial.org/">Ruby on Rails Tutorial</a>
      sample application.
    </p>
  </body>
</html>
```

Listing 3.21 uses the title tested for in Listing 3.20:

```
<title>Ruby on Rails Tutorial Sample App | Home</title>
```

As a result, the tests for the Home page should now pass. We're still Red because of the failing Contact and About tests, and we can get to Green with the code in Listing 3.22 and Listing 3.23.

Listing 3.22 The view for the Contact page with full HTML structure.
app/views/pages/contact.html.erb

```
<!DOCTYPE html>
<html>
  <head>
    <title>Ruby on Rails Tutorial Sample App | Contact</title>
  </head>
```

```
<body>
  <h1>Contact</h1>
  <p>
    Contact Ruby on Rails Tutorial about the sample app at the
    <a href="http://railstutorial.org/feedback">feedback page</a>.
  </p>
</body>
</html>
```

Listing 3.23 The view for the About page with full HTML structure.
app/views/pages/about.html.erb

```
<!DOCTYPE html>
<html>
  <head>
    <title>Ruby on Rails Tutorial Sample App | About</title>
  </head>
  <body>
    <h1>About Us</h1>
    <p>
      <a href="http://railstutorial.org/">Ruby on Rails Tutorial</a>
      is a project to make a book and screencasts to teach web development
      with <a href="http://rubyonrails.org/">Ruby on Rails</a>. This
      is the sample application for the tutorial.
    </p>
  </body>
</html>
```

These example pages introduce the *anchor* tag **a**, which creates links to the given URL (called an "href", or "hypertext reference", in the context of an anchor tag):

```
<a href="http://railstutorial.org/">Ruby on Rails Tutorial</a>
```

You can see the results in Figure 3.11.

3.3.3 Instance Variables and Embedded Ruby

We've achieved a lot already in this section, generating three valid pages using Rails controllers and actions, but they are purely static HTML and hence don't show off the power of Rails. Moreover, they suffer from terrible duplication:

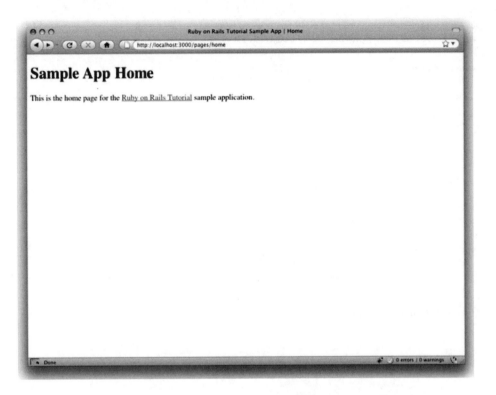

Figure 3.11   A minimal Home page for the sample app (/pages/home).

- The page titles are almost (but not quite) exactly the same.
- "Ruby on Rails Tutorial Sample App" is common to all three titles.
- The entire HTML skeleton structure is repeated on each page.

This repeated code is a violation of the important "Don't Repeat Yourself" (DRY) principle; in this section and the next we'll "DRY out our code" by removing the repetition.

Paradoxically, we'll take the first step toward eliminating duplication by first adding some more: we'll make the titles of the pages, which are currently quite similar, match *exactly*. This will make it much simpler to remove all the repetition at a stroke.

The technique involves creating *instance variables* inside our actions. Since the Home, Contact, and About page titles have a variable component, we'll set the variable `@title` (pronounced "at title") to the appropriate title for each action (Listing 3.24).

Listing 3.24 The Pages controller with per-page titles.
`app/controllers/pages_controller.rb`

```ruby
class PagesController < ApplicationController

  def home
    @title = "Home"
  end

  def contact
    @title = "Contact"
  end

  def about
    @title = "About"
  end
end
```

A statement such as

```ruby
@title = "Home"
```

is an *assignment*, in this case creating a new variable **`@title`** with value **`"Home"`**. The at sign **`@`** in **`@title`** indicates that it is an instance variable. Instance variables have a more general meaning in Ruby (see Section 4.2.3), but in Rails their role is primarily to link actions and views: any instance variable defined in the **`home`** action is automatically available in the **`home.html.erb`** view, and so on for other action/view pairs.[22]

We can see how this works by replacing the literal title "Home" with the contents of the **`@title`** variable in the **`home.html.erb`** view (Listing 3.25).

Listing 3.25 The view for the Home page with an Embedded Ruby title.
`app/views/pages/home.html.erb`

```erb
<!DOCTYPE html>
<html>
  <head>
    <title>Ruby on Rails Tutorial Sample App | <%= @title %></title>
  </head>
```

---

22. In fact, the instance variable is actually visible in *any* view, a fact we'll make use of in Section 8.2.2.

```
<body>
  <h1>Sample App</h1>
  <p>
    This is the home page for the
    <a href="http://railstutorial.org/">Ruby on Rails Tutorial</a>
    sample application.
  </p>
</body>
</html>
```

Listing 3.25 is our first example of *Embedded Ruby*, also called *ERb*. (Now you know why HTML views have the file extension **.html.erb**.) ERb is the primary mechanism in Rails for including dynamic content in web pages.[23] The code

```
<%= @title %>
```

indicates using <%= . . . %> that Rails should insert the contents of the **@title** variable, whatever it may be. When we visit /pages/home, Rails executes the body of the **home** action, which makes the assignment **@title = "Home"**, so in the present case

```
<%= @title %>
```

gets replaced with "Home". Rails then renders the view, using ERb to insert the value of **@title** into the template, which the web server then sends to your browser as HTML. The result is exactly the same as before, only now the variable part of the title is generated dynamically by ERb.

We can verify that all this works by running the tests from Section 3.3.1 and see that they still pass. Then we can make the corresponding replacements for the Contact and About pages (Listing 3.26 and Listing 3.27).

---

23. There is a second popular template system called Haml, which I personally love, but it's not *quite* standard enough yet for use in an introductory tutorial. If there is sufficient interest, I might produce a Rails Tutorial screencast series using Haml for the views. This would also allow for an introduction to Sass, Haml's sister technology, which if anything is even more awesome than Haml.

Listing 3.26 The view for the Contact page with an Embedded Ruby title.
`app/views/pages/contact.html.erb`

```
<!DOCTYPE html>
<html>
  <head>
    <title>Ruby on Rails Tutorial Sample App | <%= @title %></title>
  </head>
  <body>
    <h1>Contact</h1>
    <p>
      Contact Ruby on Rails Tutorial about the sample app at the
      <a href="http://railstutorial.org/feedback">feedback page</a>.
    </p>
  </body>
</html>
```

Listing 3.27 The view for the About page with an Embedded Ruby title.
`app/views/pages/about.html.erb`

```
<!DOCTYPE html>
<html>
  <head>
    <title>Ruby on Rails Tutorial Sample App | <%= @title %></title>
  </head>
  <body>
    <h1>About Us</h1>
    <p>
      <a href="http://railstutorial.org/">Ruby on Rails Tutorial</a>
      is a project to make a book and screencasts to teach web development
      with <a href="http://rubyonrails.org/">Ruby on Rails</a>. This
      is the sample application for the tutorial.
    </p>
  </body>
</html>
```

As before, the tests still pass.

3.3.4 Eliminating Duplication with Layouts

Now that we've replaced the variable part of the page titles with instance variables and
ERb, each of our pages looks something like this:

```
<!DOCTYPE html>
<html>
  <head>
    <title>Ruby on Rails Tutorial Sample App | <%= @title %></title>
  </head>
  <body>
    Contents
  </body>
</html>
```

In other words, *all* our pages are identical in structure, including even the title (because of Embedded Ruby), with the sole exception of the contents of each page.

Wouldn't it be nice if there were a way to factor out the common elements into some sort of global layout, with the body contents inserted on a per-page basis? Indeed, it would be nice, and Rails happily obliges using a special file called **application.html.erb**, which lives in the **layouts** directory. To capture the structural skeleton, edit **application.html.erb** and fill it with the contents of Listing 3.28.

Listing 3.28 The sample application site layout.
app/views/layouts/application.html.erb

```
<!DOCTYPE html>
<html>
  <head>
    <title>Ruby on Rails Tutorial Sample App | <%= @title %></title>
    <%= csrf_meta_tag %>
  </head>
  <body>
    <%= yield %>
  </body>
</html>
```

Note here the special line

```
<%= yield %>
```

This code is responsible for inserting the contents of each page into the layout. As with <%= @title %>, the <% ... %> tags indicate Embedded Ruby, and the equals sign in <%= ... %> ensures that the results of evaluating the expression are inserted at that exact point in the template. (Don't worry about the meaning of the word "yield"

in this context;[24] what matters is that using this layout ensures that visiting the page
/pages/home converts the contents of **home.html.erb** to HTML and then inserts it
in place of <%= yield %>.

Now that we have a site-wide layout, we've also taken this opportunity to add a
security feature to each page. Listing 3.28 adds the code

```
<%= csrf_meta_tag %>
```

which uses the Rails method **csrf_meta_tag** to prevent cross-site request forgery
(CSRF), a type of malicious web attack. Don't worry about the details (I don't); just
know that Rails is working hard to keep your application secure.

Of course, the views in Listing 3.25, Listing 3.26, and Listing 3.27 are still filled
with all the HTML structure we just hoisted into the layout, so we have to rip it out,
leaving only the interior contents. The resulting cleaned-up views appear in Listing 3.29,
Listing 3.30, and Listing 3.31.

Listing 3.29 The Home view with HTML structure removed.
app/views/pages/home.html.erb

```
<h1>Sample App</h1>
<p>
  This is the home page for the
  <a href="http://railstutorial.org/">Ruby on Rails Tutorial</a>
  sample application.
</p>
```

Listing 3.30 The Contact view with HTML structure removed.
app/views/pages/contact.html.erb

```
<h1>Contact</h1>
<p>
  Contact Ruby on Rails Tutorial about the sample app at the
  <a href="http://railstutorial.org/feedback">feedback page</a>.
</p>
```

---

24. If you've studied Ruby before, you might suspect that Rails is *yielding* the contents to a block, and your
suspicion would be correct. But, as far as developing web applications with Rails, it doesn't matter, and I've
honestly never given the meaning of <%= yield %> a second thought—or even a first one.

Listing 3.31   The About view with HTML structure removed.
`app/views/pages/about.html.erb`

```
<h1>About Us</h1>
<p>
  <a href="http://railstutorial.org/">Ruby on Rails Tutorial</a>
  is a project to make a book and screencasts to teach web development
  with <a href="http://rubyonrails.org/">Ruby on Rails</a>. This
  is the sample application for the tutorial.
</p>
```

With these views defined, the Home, Contact, and About pages are exactly the same as before—i.e., we have successfully refactored them—but they have much less duplication. And, as required, the tests still pass.

3.4   Conclusion

Seen from the outside, this chapter hardly accomplished anything: we started with static pages, and ended with... *mostly* static pages. But appearances are deceiving: by developing in terms of Rails controllers, actions, and views, we are now in a position to add arbitrary amounts of dynamic content to our site. Seeing exactly how this plays out is the task for the rest of this tutorial.

Before moving on, let's take a minute to commit our changes and merge them into the master branch. Back in Section 3.1.2 we created a Git branch for the development of static pages. If you haven't been making commits as we've been moving along, first make a commit indicating that we've reached a stopping point:

```
$ git add .
$ git commit -am "Done with static pages"
```

Then merge the changes back into the master branch using the same technique as in Section 1.3.5:

```
$ git checkout master
$ git merge static-pages
```

Once you reach a stopping point like this, it's usually a good idea to push your code up to a remote repository (which, if you followed the steps in Section 1.3.4, will be GitHub):

```
$ rspec spec/
$ git push
```

If you like, at this point you can even deploy the updated application to Heroku:

```
$ rspec spec/
$ git push heroku
```

Note that in both cases I've run **rspec spec/**, just to be sure that all the tests still pass. Running your tests before pushing or deploying is a good habit to cultivate.

3.5 Exercises

1. Make a Help page for the sample app. First write a test for the existence of a page at the URL /pages/help. Then write a second test for the title "Ruby on Rails Tutorial Sample App | Help". Get your tests to pass, and then fill in the Help page with the content from Listing 3.32.

2. You may have noticed some repetition in the Pages controller spec (Listing 3.20). In particular, the base title, "Ruby on Rails Tutorial Sample App", is the same for every title test. Using the RSpec **before(:each)** facility, which executes a block of code before each test case, fill in Listing 3.33 to define a **@base_title** instance variable that eliminates this duplication. (This code uses two new elements: a *symbol*, **:each**, and the string concatenation operator **+**. We'll learn more about both in Chapter 4, and we'll see **before(:each)** again in Section 6.2.1.) Note that, with the base title captured in an instance variable, we are now able to align **:content** with the first character inside each left parenthesis **(**. This is my preferred convention for formatting code broken into multiple lines.

Listing 3.32 Code for a proposed Help page.
app/views/pages/help.html.erb

```
<h1>Help</h1>
<p>
  Get help on Ruby on Rails Tutorial at the
  <a href="http://railstutorial.org/help">Rails Tutorial help page</a>.
```

```
  To get help on this sample app, see the
  <a href="http://railstutorial.org/book">Rails Tutorial book</a>.
</p>
```

Listing 3.33 The Pages controller spec with a base title.
spec/controllers/pages_controller_spec.rb

```ruby
require 'spec_helper'

describe PagesController do
  render_views

  before(:each) do
    #
    # Define @base_title here.
    #
  end

  describe "GET 'home'" do
    it "should be successful" do
      get 'home'
      response.should be_success
    end

    it "should have the right title" do
      get 'home'
      response.should have_selector("title",
                              :content => @base_title + " | Home")
    end
  end

  describe "GET 'contact'" do
    it "should be successful" do
      get 'contact'
      response.should be_success
    end

    it "should have the right title" do
      get 'contact'
      response.should have_selector("title",
                              :content => @base_title + " | Contact")
    end
  end

  describe "GET 'about'" do
    it "should be successful" do
```

```
    get 'about'
    response.should be_success
  end

  it "should have the right title" do
    get 'about'
    response.should have_selector("title",
                           :content => @base_title + " | About")
  end
 end
end
```

CHAPTER 4

Rails-Flavored Ruby

Grounded in examples from Chapter 3, this chapter explores some elements of Ruby important for Rails. Ruby is a big language, but fortunately the subset needed to be productive as a Rails developer is relatively small. Moreover, this subset is *different* from the usual approaches to learning Ruby, which is why, if your goal is making dynamic web applications, I recommend learning Rails first, picking up bits of Ruby along the way. To become a Rails *expert*, you need to understand Ruby more deeply, and this book gives you a good foundation for developing that expertise. As noted in Section 1.1.1, after finishing *Rails Tutorial* I suggest reading a pure Ruby book such as *Beginning Ruby*, *The Well-Grounded Rubyist*, or *The Ruby Way*.

This chapter covers a lot of material, and it's OK not to get it all on the first pass. I'll refer back to it frequently in future chapters.

4.1 Motivation

As we saw in the last chapter, it's possible to develop the skeleton of a Rails application, and even start testing it, with essentially no knowledge of the underlying Ruby language. We did this by relying on the generated controller and test code and following the examples we saw there. This situation can't last forever, though, and we'll open this chapter with a couple of additions to the site that bring us face-to-face with our Ruby limitations.

4.1.1 A `title` Helper

When we last saw our new application, we had just updated our mostly static pages to use Rails layouts to eliminate duplication in our views (Listing 4.1).

Listing 4.1 The sample application site layout.
`app/views/layouts/application.html.erb`

```erb
<!DOCTYPE html>
<html>
  <head>
    <title>Ruby on Rails Tutorial Sample App | <%= @title %></title>
    <%= csrf_meta_tag %>
  </head>
  <body>
    <%= yield %>
  </body>
</html>
```

This layout works well, but there's one part that could use a little polish. Recall that the title line

```erb
Ruby on Rails Tutorial Sample App | <%= @title %>
```

relies on the definition of **@title** in the actions, such as

```ruby
class PagesController < ApplicationController

  def home
    @title = "Home"
  end
  .
  .
  .
```

But what if we don't define an **@title** variable? It's a good convention to have a *base title* we use on every page, with an optional variable title if we want to be more specific. We've *almost* achieved that with our current layout, with one wrinkle: as you can see if you delete the **@title** assignment in one of the actions, in the absence of an **@title** variable the title appears as follows:

```
Ruby on Rails Tutorial Sample App |
```

In other words, there's a suitable base title, but there's also a trailing vertical bar character | at the end of the title.

One common way to handle this case is to define a *helper*, which is a function designed for use in views. Let's define a `title` helper that returns a base title, "Ruby on Rails Tutorial Sample App", if no `@title` variable is defined, and adds a vertical bar followed by the variable title if `@title` is defined (Listing 4.2).[1]

Listing 4.2 Defining a `title` helper.
`app/helpers/application_helper.rb`

```ruby
module ApplicationHelper

  # Return a title on a per-page basis.
  def title
    base_title = "Ruby on Rails Tutorial Sample App"
    if @title.nil?
      base_title
    else
      "#{base_title} | #{@title}"
    end
  end
end
```

This may look fairly simple to the eyes of an experienced Rails developer, but it's *full* of new Ruby ideas: modules, comments, local variable assignment, booleans, control flow, string interpolation, and return values. We'll cover each of these ideas in this chapter.

Now that we have a helper, we can use it to simplify our layout by replacing

```erb
<title>Ruby on Rails Tutorial Sample App | <%= @title %></title>
```

with

```erb
<title><%= title %></title>
```

---

1. If a helper is specific to a particular controller, you should put it in the corresponding helper file; for example, helpers for the Pages controller generally go in `app/helpers/pages_helper.rb`. In our case, we expect the `title` helper to be used on all the site's pages, and Rails has a special helper file for this case: `app/helpers/application_helper.rb`.

as seen in Listing 4.3. Note in particular the switch from the instance variable **@title** to the helper method **title** (without the **@** sign). Using Autotest or **rspec spec/**, you should verify that the tests from Chapter 3 still pass.

Listing 4.3 The sample application site layout.
app/views/layouts/application.html.erb

```
<!DOCTYPE html>
<html>
  <head>
    <title><%= title %></title>
    <%= csrf_meta_tag %>
  </head>
  <body>
    <%= yield %>
  </body>
</html>
```

4.1.2 Cascading Style Sheets

There's a second addition to our site that seems simple but adds several new Ruby concepts: including style sheets into our site layout. Though this is a book in web development, not web design, we'll be using cascading style sheets (CSS) to give the sample application some minimal styling, and we'll use the Blueprint CSS framework as a foundation for that styling.

To get started, download the latest Blueprint CSS. (For simplicity, I'll assume you download Blueprint to a **Downloads** directory, but use whichever directory is most convenient.) Using either the command line or a graphical tool, copy the Blueprint CSS directory **blueprint** into the **public/stylesheets** directory, a special directory where Rails keeps stylesheets. On my Mac, the commands looked like this, but your details may differ:

```
$ cp -r ~/Downloads/joshuaclayton-blueprint-css-<version number>/blueprint \
> public/stylesheets/
```

Here **cp** is the Unix copy command, and the **-r** flag copies recursively (needed for copying directories). (As mentioned briefly in Section 49, the tilde ~ means "home directory" in Unix.) *Note:* You should *not* paste in the > character to your terminal. If you paste in the first line with a backslash and hit return, you will see >, indicating a line continuation. You should then paste in the second line and hit return again to execute the command. Also note that you'll have to fill in the version number by hand, since that changes as Blueprint gets updated. Finally, be sure that you *don't* type

```
$ cp -r ~/Downloads/joshuaclayton-blueprint-css-<version number>/blueprint/ \
> public/stylesheets/
```

which has a trailing slash in **.../blueprint/**. This puts the *contents* of the Blueprint directory into **public/stylesheets** instead of moving the whole directory.

Once you have the stylesheets in the proper directory, Rails provides a helper for including them on our pages using Embedded Ruby (Listing 4.4).

Listing 4.4 Adding stylesheets to the sample application layout.
app/views/layouts/application.html.erb

```
<!DOCTYPE html>
<html>
  <head>
    <title><%= title %></title>
    <%= csrf_meta_tag %>
    <%= stylesheet_link_tag 'blueprint/screen', :media => 'screen' %>
    <%= stylesheet_link_tag 'blueprint/print',  :media => 'print' %>
  </head>
  <body>
    <%= yield %>
  </body>
</html>
```

Let's focus on the new lines:

```
<%= stylesheet_link_tag 'blueprint/screen', :media => 'screen' %>
<%= stylesheet_link_tag 'blueprint/print',  :media => 'print' %>
```

These use the built-in Rails helper **stylesheet_link_tag**, which you can read more about at the Rails API.[2] The first **stylesheet_link_tag** line includes the stylesheet

---

2. I don't provide links to the API because they have a tendency to go out of date quickly. Let Google be your guide. Incidentally, "API" stands for "application programming interface."

Figure 4.1   The Home page with the new Blueprint stylesheets.

blueprint/screen.css for screens (e.g., computer monitors), and the second includes **blueprint/print.css** for printing. (The helper automatically appends the **.css** extension to the filenames if absent, so I've left it off for brevity.) As with the **title** helper, to an experienced Rails developer these lines look simple, but there are at least four new Ruby ideas: built-in Rails methods, method invocation with missing parentheses, symbols, and hashes. In this chapter we'll cover these new ideas as well. (We'll see the HTML produced by these stylesheet includes in Listing 4.6 of Section 4.3.4.)

By the way, with the new stylesheets the site doesn't look much different than before, but it's a start (Figure 4.1). We'll build on this foundation starting in Chapter 5.[3]

---

3. If you're impatient, feel free to check out the Blueprint CSS Quickstart tutorial.

4.2 Strings and Methods

Our principal tool for learning Ruby will be the *Rails console*, which is a command-line tool for interacting with Rails applications. The console itself is built on top of interactive Ruby (**irb**), and thus has access to the full power of Ruby. (As we'll see in Section 4.4.4, the console also has access to the Rails environment.) Start the console at the command line as follows:[4]

```
$ rails console
Loading development environment (Rails 3.0.1)
>>
```

By default, the console starts in a *development environment*, which is one of three separate environments defined by Rails (the others are *test* and *production*). This distinction won't be important in this chapter; we'll learn more about environments in Section 6.3.1.

The console is a great learning tool, and you should feel free to explore—don't worry, you (probably) won't break anything. When using the console, type Ctrl-C if you get stuck, or Ctrl-D to exit the console altogether.

Throughout the rest of this chapter, you might find it helpful to consult the Ruby API.[5] It's packed (perhaps even *too* packed) with information; for example, to learn more about Ruby strings you can look at the Ruby API entry for the **String** class.

4.2.1 Comments

Ruby *comments* start with the pound sign **#** and extend to the end of the line. Ruby (and hence Rails) ignores comments, but they are useful for human readers (including, often, the original author!). In the code

```
# Return a title on a per-page basis.
def title
  .
  .
  .
```

the first line is a comment indicating the purpose of the subsequent function definition.

---

4. Recall that the console prompt will probably be something like **ruby-1.9.2-head >**, but the examples use **>>** since Ruby versions will vary.

5. As with the Rails API, Ruby API links go out of date, though not quite as fast. Google is still your guide.

You don't ordinarily include comments in console sessions, but for instructional purposes I'll include some comments in what follows, like this:

```
$ rails console
>> 17 + 42   # Integer addition
=> 59
```

If you follow along in this section typing or copying-and-pasting commands into your own console, you can of course omit the comments if you like; the console will ignore them in any case.

4.2.2 Strings

Strings are probably the most important data structure for web applications, since web pages ultimately consist of strings of characters sent from the server to the browser. Let's get started exploring strings with the console, this time started with **rails c**, which is a shortcut for **rails console**:

```
$ rails c
>> ""       # An empty string
=> ""
>> "foo"    # A nonempty string
=> "foo"
```

These are *string literals* (also, amusingly, called *literal strings*), created using the double quote character **"**. The console prints the result of evaluating each line, which in the case of a string literal is just the string itself.

We can also concatenate strings with the **+** operator:

```
>> "foo" + "bar"    # String concatenation
=> "foobar"
```

Here the result of evaluating **"foo"** plus **"bar"** is the string **"foobar"**.[6]

---

6. For more on the origins of "foo" and "bar"—and, in particular, the possible *non*-relation of "foobar" to "FUBAR"—see the Jargon File entry on "foo".

Another way to build up strings is via *interpolation* using the special syntax #{}:[7]

```
>> first_name = "Michael"     # Variable assignment
=> "Michael"
>> "#{first_name} Hartl"      # String interpolation
=> "Michael Hartl"
```

Here we've *assigned* the value **"Michael"** to the variable **first_name** and then interpolated it into the string **"#{first_name} Hartl"**. We could also assign both strings a variable name:

```
>> first_name = "Michael"
=> "Michael"
>> last_name = "Hartl"
=> "Hartl"
>> first_name + " " + last_name      # Concatenation, with a space in between
=> "Michael Hartl"
>> "#{first_name} #{last_name}"      # The equivalent interpolation
=> "Michael Hartl"
```

Note that the final two expressions are equivalent, but I prefer the interpolated version; having to add the single space **" "** seems a bit awkward.

Printing

To *print* a string, the most commonly used Ruby function is **puts** (pronounced "put ess", for "put string"):

```
>> puts "foo"     # put string
foo
=> nil
```

The **puts** method operates as a *side-effect*: the expression **puts "foo"** prints the string to the screen and then returns literally nothing: **nil** is a special Ruby value for "nothing at all". (In what follows, I'll sometimes suppress the **=> nil** part for simplicity.)

---

7. Programmers familiar with Perl or PHP should compare this to the automatic interpolation of dollar sign variables in expressions like **"foo $bar"**.

Using **puts** automatically appends a newline character \n to the output; the related **print** method does not:

```
>> print "foo"     # print string (same as puts, but without the newline)
foo=> nil
>> print "foo\n"   # Same as puts "foo"
foo
=> nil
```

Single-Quoted Strings

All the examples so far have used *double-quoted strings*, but Ruby also supports *single-quoted* strings. For many uses, the two types of strings are effectively identical:

```
>> 'foo'           # A single-quoted string
=> "foo"
>> 'foo' + 'bar'
=> "foobar"
```

There's an important difference, though; Ruby won't interpolate into single-quoted strings:

```
>> '#{foo} bar'        # Single-quoted strings don't allow interpolation
=> "\#{foo} bar"
```

Note how the console returns values using double-quoted strings, which requires a backslash to *escape* characters like **#**.

If double-quoted strings can do everything that single-quoted strings can do, and interpolate to boot, what's the point of single-quoted strings? They are often useful because they are truly literal, and contain exactly the characters you type. For example, the "backslash" character is special on most systems, as in the literal newline \n. If you want a variable to contain a literal backslash, single quotes make it easier:

```
>> '\n'            # A literal 'backslash n' combination
=> "\\n"
```

As with the **#** character in our previous example, Ruby needs to escape the backslash with an additional backslash; inside double-quoted strings, a literal backslash is represented with *two* backslashes.

For a small example like this, there's not much savings, but if there are lots of things to escape it can be a real help:

```
>> 'Newlines (\n) and tabs (\t) both use the backslash character \.'
=> "Newlines (\\n) and tabs (\\t) both use the backslash character \\."
```

4.2.3 Objects and Message Passing

Everything in Ruby, including strings and even **nil**, is an *object*. We'll see the technical meaning of this in Section 4.4.2, but I don't think anyone ever understood objects by reading the definition in a book; you have to build up your intuition for objects by seeing lots of examples.

It's easier to describe what objects *do*, which is respond to messages. An object like a string, for example, can respond to the message **length**, which returns the number of characters in the string:

```
>> "foobar".length        # Passing the "length" message to a string
=> 6
```

Typically, the messages that get passed to objects are *methods*, which are functions defined on those objects.[8] Strings also respond to the **empty?** method:

```
>> "foobar".empty?
=> false
>> "".empty?
=> true
```

Note the question mark at the end of the **empty?** method. This is a Ruby convention indicating that the return value is *boolean*: **true** or **false**. Booleans are especially useful

---

8. Apologies in advance for switching haphazardly between *function* and *method* throughout this chapter; in Ruby, they're the same thing: all methods are functions, and all functions are methods, because everything is an object.

for *control flow*:

```
>> s = "foobar"
>> if s.empty?
>>    "The string is empty"
>> else
>>    "The string is nonempty"
>> end
=> "The string is nonempty"
```

Booleans can also be combined using the **&&** ("and"), **||** ("or"), and **!** ("not") operators:

```
>> x = "foo"
=> "foo"
>> y = ""
=> ""
>> puts "Both strings are empty" if x.empty? && y.empty?
=> nil
>> puts "One of the strings is empty" if x.empty? || y.empty?
"One of the strings is empty"
=> nil
>> puts "x is not empty" if !x.empty?
"x is not empty"
```

Since everything in Ruby is an object, it follows that **nil** is an object, so it too can respond to methods. One example is the **to_s** method that can convert virtually any object to a string:

```
>> nil.to_s
=> ""
```

This certainly appears to be an empty string, as we can verify by *chaining* the messages we pass to **nil**:

```
>> nil.empty?
NoMethodError: You have a nil object when you didn't expect it!
You might have expected an instance of Array.
The error occurred while evaluating nil.empty?
>> nil.to_s.empty?     # Message chaining
=> true
```

We see here that the **nil** object doesn't itself respond to the **empty?** method, but **nil.to_s** does.

There's a special method for testing for **nil**-ness, which you might be able to guess:

```
>> "foo".nil?
=> false
>> "".nil?
=> false
>> nil.nil?
=> true
```

If you look back at Listing 4.2, you'll see that the **title** helper tests to see if **@title** is **nil** using the **nil?** method. This is a hint that there's something special about instance variables (variables with an **@** sign), which can best be understood by contrasting them with ordinary variables. For example, suppose we enter **title** and **@title** variables at the console without defining them first:

```
>> title          # Oops! We haven't defined a title variable.
NameError: undefined local variable or method `title'
>> @title         # An instance variable in the console
=> nil
>> puts "There is no such instance variable." if @title.nil?
There is no such instance variable.
=> nil
>> "#{@title}"    # Interpolating @title when it's nil
=> ""
```

You can see from this example that Ruby complains if we try to evaluate an undefined local variable, but issues no such complaint for an instance variable; instead, instance variables are **nil** if not defined. This also explains why the code

```
Ruby on Rails Tutorial Sample App | <%= @title %>
```

becomes

```
Ruby on Rails Tutorial Sample App |
```

when **@title** is **nil**: Embedded Ruby inserts the string corresponding to the given variable, and the string corresponding to **nil** is **""**.

The last example also shows an alternate use of the **if** keyword: Ruby allows you to write a statement that is evaluated only if the statement following **if** is true. There's a complementary **unless** keyword that works the same way:

```
>> string = "foobar"
>> puts "The string '#{string}' is nonempty." unless string.empty?
The string 'foobar' is nonempty.
=> nil
```

It's worth noting that the **nil** object is special, in that it is the *only* Ruby object that is false in a boolean context, apart from **false** itself:

```
>> if nil
>>   true
>> else
>>   false        # nil is false
>> end
=> false
```

In particular, all other Ruby objects are *true*, even 0:

```
>> if 0
>>   true          # 0 (and everything other than nil and false itself) is true
>> else
>>   false
>> end
=> true
```

4.2.4 Method Definitions

The console allows us to define methods the same way we did with the **home** action from Listing 3.6 or the **title** helper from Listing 4.2. (Defining methods in the console is a bit cumbersome, and ordinarily you would use a file, but it's convenient for demonstration purposes.) For example, let's define a function **string_message** that takes a single *argument* and returns a message based on whether the argument is empty or not:

```
>> def string_message(string)
>>   if string.empty?
>>     "It's an empty string!"
>>   else
>>     "The string is nonempty."
>>   end
>> end
=> nil
>> puts string_message("")
It's an empty string!
>> puts string_message("foobar")
The string is nonempty.
```

Note that Ruby functions have an *implicit return*, meaning they return the last statement evaluated—in this case, one of the two message strings, depending on whether the method's argument **string** is empty or not. Ruby also has an explicit return option; the following function is equivalent to the one above:

```
>> def string_message(string)
>>   return "It's an empty string!" if string.empty?
>>   return "The string is nonempty."
>> end
```

The alert reader might notice at this point that the second **return** here is actually unnecessary—being the last expression in the function, the string **"The string is nonempty."** will be returned regardless of the **return** keyword, but using **return** in both places has a pleasing symmetry to it.

4.2.5 Back to the **title** Helper

We are now in a position to understand the **title** helper from Listing 4.2:[9]

---

9. Well, there will still be *one* thing left that we don't understand, which is how Rails ties this all together: mapping URLs to actions, making the **title** helper available in views, etc. This is an interesting subject, and I encourage you to investigate it further, but knowing exactly *how* Rails works is not necessary when *using* Rails. (For a deeper understanding, I recommend *The Rails 3 Way* by Obie Fernandez.)

```
module ApplicationHelper

  # Return a title on a per-page basis.        # Documentation comment
  def title                                    # Method definition
    base_title = "Ruby on Rails Tutorial Sample App"  # Variable assignment
    if @title.nil?                             # Boolean test for nil
      base_title                               # Implicit return
    else
      "#{base_title} | #{@title}"              # String interpolation
    end
  end
end
```

These elements—function definition, variable assignment, boolean tests, control flow, and string interpolation—come together to make a compact helper method for use in our site layout. The final element is **module ApplicationHelper**: code in Ruby modules can be *mixed in* to Ruby classes. When writing ordinary Ruby, you often write modules and include them explicitly yourself, but in this case Rails handles the inclusion automatically for us. The result is that the **title** method is automagically available in all our views.

4.3 Other Data Structures

Though web apps are ultimately about strings, actually *making* those strings requires using other data structures as well. In this section, we'll learn about some Ruby data structures important for writing Rails applications.

4.3.1 Arrays and Ranges

An array is just a list of elements in a particular order. We haven't discussed arrays yet in *Rails Tutorial*, but understanding them gives a good foundation for understanding hashes (Section 4.3.3) and for aspects of Rails data modeling (such as the **has_many** association seen in Section 2.3.3 and covered more in Section 11.1.2).

So far we've spent a lot of time understanding strings, and there's a natural way to get from strings to arrays using the **split** method:

```
>> "foo bar    baz".split     # Split a string into a three-element array
=> ["foo", "bar", "baz"]
```

The result of this operation is an array of three strings. By default, **split** divides a string into an array by splitting on whitespace, but you can split on nearly anything else:

```
>> "fooxbarxbazx".split('x')
=> ["foo", "bar", "baz"]
```

As is conventional in most computer languages, Ruby arrays are *zero-offset*, which means that the first element in the array has index 0, the second has index 1, and so on:

```
>> a = [42, 8, 17]
=> [42, 8, 17]
>> a[0]                  # Ruby uses square brackets for array access.
=> 42
>> a[1]
=> 8
>> a[2]
=> 17
>> a[-1]                 # Indices can even be negative!
=> 17
```

We see here that Ruby uses square brackets to access array elements. In addition to this bracket notation, Ruby offers synonyms for some commonly accessed elements:[10]

```
>> a                     # Just a reminder of what 'a' is
=> [42, 8, 17]
>> a.first
=> 42
>> a.second
=> 8
>> a.last
=> 17
>> a.last == a[-1]       # Comparison using ==
=> true
```

This last line introduces the equality comparison operator **==**, which Ruby shares with many other languages, along with the associated **!=** ("not equal"), etc.:

---

10. The **second** method used here isn't currently part of Ruby itself, but rather is added by Rails. It works in this case because the Rails console automatically includes the Rails extensions to Ruby.

```
>> x = a.length          # Like strings, arrays respond to the 'length' method.
=> 3
>> x == 3
=> true
>> x == 1
=> false
>> x != 1
=> true
>> x >= 1
=> true
>> x < 1
=> false
```

In addition to **length** (seen in the first line above), arrays respond to a wealth of other methods:

```
>> a.sort
=> [8, 17, 42]
>> a.reverse
=> [17, 8, 42]
>> a.shuffle
=> [17, 42, 8]
```

You can also add to arrays with the "push" operator, **<<**:

```
>> a << 7                 # Pushing 7 onto an array
[42, 8, 17, 7]
>> a << "foo" << "bar"    # Chaining array pushes
[42, 8, 17, 7, "foo", "bar"]
```

This last example shows that you can chain pushes together, and also that, unlike arrays in many other languages, Ruby arrays can contain a mixture of different types (in this case, integers and strings).

Before we saw **split** convert a string to an array. We can also go the other way with the **join** method:

```
>> a
=> [42, 8, 17, 7, "foo", "bar"]
>> a.join                 # Join on nothing
=> "428177foobar"
>> a.join(', ')           # Join on comma-space
=> "42, 8, 17, 7, foo, bar"
```

Closely related to arrays are *ranges*, which can probably most easily be understood by converting them to arrays using the **to_a** method:

```
>> 0..9
=> 0..9
>> 0..9.to_a              # Oops, call to_a on 9
ArgumentError: bad value for range
>> (0..9).to_a            # Use parentheses to call to_a on the range
=> [0, 1, 2, 3, 4, 5, 6, 7, 8, 9]
```

Though **0..9** is a valid range, the second expression above shows that we need to add parentheses to call a method on it.

Ranges are useful for pulling out array elements:

```
>> a = %w[foo bar baz quux]           # Use %w to make a string array
=> ["foo", "bar", "baz", "quux"]
>> a[0..2]
=> ["foo", "bar", "baz"]
```

Ranges also work with characters:

```
>> ('a'..'e').to_a
=> ["a", "b", "c", "d", "e"]
```

4.3.2 Blocks

Both arrays and ranges respond to a host of methods that accept *blocks*, which are simultaneously one of Ruby's most powerful and most confusing features:

```
>> (1..5).each { |i| puts 2 * i }
2
4
6
8
10
=> 1..5
```

This code calls the **each** method on the range **(1..5)** and passes it the block { |i| **puts 2 * i** }. The vertical bars around the variable name in |i| are Ruby syntax for a block variable, and it's up to the method to know what to do with the block; in this

case, the range's **each** method can handle a block with a single local variable, which
we've called **i**, and it just executes the block for each value in the range.

Curly braces are one way to indicate a block, but there is a second way as well:

```
>> (1..5).each do |i|
?>   puts 2 * i
>> end
2
4
6
8
10
=> 1..5
```

Blocks can be more than one line, and often are. In *Rails Tutorial* we'll follow the
common convention of using curly braces only for short one-line blocks and the **do..end**
syntax for longer one-liners and for multi-line blocks:

```
>> (1..5).each do |number|
?>   puts 2 * number
>>   puts '--'
>> end
2
--
4
--
6
--
8
--
10
--
=> 1..5
```

Here I've used **number** in place of **i** just to emphasize that any variable name will do.

Unless you already have a substantial programming background, there is no shortcut
to understanding blocks; you just have to see them a lot, and eventually you'll get used
to them.[11] Luckily, humans are quite good at making generalizations from concrete
examples; here are a few more, including a couple using the **map** method:

---

11. Programming experts, on the other hand, might benefit from knowing that blocks are *closures*, which are
one-shot anonymous functions with data attached.

```
>> 3.times { puts "Betelgeuse!" }   # 3.times takes a block with no variables.
"Betelgeuse!"
"Betelgeuse!"
"Betelgeuse!"
=> 3
>> (1..5).map { |i| i**2 }          # The ** notation is for 'power'.
=> [1, 4, 9, 16, 25]
>> %w[a b c]                        # Recall that %w makes string arrays.
=> ["a", "b", "c"]
>> %w[a b c].map { |char| char.upcase }
=> ["A", "B", "C"]
```

As you can see, the **map** method returns the result of applying the given block to each element in the array or range.

By the way, we're now in a position to understand the line of Ruby I threw into Section 1.4.4 to generate random subdomains:

```
('a'..'z').to_a.shuffle[0..7].join
```

Let's build it up step by step:

```
>> ('a'..'z').to_a                  # An alphabet array
=> ["a", "b", "c", "d", "e", "f", "g", "h", "i", "j", "k", "l", "m", "n", "o",
"p", "q", "r", "s", "t", "u", "v", "w", "x", "y", "z"]
>> ('a'..'z').to_a.shuffle          # Shuffle it!
=> ["c", "g", "l", "k", "h", "z", "s", "i", "n", "d", "y", "u", "t", "j", "q",
"b", "r", "o", "f", "e", "w", "v", "m", "a", "x", "p"]
>> ('a'..'z').to_a.shuffle[0..7]    # Pull out the first eight elements.
=> ["f", "w", "i", "a", "h", "p", "c", "x"]
>> ('a'..'z').to_a.shuffle[0..7].join  # Join them together to make one string.
=> "mznpybuj"
```

4.3.3 Hashes and Symbols

Hashes are essentially a generalization of arrays: you can think of hashes as basically like arrays, but not limited to integer indices. (In fact, some languages, especially Perl, call hashes *associative arrays* for this reason.) Instead, hash indices, or *keys*, can be almost any object. For example, we can use strings as keys:

```
>> user = {}                          # {} is an empty hash
=> {}
>> user["first_name"] = "Michael"     # Key "first_name", value "Michael"
=> "Michael"
>> user["last_name"] = "Hartl"        # Key "last_name", value "Hartl"
=> "Hartl"
>> user["first_name"]                 # Element access is like arrays
=> "Michael"
>> user                               # A literal representation of the hash
=> {"last_name"=>"Hartl", "first_name"=>"Michael"}
```

Hashes are indicated with curly braces containing key-value pairs; a pair of braces with
no key-value pairs—i.e., {}—is an empty hash. It's important to note that the curly
braces for hashes have nothing to do with the curly braces for blocks. (Yes, this can
be confusing.) Though hashes resemble arrays, one important difference is that hashes
don't generally guarantee keeping their elements in a particular order.[12] If order matters,
use an array.

Instead of defining hashes one item at a time using square brackets, it's easy to use
their literal representation:

```
>> user = { "first_name" => "Michael", "last_name" => "Hartl" }
=> {"last_name"=>"Hartl", "first_name"=>"Michael"}
```

Here I've used the usual Ruby convention of putting an extra space at the two ends of
the hash—a convention ignored by the console output. (Don't ask me why the spaces
are conventional; probably some early influential Ruby programmer liked the look of
the extra spaces, and the convention stuck.)

So far we've used strings as hash keys, but in Rails it is much more common to use
symbols instead. Symbols look kind of like strings, but prefixed with a colon instead of
surrounded by quotes. For example, **:name** is a symbol. You can think of symbols as
basically strings without all the extra baggage:[13]

---

12. Ruby 1.9 actually guarantees that hashes keep their elements in the same order entered, but it would be
unwise ever to count on a particular ordering.

13. As a result of having less baggage, symbols are easier to compare to each other; strings need to be compared
character by character, while symbols can be compared all in one go. This makes them ideal for use as hash
keys.

```
>> "name".split('')
=> ["n", "a", "m", "e"]
>> :name.split('')
NoMethodError: undefined method `split' for :name:Symbol
>> "foobar".reverse
=> "raboof"
>> :foobar.reverse
NoMethodError: undefined method `reverse' for :foobar:Symbol
```

Symbols are a special Ruby data type shared with very few other languages, so they may seem weird at first, but Rails uses them a lot, so you'll get used to them fast.

In terms of symbols as hash keys, we can define a **user** hash as follows:

```
>> user = { :name => "Michael Hartl", :email => "michael@example.com" }
=> {:name=>"Michael Hartl", :email=>"michael@example.com"}
>> user[:name]                # Access the value corresponding to :name.
=> "Michael Hartl"
>> user[:password]            # Access the value of an undefined key.
=> nil
```

We see here from the last example that the hash value for an undefined key is simply **nil**.

Hash values can be virtually anything, even other hashes, as seen in Listing 4.5.

Listing 4.5 Nested hashes.

```
>> params = {}          # Define a hash called 'params' (short for 'parameters').
=> {}
>> params[:user] = { :name => "Michael Hartl", :email => "mhartl@example.com" }
=> {:name=>"Michael Hartl", :email=>"mhartl@example.com"}
>> params
=> {:user=>{:name=>"Michael Hartl", :email=>"mhartl@example.com"}}
>>  params[:user][:email]
=> "mhartl@example.com"
```

These sorts of hashes-of-hashes, or *nested hashes*, are heavily used by Rails, as we'll see starting in Section 8.2.

As with arrays and ranges, hashes respond to the **each** method. For example, consider a hash named **flash** with keys for two conditions, **:success** and **:error**:

```
>> flash = { :success => "It worked!", :error => "It failed. :-(" }
=> {:success=>"It worked!", :error=>"It failed. :-("}
>> flash.each do |key, value|
?>   puts "Key #{key.inspect} has value #{value.inspect}"
>> end
Key :success has value "It worked!"
Key :error has value "It failed. :-("
```

Note that, while the **each** method for arrays takes a block with only one variable, **each** for hashes takes two, a *key* and a *value*. Thus, the **each** method for a hash iterates through the hash one key-value *pair* at a time.

The last example uses the useful **inspect** method, which returns a string with a literal representation of the object it's called on:

```
>> puts (1..5).to_a          # Put an array as a string.
1
2
3
4
5
>> puts (1..5).to_a.inspect    # Put a literal array.
[1, 2, 3, 4, 5]
>> puts :name, :name.inspect
name
:name
>> puts "It worked!", "It worked!".inspect
It worked!
"It worked!"
```

By the way, using **inspect** to print an object is common enough that there's a shortcut for it, the **p** function:

```
>> p :name              # Same as 'puts :name.inspect'
:name
```

4.3.4 CSS Revisited

It's time now to revisit the lines from Listing 4.4 used in the layout to include the cascading style sheets:

```
<%= stylesheet_link_tag 'blueprint/screen', :media => 'screen' %>
<%= stylesheet_link_tag 'blueprint/print',  :media => 'print' %>
```

We are now nearly in a position to understand this. As mentioned briefly in Section 4.1.2, Rails defines a special function to include stylesheets, and

```
stylesheet_link_tag 'blueprint/screen', :media => 'screen'
```

is a call to this function. But there are two mysteries. First, where are the parentheses? In Ruby, they are optional; these two lines are equivalent:

```
# Parentheses on function calls are optional.
stylesheet_link_tag('blueprint/screen', :media => 'screen')
stylesheet_link_tag 'blueprint/screen', :media => 'screen'
```

Second, the **:media** argument sure looks like a hash, but where are the curly braces? When hashes are the *last* argument in a function call, the curly braces are optional; these two lines are equivalent:

```
# Curly braces on final hash arguments are optional.
stylesheet_link_tag 'blueprint/screen', { :media => 'screen' }
stylesheet_link_tag 'blueprint/screen', :media => 'screen'
```

So, we see now that each of the lines

```
<%= stylesheet_link_tag 'blueprint/screen', :media => 'screen' %>
<%= stylesheet_link_tag 'blueprint/print',  :media => 'print' %>
```

calls the **stylesheet_link_tag** function with two arguments: a string, indicating the path to the stylesheet, and a hash, indicating the media type (**'screen'** for the computer screen and **'print'** for a printed version). Because of the <%= %> brackets, the results are inserted into the template by ERb, and if you view the source of the page in your browser you should see the HTML needed to include a stylesheet (Listing 4.6).[14]

---

14. You may see some funky numbers, like **?1257465942**, after the CSS filenames. These are inserted by Rails to ensure that browsers reload the CSS when it changes on the server.

Listing 4.6 The HTML source produced by the CSS includes.

```
<link href="/stylesheets/blueprint/screen.css" media="screen" rel="stylesheet"
type="text/css" />
<link href="/stylesheets/blueprint/print.css" media="print" rel="stylesheet"
type="text/css" />
```

4.4 Ruby Classes

We've said before that everything in Ruby is an object, and in this section we'll finally get to define some of our own. Ruby, like many object-oriented languages, uses *classes* to organize methods; these classes are then *instantiated* to create objects. If you're new to object-oriented programming, this may sound like gibberish, so let's look at some concrete examples.

4.4.1 Constructors

We've seen lots of examples of using classes to instantiate objects, but we have yet to do so explicitly. For example, we instantiated a string using the double quote characters, which is a *literal constructor* for strings:

```
>> s = "foobar"        # A literal constructor for strings using double quotes
=> "foobar"
>> s.class
=> String
```

We see here that strings respond to the method **class**, and simply return the class they belong to.

Instead of using a literal constructor, we can use the equivalent *named constructor*, which involves calling the **new** method on the class name:[15]

```
>> s = String.new("foobar")    # A named constructor for a string
=> "foobar"
>> s.class
```

15. These results will vary based on the version of Ruby you are using. This example assumes you are using Ruby 1.9.2.

```
=> String
>> s == "foobar"
=> true
```

This is equivalent to the literal constructor, but it's more explicit about what we're doing. Arrays work the same way as strings:

```
>> a = Array.new([1, 3, 2])
=> [1, 3, 2]
```

Hashes, in contrast, are different. While the array constructor **Array.new** takes an initial value for the array, **Hash.new** takes a *default* value for the hash, which is the value of the hash for a nonexistent key:

```
>> h = Hash.new
=> {}
>> h[:foo]                # Try to access the value for the nonexistent key :foo.
=> nil
>> h = Hash.new(0)        # Arrange for nonexistent keys to return 0 instead of nil.
=> {}
>> h[:foo]
=> 0
```

4.4.2 Class Inheritance

When learning about classes, it's useful to find out the *class hierarchy* using the **superclass** method:

```
>> s = String.new("foobar")
=> "foobar"
>> s.class                          # Find the class of s.
=> String
>> s.class.superclass               # Find the superclass of String.
=> Object
>> s.class.superclass.superclass    # Ruby 1.9 uses a new BasicObject base class
=> BasicObject
>> s.class.superclass.superclass.superclass
=> nil
```

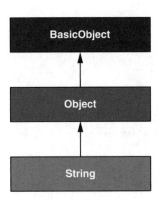

Figure 4.2   The inheritance hierarchy for the **String** class.

A diagram of this inheritance hierarchy appears in Figure 4.2. We see here that the superclass of **String** is **Object** and the superclass of **Object** is **BasicObject**, but **BasicObject** has no superclass. This pattern is true of every Ruby object: trace back the class hierarchy far enough and every class in Ruby ultimately inherits from **BasicObject**, which has no superclass itself. This is the technical meaning of "everything in Ruby is an object".

To understand classes a little more deeply, there's no substitute for making one of our own. Let's make a **Word** class with a **palindrome?** method that returns **true** if the word is the same spelled forward and backward:

```
>> class Word
>>   def palindrome?(string)
>>     string == string.reverse
>>   end
>> end
=> nil
```

We can use it as follows:

```
>> w = Word.new              # Make a new Word object
=> #<Word:0x22d0b20>
>> w.palindrome?("foobar")
=> false
>> w.palindrome?("level")
=> true
```

If this example strikes you as a bit contrived, good; this is by design. It's odd to create a new class just to create a method that takes a string as an argument. Since a word *is a* string, it's more natural to have our **Word** class *inherit* from **String**, as seen in Listing 4.7. (You should exit the console and re-enter it to clear out the old definition of **Word**.)

Listing 4.7 Defining a **Word** class in the console.

```
>> class Word < String          # Word inherits from String.
>>    # Return true if the string is its own reverse.
>>    def palindrome?
>>      self == self.reverse     # self is the string itself.
>>    end
>> end
=> nil
```

Here **Word < String** is the Ruby syntax for inheritance (discussed briefly in Section 3.1.2), which ensures that, in addition to the new **palindrome?** method, words also have all the same methods as strings:

```
>> s = Word.new("level")    # Make a new Word, initialized with "level".
=> "level"
>> s.palindrome?            # Words have the palindrome? method.
=> true
>> s.length                # Words also inherit all the normal string methods.
=> 5
```

Since the **Word** class inherits from **String**, we can use the console to see the class hierarchy explicitly:

```
>> s.class
=> Word
>> s.class.superclass
=> String
>> s.class.superclass.superclass
=> Object
```

This hierarchy is illustrated in Figure 4.3.

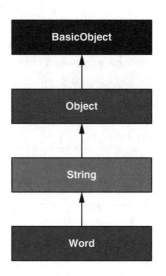

Figure 4.3   The inheritance hierarchy for the (non-built-in) **Word** class from Listing 4.7.

In Listing 4.7, note that checking that the word is its own reverse involves accessing the word inside the **Word** class. Ruby allows us to do this using the **self** keyword: inside the **Word** class, **self** is the object itself, which means we can use

```
self == self.reverse
```

to check if the word is a palindrome.[16]

4.4.3   Modifying Built-In Classes

While inheritance is a powerful idea, in the case of palindromes it might be even more natural to add the **palindrome?** method to the **String** class itself, so that (among other things) we can call **palindrome?** on a string literal, which we currently can't do:

```
>> "level".palindrome?
NoMethodError: undefined method `palindrome?' for "level":String
```

---

16. For more on Ruby classes and the **self** keyword, see the RailsTips post on "Class and Instance Variables in Ruby".

Somewhat amazingly, Ruby lets you do just this; Ruby classes can be *opened* and modified, allowing ordinary mortals such as ourselves to add methods to them:[17]

```
>> class String
>>   # Return true if the string is its own reverse.
>>   def palindrome?
>>     self == self.reverse
>>   end
>> end
=> nil
>> "deified".palindrome?
=> true
```

(I don't know which is cooler: that Ruby lets you add methods to built-in classes, or that **"deified"** is a palindrome.)

Modifying built-in classes is a powerful technique, but with great power comes great responsibility, and it's considered bad form to add methods to built-in classes without having a *really* good reason for doing so. Rails does have some good reasons; for example, in web applications we often want to prevent variables from being *blank*—e.g., a user's name should be something other than spaces and other whitespace—so Rails adds a **blank?** method to Ruby. Since the Rails console automatically includes the Rails extensions, we can see an example here (this won't work in plain **irb**):

```
>> "".blank?
=> true
>> "      ".empty?
=> false
>> "      ".blank?
=> true
>> nil.blank?
=> true
```

We see that a string of spaces is not *empty*, but it is *blank*. Note also that **nil** is blank; since **nil** isn't a string, this is a hint that Rails actually adds **blank?** to **String**'s base class, which (as we saw at the beginning of this section) is **Object** itself. We'll see some other examples of Rails additions to Ruby classes in Section 9.3.2.

---

17. For those familiar with JavaScript, this functionality is comparable to using a built-in class prototype object to augment the class. (Thanks to reader Erik Eldridge for pointing this out.)

4.4.4   A Controller Class

All this talk about classes and inheritance may have triggered a flash of recognition, because we have seen both before, in the Pages controller (Listing 3.24):

```ruby
class PagesController < ApplicationController

  def home
    @title = "Home"
  end

  def contact
    @title = "Contact"
  end

  def about
    @title = "About"
  end
end
```

You're now in a position to appreciate, at least vaguely, what this code means: **PagesController** is a class that inherits from **ApplicationController**, and comes equipped with **home**, **contact**, and **about** methods, each of which defines the instance variable **@title**. Since each Rails console session loads the local Rails environment, we can even create a controller explicitly and examine its class hierarchy:[18]

```ruby
>> controller = PagesController.new
=> #<PagesController:0x22855d0>
>> controller.class
=> PagesController
>> controller.class.superclass
=> ApplicationController
>> controller.class.superclass.superclass
=> ActionController::Base
>> controller.class.superclass.superclass.superclass
=> ActionController::Metal
>> controller.class.superclass.superclass.superclass.superclass
=> AbstractController::Base
>> controller.class.superclass.superclass.superclass.superclass.superclass
=> Object
```

A diagram of this hierarchy appears in Figure 4.4.

---

18. You don't have to know what each class in this hierarchy does. *I* don't know what they all do, and I've been programming in Ruby on Rails since 2005. This means either that (a) I'm grossly incompetent or (b) you can be a skilled Rails developer without knowing all its innards. I hope for both our sakes that it's the latter.

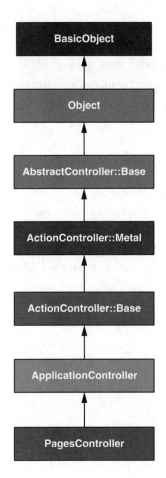

Figure 4.4   The inheritance hierarchy for the Pages controller.

We can even call the controller actions inside the console, which are just methods:

```
>> controller.home
=> "Home"
```

This return value of **"Home"** comes from the assignment **@title = "Home"** in the **home**
action.

But wait—actions don't have return values, at least not ones that matter. The point
of the **home** action, as we saw in Chapter 3, is to render a web page. And I sure don't
remember ever calling **PagesController.new** anywhere. What's going on?

What's going on is that Rails is *written in* Ruby, but Rails isn't Ruby. Some Rails classes are used like ordinary Ruby objects, but some are just grist for Rails' magic mill. Rails is *sui generis*, and should be studied and understood separately from Ruby. This is why, if your principal programming interest is writing web applications, I recommend learning Rails first, then learning Ruby, then looping back to Rails.

4.4.5   A User Class

We end our tour of Ruby with a complete class of our own, a **User** class that anticipates the User model coming up in Chapter 6.

So far we've entered class definitions at the console, but this quickly becomes tiresome; instead, create the file **example_user.rb** in your Rails root directory and fill it with the contents of Listing 4.8. (Recall from Section 1.1.3 that the Rails root is the root of your *application* directory; for example, the Rails root for my sample application is /Users/mhartl/rails_projects/sample_app.)

Listing 4.8   Code for an example user.
example_user.rb

```
class User
  attr_accessor :name, :email

  def initialize(attributes = {})
    @name  = attributes[:name]
    @email = attributes[:email]
  end

  def formatted_email
    "#{@name} <#{@email}>"
  end
end
```

There's quite a bit going on here, so let's take it step by step. The first line,

```
attr_accessor :name, :email
```

creates *attribute accessors* corresponding to a user's name and email address. This creates "getter" and "setter" methods that allow us to retrieve (get) and assign (set) **@name** and **@email** instance variables.

The first method, **initialize**, is special in Ruby: it's the method called when we execute **User.new**. This particular **initialize** takes one argument, **attributes**:

```
def initialize(attributes = {})
  @name  = attributes[:name]
  @email = attributes[:email]
end
```

Here the **attributes** variable has a *default value* equal to the empty hash, so that we can define a user with no name or email address (recall from Section 4.3.3 that hashes return **nil** for nonexistent keys, so **attributes[:name]** will be **nil** if there is no **:name** key, and similarly for **attributes[:email]**).

Finally, our class defines a method called **formatted_email** that uses the values of the assigned **@name** and **@email** variables to build up a nicely formatted version of the user's email address using string interpolation (Section 4.2.2):

```
def formatted_email
  "#{@name} <#{@email}>"
end
```

Let's fire up the console, **require** the example user code, and take our User class out for a spin:

```
>> require './example_user'     # This is how you load the example_user code.
=> ["User"]
>> example = User.new
=> #<User:0x224ceec @email=nil, @name=nil>
>> example.name                 # nil since attributes[:name] is nil
=> nil
>> example.name = "Example User"          # Assign a non-nil name
=> "Example User"
>> example.email = "user@example.com"       # and a non-nil email address
=> "user@example.com"
>> example.formatted_email
=> "Example User <user@example.com>"
```

Here the **'.'** is Unix for "current directory", and **'./example_user.rb'** tells Ruby to look for an example user file relative to that location. The subsequent code creates an empty example user and then fills in the name and email address by assigning directly to the corresponding attributes (assignments made possible by the **attr_accessor** line in Listing 4.8). When we write

```
example.name = "Example User"
```

Ruby is setting the **@name** variable to **"Example User"** (and similarly for the **email** attribute), which we then use in the **formatted_email** method.

Recalling from Section 4.3.4 we can omit the curly braces for final hash arguments, we can create another user by passing a hash to the **initialize** method to create a user with pre-defined attributes:

```
>> user = User.new(:name => "Michael Hartl", :email => "mhartl@example.com")
=> #<User:0x225167c @email="mhartl@example.com", @name="Michael Hartl">
>> user.formatted_email
=> "Michael Hartl <mhartl@example.com>"
```

We will see starting in Chapter 8 that initializing objects using a hash argument is common in Rails applications.

4.5 Exercises

1. Using Listing 4.9 as a guide, combine the **split**, **shuffle**, and **join** methods to write a function that shuffles the letters in a given string.
2. Using Listing 4.10 as a guide, add a **shuffle** method to the **String** class.
3. Create three hashes called **person1**, **person2**, and **person3**, with first and last names under the keys **:first** and **:last**. Then create a **params** hash so that **params[:father]** is **person1**, **params[:mother]** is **person2**, and **params[:child]** is **person3**. Verify that, for example, **params[:father][:first]** has the right value.
4. Find an online version of the Ruby API and read about the **Hash** method **merge**.

Listing 4.9   Skeleton for a string shuffle function.

```
>> def string_shuffle(s)
>>    s.split('').?.?
>> end
=> nil
>> string_shuffle("foobar")
```

Listing 4.10   Skeleton for a **shuffle** method attached to the **String** class.

```
>> class String
>>    def shuffle
>>      self.split('').?.?
>>    end
>> end
=> nil
>> "foobar".shuffle
```

CHAPTER 5

Filling in the Layout

In the process of taking a brief tour of Ruby in Chapter 4, we added some basic cascading style sheets to our site layout (Section 4.1.2). In this chapter, we'll add some custom styles of our own, as we fill in the layout with links to the pages (such as Home and About) that we've created so far. Along the way, we'll learn about partials, Rails routes, and integration tests. We'll end by taking a first important step toward letting users sign up to our site.

5.1 Adding Some Structure

Rails Tutorial is a book on web development, not web design, but it would be depressing to work on an application that looks like *complete* crap, so in this section we'll add some structure to the layout and give it some minimal styling with CSS. We'll also give our *code* some styling, so to speak, using *partials* to tidy up the layout once it gets a little cluttered.

When building web applications, it is often useful to get a high-level overview of the user interface as early as possible. Throughout the rest of this book, I will thus often include *mockups* (in a web context often called *wireframes*), which are rough sketches of what the eventual application will look like.[1] In this chapter, we will principally be developing the static pages introduced in Section 3.1, including a site logo, a navigation header, and a site footer. A mockup for the most important of these pages, the Home page, appears in Figure 5.1. (You can see the final result in Figure 5.8. You'll note that

---

1. The mockups in *Ruby on Rails Tutorial* are made with an excellent online mockup application called Mockingbird.

157

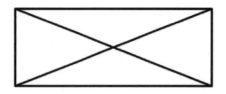

Home   Help   Sign in

Sample App

This is the home page for the sample app.

Sign up now!

About   Contact   News

Figure 5.1   A mockup of the sample application's Home page.

it differs in some details—for example, the footer has four links instead of three—but that's fine, since a mockup need not be exact.)

As usual, if you're using Git for version control, now would be a good time to make a new branch:

```
$ git checkout -b filling-in-layout
```

You might still have the **example_user.rb** file from Chapter 4 in your project directory; if so, you should probably just remove it.

5.1.1   Site Navigation

When we last saw the site layout file **application.html.erb** in Listing 4.3, we had just added Blueprint stylesheets using the Rails **stylesheet_link_tag** helper. It's time to add a couple more stylesheets, one specifically for Internet Explorer browsers and one for our (soon-to-be-added) custom CSS. We'll also add some additional divisions (**div**s), some **id**s and **class**es, and the start of our site navigation. The full file is in Listing 5.1; explanations for the various pieces follow immediately thereafter. If you'd rather not delay gratification, you can see the results in Figure 5.2. (*Note:* it's not (yet) very gratifying.)

Listing 5.1 The site layout with added structure.
app/views/layouts/application.html.erb

```erb
<!DOCTYPE html>
<html>
  <head>
    <title><%= title %></title>
    <%= csrf_meta_tag %>
    <!--[if lt IE 9]>
    <script src="http://html5shiv.googlecode.com/svn/trunk/html5.js"></script>
    <![endif]-->
    <%= stylesheet_link_tag 'blueprint/screen', :media => 'screen' %>
    <%= stylesheet_link_tag 'blueprint/print',  :media => 'print' %>
    <!--[if lt IE 8]><%= stylesheet_link_tag 'blueprint/ie' %><![endif]-->
    <%= stylesheet_link_tag 'custom', :media => 'screen' %>
  </head>
  <body>
    <div class="container">
      <header>
        <%= image_tag("logo.png", :alt => "Sample App", :class => "round") %>
        <nav class="round">
          <ul>
            <li><%= link_to "Home", '#' %></li>
            <li><%= link_to "Help", '#' %></li>
            <li><%= link_to "Sign in", '#' %></li>
          </ul>
        </nav>
      </header>
      <section class="round">
        <%= yield %>
      </section>
    </div>
  </body>
</html>
```

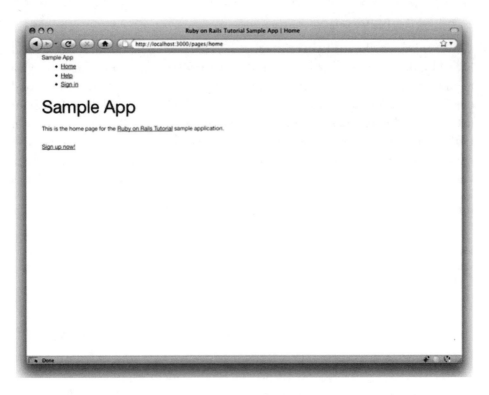

Figure 5.2 The Home page (/pages/home) with no logo image or custom CSS.

Let's look at the new elements from top to bottom. As noted briefly in Section 3.1, Rails 3 uses HTML5 by default (as indicated by the doctype `<!DOCTYPE html>`); since the HTML5 standard is new, some browsers (especially Internet Explorer) don't yet fully support it, so we include some JavaScript code (known as an "HTML5 shiv") to work around the issue:

```
<!--[if lt IE 9]>
<script src="http://html5shiv.googlecode.com/svn/trunk/html5.js"></script>
<![endif]-->
```

The somewhat odd syntax

```
<!--[if lt IE 9]>
```

includes the enclosed line only if the version of Microsoft Internet Explorer (IE) is less than 9 (**if lt IE 9**). The weird **[if lt IE 9]** syntax is *not* part of Rails; it's actually a conditional comment supported by Internet Explorer browsers for just this sort of thing. It's a good thing, too, because it means we can include the extra stylesheet *only* for IE browsers less than version 9, leaving other browsers such as Firefox, Chrome, and Safari unaffected.

After the lines to include the Blueprint stylesheets (first introduced in Listing 4.4), there is another Internet Explorer–specific line, which this time is a stylesheet that only gets included if the browser is a version of Internet Explorer less than 8 (**if lt IE 8**):

```
<!--[if lt IE 8]><%= stylesheet_link_tag 'blueprint/ie' %><![endif]-->
```

IE has a large number of idiosyncrasies (especially before version 8), and Blueprint comes with a special **ie.css** file that fixes a bunch of them.

After the IE stylesheet comes a stylesheet link for a file that doesn't exist yet, **custom.css**, where we'll put our custom CSS:

```
<%= stylesheet_link_tag 'custom', :media => 'screen' %>
```

CSS is very forgiving, and even though the file doesn't exist, our page will still work just fine. (We'll create **custom.css** in Section 5.1.2.)

The next section places a *container div* around our site navigation and content, which is a **div** tag with class **container**. This container div is needed by Blueprint (see the Blueprint tutorial for more information). Then there are **header** and **section** elements; the header contains the sample app logo (to be added below) and the site navigation (**nav**). Finally, there is **section** element containing the site's main content:

```
<div class="container">
  <header>
    <%= image_tag("logo.png", :alt => "Sample App", :class => "round") %>
    <nav class="round">
      <ul>
        <li><%= link_to "Home", '#' %></li>
        <li><%= link_to "Help", '#' %></li>
        <li><%= link_to "Sign in", '#' %></li>
      </ul>
    </nav>
```

```
  </header>
  <section class="round">
    <%= yield %>
  </section>
</div>
```

The **div** tag in HTML is a generic division; it doesn't do anything apart from divide the document into distinct parts. In older style HTML, **div** tags are used for nearly all site divisions, but HTML5 adds the **header**, **nav**, and **section** elements for divisions common to many applications. All HTML elements, including divs and the new HTML5 elements, can be assigned *classes*[2] and *ids*; these are merely labels, and are useful for styling with CSS (Section 5.1.2). The main difference between classes and ids is that classes can be used multiple times on a page, but ids can only be used once.

Inside the header is a Rails helper called **image_tag**:

```
<%= image_tag("logo.png", :alt => "Sample App", :class => "round") %>
```

Note that, as with **stylesheet_link_tag** (Section 4.3.4), we pass a hash of options, in this case setting the **alt** and **class** attributes of the image tag using symbols **:alt** and **:class**. To make this clearer, let's look at the HTML this tag produces:[3]

```
<img alt="Sample App" class="round" src="/images/logo.png" />
```

The **alt** attribute is what will be displayed if there is no image,[4] and the class will be used for styling in Section 5.1.2. (Rails helpers often take options hashes in this way, giving us the flexibility to add arbitrary HTML options without ever leaving Rails.) You can see the result in Figure 5.2; we'll add the logo image at the end of this section.

---

2. These are completely unrelated to Ruby classes.

3. You might notice that the **img** tag, rather than looking like <img>...</img>, instead looks like <img ... />. Tags that follow this form are known as *self-closing* tags.

4. The **alt** text is also what will be displayed by screen readers for the visually impaired. Though people are sometimes sloppy about including the **alt** attribute for images, it is in fact required by the HTML standard. Luckily, Rails includes a default **alt** attribute; if you don't specify the attribute in the call to **image_tag**, Rails just uses the image filename (minus extension). In this case, though, **Sample App** is more descriptive than **logo**, so I've elected to set the **alt** text explicitly.

The second element inside the layout header is a list of navigation links, made using the *unordered list* tag **ul**, together with the *list item* tag **li**:

```
<nav class="round">
  <ul>
    <li><%= link_to "Home", '#' %></li>
    <li><%= link_to "Help", '#' %></li>
    <li><%= link_to "Sign in", '#' %></li>
  </ul>
</nav>
```

This list uses the Rails helper **link_to** to create links (which we created directly with the anchor tag **a** in Section 3.3.2); the first argument is the link text, while the second is the URL. We'll fill in the URLs with *named routes* in Section 5.2.3, but for now we use the stub URL **'#'** commonly used in web design. Once Rails has processed this layout and evaluated the Embedded Ruby, the list looks like this:

```
<nav class="round">
  <ul>
    <li><a href="#">Home</a></li>
    <li><a href="#">Help</a></li>
    <li><a href="#">Sign in</a></li>
  </ul>
</nav>
```

Our layout is now complete, and we can look at the results by visiting, e.g., the Home page. In anticipation of adding users to our site in Chapter 8, let's add a signup link to the **home.html.erb** view (Listing 5.2).

Listing 5.2 The Home page with a link to the signup page.
app/views/pages/home.html.erb

```
<h1>Sample App</h1>

<p>
  This is the home page for the
  <a href="http://railstutorial.org/">Ruby on Rails Tutorial</a>
  sample application.
</p>

<%= link_to "Sign up now!", '#', :class => "signup_button round" %>
```

As with the previous uses of **link_to**, this just creates a stub link of the form

```
<a href="#" class="signup_button round">Sign up now!</a>
```

Note again the recurring theme of options hashes, in this case used to add a couple CSS classes to the anchor tag. You might notice that the **a** tag here has *two* classes, separated by a space:

```
<a href="#" class="signup_button round">
```

This is convenient for the common case of an element with two different kinds of styles.

Now we're finally ready to see the fruits of our labors (Figure 5.2).[5] Pretty underwhelming, you say? Perhaps so. Happily, though, we've done a good job of giving our HTML elements sensible classes and ids, which puts us in a great position to add style to the site with CSS.

Before we move on to CSS styling, let's replace the logo alt text with a logo image; you can download the sample application logo at

http://railstutorial.org/images/sample_app/logo.png

Put the logo in **public/images** so that Rails can find it. The result appears in Figure 5.3.

5.1.2 Custom CSS

In Section 5.1.1, you may have noticed that the CSS elements are *semantic*, that is, they have meaning in English beyond the structure of the page. For example, instead of writing that the navigation menu was "right-top" we used the element "nav". This gives us considerable flexibility in constructing a layout based on CSS.

Let's get started by filling in the **custom.css** file with Listing 5.3. (There are quite a few rules in Listing 5.3. To get a sense of what a CSS rule does, it's often helpful to comment it out using CSS comments, i.e., by putting it inside **/* ... */**, and seeing what changes.)

---

5. Note that Safari and Chrome users will see an indicator of a broken image in place of the "Sample App" alt text.

Figure 5.3 The Home page (/pages/home) with a logo image but no custom CSS.

Listing 5.3 CSS for the container, body, and links.
public/stylesheets/custom.css

```
.container {
  width: 710px;
}

body {
  background: #cff;
}

header {
  padding-top: 20px;
}

header img {
  padding: 1em;
  background: #fff;
}
```

```
section {
  margin-top: 1em;
  font-size: 120%;
  padding: 20px;
  background: #fff;
}

section h1 {
  font-size: 200%;
}

/* Links */

a {
  color: #09c;
  text-decoration: none;
}

a:hover {
  color: #069;
  text-decoration: underline;
}

a:visited {
  color: #069;
}
```

You can see the results of this CSS in Figure 5.4. There's a lot of CSS here, but it has a consistent form. Each rule refers either to a class, an id, an HTML tag, or some combination thereof, followed by a list of styling commands. For example,

```
body {
  background: #cff;
}
```

changes the background color of the **body** tag to baby blue, while

```
header img {
  padding: 1em;
  background: #fff;
}
```

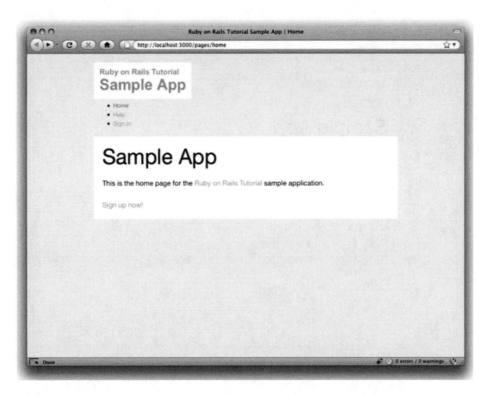

Figure 5.4   The Home page (`/pages/home`) with custom colors.

puts a padding layer of one **em** (roughly the width of the letter M) around the image (**img**) inside a **header** tag. This rule also makes the background color **#fff**, which is white.[6] Similarly,

```
.container {
  width: 710px;
}
```

6. HTML colors can be coded with three base-16 (hexadecimal) numbers, one each for the primary colors red, green, and blue. **#fff** maxes out all three colors, yielding pure white. See w3schools.com/html/html_colors.asp for more information.

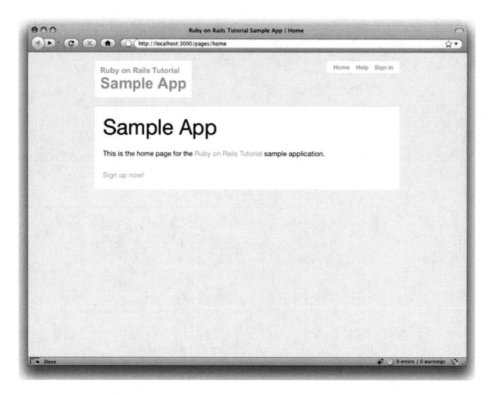

Figure 5.5   The Home page (`/pages/home`) with navigation styling.

styles an element with class **container**, in this case giving it a width of 710 pixels (corresponding to 18 Blueprint columns).[7] The dot **.** in **.container** indicates that the rule styles a *class* called "container". (As we'll see in Section 8.2.3, the pound sign **#** identifies a rule to style a CSS *id* in the same way that a dot indicates a CSS class.)

Changing colors is nice, but the navigation links are still hanging down on the left side of the page. Let's move them to a better location and give them a nicer appearance with the navigation rules in Listing 5.4. The results appear in Figure 5.5. (In some of the book's code samples, including Listing 5.4, I use three vertical dots to indicate omitted code. When typing in the code, take care not to include the dots; alternatively, if you copy-and-paste the code, make sure to remove the dots by hand.)

---

7. Blueprint CSS uses a grid of columns 40 pixels across, 30 pixels for the column itself and 10 pixels of padding. The rightmost column doesn't need padding, so 18 columns is 710 pixels: 18 * 40 − 10 = 710.

Listing 5.4 Navigation CSS.
`public/stylesheets/custom.css`

```
        .
        .
        .
/* Navigation */

nav {
  float: right;
}

nav {
  background-color: white;
  padding: 0 0.7em;
  white-space: nowrap;
}

nav ul {
  margin: 0;
  padding: 0;
}

nav ul li {
  list-style-type: none;
  display: inline-block;
  padding: 0.2em 0;
}

nav ul li a {
  padding: 0 5px;
  font-weight: bold;
}

nav ul li a:visited {
  color: #09c;
}

nav ul li a:hover {
  text-decoration: underline;
}
```

Here **nav ul** styles a **ul** tag inside a **nav** tag, **nav ul li** styles an **li** tag inside a **ul** tag inside a **nav** tag, and so on.

As the penultimate step, we'll make the link to our site's signup page a little more obvious. (Though for the sample app we don't care, on any real site it's naturally quite important to make the signup link *very* prominent.) Listing 5.5 shows CSS to make the signup link big, green, and clickable (so a click anywhere inside the box will follow the link).

Listing 5.5 CSS to make the signup button big, green, and clickable (`/pages/home`).
`public/stylesheets/custom.css`

```
.
.
.


/* Sign up button */

a.signup_button {
  margin-left: auto;
  margin-right: auto;
  display: block;
  text-align: center;
  width: 190px;
  color: #fff;
  background: #006400;
  font-size: 150%;
  font-weight: bold;
  padding: 20px;
}
```

There are a bunch of rules here; as usual, comment a line out and reload the page if you want to see what each one does. The end result is a signup link that's hard to miss (Figure 5.6).

As a final touch, we'll make use of the **round** class we've placed on many of our site elements. Although the current sharp-cornered boxes aren't terrible, it's a little friendlier to soften the corners so they won't slice up our users. We can accomplish this using the CSS code in Listing 5.6, with the results shown in Figure 5.7.

Listing 5.6 Stylesheet rules for round corners.
`public/stylesheets/custom.css`

```
.
.
.

/* Round corners */

.round {
  -moz-border-radius:      10px;
```

```
  -webkit-border-radius: 10px;
  border-radius:         10px;
}
```

It's worth noting that this trick works on Firefox, Safari, Opera, and many other browsers, but it doesn't work on Internet Explorer. There *are* ways of getting round corners that work on all browsers, but there's no other technique that's even *close* to this easy, so we'll just risk leaving our IE users with a few tiny cuts.

5.1.3 Partials

Though the layout in Listing 5.1 serves its purpose, it's getting a little cluttered: there are several lines of CSS includes and even more lines of header for what are logically only two ideas. We can tuck these sections away using a convenient Rails facility called *partials*. Let's first take a look at what the layout looks like after the partials are defined (Listing 5.7).

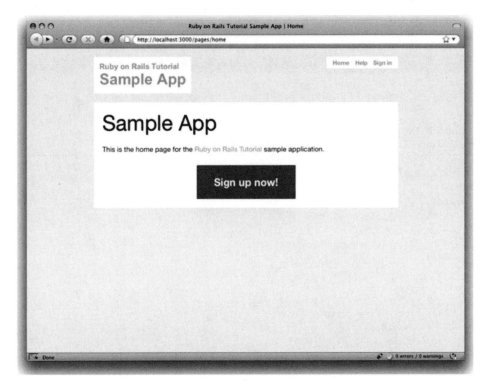

Figure 5.6 The Home page (/pages/home) with a signup button.

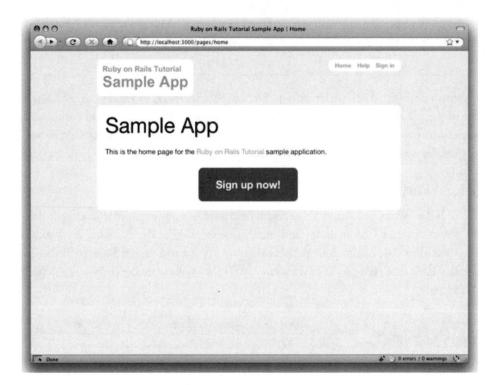

Figure 5.7   The Home page (/pages/home) with round corners.

Listing 5.7   The site layout with partials for the stylesheets and header.
app/views/layouts/application.html.erb

```
<!DOCTYPE html>
<html>
  <head>
    <title><%= title %></title>
    <%= csrf_meta_tag %>
    <%= render 'layouts/stylesheets' %>
  </head>
  <body>
    <div class="container">
      <%= render 'layouts/header' %>
      <section class="round">
        <%= yield %>
      </section>
    </div>
  </body>
</html>
```

In Listing 5.7, we've replaced the stylesheet lines with a single call to a Rails helper called **render**:

```
<%= render 'layouts/stylesheets' %>
```

The effect of this line is to look for a file called **app/views/layouts/_stylesheets. html.erb**, evaluate its contents, and insert the results into the view.[8] (Recall that <%= ... %> is the Embedded Ruby syntax needed to evaluate a Ruby expression and then insert the results into the template.) Note the leading underscore on the filename **_stylesheets.html.erb**; this underscore is the universal convention for naming partials, and among other things makes it possible to identify all the partials in a directory at a glance.

Of course, to get the partial to work, we have to fill it with some content; in the case of the stylesheet partial, this is just the four lines of stylesheet includes from Listing 5.1; the result appears in Listing 5.8. (Technically, the HTML5 shiv includes JavaScript, not CSS. On the other hand, its purpose is to allow Internet Explorer to understand CSS with HTML5, so logically it still belongs in the stylesheet partial.)

Listing 5.8 A partial for stylesheet includes.
app/views/layouts/_stylesheets.html.erb

```
<!--[if lt IE 9]>
<script src="http://html5shiv.googlecode.com/svn/trunk/html5.js"></script>
<![endif]-->
<%= stylesheet_link_tag 'blueprint/screen', :media => 'screen' %>
<%= stylesheet_link_tag 'blueprint/print',  :media => 'print' %>
<!--[if lt IE 8]><%= stylesheet_link_tag 'blueprint/ie' %><![endif]-->
<%= stylesheet_link_tag 'custom', :media => 'screen' %>
```

Similarly, we can move the header material into the partial shown in Listing 5.9 and insert it into the layout with another call to **render**:

---

8. Many Rails developers use a **shared** directory for partials shared across different views. I prefer to use the **shared** folder for utility partials that are useful on multiple views, while putting partials that are literally on every page (as part of the site layout) in the **layouts** directory. (We'll create the **shared** directory starting in Chapter 8.) That seems to me a logical division, but putting them all in the **shared** folder certainly works fine, too.

```
<%= render 'layouts/header' %>
```

Listing 5.9 A partial for the site header.
app/views/layouts/_header.html.erb

```
<header>
  <%= image_tag("logo.png", :alt => "Sample App", :class => "round") %>
  <nav class="round">
    <ul>
      <li><%= link_to "Home", '#' %></li>
      <li><%= link_to "Help", '#' %></li>
      <li><%= link_to "Sign in", '#' %></li>
    </ul>
  </nav>
</header>
```

Now that we know how to make partials, let's add a site footer to go along with the header. By now you can probably guess that we'll call it **_footer.html.erb** and put it in the layouts directory (Listing 5.10).

Listing 5.10 A partial for the site footer.
app/views/layouts/_footer.html.erb

```
<footer>
  <nav class="round">
    <ul>
      <li><%= link_to "About", '#' %></li>
      <li><%= link_to "Contact", '#' %></li>
      <li><a href="http://news.railstutorial.org/">News</a></li>
      <li><a href="http://www.railstutorial.org/">Rails Tutorial</a></li>
    </ul>
  </nav>
</footer>
```

As with the header, in the footer we've used **link_to** for the internal links to the About and Contact pages and stubbed out the URLs with **'#'** for now. (As with **header**, the **footer** tag is new in HTML5.)

We can render the footer partial in the layout by following the same pattern as the stylesheets and header partials (Listing 5.11).

Listing 5.11   The site layout with a footer partial.
`app/views/layouts/application.html.erb`

```
<!DOCTYPE html>
<html>
  <head>
    <title><%= title %></title>
    <%= csrf_meta_tag %>
    <%= render 'layouts/stylesheets' %>
  </head>
  <body>
    <div class="container">
      <%= render 'layouts/header' %>
      <section class="round">
        <%= yield %>
      </section>
      <%= render 'layouts/footer' %>
    </div>
  </body>
</html>
```

Of course, the footer will be ugly without some styling (Listing 5.12). The results appear in Figure 5.8.

Listing 5.12   Adding the CSS for the site footer.
`public/stylesheets/custom.css`

```
.
.
.
footer {
  text-align: center;
  margin-top: 10px;
  width: 710px;
  margin-left: auto;
  margin-right: auto;
}

footer nav {
  float: none;
}
```

Note here the rule

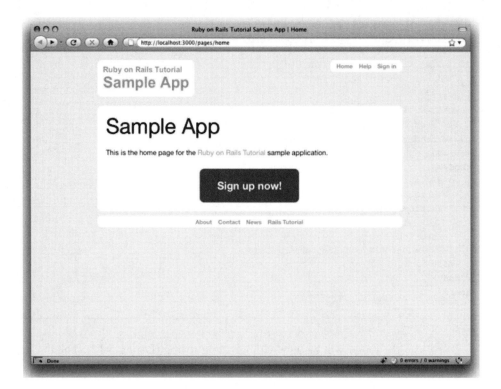

Figure 5.8   The Home page (/pages/home) with an added footer.

```
footer nav {
  float: none;
}
```

that overrides the previous rule

```
nav {
  float: right;
}
```

so that the footer is centered in the bottom of the page rather than pushed off to the right like the navigation in the header. This convention of having a succession of rules, with subsequent rules possibly overriding previous ones, is what puts the *cascading* in cascading style sheets.

5.2 Layout Links

Now that we've finished a site layout with decent styling, it's time to start filling in the links we've stubbed out with '**#**'. Of course, we could hard-code links like

```
<a href="/pages/about">About</a>
```

but that isn't the Rails Way. For one, it would be nice if the URL for the about page were /about rather than /pages/about; moreover, Rails conventionally uses *named routes*, which involves code like

```
<%= link_to "About", about_path %>
```

This way the code has a more transparent meaning, and it's also more flexible since we can change the definition of **about_path** and have the URL change everywhere **about_path** is used.

The full list of our planned links appears in Table 5.1, along with their mapping to URLs and routes. We'll implement all but the last one by the end of this chapter. (We'll make the last one in Chapter 9.)

Table 5.1 Route and URL mapping for site links

Page	URL	Named route
Home	/	**root_path**
About	/about	**about_path**
Contact	/contact	**contact_path**
Help	/help	**help_path**
Sign up	/signup	**signup_path**
Sign in	/signin	**signin_path**

5.2.1 Integration Tests

Before writing the routes for our application, we'll continue with our test-driven development by writing some tests for them. There are several ways to test routes, and we're going to take this opportunity to introduce *integration tests*, which give us a way to simulate a browser accessing our application and thereby test it from end to end. As we'll see starting in Section 8.4, testing routes is just the beginning.

We start by generating an integration test for the sample application's layout links:

```
$ rails generate integration_test layout_links
      invoke  rspec
      create    spec/requests/layout_links_spec.rb
```

Note that the generator automatically appends **_spec.rb** to the name of our test file, yielding **spec/requests/layout_links_spec.rb**. (In RSpec, integration tests are also called *request specs*; the origins of this terminology are obscure to me.)

Our integration test will use the same **get** function we used in Section 3.2 in the Pages controller spec, with code like this:

```
describe "GET 'home'" do
  it "should be successful" do
    get 'home'
    response.should be_success
  end
end
```

In this section, we want to test URLs like / and /about, but you can't **get** these URLs inside a controller test—controller tests only know about URLs defined for that exact controller. In contrast, integration tests are bound by no such restriction, since they are designed as *integrated* tests for the whole application and hence can **get** any page they want.

Following the model of the Pages controller spec, we can write an integration spec for each of the pages in Table 5.1 that we've already created, namely, Home, About, Contact, and Help. To make sure the right page (i.e., view) is rendered in each case, we'll check for the correct title using **have_selector**. The test definitions appear in Listing 5.13.

Listing 5.13 Integration test for routes.
`spec/requests/layout_links_spec.rb`

```ruby
require 'spec_helper'

describe "LayoutLinks" do

  it "should have a Home page at '/'" do
    get '/'
    response.should have_selector('title', :content => "Home")
  end

  it "should have a Contact page at '/contact'" do
    get '/contact'
    response.should have_selector('title', :content => "Contact")
  end

  it "should have an About page at '/about'" do
    get '/about'
    response.should have_selector('title', :content => "About")
  end

  it "should have a Help page at '/help'" do
    get '/help'
    response.should have_selector('title', :content => "Help")
  end
end
```

Of course, at this point they should fail (Red); we'll get them to Green in Section 5.2.2.

By the way, if you don't have a Help page at this point, now would be a good time to add one. (If you solved the Chapter 3 exercises in Section 3.5, you already have one.) First, add the **help** action to the Pages controller (Listing 5.14). Then, create the corresponding view (Listing 5.15).

Listing 5.14 Adding the **help** action to the Pages controller.
`app/controllers/pages_controller.rb`

```ruby
class PagesController < ApplicationController
  .
  .
  .
  def help
    @title = "Help"
  end
end
```

Listing 5.15 Adding a view for the Help page.
`app/views/pages/help.html.erb`

```
<h1>Help</h1>
<p>
  Get help on Ruby on Rails Tutorial at the
  <a href="http://railstutorial.org/help">Rails Tutorial help page</a>.
  To get help on this sample app, see the
  <a href="http://railstutorial.org/book">Rails Tutorial book</a>.
</p>
```

There's one final detail to deal with before moving on: if you're running Autotest, you might notice that it doesn't run the integration test. This is by design, since integration tests can be slow and hence can disrupt the red-green-refactor cycle, but I still find it preferable to have Autotest run the integration tests. To arrange for this to happen, you just have to tell Autotest to run tests in the **spec/requests** directory (Listing 5.16 or Listing 5.17).

Listing 5.16 Additions to `.autotest` needed to run integration tests with Autotest on OS X.

```
Autotest.add_hook :initialize do |autotest|
  autotest.add_mapping(/^spec\/requests\/.*_spec\.rb$/) do
    autotest.files_matching(/^spec\/requests\/.*_spec\.rb$/)
  end
end
```

Listing 5.17 Additions to `.autotest` needed to run integration tests with Autotest on Ubuntu Linux.

```
Autotest.add_hook :initialize do |autotest|
  autotest.add_mapping(%r%^spec/(requests)/.*rb$%) do|filename, _|
    filename
  end
end
```

Don't worry about where this code comes from; I don't know the Autotest API either. At some point I Googled around with search terms like "rspec autotest integration" and found it, and when I dropped it into my `.autotest` file, it worked.

5.2.2 Rails Routes

Now that we have tests for the URLs we want, it's time to get them to work. As noted in Section 3.1.2, the file Rails uses for URL mappings is **config/routes.rb**. If you take a look at the default routes file, you'll see that it's quite a mess, but it's a useful mess—full of commented-out example route mappings. I suggest reading through it at some point, and I also suggest taking a look at the Rails Guides article "Rails Routing from the outside in" for a much more in-depth treatment of routes. For now, though, we'll stick with the examples in Listing 5.18.[9]

Listing 5.18 Routes for static pages.
config/routes.rb

```
SampleApp::Application.routes.draw do
  match '/contact', :to => 'pages#contact'
  match '/about',   :to => 'pages#about'
  match '/help',    :to => 'pages#help'
  .
  .
  .
end
```

If you read this code carefully, you can probably figure out what it does; for example, you can see that

```
match '/about', :to => 'pages#about'
```

matches **'/about'** and routes it to the **about** action in the Pages controller. Before, this was more explicit: we used get 'pages/about' to get to the same place, but /about is more succinct. What isn't obvious is that **match '/about'** also automatically creates *named routes* for use in the controllers and views:

```
about_path => '/about'
about_url  => 'http://localhost:3000/about'
```

---

9. In the line **SampleApp::Application.routes.draw do** you might recognize that the **draw** method takes a *block*, a construction we last saw in Section 4.3.2.

Note that **about_url** is the *full* URL http://localhost:3000/about (with **local-host:3000** being replaced with the domain name, such as **example.com**, for a fully deployed site). As discussed in Section 5.2, to get just /about, you use **about_path**. (*Rails Tutorial* uses the **path** form for consistency, but the difference rarely matters in practice.)

With these routes now defined, the tests for the About, Contact, and Help pages should pass. (As usual, use Autotest or **rspec spec/** to check.) This leaves the test for the Home page.

To establish the route mapping for the Home page, we *could* use code like this:

```
match '/', :to => 'pages#home'
```

This is unnecessary, though; Rails has special instructions for the root URL / ("slash") located lower down in the file (Listing 5.19).

Listing 5.19 The commented-out hint for defining the root route.
config/routes.rb

```
SampleApp::Application.routes.draw do
  .
  .
  .
  # You can have the root of your site routed with "root"
  # just remember to delete public/index.html.
  # root :to => "welcome#index"
  .
  .
  .
end
```

Using Listing 5.19 as a model, we arrive at Listing 5.20 to route the root URL / to the Home page.

Listing 5.20 Adding a mapping for the root route.
config/routes.rb

```
SampleApp::Application.routes.draw do
  match '/contact', :to => 'pages#contact'
  match '/about',   :to => 'pages#about'
  match '/help',    :to => 'pages#help'
```

```
root :to => 'pages#home'
  .
  .
  .
end
```

This code maps the root URL / to /pages/home, and also gives URL helpers as follows:

```
root_path => '/'
root_url  => 'http://localhost:3000/'
```

We should also heed the comment in Listing 5.19 and delete **public/index.html** to prevent Rails from rendering the default page (Figure 1.3) when we visit /. You can of course simply remove the file by trashing it, but if you're using Git for version control there's a way to tell Git about the removal at the same time using **git rm**:

```
$ git rm public/index.html
$ git commit -am "Removed default Rails page"
```

With that, all of the routes for static pages are working, and the tests should pass. Now we just have to fill in the links in the layout.

5.2.3 Named Routes

Let's put the named routes created in Section 5.2.2 to work in our layout. This will entail filling in the second arguments of the **link_to** functions with the proper named routes. For example, we'll convert

```
<%= link_to "About", '#' %>
```

to

```
<%= link_to "About", about_path %>
```

and so on.

We'll start in the header partial, **_header.html.erb** (Listing 5.21), which has links to the Home and Help pages. While we're at it, we'll follow a common web convention and link the logo image to the Home page as well.

Listing 5.21 Header partial with links.
app/views/layouts/_header.html.erb

```
<header>
  <% logo = image_tag("logo.png", :alt => "Sample App", :class => "round") %>
  <%= link_to logo, root_path %>
  <nav class="round">
    <ul>
      <li><%= link_to "Home", root_path %></li>
      <li><%= link_to "Help", help_path %></li>
      <li><%= link_to "Sign in", '#' %></li>
    </ul>
  </nav>
</header>
```

We won't have a named route for the "Sign in" link until Chapter 9, so we've left it as **'#'** for now. Note that this code defines the local variable **logo** for the logo image tag, and then links to it in the next line:

```
  <% logo = image_tag("logo.png", :alt => "Sample App", :class => "round") %>
  <%= link_to logo, root_path %>
```

This is a little cleaner than stuffing it all into one line. It's especially important to notice that the ERb for the variable assignment doesn't have an equals sign; it's just <% . . . %>, because we don't want that line inserted into the template. (Using a local variable in this manner is only one way to do it. An even cleaner way might be to define a **logo** helper; see Section 5.5.)

The other place with links is the footer partial, **_footer.html.erb**, which has links for the About and Contact pages (Listing 5.22).

Listing 5.22 Footer partial with links.
app/views/layouts/_footer.html.erb

```
<footer>
  <nav class="round">
    <ul>
      <li><%= link_to "About", about_path %></li>
```

```
        <li><%= link_to "Contact", contact_path %></li>
        <li><a href="http://news.railstutorial.org/">News</a></li>
        <li><a href="http://www.railstutorial.org/">Rails Tutorial</a></li>
      </ul>
    </nav>
</footer>
```

With that, our layout has links to all the static pages created in Chapter 3, so that, for example, /about goes to the About page (Figure 5.9).

By the way, it's worth noting that, although we haven't actually tested for the presence of the links on the layout, our tests will fail if the routes aren't defined. You can check this by commenting out the routes in Listing 5.18 and running your test suite. For a testing method that actually makes sure the links go to the right places, see Section 5.5.

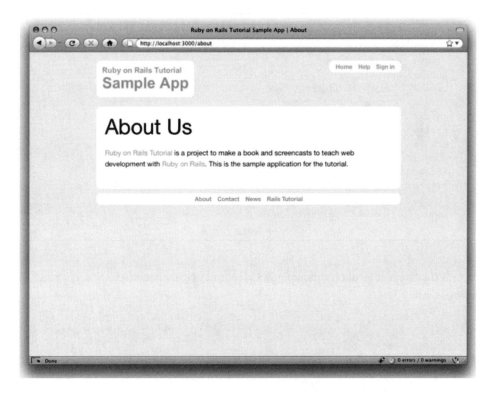

Figure 5.9 The About page at /about.

5.3 User Signup: A First Step

As a capstone to our work on the layout and routing, in this section we'll make a route for the signup page, which will mean creating a second controller along the way. This is a first important step toward allowing users to register for our site; we'll take the next step, modeling users, in Chapter 6, and we'll finish the job in Chapter 8.

5.3.1 Users Controller

It's been a while since we created our first controller, the Pages controller, way back in Section 3.1.2. It's time to create a second one, the Users controller. As before, we'll use **generate** to make the simplest controller that meets our present needs, namely, one with a stub signup page for new users. Following the conventional REST architecture favored by Rails, we'll call the action for new users **new** and pass it as an argument to **generate controller** to create it automatically (Listing 5.23).

Listing 5.23 Generating a Users controller (with a **new** action).

```
$ rails generate controller Users new
      create  app/controllers/users_controller.rb
       route  get "users/new"
      invoke  erb
      create    app/views/users
      create    app/views/users/new.html.erb
      invoke  rspec
      create    spec/controllers/users_controller_spec.rb
      create    spec/views/users
      create    spec/views/users/new.html.erb_spec.rb
      invoke  helper
      create    app/helpers/users_helper.rb
      invoke    rspec
      create    spec/helpers/users_helper_spec.rb
```

As with the Pages controller, this generates view and helper specs that we won't need, so remove them:

```
$ rm -rf spec/views
$ rm -rf spec/helpers
```

The controller generator makes both the Users controller and a useful default test, which verifies that the **new** action responds properly to a GET request (Box 3.1); the code appears in Listing 5.24. This code should look familiar; it follows the exact same form as the Pages controller spec last seen in Section 3.3.1 (Listing 3.20).

Listing 5.24 Testing the signup page.
`spec/controllers/users_controller_spec.rb`

```ruby
require 'spec_helper'

describe UsersController do

  describe "GET 'new'" do
    it "should be successful" do
      get 'new'
      response.should be_success
    end
  end
end
```

By construction, the Users controller already has the proper **new** action and **new.html.erb** template to get this test to pass (Listing 5.25). (To view the page at /users/new, you might have to restart the server.)

Listing 5.25 Action for the new user (signup) page.
`app/controllers/users_controller.rb`

```ruby
class UsersController < ApplicationController

  def new
  end

end
```

To get back in the spirit of test-driven development, let's add a second (failing) test of our own by testing for a title that contains the string **"Sign up"** (Listing 5.26). Be sure to add **render_views** as we did in the Pages controller spec (Listing 3.20); otherwise, the test won't pass even after we add the proper title.

Listing 5.26 A test for the signup page title.
spec/controllers/users_controller_spec.rb

```
require 'spec_helper'

describe UsersController do
  render_views

  describe "GET 'new'" do
    it "should be successful" do
      get 'new'
      response.should be_success
    end

    it "should have the right title" do
      get 'new'
      response.should have_selector("title", :content => "Sign up")
    end
  end
end
```

This test uses the **have_selector** method we've seen before (Section 3.3.1); note that, as in Section 3.3.1, **have_selector** needs the **render_views** line since it tests the view along with the action.

Of course, by design this test currently fails (Red). To get a custom title, we need to make an **@title** instance variable as in Section 3.3.3. We can thus get to Green with the code in Listing 5.27.

Listing 5.27 Setting the custom title for the new user page.
app/controllers/users_controller.rb

```
class UsersController < ApplicationController

  def new
    @title = "Sign up"
  end
end
```

5.3.2 Signup URL

With the code from Section 5.3.1, we already have a working page for new users at /users/new, but recall from Table 5.1 that we want the URL to be /signup instead. As in Section 5.2, we'll first write a test (Listing 5.28).

Listing 5.28 Simple integration test for user signup link.
`spec/requests/layout_links_spec.rb`

```
require 'spec_helper'

describe "LayoutLinks" do
  .
  .
  .
  it "should have a signup page at '/signup'" do
    get '/signup'
    response.should have_selector('title', :content => "Sign up")
  end
end
```

Note that this is the *same* file as the one used for the other layout links, even though the Signup page is in a different controller. Being able to hit pages in multiple controllers is one of the advantages of using integration tests.

The last step is to make a named route for signups. We'll follow the examples from Listing 5.18 and add a **match '/signup'** rule for the signup URL (Listing 5.29).

Listing 5.29 A route for the signup page.
`config/routes.rb`

```
SampleApp::Application.routes.draw do
  get "users/new"

  match '/signup',  :to => 'users#new'

  match '/contact', :to => 'pages#contact'
  match '/about',   :to => 'pages#about'
  match '/help',    :to => 'pages#help'

  root :to => 'pages#home'
  .
  .
  .
end
```

Note that we have kept the rule **get "users/new"**, which was generated automatically by the Users controller generation in Listing 5.23. Currently, this rule is necessary to route /users/new correctly, but it doesn't follow the proper REST conventions (Table 2.2), and we will eliminate it in Section 6.3.3.

At this point, the signup test in Listing 5.28 should pass. All that's left is to add the proper link to the button on the Home page. As with the other routes, **match '/signup'** gives us the named route **signup_path**, which we put to use in Listing 5.30.

Listing 5.30 Linking the button to the Signup page.
app/views/pages/home.html.erb

```
<h1>Sample App</h1>

<p>
  This is the home page for the
  <a href="http://railstutorial.org/">Ruby on Rails Tutorial</a>
  sample application.
</p>

<%= link_to "Sign up now!", signup_path, :class => "signup_button round" %>
```

With that, we're done with the links and named routes, at least until we add a route for signing in (Chapter 9). The resulting new user page (at the URL /signup) appears in Figure 5.10.

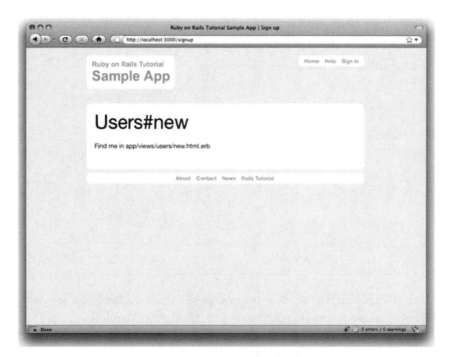

Figure 5.10 The new signup page at /signup.

5.4 Conclusion

In this chapter, we've hammered our application layout into shape and polished up the routes. The rest of the book is dedicated to fleshing out the sample application: first, by adding users who can sign up, sign in, and sign out; next, by adding user microposts; and, finally, by adding user relationships.

If you're following along with Git, be sure to commit and merge (and, just to be paranoid, run your tests first):

```
$ rspec spec/
$ git add .
$ git commit -am "Finished layout and routes"
$ git checkout master
$ git merge filling-in-layout
```

You might also want to push up to GitHub, or deploy to Heroku:

```
$ git push
$ git push heroku
```

5.5 Exercises

1. Replace the local variable **logo** in Listing 5.21 with a helper method of the same name, so that the new partial looks like Listing 5.31. Use the code in Listing 5.32 to help you get started.
2. You may have noticed that our tests for the layout links test the routing but don't actually check that the links on the layout go to the right pages. One way to implement these tests is to use **visit** and **click_link** inside the RSpec integration test. Fill in the code in Listing 5.33 to verify that all the layout links are properly defined.

Listing 5.31 Header partial with the logo helper from Listing 5.32.
app/views/layouts/_header.html.erb

```
<header>
  <%= link_to logo, root_path %>
  <nav class="round">
    <ul>
      <li><%= link_to "Home", root_path %></li>
      <li><%= link_to "Help", help_path %></li>
      <li><%= link_to "Sign in", '#' %></li>
```

```
      </ul>
    </nav>
  </header>
```

Listing 5.32 A template for the **logo** helper.
app/helpers/application_helper.rb

```
module ApplicationHelper

  def logo
    # Fill in.
  end

  # Return a title on a per-page basis.
  def title
    .
    .
    .
  end
end
```

Listing 5.33 A test for the links on the layout.
spec/requests/layout_links_spec.rb

```
require 'spec_helper'

describe "LayoutLinks" do
  .
  .
  .
  it "should have the right links on the layout" do
    visit root_path
    click_link "About"
    response.should have_selector('title', :content => "About")
    click_link "Help"
    response.should # fill in
    click_link "Contact"
    response.should # fill in
    click_link "Home"
    response.should # fill in
    click_link "Sign up now!"
    response.should # fill in
  end
end
```

## CHAPTER 6

Modeling and Viewing Users, Part I

In Chapter 5, we ended with a stub page for creating new users (Section 5.3); over the course of the next three chapters, we'll fulfill the promise implicit in this incipient signup page. The first critical step is to create a *data model* for users of our site, together with a way to store that data. Completing this task is the goal for this chapter and the next (Chapter 7), and we'll give users the ability to sign up in Chapter 8. Once the sample application can create new users, we'll let them sign in and sign out (Chapter 9), and in Chapter 10 (Section 10.2) we'll learn how to protect pages from improper access.

Taken together, the material in Chapter 6 through Chapter 10 develops a full Rails login and authentication system. As you may know, there are various pre-built authentication solutions out there in Rails land; Box 6.1 explains why (at least at first) it's a good idea to roll your own.

Box 6.1   Roll Your Own Authentication System

Virtually all web applications nowadays require a login and authentication system of some sort. Unsurprisingly, most web frameworks have a plethora of options for implementing such systems, and Rails is no exception. Examples of authentication and authorization systems include Clearance, Authlogic, Devise, and CanCan (as well as non-Rails-specific solutions built on top of OpenID or OAuth). It's reasonable to ask why we should reinvent the wheel. Why not just use an off-the-shelf solution instead of rolling our own?

There are several reasons why building our own authentication system is a good idea. First, there is no standard answer to Rails authentication; tying the tutorial to a specific project would leave us open to the risk that the our particular choice would go out of fashion or out of date. Moreover, even if we guessed right, the project's code-base would continue to evolve, rendering any tutorial explanation quickly obsolete.

> Finally, introducing all the authentication machinery at once would be a pedagogi-cal disaster—to take one example, Clearance contains more than 1,000 lines of code and creates a complicated data model right from the start. Authentication systems are a challenging and rich programming exercise; rolling our own means that we can consider one small piece at a time, leading to a far deeper understanding—of both authentication and of Rails.
>
> I encourage you to study Chapter 6 through Chapter 10 to give yourself a good foundation for future projects. When the time comes, if you decide to use an off-the-shelf authentication system for your own applications, you will be in a good position both to understand it and to tailor it to meet your specific needs.

In parallel with our data modeling, we'll also develop a web page for *showing* users, which will serve as the first step toward implementing the REST architecture for users (discussed briefly in Section 2.2.2). Though we won't get very far in this chapter, our eventual goal for the user profile pages is to show the user's profile image, basic user data, and a list of microposts, as mocked up in Figure 6.1.[1] (Figure 6.1 has our first example of *lorem ipsum* text, which has a fascinating story that you should definitely read about some time.) In this chapter, we'll lay the essential foundation for the user show page, and we'll start filling in the details starting in Chapter 7.

As usual, if you're following along using Git for version control, now would be a good time to make a topic branch for modeling users:

```
$ git checkout master
$ git checkout -b modeling-users
```

(The first line here is just to make sure that you start on the master branch, so that the `modeling-users` topic branch is based on `master`. You can skip that command if you're already on the master branch.)

6.1 User Model

Although the ultimate goal of the next three chapters is to make a signup page for our site, it would do little good to accept signup information now, since we don't currently have any place to put it. Thus, the first step in signing up users is to make a data structure

---

1. Mockingbird doesn't support custom images like the profile photo in Figure 6.1; I put that in by hand using Adobe Fireworks. The hippo here is from http://www.flickr.com/photos/43803060@N00/24308857/.

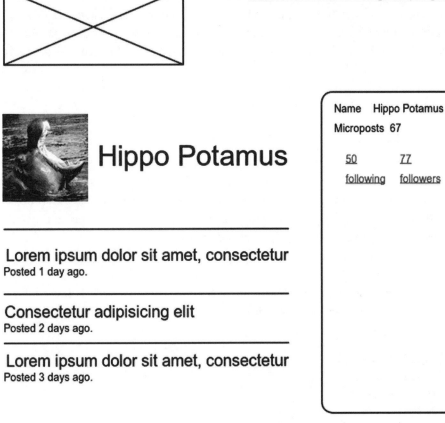

Figure 6.1 A mockup of our best guess at the user show page.

to capture and store their information. In Rails, the default data structure for a data model is called, naturally enough, a *model* (the M in MVC from Section 1.2.6). The default Rails solution to the problem of persistence is to use a *database* for long-term data storage, and the default library for interacting with the database is called *Active Record*.[2]

Active Record comes with a host of methods for creating, saving, and finding data objects, all without having to use the structured query language (SQL)[3] used by relational

---

2. The name comes from the "active record pattern", identified and named in *Patterns of Enterprise Application Architecture* by Martin Fowler.

3. Pronounced "ess-cue-ell", though the alternate pronunciation "sequel" is also common.

databases. Moreover, Rails has a feature called *migrations* to allow data definitions to be written in pure Ruby, without having to learn an SQL data definition language (DDL).[4] The effect is that Rails insulates you almost entirely from the details of the data store. In this book, by using SQLite for development and Heroku for deployment (Section 1.4), we have developed this theme even further, to the point where we barely ever have to think about how Rails stores data, even for production applications.[5]

6.1.1 Database Migrations

You may recall from Section 4.4.5 that we have already encountered, via a custom-built **User** class, user objects with **name** and **email** attributes. That class served as a useful example, but it lacked the critical property of *persistence*: when we created a User object at the Rails console, it disappeared as soon as we exited. Our goal in this section is to create a model for users that won't disappear quite so easily.

As with the User class in Section 4.4.5, we'll start by modeling a user with two attributes, a **name** and an **email** address, the latter of which we'll use as a unique username.[6] (We'll add a password attribute in Section 7.1.) In Listing 4.8, we did this with Ruby's **attr_accessor** keyword:

```
class User
  attr_accessor :name, :email
  .
  .
  .
end
```

---

4. In its earliest incarnations, Rails did require knowledge of an SQL DDL. Even after Rails added migrations, setting up the old default database (MySQL) was quite involved. Happily, as noted in Section 1.2.5, Rails now uses SQLite by default, which stores its data as a simple file—no setup required.

5. Occasionally, it is necessary to pierce this abstraction layer, but one design goal of this tutorial is to make all the code database-independent. (Indeed, this is a worthy goal in general.) In case you ever do need to write database-specific code to deploy on Heroku, you should know that they use the excellent PostgreSQL ("post-gres-cue-ell") database. PostgreSQL is free, open-source, and cross-platform; if you develop PostgreSQL-specific applications, you can install it locally, and configure Rails to use it in development by editing the **config/database.yml** file. Such configuration is beyond the scope of this tutorial, but there are lots of resources on the web; use a search engine to find the most up-to-date information for your platform.

6. By using an email address as the username, we open the theoretical possibility of communicating with our users at a future date.

In contrast, when using Rails to model users we don't need to identify the attributes explicitly. As noted briefly above, to store data Rails uses a relational database by default, which consists of *tables* composed of data *rows*, where each row has *columns* of data attributes. For example, to store users with names and email addresses, we'll create a **users** table with **name** and **email** columns (with each row corresponding to one user). By naming the columns in this way, we'll let Active Record figure out the User object attributes for us.

Let's see how this works. (If this discussion gets too abstract for your taste, be patient; the console examples starting in Section 6.1.3 and the database browser screenshots in Figure 6.3 and Figure 6.8 should make things clearer.) In Section 5.3.1, recall (Listing 5.23) that we created a Users controller (along with a **new** action) using the command

```
$ rails generate controller Users new
```

There is an analogous command for making a model: **generate model**; Listing 6.1 shows the command to generate a User model with two attributes, **name** and **email**.

Listing 6.1 Generating a User model.

```
$ rails generate model User name:string email:string
      invoke  active_record
      create    db/migrate/<timestamp>_create_users.rb
      create    app/models/user.rb
      invoke    rspec
      create      spec/models/user_spec.rb
```

(Note that, in contrast to the plural convention for controller names, model names are singular: a Users controller, but a User model.) By passing the optional parameters **name:string** and **email:string**, we tell Rails about the two attributes we want, along with what types those attributes should be (in this case, **string**). Compare this with including the action names in Listing 3.4 and Listing 5.23.

One of the results of the **generate** command in Listing 6.1 is a new file called a *migration*. Migrations provide a way to alter the structure of the database incrementally, so that our data model can adapt to changing requirements. In the case of the User model, the migration is created automatically by the model generation script; it creates a **users** table with two columns, **name** and **email**, as shown in Listing 6.2. (We'll see in Section 6.2.4 how to make a migration from scratch.)

Listing 6.2 Migration for the User model (to create a **users** table).
db/migrate/<timestamp>_create_users.rb

```ruby
class CreateUsers < ActiveRecord::Migration
  def self.up
    create_table :users do |t|
      t.string :name
      t.string :email

      t.timestamps
    end
  end

  def self.down
    drop_table :users
  end
end
```

Note that the name of the migration is prefixed by a *timestamp* based on when the migration was generated. In the early days of migrations, the filenames were prefixed with incrementing integers, which caused conflicts for collaborating teams if multiple programmers had migrations with the same number. Barring highly improbable millisecond-level simultaneity, using timestamps conveniently avoids such collisions.

Let's focus on the **self.up** method, which uses a Rails method called **create_table** to create a *table* in the database for storing users. (The use of **self** in **self.up** identifies it as a *class method*. This doesn't matter now, but we'll learn about class methods when we make one of our own in Section 7.2.4.) The **create_table** method accepts a block (Section 4.3.2) with one block variable, in this case called **t** (for "table"). Inside the block, the **create_table** method uses the **t** object to create **name** and **email** columns in the database, both of type **string**.[7] Here the table name is plural (**users**) even though the model name is singular (User), which reflects a linguistic convention followed by Rails: a model represents a single user, whereas a database table consists of many users. The final line in the block, **t.timestamps**, is a special command that creates two *magic columns* called **created_at** and **updated_at**, which are timestamps that automatically record when a given user is created and updated. (We'll see concrete examples of the magic columns starting in Section 6.1.3.) The full data model represented by this migration is shown in Figure 6.2.

---

7. Don't worry about exactly how the **t** object manages to do this; the beauty of *abstraction layers* is that we don't have to know. We can just trust the **t** object to do its job.

users	
id	integer
name	string
email	string
created_at	datetime
updated_at	datetime

Figure 6.2   The users data model produced by Listing 6.2.

We can run the migration, known as "migrating up", using the **rake** command (Box 2.1) as follows:[8]

```
$ rake db:migrate
```

(You may recall that we have run this command before, in Section 1.2.5 and again in Chapter 2.) The first time **db:migrate** is run, it creates a file called **db/development.sqlite3**, which is an SQLite[9] database. We can see the structure of the database using the excellent SQLite Database Browser to open the **db/development.sqlite3** file (Figure 6.3); compare with the diagram in Figure 6.2. You might note that there's one column in Figure 6.3 not accounted for in the migration: the **id** column. As noted briefly in Section 2.2, this column is created automatically, and is used by Rails to identify each row uniquely.

You've probably inferred that running **db:migrate** executes the **self.up** command in the migration file. What, then, of **self.down**? As you might guess, **down** migrates *down*, reversing the effects of migrating up. In our case, this means *dropping* the **users** table from the database:

```
class CreateUsers < ActiveRecord::Migration
  .
  .
  .
  def self.down
    drop_table :users
  end
end
```

---

8. We'll see how to migrate up on a remote Heroku server in Section 7.4.2.

9. Officially pronounced "ess-cue-ell-ite", although the (mis)pronunciation "sequel-ite" is also common.

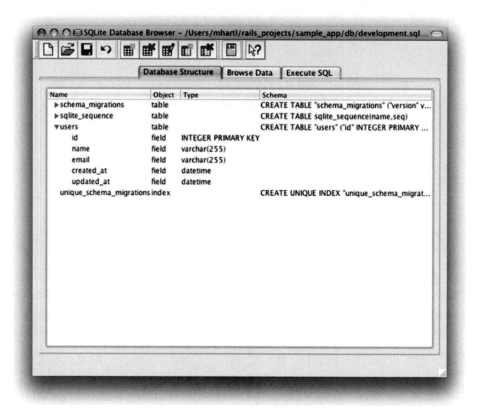

Figure 6.3   The SQLite Database Browser with our new **users** table.

You can execute **down** with **rake** using the argument **db:rollback**:

```
$ rake db:rollback
```

This is often useful if you realize there's another column you want to add but don't want the trouble of making a new migration: you can roll back the migration, add the desired column, and then migrate back up. (This isn't always convenient, and we'll learn how to add columns to an existing table in Section 7.1.2.)

If you rolled back the database, migrate up again before proceeding:

```
$ rake db:migrate
```

6.1.2 The Model File

We've seen how the User model generation in Listing 6.1 generated a migration file (Listing 6.2), and we saw in Figure 6.3 the results of running this migration: it updated a file called **development.sqlite3** by creating a table **users** with columns **id**, **name**, **email**, **created_at**, and **updated_at**. Listing 6.1 also created the model itself; the rest of this section is dedicated to understanding it.

We begin by looking at the code for the User model, which lives in the file **user.rb** inside the **app/models/** directory; it is, to put it mildly, very compact (Listing 6.3).

Listing 6.3 The brand new User model.
app/models/user.rb

```
class User < ActiveRecord::Base
end
```

Recall from Section 4.4.2 that the syntax **class User < ActiveRecord::Base** means that the **User** class *inherits* from **ActiveRecord::Base**, so that the User model automatically has all the functionality of the **ActiveRecord::Base** class. Of course, knowledge of this inheritance doesn't do any good unless we know what **ActiveRecord::Base** contains, and we'll get a first taste starting momentarily. Before we move on, though, there are two tasks to complete.

Model Annotation

Though it's not strictly necessary, you might find it convenient to *annotate* your Rails models using the annotate-models gem (Listing 6.4).

Listing 6.4 Adding the annotate-models gem to the **Gemfile**.

```
source 'http://rubygems.org'
 .
 .
 .
group :development do
  gem 'rspec-rails', '2.0.1'
  gem 'annotate-models', '1.0.4'
end

group :test do
  .
  .
  .
end
```

(We place the `annotate-models` gem in a **group :development** block (analogous to **group :test**) because the annotations aren't needed in production applications.) We next install it with **bundle**:

```
$ bundle install
```

This gives us a command called **annotate**, which simply adds comments containing the data model to the model file:

```
$ annotate
Annotated User
```

The results appear in Listing 6.5.

Listing 6.5   The annotated User model.
app/models/user.rb

```
# == Schema Information
# Schema version: <timestamp>
#
# Table name: users
#
#  id         :integer          not null, primary key
#  name       :string(255)
#  email      :string(255)
#  created_at :datetime
#  updated_at :datetime
#

class User < ActiveRecord::Base
end
```

I find that having the data model visible in the model files helps remind me which attributes the model has, but future code listings will usually omit the annotations for brevity.

Accessible Attributes

Another step that isn't strictly necessary but is a really good idea is to tell Rails which attributes of the model are accessible, i.e., which attributes can be modified by outside users (such as users submitting requests with web browsers). We do this with the **attr_accessible** method (Listing 6.6). We'll see in Chapter 10 that using **attr_accessible** is important for preventing a *mass assignment* vulnerability, a distressingly common and often serious security hole in many Rails applications.

Listing 6.6 Making the **name** and **email** attributes accessible.
app/models/user.rb

```
class User < ActiveRecord::Base
  attr_accessible :name, :email
end
```

6.1.3   Creating User Objects

We've done some good prep work, and now it's time to cash in and learn about Active Record by playing with our newly created User model. As in Chapter 4, our tool of choice is the Rails console. Since we don't (yet) want to make any changes to our database, we'll start the console in a *sandbox*:

```
$ rails console --sandbox
Loading development environment in sandbox (Rails 3.0.1)
Any modifications you make will be rolled back on exit
>>
```

As indicated by the helpful message "Any modifications you make will be rolled back on exit", when started in a sandbox the console will "roll back" (i.e., undo) any database changes introduced during the session.

When working at the console, it's useful to keep an eye on the *development log*, which records the actual low-level SQL statements being issued by Active Record, as shown in Figure 6.4. The way to get this output at a Unix command line is to **tail** the log:

```
$ tail -f log/development.log
```

The **-f** flag ensures that **tail** will display additional lines as they are written. I recommend keeping an open terminal window for tailing the log whenever working at the console.

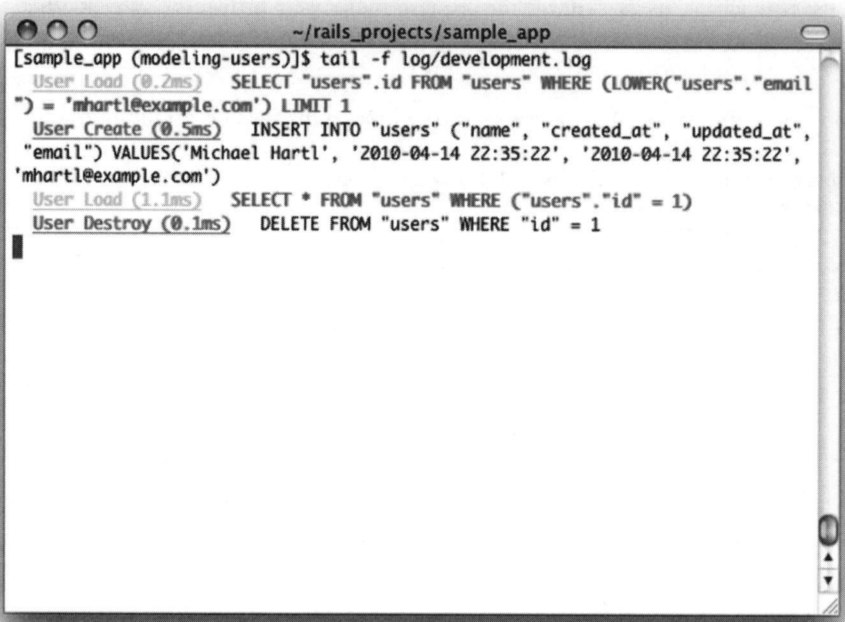

Figure 6.4   Tailing the development log.

In the console session in Section 4.4.5, we created a new user object with **User.new**, which we had access to only after requiring the example user file in Listing 4.8. With models, the situation is different; as you may recall from Section 4.4.4, the Rails console automatically loads the Rails environment, which includes the models. This means that we can make a new user object without any further work:

```
>> User.new
=> #<User id: nil, name: nil, email: nil, created_at: nil, updated_at: nil>
```

We see here the default console representation of a user object, which prints out the same attributes shown in Figure 6.3 and Listing 6.5.

When called with no arguments, **User.new** returns an object with all **nil** attributes. In Section 4.4.5, we designed the example User class to take an *initialization hash* to set the object attributes; that design choice was motivated by Active Record, which allows objects to be initialized in the same way:

```
>> user = User.new(:name => "Michael Hartl", :email => "mhartl@example.com")
=> #<User id: nil, name: "Michael Hartl", email: "mhartl@example.com",
created_at: nil, updated_at: nil>
```

Here we see that the name and email attributes have been set as expected.

If you've been tailing the development log, you may have noticed that no new lines have shown up yet. This is because calling **User.new** doesn't touch the database; it simply creates a new Ruby object in memory. To save the user object to the database, we call the **save** method on the **user** variable:

```
>> user.save
=> true
```

The **save** method returns **true** if it succeeds and **false** otherwise. (Currently, all saves should succeed; we'll see cases in Section 6.2 when some will fail.) As soon as you save, you should see a line in the development log with the SQL command to **INSERT INTO** **"users"**. Because of the many methods supplied by Active Record, we won't ever need raw SQL in this book, and I'll omit discussion of the SQL commands from now on. But you can learn a lot by watching the log.

You may have noticed that the new user object had **nil** values for the **id** and the magic columns **created_at** and **updated_at** attributes. Let's see if our **save** changed anything:

```
>> user
=> #<User id: 1, name: "Michael Hartl", email: "mhartl@example.com",
created_at: "2010-01-05 00:57:46", updated_at: "2010-01-05 00:57:46">
```

We see that the **id** has been assigned a value of **1**, while the magic columns have been assigned the current time and date.[10] Currently, the created and updated timestamps are identical; we'll see them differ in Section 6.1.5.

---

10. In case you're curious about **"2010-01-05 00:57:46"**, I'm not writing this after midnight; the timestamps are recorded in Coordinated Universal Time (UTC), which for most practical purposes is the same as Greenwich Mean Time. From the NIST Time and Frequency FAQ: **Q:** Why is UTC used as the acronym for Coordinated Universal Time instead of CUT? **A:** In 1970 the Coordinated Universal Time system was devised by an international advisory group of technical experts within the International Telecommunication Union (ITU). The ITU felt it was best to designate a single abbreviation for use in all languages in order to minimize confusion. Since unanimous agreement could not be achieved on using either the English word order, CUT, or the French word order, TUC, the acronym UTC was chosen as a compromise.

As with the User class in Section 4.4.5, instances of the User model allow access to their attributes using a dot notation:[11]

```
>> user.name
=> "Michael Hartl"
>> user.email
=> "mhartl@example.com"
>> user.updated_at
=> Tue, 05 Jan 2010 00:57:46 UTC +00:00
```

As we'll see in Chapter 8, it's often convenient to make and save a model in two steps as we have above, but Active Record also lets you combine them into one step with **User.create**:

```
>> User.create(:name => "A Nother", :email => "another@example.org")
=> #<User id: 2, name: "A Nother", email: "another@example.org", created_at:
"2010-01-05 01:05:24", updated_at: "2010-01-05 01:05:24">
>> foo = User.create(:name => "Foo", :email => "foo@bar.com")
=> #<User id: 3, name: "Foo", email: "foo@bar.com", created_at: "2010-01-05
01:05:42", updated_at: "2010-01-05 01:05:42">
```

Note that **User.create**, rather than returning **true** or **false**, returns the User object itself, which we can optionally assign to a variable (such as **foo** in the second command above).

The inverse of **create** is **destroy**:

```
>> foo.destroy
=> #<User id: 3, name: "Foo", email: "foo@bar.com", created_at: "2010-01-05
01:05:42", updated_at: "2010-01-05 01:05:42">
```

Oddly, **destroy**, like **create**, returns the object in question, though I can't recall ever having used the return value of **destroy**. Even odder, perhaps, is that the **destroy**ed object still exists in memory:

---

11. Note the value of **user.updated_at**. Told you the timestamp was in UTC.

```
>> foo
=> #<User id: 3, name: "Foo", email: "foo@bar.com", created_at: "2010-01-05
01:05:42", updated_at: "2010-01-05 01:05:42">
```

How do we know if we really destroyed an object? And for saved and non-destroyed objects, how can we retrieve users from the database? It's time to learn how to use Active Record to find user objects.

6.1.4   Finding User Objects

Active Record provides several options for finding objects. Let's use them to find the first user we created while verifying that the third user (**foo**) has been destroyed. We'll start with the existing user:

```
>> User.find(1)
=> #<User id: 1, name: "Michael Hartl", email: "mhartl@example.com",
created_at: "2010-01-05 00:57:46", updated_at: "2010-01-05 00:57:46">
```

Here we've passed the id of the user to **User.find**; Active Record returns the user with that **id** attribute.

Let's see if the user with an **id** of **3** still exists in the database:

```
>> User.find(3)
ActiveRecord::RecordNotFound: Couldn't find User with ID=3
```

Since we destroyed our third user in Section 6.1.3, Active Record can't find it in the database. Instead, **find** raises an *exception*, which is a way of indicating an exceptional event in the execution of a program—in this case, a nonexistent Active Record id, which causes **find** to raise an **ActiveRecord::RecordNotFound** exception.[12]

In addition to the generic **find**, Active Record also allows us to find users by specific attributes:

---

12. Exceptions and exception handling are somewhat advanced Ruby subjects, and we won't need them much in this book. They are important, though, and I suggest learning about them using one of the Ruby books recommended in Section 1.1.1.

```
>> User.find_by_email("mhartl@example.com")
=> #<User id: 1, name: "Michael Hartl", email: "mhartl@example.com",
created_at: "2010-01-05 00:57:46", updated_at: "2010-01-05 00:57:46">
```

Since we will be using email addresses as usernames, this sort of find will be useful when we learn how to let users sign in to our site (Chapter 8).[13]

We'll end with a couple of more general ways of finding users. First, there's **first**:

```
>> User.first
=> #<User id: 1, name: "Michael Hartl", email: "mhartl@example.com",
created_at: "2010-01-05 00:57:46", updated_at: "2010-01-05 00:57:46">
```

Naturally, **first** just returns the first user in the database. There's also **all**:

```
>> User.all
=> [#<User id: 1, name: "Michael Hartl", email: "mhartl@example.com",
created_at: "2010-01-05 00:57:46", updated_at: "2010-01-05 00:57:46">,
#<User id: 2, name: "A Nother", email: "another@example.org", created_at:
"2010-01-05 01:05:24", updated_at: "2010-01-05 01:05:24">]
```

No prizes for inferring that **all** returns an array (Section 4.3.1) of all users in the database.

6.1.5 Updating User Objects

Once we've created objects, we often want to update them. There are two basic ways to do this. First, we can assign attributes individually, as we did in Section 4.4.5:

```
>> user            # Just a reminder about our user's attributes
=> #<User id: 1, name: "Michael Hartl", email: "mhartl@example.com",
created_at: "2010-01-05 00:57:46", updated_at: "2010-01-05 00:57:46">
>> user.email = "mhartl@example.net"
=> "mhartl@example.net"
>> user.save
=> true
```

---

13. To those worried that **find_by_email** will be inefficient if there are a large number of users, you're ahead of the game. We'll cover this issue, and its solution via database indices, in Section 6.2.4.

Note that the final step is necessary to write the changes to the database. We can see what happens without a save by using **reload**, which reloads the object based on the database information:

```
>> user.email
=> "mhartl@example.net"
>> user.email = "foo@bar.com"
=> "foo@bar.com"
>> user.reload.email
=> "mhartl@example.net"
```

Now that we've updated the user, the magic columns differ, as promised in Section 6.1.3:

```
>> user.created_at
=> "2010-01-05 00:57:46"
>> user.updated_at
=> "2010-01-05 01:37:32"
```

The second way to update attributes is to use **update_attributes**:

```
>> user.update_attributes(:name => "The Dude", :email => "dude@abides.org")
=> true
>> user.name
=> "The Dude"
>> user.email
=> "dude@abides.org"
```

The **update_attributes** method accepts a hash of attributes, and on success performs both the update and the save in one step (returning **true** to indicate that the save went through). It's worth noting that, once you have defined some attributes as accessible using **attr_accessible** (Section 6.1.2), *only* those attributes can be modified using **update_attributes**. If you ever find that your models mysteriously start refusing to update certain columns, check to make sure that those columns are included in the call to **attr_accessible**.

6.2 User Validations

The User model we created in Section 6.1 now has working **name** and **email** attributes, but they are completely generic: any string (including an empty one) is currently valid in either case. And yet, names and email addresses are more specific than this. For example, **name** should be non-blank, and **email** should match the specific format characteristic of email addresses. Moreover, since we'll be using email addresses as unique usernames when users sign in, we shouldn't allow email duplicates in the database.

In short, we shouldn't allow **name** and **email** to be just any strings; we should enforce certain constraints on their values. Active Record allows us to impose such constraints using *validations*. In this section, we'll cover several of the most common cases, validating *presence, length, format* and *uniqueness*. In Section 7.1.1 we'll add a final common validation, *confirmation*. And we'll see in Section 8.2 how validations give us convenient error messages when users make submissions that violate them.

As with the other features of our sample app, we'll add User model validations using test-driven development. Since we've changed the data model, it's a good idea to prepare the test database before proceeding:

```
$ rake db:test:prepare
```

This just ensures that the data model from the development database, **db/development. sqlite3**, is reflected in the test database, **db/test.sqlite3**.

6.2.1 Validating Presence

We'll start with a test for the presence of a **name** attribute. Although the first step in TDD is to write a *failing* test (Section 3.2.2), in this case we don't yet know enough about validations to write the proper test, so we'll write the validation first, using the console to understand it. Then we'll comment out the validation, write a failing test, and verify that uncommenting the validation gets the test to pass. This procedure may seem pedantic for such a simple test, but I have seen[14] *many* "simple" tests that test the wrong thing; being meticulous about TDD is simply the *only* way to be confident that we're testing the right thing. (This comment-out technique is also useful when rescuing an application whose application code is already written but—*quelle horreur!*—has no tests.)

---

14. (and written)

The way to validate the presence of the name attribute is to use the **validates** method with argument **:presence => true**, as shown in Listing 6.7. The **:presence => true** argument is a one-element *options hash*; recall from Section 4.3.4 that curly braces are optional when passing hashes as the final argument in a method. (As noted in Section 5.1.1, the use of options hashes is a recurring theme in Rails.)

Listing 6.7 Validating the presence of a **name** attribute.
app/models/user.rb

```
class User < ActiveRecord::Base
  attr_accessible :name, :email

  validates :name, :presence => true
end
```

As discussed briefly in Section 2.3.2, the use of **validates** is characteristic of Rails 3. (In Rails 2.3, we would write **validates_presence_of :name** instead.)

Listing 6.7 may look like magic, but **validates** is just a method, as indeed is **attr_accessible**. An equivalent formulation of Listing 6.7 using parentheses is as follows:

```
class User < ActiveRecord::Base
  attr_accessible(:name, :email)

  validates(:name, :presence => true)
end
```

Let's drop into the console to see the effects of adding a validation to our User model:[15]

```
$ rails console --sandbox
>> user = User.new(:name => "", :email => "mhartl@example.com")
>> user.save
=> false
>> user.valid?
=> false
```

---

15. I'll omit the output of console commands when they are not particularly instructive—for example, the results of **User.new**.

Here **user.save** returns **false**, indicating a failed save. In the final command, we use the **valid?** method, which returns **false** when the object fails one or more validations, and **true** when all validations pass. (Recall from Section 4.2.3 that Ruby uses a question mark to indicate such true/false *boolean* methods.) In this case, we only have one validation, so we know which one failed, but it can still be helpful to check using the **errors** object generated on failure:

```
>> user.errors.full_messages
=> ["Name can't be blank"]
```

(The error message is a hint that Rails validates the presence of an attribute using the **blank?** method, which we saw at the end of Section 4.4.2.)

Now for the failing test. To ensure that our incipient test will fail, let's comment out the validation at this point (Listing 6.8).

Listing 6.8 Commenting out a validation to ensure a failing test.
app/models/user.rb

```ruby
class User < ActiveRecord::Base
  attr_accessible :name, :email

  # validates :name, :presence => true
end
```

As in the case of controller generation (e.g., Listing 5.23), the model generate command in Listing 6.1 produces an initial spec for testing users, but in this case it's practically blank (Listing 6.9).

Listing 6.9 The practically blank default User spec.
spec/models/user_spec.rb

```ruby
require 'spec_helper'

describe User do
  pending "add some examples to (or delete) #{__FILE__}"
end
```

This simply uses the **pending** method to indicate that we should fill the spec with something useful. We can see its effect by running the User model spec:

```
$ rspec spec/models/user_spec.rb
*




Finished in 0.01999 seconds
1 example, 0 failures, 1 pending

Pending:
  User add some examples to (or delete)
  /Users/mhartl/rails_projects/sample_app/spec/models/user_spec.rb
  (Not Yet Implemented)
```

We'll follow the advice of the default spec by filling it in with some RSpec examples, shown in Listing 6.10.

Listing 6.10 The initial user spec.
spec/models/user_spec.rb

```ruby
require 'spec_helper'

describe User do

  before(:each) do
    @attr = { :name => "Example User", :email => "user@example.com" }
  end

  it "should create a new instance given valid attributes" do
    User.create!(@attr)
  end

  it "should require a name"
end
```

We've seen **require** and **describe** before, most recently in Listing 5.28. The next line is a **before(:each)** block; this was covered briefly in an exercise (Listing 3.33), and all it does is run the code inside the block before each example—in this case setting the **@attr** instance variable to an initialization hash.

The first example is just a sanity check, verifying that the User model is basically working. It uses **User.create!** (read "create bang"), which works just like the **create** method we saw in Section 6.1.3 except that it raises an **ActiveRecord::Record-Invalid** exception if the creation fails (similar to the **ActiveRecord::RecordNot-Found** exception we saw in Section 6.1.4). As long as the attributes are valid, it won't raise any exceptions, and the test will pass.

The final line is the test for the presence of the **name** attribute—or rather, it *would* be the actual test, if it had anything in it. Instead, the test is just a stub, but a useful stub it is: it's a *pending spec*, which is a way to write a description of the application's behavior without worrying yet about the implementation. Listing 6.9 shows an example of a pending spec using an explicit call to the **pending** method; in this case, since we have included only the **it** part of the example,

```
it "should require a name"
```

RSpec infers the existence of a pending spec.

Pending specs are handled well by programs for running specs, as seen for Autotest in Figure 6.5, and the output of **rspec spec/** is similarly useful. Pending specs are

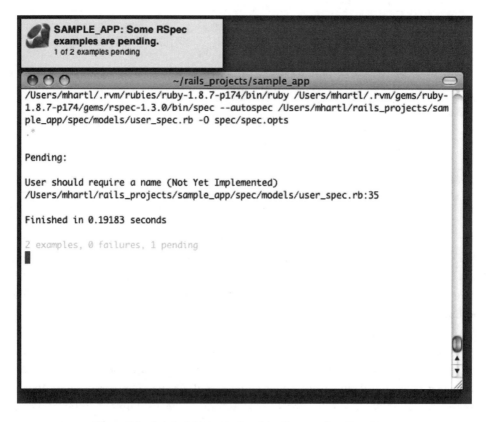

Figure 6.5   Autotest (via **autotest**) with a pending User spec.

useful as placeholders for tests we know we need to write at some point but don't want to deal with right now.

In order to fill in the pending spec, we need a way to make an attributes hash with an invalid name. (The **@attr** hash is valid by construction, with a non-blank **name** attribute.) The **Hash** method **merge** does the trick, as we can see with **rails console**:

```
>> @attr = { :name => "Example User", :email => "user@example.com" }
=> {:name => "Example User", :email => "user@example.com"}
>> @attr.merge(:name => "")
=> {:name => "", :email => "user@example.com"}
```

With **merge** in hand, we're ready to make the new spec (using a trick I'll explain momentarily), as seen in Listing 6.11.

Listing 6.11 A failing test for validation of the **name** attribute.
spec/models/user_spec.rb

```
describe User do

  before(:each) do
    @attr = { :name => "Example User", :email => "user@example.com" }
  end
  .
  .
  .
  it "should require a name" do
    no_name_user = User.new(@attr.merge(:name => ""))
    no_name_user.should_not be_valid
  end
end
```

Here we use **merge** to make a new user called **no_name_user** with a blank name. The second line then uses the RSpec **should_not** method to verify that the resulting user is *not* valid. The trick I alluded to above is related to **be_valid**: we know from earlier in this section that a User object responds to the **valid?** boolean method. RSpec adopts the useful convention of allowing us to test *any* boolean method by dropping the question mark and prepending **be_**. In other words,

```
no_name_user.should_not be_valid
```

is equivalent to

```
no_name_user.valid?.should_not == true
```

Since it sounds more like natural language, writing **should_not be_valid** is definitely more idiomatically correct RSpec.

With that, our new test should fail, which we can verify with Autotest or by running the **user_spec.rb** file using the **spec** script:

```
$ rspec spec/models/user_spec.rb
.F

1)
'User should require a name' FAILED
expected valid? to return false, got true
./spec/models/user_spec.rb:14:

2 examples, 1 failure
```

Now uncomment the validation (i.e., revert Listing 6.8 back to Listing 6.7) to get the test to pass:

```
$ rspec spec/models/user_spec.rb
..

2 examples, 0 failures
```

Of course, we also want to validate the presence of email addresses. The test (Listing 6.12) is analogous to the one for the **name** attribute.

Listing 6.12 A test for presence of the **email** attribute.
spec/models/user_spec.rb

```
describe User do

  before(:each) do
    @attr = { :name => "Example User", :email => "user@example.com" }
  end

  .
```

```
  .
  .
it "should require an email address" do
  no_email_user = User.new(@attr.merge(:email => ""))
  no_email_user.should_not be_valid
  end
end
```

The implementation is also virtually the same, as seen in Listing 6.13.

Listing 6.13 Validating the presence of the **name** and **email** attributes.
app/models/user.rb

```
class User < ActiveRecord::Base
  attr_accessible :name, :email

  validates :name,  :presence => true
  validates :email, :presence => true
end
```

Now all the tests should pass, and the "presence" validations are complete.

6.2.2 Length Validation

We've constrained our User model to require a name for each user, but we should go further: the user's names will be displayed on the sample site, so we should enforce some limit on their length. With all the work we did in Section 6.2.1, this step is easy.

We start with a test. There's no science to picking a maximum length; we'll just pull **50** out of thin air as a reasonable upper bound, which means verifying that names of **51** characters are too long (Listing 6.14).

Listing 6.14 A test for **name** length validation.
spec/models/user_spec.rb

```
describe User do

  before(:each) do
    @attr = { :name => "Example User", :email => "user@example.com" }
  end
  .
  .
  .
  it "should reject names that are too long" do
```

```
    long_name = "a" * 51
    long_name_user = User.new(@attr.merge(:name => long_name))
    long_name_user.should_not be_valid
  end
end
```

For convenience, we've used "string multiplication" in Listing 6.14 to make a string 51 characters long. We can see how this works using the console:

```
>> s = "a" * 51
=> "aaaaaaaaaaaaaaaaaaaaaaaaaaaaaaaaaaaaaaaaaaaaaaaaaaa"
>> s.length
=> 51
```

The test in Listing 6.14 should fail. To get it to pass, we need to know about the validation argument to constrain length, **:length**, along with the **:maximum** parameter to enforce the upper bound (Listing 6.15).

Listing 6.15   Adding a length validation for the **name** attribute.
app/models/user.rb

```
class User < ActiveRecord::Base
  attr_accessible :name, :email

  validates :name,  :presence => true,
                    :length   => { :maximum => 50 }
  validates :email, :presence => true
end
```

With our test suite passing again, we can move on to a more challenging validation: email format.

6.2.3   Format Validation

Our validations for the **name** attribute enforce only minimal constraints—any non-blank name under 51 characters will do—but of course the **email** attribute must satisfy more stringent requirements. So far we've only rejected blank email addresses; in this section, we'll require email addresses to conform to the familiar pattern **user@example.com**.

Neither the tests nor the validation will be exhaustive, just good enough to accept most valid email addresses and reject most invalid ones. We'll start with a couple tests involving collections of valid and invalid addresses. To make these collections, it's worth knowing about a useful method for making arrays of strings, as seen in this console session:

```
>> %w[foo bar baz]
=> ["foo", "bar", "baz"]
>> addresses = %w[user@foo.com THE_USER@foo.bar.org first.last@foo.jp]
=> ["user@foo.com", "THE_USER@foo.bar.org", "first.last@foo.jp"]
>> addresses.each do |address|
?>   puts address
>> end
user@foo.com
THE_USER@foo.bar.org
first.last@foo.jp
```

Here we've iterated over the elements of the **addresses** array using the **each** method (Section 4.3.2). With this technique in hand, we're ready to write some basic email format validation tests (Listing 6.16).

Listing 6.16 Tests for email format validation.
spec/models/user_spec.rb

```
describe User do

  before(:each) do
    @attr = { :name => "Example User", :email => "user@example.com" }
  end
  .
  .
  .
  it "should accept valid email addresses" do
    addresses = %w[user@foo.com THE_USER@foo.bar.org first.last@foo.jp]
    addresses.each do |address|
      valid_email_user = User.new(@attr.merge(:email => address))
      valid_email_user.should be_valid
    end
  end

  it "should reject invalid email addresses" do
    addresses = %w[user@foo,com user_at_foo.org example.user@foo.]
    addresses.each do |address|
      invalid_email_user = User.new(@attr.merge(:email => address))
      invalid_email_user.should_not be_valid
    end
  end
end
```

As noted earlier, these are far from exhaustive, but we do check the common valid email forms **user@foo.com**, **THE_USER@foo.bar.org** (uppercase, underscores, and compound domains), and **first.last@foo.jp** (the standard corporate username **first.last**, with a two-letter top-level domain **jp**), along with several invalid forms.

The application code for email format validation uses a *regular expression* (or *regex*) to define the format, along with the **:format** argument to the **validates** method (Listing 6.17).

Listing 6.17 Validating the email format with a regular expression.
app/models/user.rb

```
class User < ActiveRecord::Base
  attr_accessible :name, :email

  email_regex = /\A[\w+\-.]+@[a-z\d\-.]+\.[a-z]+\z/i

  validates :name,  :presence => true,
                    :length   => { :maximum => 50 }
  validates :email, :presence => true,
                    :format   => { :with => email_regex }
end
```

Here **email_regex** is a *regular expression*, also known as a *regex*. The code

```
  email_regex = /\A[\w+\-.]+@[a-z\d\-.]+\.[a-z]+\z/i
  .
  .
  .
  validates :email, :presence => true,
                    :format   => { :with => email_regex }
```

ensures that only email addresses that match the pattern will be considered valid.

So, where does the pattern come from? Regular expressions consist of a terse (some would say unreadable) language for matching text patterns; learning to construct regexes is an art, and to get you started I've broken **email_regex** into bite-sized pieces (Table 6.1).[16] To really learn about regular expressions, though, I consider the amazing Rubular regular expression editor (Figure 6.6) to be simply essential.[17] The Rubular

16. Note that, in Table 6.1, "letter" really means "lower-case letter", but the **i** at the end of the regex enforces case-insensitive matching.

17. If you find it as useful as I do, I encourage you to donate to Rubular to reward developer Michael Lovitt for his wonderful work.

Table 6.1 Breaking down the email regex from Listing 6.17

Expression	Meaning
`/\A[\w+\-.]+@[a-z\d\-.]+\.[a-z]+\z/i`	full regex
`/`	start of regex
`\A`	match start of a string
`[\w+\-.]+`	at least one word character, plus, hyphen, or dot
`@`	literal "at sign"
`[a-z\d\-.]+`	at least one letter, digit, hyphen, or dot
`\.`	literal dot
`[a-z]+`	at least one letter
`\z`	match end of a string
`/`	end of regex
`i`	case insensitive

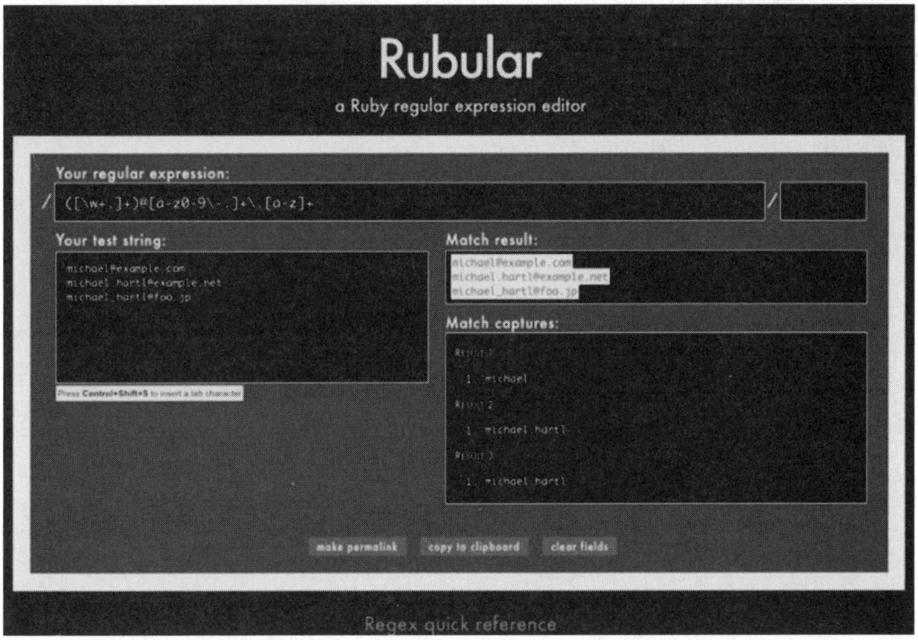

Figure 6.6 The awesome Rubular regular expression editor.

website has a beautiful interactive interface for making regular expressions, along with a handy regex quick reference. I encourage you to study Table 6.1 with a browser window open to Rubular—no amount of reading about regular expressions can replace a couple of hours playing with Rubular.

By the way, there actually exists a full regex for matching email addresses according to the official standard, but it's really not worth the trouble. The one in Listing 6.17 is fine, maybe even better than the official one.[18]

The tests should all be passing now. (In fact, the tests for valid email addresses should have been passing all along; since regexes are notoriously error-prone, the valid email tests are there mainly as a sanity check on **email_regex**.) This means that there's only one constraint left: enforcing the email addresses to be unique.

6.2.4 Uniqueness Validation

To enforce uniqueness of email addresses (so that we can use them as usernames), we'll be using the **:unique** option to the **validates** method. But be warned: there's a *major* caveat, so don't just skim this section—read it carefully.

We'll start, as usual, with our tests. In our previous model tests, we've mainly used **User.new**, which just creates a Ruby object in memory, but for uniqueness tests we actually need to put a record into the database.[19] The (first) duplicate email test appears in Listing 6.18.

Listing 6.18 A test for the rejection of duplicate email addresses.
spec/models/user_spec.rb

```
describe User do

  before(:each) do
    @attr = { :name => "Example User", :email => "user@example.com" }
  end
  .
  .
```

---

18. Did you know that **"Michael Hartl"@example.com**, with quotation marks and a space in the middle, is a valid email address according to the standard? Incredibly, it is—but it's absurd. If you don't have an email address that contains only letters, numbers, underscores, and dots, then get one. N.B. The regex in Listing 6.17 allows plus signs, too, because Gmail (and possibly other email services) does something useful with them: for example, to filter orders from Amazon, you can use username+amazon@gmail.com, which will go to the Gmail address username@gmail.com, allowing you to filter on the string amazon.

19. As noted briefly in the introduction to this section, there is a dedicated test database, **db/test.sqlite3**, for this purpose.

```
    .
  it "should reject duplicate email addresses" do
    # Put a user with given email address into the database.
    User.create!(@attr)
    user_with_duplicate_email = User.new(@attr)
    user_with_duplicate_email.should_not be_valid
  end
end
```

The method here is to create a user and then try to make another one with the same email address. (We use the noisy method **create!**, first seen in Listing 6.10, so that it will raise an exception if anything goes wrong. Using **create**, without the bang **!**, risks having a silent error in our test, a potential source of elusive bugs.) We can get this test to pass with the code in Listing 6.19.[20]

Listing 6.19 Validating the uniqueness of email addresses.
app/models/user.rb

```
class User < ActiveRecord::Base
  .
  .
  .
  validates :email, :presence   => true,
                    :format     => { :with => email_regex },
                    :uniqueness => true
end
```

We're not quite done, though. Email addresses are case-insensitive—**foo@bar.com** goes to the same place as **FOO@BAR.COM** or **FoO@BAr.coM**—so our validation should cover this case as well. We test for this with the code in Listing 6.20.

Listing 6.20 A test for the rejection of duplicate email addresses, insensitive to case.
spec/models/user_spec.rb

```
describe User do

  before(:each) do
    @attr = { :name => "Example User", :email => "user@example.com" }
```

20. If you're wondering why the **create!** line in Listing 6.10 doesn't cause this to fail by creating a duplicate user, it's because Rails tests are *transactional*: each test is wrapped in a transaction, which *rolls back* the database after the test executes. This way, each test runs against a fresh database.

```
  end
  .
  . .
  .
  it "should reject email addresses identical up to case" do
    upcased_email = @attr[:email].upcase
    User.create!(@attr.merge(:email => upcased_email))
    user_with_duplicate_email = User.new(@attr)
    user_with_duplicate_email.should_not be_valid
  end
end
```

Here we are using the **upcase** method on strings (seen briefly in Section 4.3.2). This test does the same thing as the first duplicate email test, but with an upper-case email address instead. If this test feels a little abstract, go ahead and fire up the console:

```
$ rails console --sandbox
>> @attr = { :name => "Example User", :email => "user@example.com" }
=> {:name => "Example User", :email => "user@example.com"}
>> upcased_email = @attr[:email].upcase
=> "USER@EXAMPLE.COM"
>> User.create!(@attr.merge(:email => upcased_email))
>> user_with_duplicate_email = User.new(@attr)
>> user_with_duplicate_email.valid?
=> true
```

Of course, currently **user_with_duplicate_email.valid?** is **true**, since this is a failing test, but we want it to be **false**. Fortunately, **:uniqueness** accepts an option, **:case_sensitive**, for just this purpose (Listing 6.21).

Listing 6.21 Validating the uniqueness of email addresses, ignoring case.
app/models/user.rb

```
class User < ActiveRecord::Base
  .
  .
  .
  validates :email, :presence   => true,
                    :format     => { :with => email_regex },
                    :uniqueness => { :case_sensitive => false }
end
```

Note that we have simply replaced **true** with **:case_sensitive => false**; Rails infers in this case that **:uniqueness** should be **true**. At this point, our application (sort of) enforces email uniqueness, and our test suite should pass.

The Uniqueness Caveat

There's just one small problem, the caveat alluded to above:

Using validates :uniqueness does not guarantee uniqueness.

D'oh! But what can go wrong? Here's what:

1. Alice signs up for the sample app, with address **alice@wonderland.com**.
2. Alice accidentally clicks on "Submit" *twice*, sending two requests in quick succession.
3. The following sequence occurs: request 1 creates a user in memory that passes validation; request 2 does the same; request 1's user gets saved; request 2's user gets saved.
4. Result: two user records with the exact same email address, despite the uniqueness validation.

If the above sequence seems implausible, believe me, it isn't: it happens on any Rails website with significant traffic.[21] Luckily, the solution is straightforward to implement; we just need to enforce uniqueness at the database level as well. Our method is to create a database *index* on the email column, and then require that the index be unique.

The email index represents an update to our data modeling requirements, which (as discussed in Section 6.1.1) is handled in Rails using migrations. We saw in Section 6.1.1 that generating the User model automatically created a new migration (Listing 6.2); in the present case, we are adding structure to an existing model, so we need to create a migration directly using the **migration** generator:

```
$ rails generate migration add_email_uniqueness_index
```

Unlike the migration for users, the email uniqueness migration is not pre-defined, so we need to fill in its contents with Listing 6.22.[22]

---

21. Yes, it happened to me. How do you think I found out about this issue?

22. Of course, we could just edit the migration file for the **users** table in Listing 6.2 but that would require rolling back and then migrating back up. The Rails Way is to use migrations every time we discover that our data model needs to change.

Listing 6.22 The migration for enforcing email uniqueness.
`db/migrate/<timestamp>_add_email_uniqueness_index.rb`

```
class AddEmailUniquenessIndex < ActiveRecord::Migration
  def self.up
    add_index :users, :email, :unique => true
  end

  def self.down
    remove_index :users, :email
  end
end
```

This uses a Rails method called **add_index** to add an index on the **email** column of the **users** table. The index by itself doesn't enforce uniqueness, but the option **:unique => true** does.

The final step is to migrate the database:

```
$ rake db:migrate
```

Now the Alice scenario above will work fine: the database will save a user record based on the first request, and will reject the second save for violating the uniqueness constraint. (An error will appear in the Rails log, but that doesn't do any harm. You can actually catch the **ActiveRecord::StatementInvalid** exception that gets raised—see Insoshi for an example—but in this tutorial we won't bother with this step.) Adding this index on the email attribute accomplishes a second goal, alluded to briefly in Section 6.1.4: it fixes an efficiency problem in **find_by_email** (Box 6.2).

Box 6.2 Database Indices

When creating a column in a database, it is important to consider if we will need to *find* records by that column. Consider, for example, the **email** attribute created by the migration in Listing 6.2. When we allow users to sign in to the sample app starting in Chapter 8, we will need to find the user record corresponding to the submitted email address; unfortunately, based on the naïve data model, the only way to find a user by email address is to look through *each* user row in the database and compare its email attribute to the given email. This is known in the database business as a *full-table scan*, and for a real site with thousands of users it is a Bad Thing.

Putting an index on the email column fixes the problem. To understand a database index, it's helpful to consider the analogy of a book index. In a book, to find all the occurrences of a given string, say "foobar", you would have to scan each page for "foobar". With a book index, on the other hand, you can just look up "foobar" in the index to see all the pages containing "foobar". A database index works essentially the same way.

6.3 Viewing Users

We're not quite done with the basic user model—we still need to add passwords, a task for Chapter 7—but we do have enough in place to make a minimalist page for showing user information. This will allow a gentle introduction to the REST style of organizing the actions for our site's users. Since this is just a rough demonstration for now, there are no tests in this section; we'll add tests when we flesh out the user view in Section 7.3.

6.3.1 Debug and Rails Environments

As preparation for adding dynamic pages to our sample application, now is a good time to add some debug information to our site layout (Listing 6.23). This displays some useful information about each page using the built-in **debug** method and **params** variable (which we'll learn more about in Section 6.3.2), as seen in Figure 6.7.

Listing 6.23 Adding some debug information to the site layout.
app/views/layouts/application.html.erb

```
<!DOCTYPE html>
<html>
    .
    .
    .
  <body>
    <div class="container">
      .
      .
      .
      <%= render 'layouts/footer' %>
      <%= debug(params) if Rails.env.development? %>
    </div>
  </body>
</html>
```

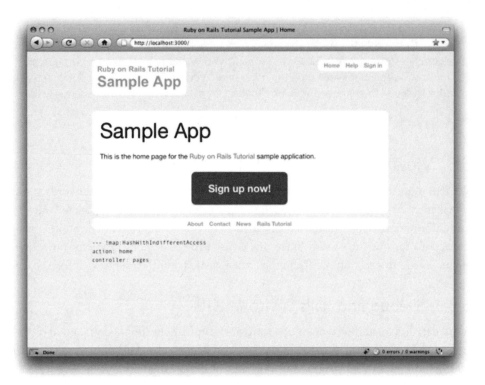

Figure 6.7 The sample application Home page (/) with debug information at the bottom.

Since we don't want to display debug information to users of a deployed application, we use

```
if Rails.env.development?
```

to restrict the debug information to the *development environment*. Though we've seen evidence of Rails environments before (most recently in Section 6.1.3), this is the first time it has mattered to us.

Rails comes equipped with three environments: **test**, **development**, and **production**.[23] The default environment for the Rails console is **development**:

---

23. You can define your own custom environments as well; see the Railscast on adding an environment for details.

```
$ rails console
Loading development environment (Rails 3.0.1)
>> Rails.env
=> "development"
>> Rails.env.development?
=> true
>> Rails.env.test?
=> false
```

As you can see, Rails provides a **Rails** object with an **env** attribute and associated environment boolean methods. In particular, **Rails.env.development?** is **true** only in a development environment, so the Embedded Ruby

```
<%= debug(params) if Rails.env.development? %>
```

won't be inserted into production applications or tests. (Inserting the debug information into tests probably doesn't do any harm, but it probably doesn't do any good, either, so it's best to restrict the debug display to development only.)

If you ever need to run a console in a different environment (to debug a test, for example), you can pass the environment as a parameter to the **console** script:

```
$ rails console test
Loading test environment (Rails 3.0.0)
>> Rails.env
=> "test"
```

As with the console, **development** is the default environment for the local Rails server, but you can also run it in a different environment:

```
$ rails server --environment production
```

If you view your app running in production, it won't work without a production database, which we can create by running **rake db:migrate** in production:

```
$ rake db:migrate RAILS_ENV=production
```

(I find it confusing that the console, server, and migrate commands specify non-default environments in three mutually incompatible ways, which is why I bothered showing all three.)

By the way, if you have deployed your sample app to Heroku, you can see its environment using the **heroku** command, which provides its own (remote) console:

```
$ heroku console
Ruby console for yourapp.heroku.com
>> Rails.env
=> "production"
>> Rails.env.production?
=> true
```

Naturally, since Heroku is a platform for production sites, it runs each application in a production environment.

6.3.2 User Model, View, Controller

In order to make a page to view a user, we'll use the User *model* to put a user into the database, make a *view* to display some user information, and then add an action to the Users *controller* to handle the browser request. In other words, for the first time in this tutorial, we'll see in one place all three elements of the model-view-controller architecture first discussed in Section 1.2.6.

Our first step is to create a user using the console, which we'll take care *not* to start in a sandbox since this time the whole point is to save a record to the database:

```
$ rails console
Loading development environment (Rails 3.0.1)
>> User.create!(:name => "Michael Hartl", :email => "mhartl@example.com")
=> #<User id: 1, name: "Michael Hartl", email: "mhartl@example.com",
created_at: "2010-01-07 23:05:14", updated_at: "2010-01-07 23:05:14">
```

To double-check that this worked, let's look at the row in the development database using the SQLite Database Browser (Figure 6.8). Note that the columns correspond to the attributes of the data model defined in Section 6.1.

Next comes the view, which is minimalist to emphasize that this is just a demonstration (Listing 6.24). We use the standard Rails location for showing a user, **app/views/users/show.html.erb**; unlike the **new.html.erb** view, which we

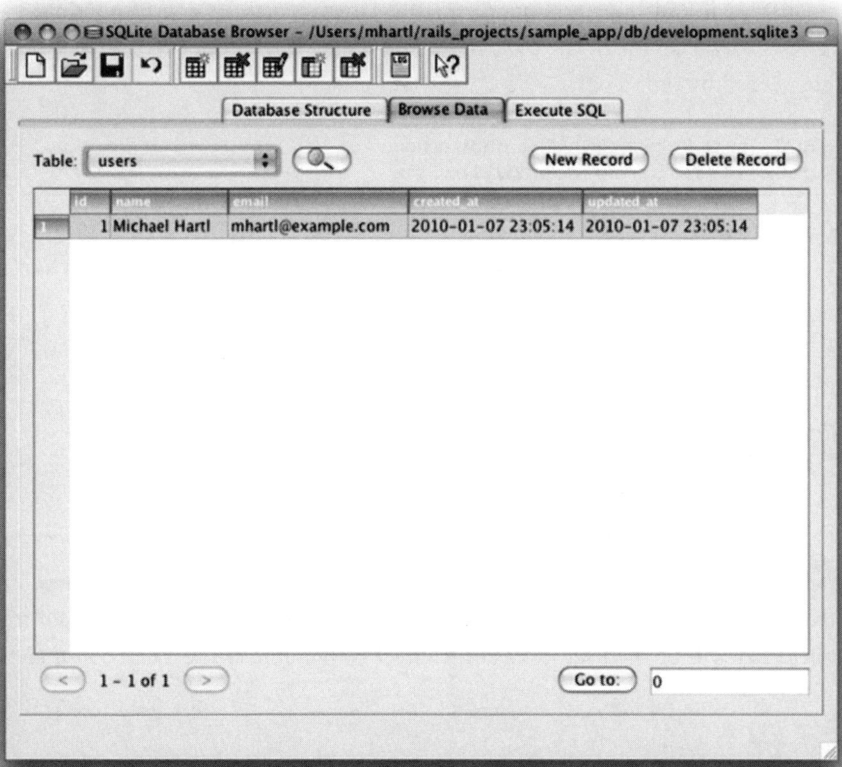

Figure 6.8 A user row in the SQLite database `db/development.sqlite3`.

created with the generator in Listing 5.23, the **show.html.erb** file doesn't currently exist, so you'll have to create it by hand.

Listing 6.24 A stub view for showing user information.
app/views/users/show.html.erb

```
<%= @user.name %>, <%= @user.email %>
```

This view uses Embedded Ruby to display the user's name and email address, assuming the existence of an instance variable called **@user**. Of course, eventually the real user show page will look very different, and won't display the email address publicly.

Finally, we'll add the **show** action to the Users controller (corresponding to the **show.html.erb** view) with the code in Listing 6.25, which defines the **@user** instance variable needed by the view.

Listing 6.25 The Users controller with a **show** action.
app/controllers/users_controller.rb

```
class UsersController < ApplicationController

  def show
    @user = User.find(params[:id])
  end

  def new
    @title = "Sign up"
  end
end
```

Here we've gotten a little ahead of ourselves by using the standard Rails **params** object to retrieve the user id. When we make the appropriate request to the Users controller, **params[:id]** will be the user id **1**, so the effect is the same as the **find** command

```
User.find(1)
```

we saw in Section 6.1.4.

Although the **show** view and action are now both defined, we still don't have a way to view the page itself. This requires defining the proper rule in the Rails routes file, as we'll see in the next section.

6.3.3 A Users Resource

Our method for displaying the user show page will follow the conventions of the REST architecture favored in Rails applications. This style is based on the ideas of *representational state transfer* identified and named by computer scientist Roy Fielding in his doctoral dissertation *Architectural Styles and the Design of Network Based Software Architectures.*[24]

---

24. Fielding, Roy Thomas. *Architectural Styles and the Design of Network Based Software Architectures.* Doctoral dissertation, University of California, Irvine, 2000.

Figure 6.9   The initial effect of hitting `/users/1`.

The REST design style emphasizes representing data as *resources* that can be created, shown, updated, or destroyed—four actions corresponding to the four fundamental operations POST, GET, PUT, and DELETE defined by the HTTP standard (Box 3.1).

When following REST principles, resources are typically referenced using the resource name and a unique identifier. What this means in the context of users—which we're now thinking of as a Users *resource*—is that we should view the user with id **1** by issuing a GET request to the URL /users/1. Here the **show** action is *implicit* in the type of request—when Rails' REST features are activated, GET requests are automatically handled by the **show** action.

Unfortunately, the URL /users/1 doesn't work quite yet due to a routing error (Figure 6.9). We can get the REST-style Users URL to work by adding users as a resource to **config/routes.rb**, as seen in Listing 6.26.

Listing 6.26 Adding a Users resource to the routes file.
`config/routes.rb`

```
SampleApp::Application.routes.draw do
  resources :users

  match '/signup',  :to => 'users#new'
  .
  .
  .
end
```

After adding the routes for the Users resource, the URL `/users/1` works perfectly (Figure 6.10).

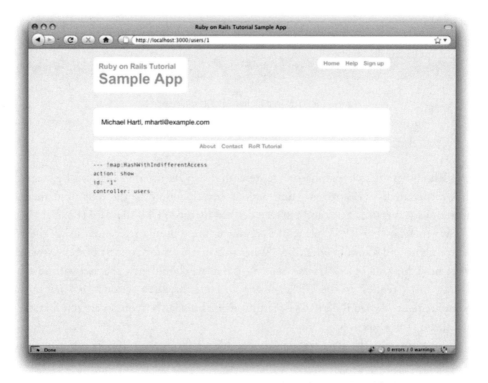

Figure 6.10   The user show page at `/users/1` after adding a Users resource.

Table 6.2 RESTful routes provided by the Users resource in Listing 6.26

HTTP Request	URL	Action	Named Route	Purpose
GET	/users	**index**	**users_path**	page to list all users
GET	/users/1	**show**	**user_path(1)**	page to show user with id **1**
GET	/users/new	**new**	**new_user_path**	page to make a new user (signup)
POST	/users	**create**	**users_path**	create a new user
GET	/users/1 /edit	**edit**	**edit_user_path(1)**	page to edit user with id **1**
PUT	/users/1	**update**	**user_path(1)**	update user with id **1**
DELETE	/users/1	**destroy**	**user_path(1)**	delete user with id **1**

You might have noticed that Listing 6.26 removed the line

```
get "users/new"
```

last seen in Listing 5.29. This is because the one additional resource line in Listing 6.26 doesn't just add a working /users/1 URL; it endows our sample application with all the actions needed for a RESTful Users resource,[25] along with a large number of named routes (Section 5.2.3) for generating user URLs. The resulting correspondence of URLs, actions, and named routes is shown in Table 6.2. (Compare to Table 2.2.) Over the course of the next three chapters, we'll cover all of the other entries in Table 6.2 as we fill in all the actions necessary to make Users a fully RESTful resource.

`params` in `debug`

Before leaving the user show page, we'll take a moment to examine the debug information produced by Listing 6.23. If you look closely at Figure 6.10, you'll see that it includes useful information about the page being rendered:[26]

---

25. This means that the *routing* works, but the corresponding pages don't necessarily work at this point. For example, /users/1/edit gets routed properly to the **edit** action of the Users controller, but since the **edit** action doesn't exist yet actually hitting that URL will return an error.

26. Some of this tutorial's screenshots show debug information with output like **!map:HashWithIndifferent-Access** instead of **!map:ActiveSupport::HashWithIndifferentAccess**. This is simply a minor difference between Rails 2.3 and Rails 3. Since the rendered web pages are otherwise identical between Rails versions, this one footnote saves me the trouble of redoing all the screenshots.

```
--- !map:ActiveSupport::HashWithIndifferentAccess
action: show
id: "1"
controller: users
```

This is a YAML[27] representation of **params**, which (as hinted at by the name **Hash-WithIndifferentAccess**) is basically a hash. We see that its controller is **users**, its action is **show**, and its **id** attribute is **"1"**. Although you will rarely have occasion to use **params[:controller]** or **params[:action]**, using **params[:id]** to pull out the id from the URL is a common Rails idiom. In particular, we used the code

```
User.find(params[:id])
```

in Listing 6.25 to find the user with id **1**. (The **find** method knows how to convert the string **"1"** into the integer **1**.)

The **debug** information often provides useful feedback when developing Rails application, and I suggest getting in the habit of checking it whenever your application doesn't behave as expected.

6.4 Conclusion

This chapter is the first half of the two-step process of creating a working User model. Our users now have **name** and **email** attributes, together with validations enforcing several important constraints on their values. We've also taken a first small step toward a working user show page and a Users resource based on the principles of representational state transfer (REST). In Chapter 7, we'll complete the process by adding user passwords and a more useful user view.

If you're using Git, now would be a good time to commit if you haven't done so in a while:

```
$ git add .
$ git commit -am "Finished first cut of the User model"
```

---

27. The Rails **debug** information is shown as YAML (a recursive acronym standing for "YAML Ain't Markup Language"), which is a friendly data format designed to be both machine- *and* human-readable.

6.5 Exercises

1. Read through the Rails API entry for **`ActiveRecord::Base`** to get a sense of its capabilities.
2. Study the entry in the Rails API for the **`validates`** method to learn more about its capabilities and options.
3. Spend a couple hours playing with Rubular.

## CHAPTER 7

Modeling and Viewing Users, Part II

In Chapter 6, we created the first iteration of a User model to represent users of our application, but the job is only half-done. Virtually any website with users, including ours, needs *authentication* as well, but currently any user signing up for the site would only have a name and email address, with no way to verify their identity. In this chapter, we'll add the **password** attribute needed for an initial user signup (Chapter 8) and for signing in with an email/password combination (Chapter 9). In the process, we'll re-use several of the ideas from Chapter 6, including migrations and validations, and also introduce some new ideas such as virtual attributes, private methods, and Active Record callbacks.

Once we have a working **password** attribute, we'll make a working action and view for showing user profiles (Section 7.3). By the end of the chapter, our user profiles will display names and profile photos (as indicated by the mockup in Figure 7.1), and they will be nicely tested with user *factories*.

7.1 Insecure Passwords

Making industrial-strength passwords requires a lot of machinery, so we'll break the process into two main steps. In this section, we'll make a **password** attribute and add validations. The resulting User model will be functionally complete but badly insecure, with the passwords stored as plain text in the database. In Section 7.2, we'll fix this problem by encrypting the passwords before saving them, thereby protecting our site against potential attackers.

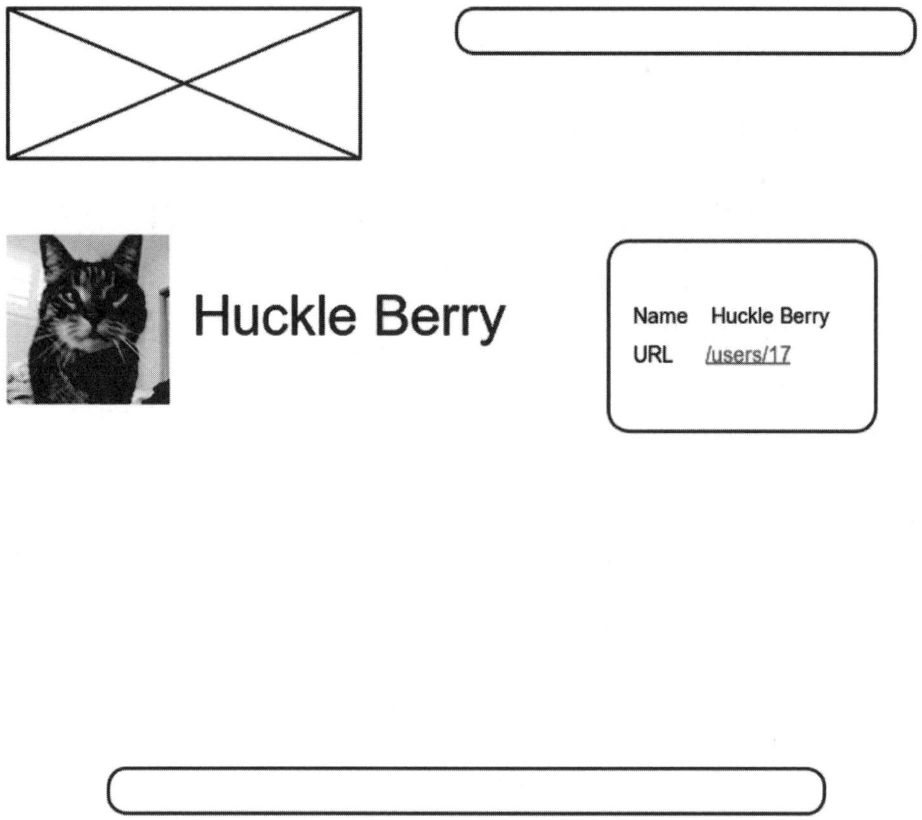

Figure 7.1   A mockup of the user profile made in Section 7.3.

7.1.1 Password Validations

Even though we have yet even to add a column for passwords to our database, we're already going to start writing tests for them. Our initial plan is to have tests to validate the presence, length, and confirmation of passwords. This is our biggest single block of tests so far, so see if you can read it all in one go. If you get stuck, it might help to review the analogous validations from Section 6.2 or skip ahead to the application code in Listing 7.2.

In order to minimize typos in passwords, when making a user signup page in Chapter 8 we'll adopt the common convention of requiring that users *confirm* their passwords. To get started, let's review the user attributes hash last seen in Listing 6.20:

```
describe User do

  before(:each) do
    @attr = { :name => "Example User", :email => "user@example.com" }
  end
    .
    .
    .
end
```

To write tests for passwords, we'll need to add *two* new attributes to the **@attr** hash, **password** and **password_confirmation**. As you can probably guess, the **password_confirmation** attribute will be used for the password confirmation step.

Let's write tests for the presence of the password and its confirmation, together with tests confirming that the password is a valid length (restricted somewhat arbitrarily to be between 6 and 40 characters long). The results appear in Listing 7.1.

Listing 7.1 Tests for password validations.
spec/models/user_spec.rb

```
require 'spec_helper'

describe User do

  before(:each) do
    @attr = {
      :name => "Example User",
      :email => "user@example.com",
      :password => "foobar",
      :password_confirmation => "foobar"
    }
  end

  it "should create a new instance given valid attributes" do
    User.create!(@attr)
  end
    .
    .
    .
  describe "password validations" do

    it "should require a password" do
      User.new(@attr.merge(:password => "", :password_confirmation => "")).
        should_not be_valid
    end
```

```
  it "should require a matching password confirmation" do
    User.new(@attr.merge(:password_confirmation => "invalid")).
      should_not be_valid
  end

  it "should reject short passwords" do
    short = "a" * 5
    hash = @attr.merge(:password => short, :password_confirmation => short)
    User.new(hash).should_not be_valid
  end

  it "should reject long passwords" do
    long = "a" * 41
    hash = @attr.merge(:password => long, :password_confirmation => long)
    User.new(hash).should_not be_valid
  end
 end
end
```

Note in Listing 7.1 how we first collect a set of valid user attributes in **@attr**. If for some reason those attributes aren't valid—as would be the case, for example, if we didn't implement password confirmations properly—then the first test

```
  it "should create a new instance given valid attributes" do
    User.create!(@attr)
  end
```

would catch the error. The subsequent tests then check each validation in turn, using the same **@attr.merge** technique first introduced in Listing 6.11.

Now for the application code, which contains a trick. Actually, it contains *two* tricks. First, you might expect at this point that we would run a migration to add a **password** attribute to the User model, as we did with the **name** and **email** attributes in Listing 6.1. But this is not the case: we will store only an *encrypted* password in the database; for the password, we will introduce a *virtual attribute* (that is, an attribute not corresponding to a column in the database) using the **attr_accessor** keyword, much as we did with the original **name** and **email** attributes for the example user in Section 4.4.5. The **password** attribute will not ever be written to the database, but will exist only in memory for use in performing the password confirmation step (implemented next) and the encryption step (implemented in Section 7.1.2 and Section 7.2).

The second trick is that we will *not* introduce a **password_confirmation** attribute, not even a virtual one. Instead, we will use the special validation

```
validates :password, :confirmation => true
```

which will *automatically* create a virtual attribute called **password_confirmation**, while confirming that it matches the **password** attribute at the same time.

Thus prepared to understand the implementation, let's take a look at the code itself (Listing 7.2).

Listing 7.2 Validations for the **password** attribute.
app/models/user.rb

```
class User < ActiveRecord::Base
  attr_accessor :password
  attr_accessible :name, :email, :password, :password_confirmation
  .
  .
  .
  # Automatically create the virtual attribute 'password_confirmation'.
  validates :password, :presence     => true,
                       :confirmation => true,
                       :length       => { :within => 6..40 }
end
```

As promised, we use **attr_accessor :password** to create a virtual **password** attribute (as in Section 4.4.5). Then, since we'll be accepting passwords and password confirmations as part of the signup process in Chapter 8, we need to add the password and its confirmation to the list of accessible attributes (first mentioned in Section 6.1.2), which we've done in the line

```
attr_accessible :name, :email, :password, :password_confirmation
```

Next come the password validations. They require the presence of a **:password** (as in, e.g., Listing 6.7) and include **:confirmation => true** to reject users whose password and password confirmations don't match. We also have a second application of

length validation; in Listing 6.15 we constrained the **name** attribute to be 50 characters
or less using the **:maximum** option:

```
validates :name,   :presence => true,
                   :length   => { :maximum => 50 }
```

For the password length validation, instead we've used the **:within** option, passing it
the *range*[1] **6..40** to enforce the desired length constraints.

7.1.2 A Password Migration

At this point, you may be concerned that we're not storing user passwords anywhere;
since we've elected to use a virtual password, rather than storing it in the database, it exists
only in memory. How can we use this password for authentication? The solution is to
create a separate attribute dedicated to password storage, and our strategy will be to use
the virtual password as raw material for an *encrypted password*, which we *will* store in the
database upon user signup (Chapter 8) and retrieve later for use in user authentication
(Chapter 9).

Let's plan to store the encrypted password using an **encrypted_password** attribute
in our User model. We'll discuss the implementation details in Section 7.2, but we can
get started with our encrypted password tests by noting that the encrypted password
should at the least *exist*. We can test this using the Ruby method **respond_to?**, which
accepts a symbol and returns **true** if the object responds to the given method or attribute
and **false** otherwise:

```
$ rails console --sandbox
>> user = User.new
>> user.respond_to?(:password)
=> true
>> user.respond_to?(:encrypted_password)
=> false
```

---

1. We saw ranges before in Section 4.3.1.

We can test the existence of an **encrypted_password** attribute with the code in Listing 7.3, which uses RSpec's **respond_to** helper method.

Listing 7.3 Testing for the existence of an **encrypted_password** attribute. **spec/models/user_spec.rb**

```
describe User do
  .
  .
  .
  describe "password encryption" do

    before(:each) do
      @user = User.create!(@attr)
    end

    it "should have an encrypted password attribute" do
      @user.should respond_to(:encrypted_password)
    end
  end
end
```

Note that in the **before(:each)** block we *create* a user, rather than just calling **User.new**. We could actually get this test to pass using **User.new**, but (as we'll see momentarily) *setting* the encrypted password will require that the user be saved to the database. Using **create!** in this first case does no harm, and putting it in **before(:each)** will allow us to keep all the encrypted password tests in one **describe** block.

To get this test to pass, we'll need a migration to add the **encrypted_password** attribute to the **users** table:

```
$ rails generate migration add_password_to_users encrypted_password:string
```

Here the first argument is the migration name, and we've also supplied a second argument with the name and type of attribute we want to create. (Compare this to the original generation of the **users** table in Listing 6.1.) We can choose any migration name we want, but it's convenient to end the name with **_to_users**, since in this case Rails can automatically construct a migration to add columns to the **users** table. Moreover, by including the second argument, we've given Rails enough information to construct the entire migration for us, as seen in Listing 7.4.

Listing 7.4 The migration to add an **encrypted_password** column to the **users** table.
db/migrate/<timestamp>_add_password_to_users.rb

```ruby
class AddPasswordToUsers < ActiveRecord::Migration
  def self.up
    add_column :users, :encrypted_password, :string
  end

  def self.down
    remove_column :users, :encrypted_password
  end
end
```

This code uses the **add_column** method to add an **encrypted_password** column to the **users** table (and the complementary **remove_column** method to remove it when migrating down). The result is the data model shown in Figure 7.2.

Now if we run the migration and prepare the test database, the test should pass, since the User model will respond to the **encrypted_password** attribute. (Be sure to close any Rails consoles started in a sandbox; the sandbox locks the database and prevents the migration from going through.)

```
$ rake db:migrate
$ rake db:test:prepare
```

Of course, we can run the full test suite with **rspec spec/**, but sometimes it's convenient to run just *one* RSpec example, which we can do with the **-e** ("example") flag:

```
$ rspec spec/models/user_spec.rb \
> -e "should have an encrypted password attribute"
.

1 example, 0 failures
```

users	
id	integer
name	string
email	string
encrypted_password	string
created_at	datetime
updated_at	datetime

Figure 7.2 The User model with an added (encrypted) password attribute.

7.1.3   An Active Record Callback

Now that our User model has an attribute for storing the password, we need to arrange to generate and save the encrypted password when Active Record saves the user to the database. We'll do this with a technique called a *callback*, which is a method that gets invoked at a particular point in the lifetime of an Active Record object. In the present case, we'll use a **before_save** callback to create **encrypted_password** just before the user is saved.[2]

We start with a test for the encrypted password attribute. Since we're deferring the implementation details—and, in particular, the method of encryption—to Section 7.2, in this section we'll just make sure that a saved user's **encrypted_password** attribute is not blank. We do this by combining the **blank?** method on strings (Section 4.4.2) with the RSpec convention for boolean methods (first seen in the context of **valid?/be_valid** in Listing 6.11), yielding the test in Listing 7.5.

Listing 7.5 Testing that the **encrypted_password** attribute is nonempty.
spec/models/user_spec.rb

```
describe User do
  .
  .
  .
  describe "password encryption" do

    before(:each) do
      @user = User.create!(@attr)
    end
    .
    .
    .
    it "should set the encrypted password" do
      @user.encrypted_password.should_not be_blank
    end
  end
end
```

This code verifies that **encrypted_password.blank?** is not true using the construction **should_not be_blank**.

---

2. For more details on the kind of callbacks supported by Active Record, see the discussion of callbacks at the Rails Guides.

To get this test to pass, we *register* a callback called **encrypt_password** by passing a symbol of that name to the **before_save** method, and then define an **encrypt_-password** method to perform the encryption. With the **before_save** in place, Active Record will automatically call the corresponding method before saving the record. The result appears in Listing 7.6.

Listing 7.6   A **before_save** callback to create the **encrypted_password** attribute.
app/models/user.rb

```
class User < ActiveRecord::Base
  .
  .
  .
  validates :password, :presence     => true,
                       :confirmation => true,
                       :length       => { :within => 6..40 }

  before_save :encrypt_password

  private

    def encrypt_password
      self.encrypted_password = encrypt(password)
    end

    def encrypt(string)
      string # Only a temporary implementation!
    end
end
```

Here the **encrypt_password** callback delegates the actual encryption to an **encrypt** method; as noted in the comment, this is only a temporary implementation—as currently constructed, Listing 7.6 simply sets the encrypted to the *unencrypted* password, which kind of defeats the purpose. But it's enough to get our test to pass, and we'll make the **encrypt** method do some actual encryption in Section 7.2.

Before trying to understand the implementation, first note that the encryption methods appear after the **private** keyword; inside a Ruby class, all methods defined *after* **private** are used internally by the object and are not intended for public use.[3] For an

---

3. The extra level of indentation is a typographical reminder that we're in a private section; otherwise, it's easy to miss the **private** keyword and be confused when trying to access a private method that you think is public. I thought the extra indentation was a stupid convention until I burned an hour on just this problem a couple years back. Now I add the extra indentation...

example, we can look at a User object in the console:

```
>> user = User.new
>> user.encrypt_password
NoMethodError: Attempt to call private method
```

Here Ruby raises a **NoMethodError** exception and issues a warning that the **encrypt_-password** method is private.

In the present context, making the **encrypt_password** and **encrypt** methods private isn't strictly necessary, but it's a good practice to make them private unless they are needed for the public interface.[4]

Now that we understand the **private** keyword, let's take another look at the **encrypt_password** method:

```
def encrypt_password
  self.encrypted_password = encrypt(password)
end
```

This is a one-line method (the best kind!), but it contains not one but *two* subtleties. First, the left-hand side of the statement explicitly assigns the **encrypted_password** attribute using the **self** keyword. (Recall from Section 4.4.2 that inside the class **self** refers to the object itself, which for the User model is just the user.) The use of **self** is *required* in this context; if we omitted **self** and wrote

```
def encrypt_password
  encrypted_password = encrypt(password)
end
```

Ruby would create a *local variable* called **encrypted_password**, which isn't what we want at all.

---

4. Ruby has a closely related keyword called **protected** that differs subtly from **private**. As far as I can tell, the only reason to learn the difference is so that you can ace a job interview that asks you "In Ruby, what is the difference between **private** and **protected**?" But do you really want to work at a company that asks you such a lame interview question? At his keynote at RubyConf in 2008, Dave Thomas (author of *Programming Ruby*) suggested eliminating **protected** from future versions of Ruby, and I agree with the sentiment. Just use **private** and you'll be fine.

Second, the right-hand side of the assignment calls **encrypt** on **password**, but there is no **password** in sight. In the console, we would access the password attribute through a user object.

```
>> user = User.new(:password => "foobar")
>> user.password
=> "foobar"
```

Inside the User class, the user object is just **self**, and we could write

```
def encrypt_password
  self.encrypted_password = encrypt(self.password)
end
```

in analogy with the console example, just replacing **user** with **self**. But the **self** is optional, so for brevity we can write simply

```
def encrypt_password
  self.encrypted_password = encrypt(password)
end
```

as in Listing 7.6 above. (Of course, as we've noted, the **self** is *not* optional when assigning to an attribute, so we have to write **self.encrypted_password** in this case.)

7.2 Secure Passwords

With the code from Section 7.1, in principle we are done: although the "encrypted" password is the same as the unencrypted password, as long as we are willing to store unencrypted passwords in the database we have the necessary foundation for user login and authentication.[5] Our standards in *Rails Tutorial* are much loftier, though: any web developer worth his salt should know how to implement a password system with *secure one-way hashing*. In this section, we will build on the material from Section 7.1 to implement just such an industrial-strength password system.

---

5. I am ashamed to admit that this is how we implemented passwords in *RailsSpace*. Consider this section my penance.

7.2.1   A Secure Password Test

As hinted at in Section 7.1.3, all of the machinery for password encryption will be tucked away in the **private** regions of the User model, which presents a challenge for testing it. What we need is some sort of *public interface* that we can expose to the rest of the application. One useful aspect of test-driven development is that, by acting as a client for our application code, the tests motivate us to design a useful interface right from the start.

Authenticating users involves comparing the encrypted version of a submitted password to the (encrypted) password of a given user. This means we need to define some method to perform the comparison, which we'll call **has_password?**; this will be our public interface to the encryption machinery.[6] The **has_password?** method will test whether a user has the same password as one submitted on a sign-in form (to be written in Chapter 9); a skeleton method for **has_password?** appears in Listing 7.7.

Listing 7.7 A **has_password?** method for users.
app/models/user.rb

```
class User < ActiveRecord::Base
  .
  .
  .

  before_save :encrypt_password

  # Return true if the user's password matches the submitted password.
  def has_password?(submitted_password)
    # Compare encrypted_password with the encrypted version of
    # submitted_password.
  end

  private
  .
  .
  .
end
```

6. The alert reader may notice that none of what we do in this section *requires* encryption, but, once we develop some of the theory of secure passwords and write a basic implementation (Section 7.2.2), the only way for the **has_password?** method to work properly is for all the encryption machinery to work properly as well.

With this method, we can write tests as in Listing 7.8, which uses the RSpec methods **be_true** and **be_false** to test that **has_password?** returns **true** or **false** in the proper cases.

Listing 7.8 Tests for the **has_password?** method.
spec/models/user_spec.rb

```
describe User do
  .
  .
  .
  describe "password encryption" do

    before(:each) do
      @user = User.create!(@attr)
    end
    .
    .
    .
    describe "has_password? method" do

      it "should be true if the passwords match" do
        @user.has_password?(@attr[:password]).should be_true
      end

      it "should be false if the passwords don't match" do
        @user.has_password?("invalid").should be_false
      end
    end
  end
end
```

In Section 7.2.3, we'll complete the implementation of **has_password?** (and get the test to pass in the process). But first we need to learn a little more about secure passwords.

7.2.2 Some Secure Password Theory

The basic idea of encrypted passwords is simple: rather than storing a raw password in the database (known as "cleartext"), we store a string generated using a cryptographic hash function, which is essentially irreversible, so that even an attacker in possession of the hashed password will be unable to infer the original. To verify that a submitted password matches the user's password, we first encrypt the submitted string and then compare the hashes. Let's drop into a console session to see how this works:

```
$ rails console
>> require 'digest'
>> def secure_hash(string)
>>   Digest::SHA2.hexdigest(string)
>> end
=> nil
>> password = "secret"
=> "secret"
>> encrypted_password = secure_hash(password)
=> "2bb80d537b1da3e38bd30361aa855686bde0eacd7162fef6a25fe97bf527a25b"
>> submitted_password = "secret"
=> "secret"
>> encrypted_password == secure_hash(submitted_password)
=> true
```

Here we've defined a function called **secure_hash** that uses a cryptographic hash function called SHA2, part of the SHA family of hash functions, which we include into Ruby through the **digest** library.[7] It's not important to know exactly how these hash functions work; for our purposes what's important is that they are one-way: there is no computationally tractable way to discover that

2bb80d537b1da3e38bd30361aa855686bde0eacd7162fef6a25fe97bf527a25b

is the SHA2 hash of the string **"secret"**.

If you think about it, though, we still have a problem: if an attacker ever got hold of the hashed passwords, he would still have a chance at discovering the originals. For example, he could guess that we used SHA2, and so write a program to compare a given hash to the hashed values of potential passwords:

```
>> hash = "2bb80d537b1da3e38bd30361aa855686bde0eacd7162fef6a25fe97bf527a25b"
>> secure_hash("secede") == hash
=> false
>> secure_hash("second") == hash
=> false
>> secure_hash("secret") == hash
=> true
```

---

7. In my setup, the **require 'digest'** line is unnecessary, but several readers have reported getting a **NameError** exception if they don't include it explicitly. It does no harm in any case, so I've included the explicit **require** just to be safe.

So our attacker has a match—bad news for any users with password **"secret"**. This technique is known as a *rainbow attack*.

To foil a potential rainbow attack, we can use a *salt*, which is a different unique string for each user.[8] One common way to (nearly) ensure uniqueness is to hash the current time (in UTC to be time-zone–independent) along with the password, so that two users will have the same salt only if they are created at exactly the same time *and* have the same password. Let's see how this works using the **secure_hash** function defined in the console above:

```
>> Time.now.utc
=> Fri Jan 29 18:11:27 UTC 2010
>> password = "secret"
=> "secret"
>> salt = secure_hash("#{Time.now.utc}--#{password}")
=> "d1a3eb8c9aab32ec19cfda810d2ab351873b5dca4e16e7f57b3c1932113314c8"
>> encrypted_password = secure_hash("#{salt}--#{password}")
=> "69a98a49b7fd103058639be84fb88c19c998c8ad3639cfc5deb458018561c847"
```

In the last line, we've hashed the salt with the password, yielding an encrypted password that is virtually impossible to crack. (For clarity, arguments to hashing functions are often separated with --.)

7.2.3 Implementing `has_password?`

Having finished with the theory, we're now ready for the implementation. Let's look ahead a little to see where we're going. Each user object knows its own encrypted password, so to check for a match with a submitted password we can define `has_password?` as follows:

```
def has_password?(submitted_password)
  encrypted_password == encrypt(submitted_password)
end
```

As long as we encrypt the submitted password using the same salt used to encrypt the original password, this function will be true if and only if the submitted password matches.

---

8. Technically, rainbow attacks could still succeed, but using a salted hash makes them computationally unfeasible.

Since comparing a user password with a submitted password will involve encrypting the submitted password with the salt, we need to store the salt somewhere, so the first step is to add a **salt** column to the **users** table:

```
$ rails generate migration add_salt_to_users salt:string
```

As with the **encrypted_password** migration (Section 7.1.2), this migration has a name that ends in **_to_users** and passes a second argument containing the attribute name and type, so Rails automatically constructs the right migration (Listing 7.9).

Listing 7.9 The migration to add a **salt** column to the **users** table.
db/migrate/<timestamp>_add_salt_to_users.rb

```
class AddSaltToUsers < ActiveRecord::Migration
  def self.up
    add_column :users, :salt, :string
  end

  def self.down
    remove_column :users, :salt
  end
end
```

Then we migrate the database and prepare the test database as usual:

```
$ rake db:migrate
$ rake db:test:prepare
```

The result is a database with the data model shown in Figure 7.3.

Finally, we're ready for the full implementation. When last we saw the **encrypt** function (Listing 7.6), it did nothing, simply returning the string in its argument. With the ideas from Section 7.2.2, we're now in a position to use a secure hash instead (Listing 7.10).[9]

---

9. As noted in Section 7.2.2, the explicit **require 'digest'** line is unnecessary on some systems, but it does no harm to include it.

users	
id	integer
name	string
email	string
encrypted_password	string
salt	string
created_at	datetime
updated_at	datetime

Figure 7.3   The User model with an added salt.

Listing 7.10 The **has_password?** method with secure encryption.
app/models/user.rb

```ruby
require 'digest'
class User < ActiveRecord::Base
  .
  .
  .
  before_save :encrypt_password

  def has_password?(submitted_password)
    encrypted_password == encrypt(submitted_password)
  end

  private

    def encrypt_password
      self.salt = make_salt if new_record?
      self.encrypted_password = encrypt(password)
    end

    def encrypt(string)
      secure_hash("#{salt}--#{string}")
    end

    def make_salt
      secure_hash("#{Time.now.utc}--#{password}")
    end

    def secure_hash(string)
      Digest::SHA2.hexdigest(string)
    end
end
```

This code contains the same two subtleties mentioned in Section 7.1.3, namely, the assignment to an Active Record attribute in the line

```
self.salt = make_salt if new_record?
```

and the omission of the **self** keyword in the **encrypt** method:

```
def encrypt(string)
  secure_hash("#{salt}--#{string}")
end
```

Since we're inside the User class, Ruby knows that **salt** refers to the user's **salt** attribute.

It's also important to note the use of Active Record's **new_record?** boolean method, which returns true if the object has not yet been saved to the database. Since the salt is a unique identifier for each user, we don't want it to change every time the user is updated (as in Section 10.1), and by including **new_record?** we ensure that the salt is only created *once*, when the user is first created.[10] (This subtlety doesn't matter now, but it will when we implement a "remember me" signin feature in Section 9.3.2.)

At this point, the tests from Listing 7.8 should pass:

```
$ rspec spec/models/user_spec.rb -e "should be true if the passwords match"
.

1 example, 0 failures

$ rspec spec/models/user_spec.rb \
> -e "should be false if the passwords don't match"
.

1 example, 0 failures
```

We can also run all the examples in a particular **describe** block, but we do have to be careful to *escape* any special regular expression characters—in this case, the question

---

10. In past versions of Rails, we could have used the **after_validation_before_create** callback to set the salt, but it has been eliminated in Rails 3. Meanwhile, we can't use the **before_create** callback because it executes *after* the **before_save** callback, and the **before_save** callback needs the salt.

mark **?** in **"has_password? method"**:

```
$ rspec spec/models/user_spec.rb -e "has_password\? method"
Run filtered using {:full_description=>/(?-mix:has_password\? method)/}
..

2 examples, 0 failures
```

The backslash before the question mark ensures that RSpec's regular expression matcher interprets the string correctly, thereby running the tests associated with the given **describe** block.

7.2.4   An Authenticate Method

Having a **has_password?** method for each user is nice, but by itself it isn't very useful. We'll end our discussion of passwords by using **has_password?** to write a method to authenticate a user based on an email/password combination. In Chapter 9, we'll use this **authenticate** method when signing users in to our site.

We can get a hint of how this will work by using the console. First, we'll create a user, and then retrieve that user by email address to verify that it has a given password:[11]

```
$ rails console --sandbox
>> User.create(:name => "Michael Hartl", :email => "mhartl@example.com",
?>             :password => "foobar", :password_confirmation => "foobar")
>> user = User.find_by_email("mhartl@example.com")
>> user.has_password?("foobar")
=> true
```

Using these ideas, let's write a method that will return an authenticated user on password match, and **nil** otherwise. We should be able to use the resulting **authenticate** class method as follows:

```
User.authenticate(email, submitted_password)
```

_____

11. Recall from Box 6.2 that the *index* on the **email** column ensures that this retrieval is efficient.

We start with the tests, which we'll use to specify the behavior we expect from **User.authenticate**. There are three cases to check: **authenticate** (1) should return **nil** when the email/password combination is invalid or (2) when no user exists with the given email address, and (3) should return the user object itself on success. With this information, we can write the tests for **authenticate** as in Listing 7.11.

Listing 7.11 Tests for the **User.authenticate** method.
spec/models/user_spec.rb

```
describe User do
  .
  .
  .
  describe "password encryption" do
    .
    .
    .
    describe "authenticate method" do

      it "should return nil on email/password mismatch" do
        wrong_password_user = User.authenticate(@attr[:email], "wrongpass")
        wrong_password_user.should be_nil
      end

      it "should return nil for an email address with no user" do
        nonexistent_user = User.authenticate("bar@foo.com", @attr[:password])
        nonexistent_user.should be_nil
      end

      it "should return the user on email/password match" do
        matching_user = User.authenticate(@attr[:email], @attr[:password])
        matching_user.should == @user
      end
    end
  end
end
```

Now we're ready for the implementation, which will get our tests to pass and show how to define a *class method* as a bonus. We've mentioned class methods several times before, most recently in Section 6.1.1; a class method is simply a method attached to a class, rather than an instance of that class. For example, **new**, **find**, and **find_by_email** are all class methods on the User class. Outside of the class, they are invoked using the class name, as in **User.find**, but inside the class we can omit the class name.

Box 7.1   What is `self`?

We've talked about how `self` is "the object itself", but exactly what that means depends on context. Inside of an ordinary method, `self` refers to an *instance* of the class, that is, the object itself. For example, in Listing 7.10, `self` is a *user*:

```
def encrypt_password
  self.salt = make_salt if new_record?
  self.encrypted_password = encrypt(password)
end
```

Inside the **`encrypt_password`** method, `self` is a user object, so `self.salt` is the same as **`user.salt`** outside the method:

```
$ rails console
>> user = User.first
>> user.salt
=> "d3b9af261c502947fbf32f78cb8179b16e62eabacf059451efee404328b2f537"
```

On the other hand, Listing 7.12 shows the definition of **`authenticate`**, which uses `self` to define a *class method*; here, `self` is the **`User`** class itself:

```
def self.authenticate(email, submitted_password)
  .
  .
  .
end
```

Because it is defined on the **`User`** class, **`authenticate`** gets invoked directly on **`User`**:

```
>> user = User.authenticate('example@railstutorial.org', 'foobar')
>> user.name
=> "Example User"
```

It's worth noting two alternative ways of defining an **`authenticate`** class method equivalent to the one shown in Listing 7.12. First, we could indicate the **`User`** class explicitly by name:

```
def User.authenticate(email, submitted_password)
  .
  .
  .
end
```

(Some people might find this syntax clearer, but it's not as idiomatically correct.) Second, we could use the following code, which quite frankly melts my brain:

```
class << self
  def authenticate(email, submitted_password)
     .
     .
     .
  end
end
```

The weird **class << self** starts a block in which all new methods are automatically class methods. I find this syntax rather confusing, but it's possible you'll encounter it in others' code, so it's worth knowing what it does. (I recommend *The Well-Grounded Rubyist* by David A. Black if you want to dig into Ruby details like this one.)

The way to define a class method is to use the **self** keyword in the method definition. (This **self** is not the same as the **self** shown in Listing 7.10; see Box 7.1.) Listing 7.12 shows this construction in the context of the **authenticate** method. Note the call to **find_by_email**, in which we omit the explicit **User** class name since this method is already inside the **User** class.

Listing 7.12 The **User.authenticate** method.
app/models/user.rb

```
class User < ActiveRecord::Base
  .
  .
  .
  def has_password?(submitted_password)
    encrypted_password == encrypt(submitted_password)
  end

  def self.authenticate(email, submitted_password)
    user = find_by_email(email)
    return nil  if user.nil?
    return user if user.has_password?(submitted_password)
  end

  private
  .
  .
  .
end
```

There are several equivalent ways to write the **authenticate** method, but I find the implementation above the clearest. It handles two cases (invalid email and a successful match) with explicit **return** keywords, and handles the third case (password mismatch) implicitly, since in that case we reach the end of the method, which automatically returns **nil**. See Section 7.5 for some of the other possible ways to implement this method.

7.3 Better User Views

Now that User model is effectively complete,[12] we are in a position to add a sample user to the development database and make a **show** page to show some of that user's information. Along the way, we'll add some tests to the Users controller spec started in Section 5.3.1.

Before continuing, it's helpful to see where we left off by recalling what the Users controller spec looks like right now (Listing 7.13). Our tests for the user show page will follow this example, but we'll find that, unlike the tests for the **new** action, the tests for the **show** action will require the use of an instance of the User model. We'll meet this challenge using a technique called *factories*.

Listing 7.13 The current Users controller spec.
spec/controllers/users_controller_spec.rb

```
require 'spec_helper'

describe UsersController do
  render_views

  describe "GET 'new'" do

    it "should be successful" do
      get 'new'
      response.should be_success
    end

    it "should have the right title" do
      get 'new'
      response.should have_selector("title", :content => "Sign up")
    end
  end
end
```

---

12. We'll plan to add a couple more attributes (one to identify administrative users and one to allow a "remember me" feature), but they are not strictly necessary. All the *essential* user attributes have now been defined.

7.3.1 Testing the User Show Page (With Factories)

Tests for the Users controller will need instances of User model objects, preferably with pre-defined values. For example, as seen in Listing 7.14, the Users controller **show** action needs an instance of the User class, so the tests for this action will require that we create an **@user** variable somehow. We'll accomplish this goal with a user *factory*, which is a convenient way to define a user object and insert it into our test database.[13]

Listing 7.14 The user **show** action from Listing 6.25.
app/controllers/users_controller.rb

```
class UsersController < ApplicationController

  def show
    @user = User.find(params[:id])
  end
  .
  .
  .
end
```

We'll be using the factories generated by Factory Girl,[14] a Ruby gem produced by the good people at thoughtbot. As with other Ruby gems, we can install it by adding a line to the **Gemfile** used by Bundler (Listing 7.15). (Since Factory Girl is only needed in the tests, we've included it in the **:test** group.)

Listing 7.15 Adding Factory Girl to the **Gemfile**.

```
source 'http://rubygems.org'
.
.
.
group :test do
  .
  .
  .
  gem 'factory_girl_rails', '1.0'
end
```

---

13. Many experienced Rails programmers find that this factory approach is much more flexible than *fixtures*, which Rails uses by default but can be brittle and difficult to maintain.

14. Presumably "Factory Girl" is a reference to the movie of the same name.

Then install as usual:

```
$ bundle install
```

Now we're ready to create the file **spec/factories.rb** and define a User factory, as shown in Listing 7.16. By putting the **factories.rb** file in the **spec/** directory, we arrange for RSpec to load our factories automatically whenever the tests run.

Listing 7.16   A factory to simulate User model objects.
spec/factories.rb

```
# By using the symbol ':user', we get Factory Girl to simulate the User model.
Factory.define :user do |user|
  user.name                 "Michael Hartl"
  user.email                "mhartl@example.com"
  user.password             "foobar"
  user.password_confirmation "foobar"
end
```

With the definition in Listing 7.16, we can create a User factory in the tests like this:

```
@user = Factory(:user)
```

As noted in the comment in the first line of Listing 7.16, by using the symbol **:user** we ensure that Factory Girl will guess that we want to use the User model, so in this case **@user** will simulate an instance of **User**.

To use our new User factory in the Users controller spec, we'll create an **@user** variable in a **before(:each)** block and then **get** the show page and verify success (just as we did with the **new** page in Listing 7.13), while also verifying that the **show** action pulls the correct user out of the database. The result appears in Listing 7.17. (If you're using Spork, you might have to restart it to get these tests to pass.)

Listing 7.17   A test for **get**ting the user **show** page, with a user factory.
spec/controllers/users_controller_spec.rb

```
require 'spec_helper'

describe UsersController do
  render_views
```

```
describe "GET 'show'" do

  before(:each) do
    @user = Factory(:user)
  end

  it "should be successful" do
    get :show, :id => @user
    response.should be_success
  end

  it "should find the right user" do
    get :show, :id => @user
    assigns(:user).should == @user
  end
end
  .
  .
  .
end
```

Apart from the first use of a factory, the real novelty here is the use of a **assigns(:user)**, which is a facility provided by RSpec (via the underlying Test::Unit library). The **assigns** method takes in a symbol argument and returns the value of the corresponding *instance* variable in the controller action. In other words, in Listing 7.17 the code

```
assigns(:user)
```

returns the value of the instance variable

```
@user
```

in the **show** action of the Users controller. The test

```
assigns(:user).should == @user
```

then verifies that the variable retrieved from the database in the action corresponds to the **@user** instance created by Factory Girl. It's worth noting that not all Rails programmers use **assigns** in this context, preferring instead to use a technique called *stubbing* (Box 7.2).

Box 7.2　To stub! or not to stub!.

The code in Listing 7.17 relies on the **User.find** method in the controller action to retrieve the right user from the test database. A second way to achieve this same result is using a technique called *stubbing*, using RSpec's **stub!** method:

```
before(:each)
  @user = Factory(:user)
  User.stub!(:find, @user.id).and_return(@user)
end
```

This code ensures that any call to **User.find** with the given **id** will return **@user**. Since this is just what we have in the application code (Listing 7.14), the stub will cause RSpec to intercept the call to **User.find** and, instead of hitting the database, return **@user** instead.

　　Many Rails programmers, especially RSpec users, prefer this stubbing approach because it separates the controller tests from the model layer. Indeed, the Rails 2.3 version of this book uses stubs, along with the closely related technique of *message expectations*. After gaining more experience with stubs and expectations, and especially after fielding lots of questions from readers of the *Rails 2.3 Tutorial* confused by these issues, I have concluded that stubbing and related techniques are not worth the trouble.

　　Figuring out exactly when to stub things out is difficult, and message expectations are incredibly subtle and error-prone (see, e.g., Box 8.1 in the Rails 2.3 Tutorial book). To the common objection, "But now the controller tests hit the test database!", I now find myself saying: "So what?" In my experience it has never mattered. I see no compelling reason not to hit the model layer in the controller tests, especially when it leads to much simpler tests. If you are interested in learning stubbing and message expectation techniques, I recommend reading the *Ruby on Rails 2.3 Tutorial* book. Otherwise, I suggest not worrying about enforcing a full separation of the model and controller layers in Rails tests. Although the controller tests in the rest of this book will hit the test database, at a *conceptual* level it will always be clear which part of MVC is being tested.

　　By the way, in principle the tests should run faster when the controllers don't hit the database, and for the full *Rails Tutorial* sample application test suite they do—by around two-tenths of a second.

There are two other details in Listing 7.17 worth noting. First, in the call to **get**, the test uses the *symbol* **:show** instead of the string **'show'**, which is different from the convention in the other tests (for example, in Listing 3.10 we wrote **get 'home'**). Both

```
get :show
```

and

```
get 'show'
```

do the same thing, but when testing the canonical REST actions (Table 6.2) I prefer to use symbols, which for some reason feel more natural in this context.[15] Second, note that the value of the hash key **:id**, instead of being the user's **id** attribute **@user.id**, is the user object itself:

```
get :show, :id => @user
```

We could use the code

```
get :show, :id => @user.id
```

to accomplish the same thing, but in this context Rails automatically converts the user object to the corresponding id.[16] Using the more succinct construction

```
get :show, :id => @user
```

is a very common Rails idiom.

Because of the code we added in Listing 6.25, the test in this section already passes. If you're feeling paranoid, you can comment out the line

```
@user = User.find(params[:id])
```

---

15. I used **get 'new'** in Listing 5.24 and subsequent tests for the **new** action because at that point we had yet to encounter the idea of standard REST actions. I'll switch to **get :new** in future tests.

16. It does this by calling the **to_param** method on the **@user** variable.

and verify that the test fails, then uncomment it to get it to pass. (We went through this same process once before, in Section 6.2.1.)

7.3.2 A Name and a Gravatar

In this section, we'll improve the look of the user show page by adding a heading with the user's name and profile image. This is one of those situations where I can go either way on test-driven development, and often when making views I'll experiment with the HTML before bothering with tests. Let's stick with the TDD theme for now, and test for a top-level heading (**h1** tag) containing the user's name and an **img** tag of class **gravatar**. (We'll talk momentarily about what this second part means.)

To view a working user show page in a browser, we'll need to create a sample user in the development database. To do this, first reset the database with **rake db:reset**, which will clear out any old sample users from previous sessions, and then start the console (*not* in a sandbox this time) and create the user:

```
$ rake db:reset
$ rails console
>> User.create(:name => "Example User", :email => "user@example.com",
?>              :password => "foobar", :password_confirmation => "foobar")
```

The tests in this section are similar to the tests for the **new** page seen in Listing 5.26. In particular, we use the **have_selector** method to check the title and the content of the **h1** tag, as seen in Listing 7.18.

Listing 7.18 Tests for the user show page.
spec/controllers/users_controller_spec.rb

```
require 'spec_helper'

describe UsersController do
  render_views

  describe "GET 'show'" do
    .
    .
    .
    it "should have the right title" do
      get :show, :id => @user
      response.should have_selector("title", :content => @user.name)
    end
```

```
    it "should include the user's name" do
      get :show, :id => @user
      response.should have_selector("h1", :content => @user.name)
    end

    it "should have a profile image" do
      get :show, :id => @user
      response.should have_selector("h1>img", :class => "gravatar")
    end
  end
  .
  .
  .
end
```

Here RSpec's **have_selector** method verifies the presence of a **title** and **h1** tags containing the user's name. The third example introduces a new element through the code **h1>img**, which makes sure that the **img** tag is *inside* the **h1** tag.[17] In addition, we see that **have_selector** can take a **:class** option to test the CSS class of the element in question.

We can get the first test to pass by setting the **@title** variable for use in the **title** helper (Section 4.1.1), in this case setting it to the user's name (Listing 7.19).

Listing 7.19 A title for the user show page.
app/controllers/users_controller.rb

```
class UsersController < ApplicationController

  def show
    @user = User.find(params[:id])
    @title = @user.name
  end
  .
  .
  .
end
```

17. It's not necessarily always a good idea to make HTML tests this specific, since we don't always want to constrain the HTML layout this tightly. Feel free to experiment and find the right level of detail for your projects and tastes.

This code introduces a potential problem: a user could enter a name with malicious code—called a cross-site scripting attack—which would be injected into our application by the **title** helper defined in Listing 4.2. Before Rails 3, the solution was to *escape* potentially problematic code using the **h** method (short for **html_escape**), but as of Rails 3.0 all Embedded Ruby text is escaped by default.[18] For example, if a user tried to inject a malicious JavaScript program by using **<script>** in his name, the automatic HTML escaping would convert it to **<script>**, rendering it completely harmless.

Now for the other tests. Creating an **h1** with the (auto-escaped) user name is easy (Listing 7.20).

Listing 7.20   The user show view with the user's name.
app/views/users/show.html.erb

```
<h1>
  <%= @user.name %>
</h1>
```

Getting the **img** test to pass is trickier. The first step is to install the gravatar_image_tag gem to handle each user's Gravatar,[19] which is a "globally recognized avatar".[20] As usual, we will include the gem dependency in the **Gemfile** (Listing 7.21).

Listing 7.21   Adding a Gravatar gem to the **Gemfile**.

```
source 'http://rubygems.org'

gem 'rails', '3.0.0'
gem 'sqlite3-ruby', '1.2.5', :require => 'sqlite3'
gem 'gravatar_image_tag', '0.1.0'
.
.
.
```

---

18. Instead, if you want *unescaped* text you have to use the **raw** method, as in <%= raw @title %>.

19. Gravatar was originally created by Tom Preston-Werner, cofounder of GitHub, and was acquired and scaled by Automattic (best known as the makers of WordPress).

20. In Hinduism, an avatar is the manifestation of a deity in human or animal form. By extension, the term *avatar* is commonly used to mean some kind of personal representation, especially in a virtual environment. But you've seen the movie by now, so you already knew this.

Then install it with **bundle**:

```
$ bundle install
```

You should also restart your web server at this point to load the new Gravatar gem properly. Gravatars are a convenient way to include user profile images without going through the trouble of managing image upload, cropping, and storage.[21] Each Gravatar is associated with an email address, so the Gravatar gem comes with a helper method called **gravatar_image_tag** that takes an email address as an argument:

```
<%= gravatar_image_tag 'example@railstutorial.org' %>
```

For the moment, we'll use this directly in our user show view, as seen in Listing 7.22. (We'll make a helper method for it in a moment.) The result appears in Figure 7.4, which shows our example user with the default Gravatar image.

Listing 7.22 The user show view with name and Gravatar.
app/views/users/show.html.erb

```
<h1>
  <%= gravatar_image_tag @user.email %>
  <%= @user.name %>
</h1>
```

This Gravatar business might seem like magic, so let's fire up the console to get a little more insight into what's going on:

```
$ rails console
>> user = User.first
>> user.update_attributes(:email => "example@railstutorial.org",
?>                        :password => "foobar",
?>                        :password_confirmation => "foobar")
=> true
```

---

21. If your application does need to handle images or other file uploads, Paperclip is the way to go. Like Factory Girl, Paperclip is brought to you by thoughtbot. (Though I do know several people there, I have no vested interest in promoting thoughtbot; they just make good software.)

Figure 7.4 The initial user show page /users/1 with the default Gravatar.

Note that we can pull out the first (and, at this point, only) user in the database with the handy **User.first** method. In the **update_attributes** step we've reassigned the user's email address, changing it to **example@railstutorial.org**. As you can see from Figure 7.5, this change results in a new Gravatar being displayed: the Rails Tutorial logo. What's going on is that Gravatar works by associating images with email addresses; since **user@example.com** is an invalid email address (the example.com domain is reserved for examples), there is no Gravatar for that email address. But at my Gravatar account I've associated the address **example@railstutorial.org** with the Rails Tutorial logo, so when updating the example user with that email address the Gravatar changes automatically.

A Gravatar Helper
At this point, the Gravatar displays properly, but the final example from Listing 7.18 still doesn't pass. This is because the **"gravatar"** class, which we want for styling the

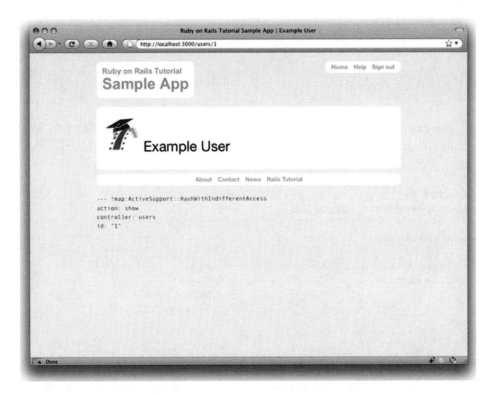

Figure 7.5   The user show page /users/1 with the Rails Tutorial Gravatar.

Gravatar with CSS, isn't yet present in the Gravatar's **img** tag. We could arrange for the test to pass by including an option to the **gravatar_image_tag** method:

```
<%= gravatar_image_tag @user.email, :class => "gravatar" %>
```

On the other hand, since we expect the Gravatars to appear in multiple places in our application, it would be repetitive to put the class in everywhere by hand. It would be better to make a helper method to eliminate this duplication preemptively.

   This situation may remind you of the repetition in the site's base title ("Ruby on Rails Tutorial Sample App"), which we solved with a **title** helper in the Application helper (Listing 4.2). The solution here is similar; since Gravatars are naturally associated with users, we'll define a **gravatar_for** method in the Users helper. (The choice to use the Users helpers instead of the Application helper is just for conceptual convenience;

Rails makes all helpers available in all views.) The result will be concise view code like

```
<%= gravatar_for @user %>
```

The **gravatar_for** helper should take in a **user** object and then pass some default options to the **gravatar_image_tag** helper. The implementation appears in Listing 7.23.

Listing 7.23 Defining a **gravatar_for** helper method.
app/helpers/users_helper.rb

```
module UsersHelper

  def gravatar_for(user, options = { :size => 50 })
    gravatar_image_tag(user.email.downcase, :alt => user.name,
                                            :class => 'gravatar',
                                            :gravatar => options)
  end
end
```

The first argument in the call to **gravatar_image_tag** passes in the lower-case version of the user's email address (using the **downcase** method).[22] Then the first option to **gravatar_image_tag** assigns the user's name to the **img** tag's **alt** attribute (which gets displayed in devices that can't render images), while the second option sets the CSS class of the resulting Gravatar. The third option passes the **options** hash using the **:gravatar** key, which (according to the gravatar_image_tag gem documentation) is how to set the options for **gravatar_image_tag**. Note that the function definition sets a *default option*[23] for the size of the Gravatar[24] using

```
option = { :size => 50 }
```

This sets the default Gravatar size to 50x50, while also allowing us to override the default size using code like

---

22. Thanks to the anonymous reader who noted that the Gravatar plugin is case-sensitive in this context.

23. There's actually a way to reset the default size in a configuration file, but I find this way clearer.

24. Gravatars are square, so a single parameter determines their size uniquely.

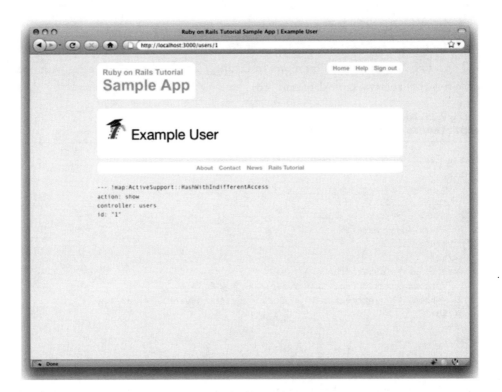

Figure 7.6   The user show page with `gravatar_for`.

```erb
<%= gravatar_for @user, :size => 30 %>
```

If we now update the user show template with the code in Listing 7.24, the user show page appears as in Figure 7.6. And since the `gravatar_for` helper assigns the **img** tag the class **"gravatar"**, the tests from Listing 7.18 should now pass.

Listing 7.24   Updating the user show template to use `gravatar_for`.
app/views/users/show.html.erb

```erb
<h1>
  <%= gravatar_for @user %>
  <%= @user.name %>
</h1>
```

7.3.3   A User Sidebar

Even though our tests are now passing, and the user show page is much improved, it's still nice to polish it up just a bit more. In Listing 7.25, we have a **table** tag with one table row (**tr**) and two table data cells (**td**).[25]

Listing 7.25   Adding a sidebar to the user **show** view.
`app/views/users/show.html.erb`

```erb
<table class="profile" summary="Profile information">
  <tr>
    <td class="main">
      <h1>
        <%= gravatar_for @user %>
        <%= @user.name %>
      </h1>
    </td>
    <td class="sidebar round">
      <strong>Name</strong> <%= @user.name %><br />
      <strong>URL</strong>   <%= link_to user_path(@user), @user %>
    </td>
  </tr>
</table>
```

Here we've used an HTML break tag **
** to put a break between the user's name and URL. Also note the use of **user_path** to make a clickable link so that users can easily share their profile URLs. This is only the first of many named routes (Section 5.2.2) associated with the User resource (Listing 6.26); we'll see many more in the next few chapters. The code

```
user_path(@user)
```

returns the path to the user, in this case `/users/1`. The related code

```
user_url(@user)
```

---

25. If anyone gives you grief for using, horror of horrors, *tables for layout*, have them point their Firebug inspector at Twitter's profile sidebar and tell you what they see. In fact, you'll find that, while "semantic markup" using **div**s and **span**s is increasingly common, virtually all sites resort to **table**s for layout on occasion. In the present case, getting the vertical alignment just right is *much* easier with tables.

Table 7.1 Named routes provided by the users resource in Listing 6.26

Named route	Path
users_path	/users
user_path(@user)	/users/1
new_user_path	/users/new
edit_user_path(@user)	/users/1/edit
users_url	http://localhost:3000/users
user_url(@user)	http://localhost:3000/users/1
new_user_url	http://localhost:3000/users/new
edit_user_url(@user)	http://localhost:3000/users/1/edit

just returns the entire URL, `http://localhost:3000/users/1`. (Compare to the routes created in Section 5.2.2.) Both are examples of the named routes created by the users resource in Listing 6.26; a list of all the named routes appears in Table 7.1.

Note that in

```
<%= link_to user_path(@user), @user %>
```

user_path(@user) is the link *text*, while the address is just **@user**. In the context of a **link_to**, Rails converts **@user** to the appropriate URL; in other words, the code above is equivalent to the code

```
<%= link_to user_path(@user), user_path(@user) %>
```

Either way works fine, but, as in the **:id => @user** idiom from Listing 7.17, using just **@user** is a common Rails convention. In both cases, the Embedded Ruby produces the HTML

```
<a href="/users/1">/users/1</a>
```

With the HTML elements and CSS classes in place, we can style the show page with the CSS shown in Listing 7.26. The resulting page is shown in Figure 7.7.

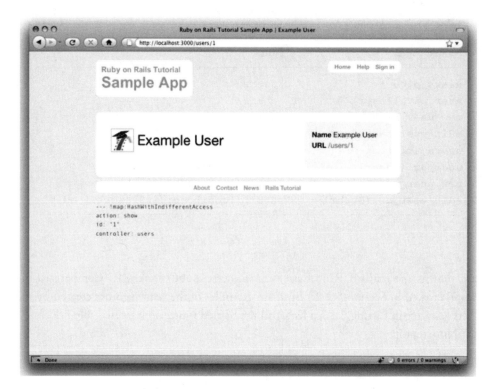

Figure 7.7   The user show page /users/1 with a sidebar and CSS.

Listing 7.26 CSS for styling the user show page, including the sidebar.
public/stylesheets/custom.css

```
.
.
.
/* User show page */

table.profile {
  width: 100%;
  margin-bottom: 0;
}

td.main {
  width: 70%;
  padding: 1em;
}
```

```
td.sidebar {
  width: 30%;
  padding: 1em;
  vertical-align: top;
  background: #ffc;
}

.profile img.gravatar {
  border: 1px solid #999;
  margin-bottom: -15px;
}
```

7.4 Conclusion

In this chapter, we've effectively finished the User model, so we're now fully prepared to sign up new users and to let them sign in securely with an email/password combination. Moreover, we have a nice first cut of the user profile page, so after signing in users will have a place to go.

7.4.1 Git Commit

Before moving on, we should close the Git loop opened in the introduction to Chapter 6 by making a final commit to the **modeling-users** branch and then merging into **master**.[26] First, verify that we are on the **modeling-users** branch:

```
$ git branch
  master
* modeling-users
```

As noted in Section 1.3.5, the asterisk here identifies the present branch, so we are indeed ready to commit and merge:[27]

```
$ git add .
$ git commit -am "User model with passwords, and user show page"
$ git checkout master
$ git merge modeling-users
```

---

26. Ordinarily, I recommend making more frequent, smaller commits, but frequent Git commits throughout the tutorial would be hard to maintain and would break up the flow of the discussion.

27. If you're *not* on the right branch, run **git checkout modeling-users** before proceeding.

7.4.2 Heroku Deploy

If you've deployed your sample application to Heroku, you can push it up at this point:

```
$ git push heroku
```

Then migrate the database on the remote server using the **heroku** command:

```
$ heroku rake db:migrate
```

Now if you want to create a sample user on Heroku, you can use the Heroku console:

```
$ heroku console
>> User.create(:name => "Example User", :email => "user@example.com",
?>              :password => "foobar", :password_confirmation => "foobar")
```

7.5 Exercises

1. Copy each of the variants of the **authenticate** method from Listing 7.27 through Listing 7.31 into your User model, and verify that they are correct by running your test suite.
2. The final **authenticate** example (Listing 7.31) is particularly challenging. Experiment with the console to see if you can understand how it works.
3. How could you get the Gravatar helper **gravatar_for** to work if our User model used **email_address** instead of **email** to represent email addresses?

Listing 7.27 The **authenticate** method with **User** in place of **self**.

```
def User.authenticate(email, submitted_password)
  user = find_by_email(email)
  return nil  if user.nil?
  return user if user.has_password?(submitted_password)
end
```

Listing 7.28 The **authenticate** method with an explicit third **return**.

```
def self.authenticate(email, submitted_password)
  user = find_by_email(email)
  return nil  if user.nil?
  return user if user.has_password?(submitted_password)
  return nil
end
```

Listing 7.29 The **authenticate** method using an **if** statement.

```
def self.authenticate(email, submitted_password)
  user = find_by_email(email)
  if user.nil?
    nil
  elsif user.has_password?(submitted_password)
    user
  else
    nil
  end
end
```

Listing 7.30 The **authenticate** method using an **if** statement and an implicit return.

```
def self.authenticate(email, submitted_password)
  user = find_by_email(email)
  if user.nil?
    nil
  elsif user.has_password?(submitted_password)
    user
  end
end
```

Listing 7.31 The **authenticate** method using the ternary operator.

```
def self.authenticate(email, submitted_password)
  user = find_by_email(email)
  user && user.has_password?(submitted_password) ? user : nil
end
```

CHAPTER 8

Sign Up

Now that we have a working User model, it's time to add an ability few websites can live with out: letting users sign up for the site—thus fulfilling the promise implicit in Section 5.3, "User signup: A first step". We'll use an HTML *form* to submit user signup information to our application in Section 8.1, which will then be used to create a new user and save its attributes to the database in Section 8.3. As usual, we'll write tests as we develop, and in Section 8.4 we'll use RSpec's support for web navigation syntax to write succinct and expressive integration tests.

Since we'll be creating a new user in this chapter, you might want to reset the database to clear out any users created at the console (e.g., in Section 7.3.2), so that your results will match those shown in the tutorial. You can do this as follows:

```
$ rake db:reset
```

If you're following along with version control, make a topic branch as usual:

```
$ git checkout master
$ git checkout -b signing-up
```

8.1 Signup Form

Recall from Section 5.3.1 that we already have tests for the new users (signup) page, originally seen in Listing 5.26 and reproduced in Listing 8.1. (As promised in Section 7.3.1, we've switched from **get 'new'** to **get :new** because that's what my fingers want to type.) In addition, we saw in Figure 5.10 (shown again in Figure 8.1) that this signup

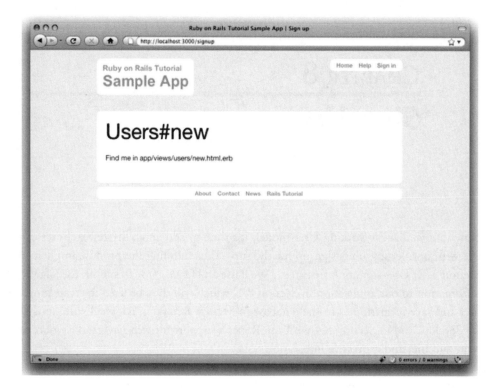

Figure 8.1   The current state of the signup page /signup.

page is currently blank: useless for signing up new users. The goal of this section is to start changing this sad state of affairs by producing the signup form mocked up in Figure 8.2.

Listing 8.1   The tests for the new users page (first seen in Listing 5.26).
spec/controllers/users_controller_spec.rb

```
require 'spec_helper'

describe UsersController do
  render_views
  .
  .
  .
  describe "GET 'new'" do

    it "should be successful" do
      get :new
      response.should be_success
```

```
    end

  it "should have the right title" do
    get :new
    response.should have_selector("title", :content => "Sign up")
  end
end
  .
  .
  .
end
```

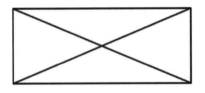

Sign up

Name

Email

Password

Confirmation

Sign up

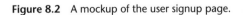

Figure 8.2   A mockup of the user signup page.

8.1.1 Using `form_for`

The HTML element needed for submitting information to a remote website is a *form*, which suggests a good first step toward registering users is to make a form to accept their signup information. We can accomplish this in Rails with the `form_for` helper method; the result appears in Listing 8.2. (Readers familiar with Rails 2.x should note that `form_for` now uses the "percent-equals" ERb syntax for inserting content; that is, where Rails 2.x used <% form_for ... %>, Rails 3 uses <%= form_for ... %> instead.)

Listing 8.2 A form to sign up new users.
app/views/users/new.html.erb

```
<h1>Sign up</h1>

<%= form_for(@user) do |f| %>
  <div class="field">
    <%= f.label :name %><br />
    <%= f.text_field :name %>
  </div>
  <div class="field">
    <%= f.label :email %><br />
    <%= f.text_field :email %>
  </div>
  <div class="field">
    <%= f.label :password %><br />
    <%= f.password_field :password %>
  </div>
  <div class="field">
    <%= f.label :password_confirmation, "Confirmation" %><br />
    <%= f.password_field :password_confirmation %>
  </div>
  <div class="actions">
    <%= f.submit "Sign up" %>
  </div>
<% end %>
```

Let's break this down into pieces. The presence of the `do` keyword indicates that `form_for` takes a block (Section 4.3.2), which has one variable, which we've called `f` for "form". Inside of the `form_for` helper, `f` is an object that represents a form; as is usually the case with Rails helpers, we don't need to know any details about the implementation, but what we *do* need to know is what the `f` object does: when called with a method corresponding to an HTML form element—such as a text field, radio button, or password field—it returns code for that element specifically designed to set an attribute of the **@user** object. In other words,

```
<div class="field">
  <%= f.label :name %><br />
  <%= f.text_field :name %>
</div>
```

creates the HTML needed to make a labeled text field element appropriate for setting the **name** attribute of a User model.

To see this in action, we need to drill down and look at the actual HTML produced by this form, but here we have a problem: the page currently breaks, because we have not set the **@user** variable—like all undefined instance variables (Section 4.2.3), **@user** is currently **nil**. Appropriately, if you run your test suite at this point, you'll see that the signup page tests fail. To get them to pass and get our form to render, we must define an **@user** variable in the controller action corresponding to **new.html.erb**, i.e., the **new** action in the Users controller. The **form_for** helper expects **@user** to be a User object, and since we're creating a *new* user we simply use **User.new**, as seen in Listing 8.3.

Listing 8.3 Adding an **@user** variable to the **new** action.
app/controllers/users_controller.rb

```
class UsersController < ApplicationController
  .
  .
  .
  def new
    @user = User.new
    @title = "Sign up"
  end
end
```

With the **@user** variable so defined, the tests should be passing again,[1] and now the form (with the tiny bit of styling from Listing 8.4) appears as in Figure 8.3.

---

1. If you get an error like **views/users/new.html.erb_spec.rb fails**, remove those accursed view specs with **$ rm -rf spec/views**.

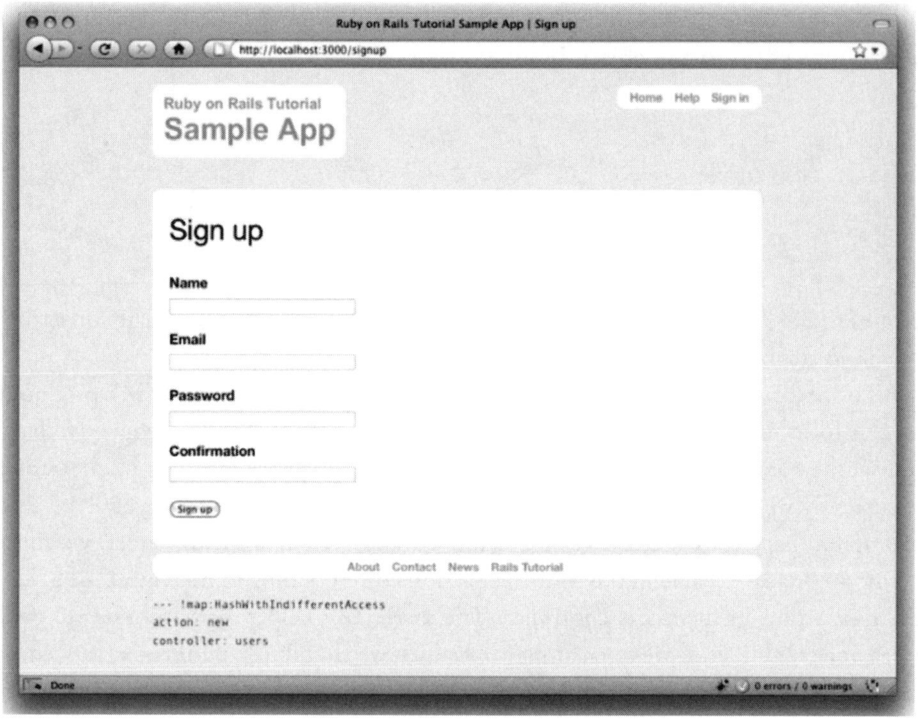

Figure 8.3   The signup form /signup for new users.

Listing 8.4 A wafer-thin amount of CSS for the signup form.
public/stylesheets/custom.css

```
.
.
.
div.field, div.actions {
  margin-bottom: 10px;
}
```

8.1.2   The Form HTML

As indicated by Figure 8.3, the signup page now renders properly, indicating that the
form_for code in Listing 8.2 is producing valid HTML. If you look at the HTML
for the generated form (using either Firebug or the "view page source" feature of your

browser), you should see markup as in Listing 8.5. Although many of the details are irrelevant for our purposes, let's take a moment to highlight the most important parts of its structure.

Listing 8.5 The HTML for the form in Figure 8.3.

```
<form action="/users" class="new_user" id="new_user" method="post">
<div style="margin:0;padding:0;display:inline">
<input name="authenticity_token" type="hidden"
       value="rB82sI7Qw5J9J1UMILG/VQL411vH5putR+JwlxLScMQ=" />
</div>

  <div class="field">
    <label for="user_name">Name</label><br />
    <input id="user_name" name="user[name]" size="30" type="text" />
  </div>

  <div class="field">
    <label for="user_email">Email</label><br />
    <input id="user_email" name="user[email]" size="30" type="text" />
  </div>
  <div class="field">
    <label for="user_password">Password</label><br />
    <input id="user_password" name="user[password]" size="30" type="password" />
  </div>

  <div class="field">
    <label for="user_password_confirmation">Confirmation</label><br />
    <input id="user_password_confirmation" name="user[password_confirmation]"
           size="30" type="password" />
  </div>
  <div class="actions">
    <input id="user_submit" name="commit" type="submit" value="Sign up" />
  </div>
</form>
```

We'll start with the internal structure. Comparing Listing 8.2 with Listing 8.5, we see that the Embedded Ruby

```
<div class="field">
  <%= f.label :name %><br />
  <%= f.text_field :name %>
</div>
```

produces the HTML

```
<div class="field">
  <label for="user_name">Name</label><br />
  <input id="user_name" name="user[name]" size="30" type="text" />
</div>
```

and

```
<div class="field">
  <%= f.label :password %><br />
  <%= f.password_field :password %>
</div>
```

produces the HTML

```
<div class="field">
  <label for="user_password">Password</label><br />
  <input id="user_password" name="user[password]" size="30" type="password" />
</div>
```

As seen in Figure 8.4, text fields (`type="text"`) simply display their contents, whereas password fields (`type="password"`) obscure the input for security purposes, as seen in Figure 8.4.

As we'll see in Section 8.3, the key to creating a user is the special **name** attribute in each **input**:

```
<input id="user_name" name="user[name]" - - - />
.
.
.
<input id="user_password" name="user[password]" - - - />
```

These **name** values allow Rails to construct an initialization hash (via the **params** variable first seen in Section 6.3.2) for creating users using the values entered by the user, as we'll see in Section 8.2.

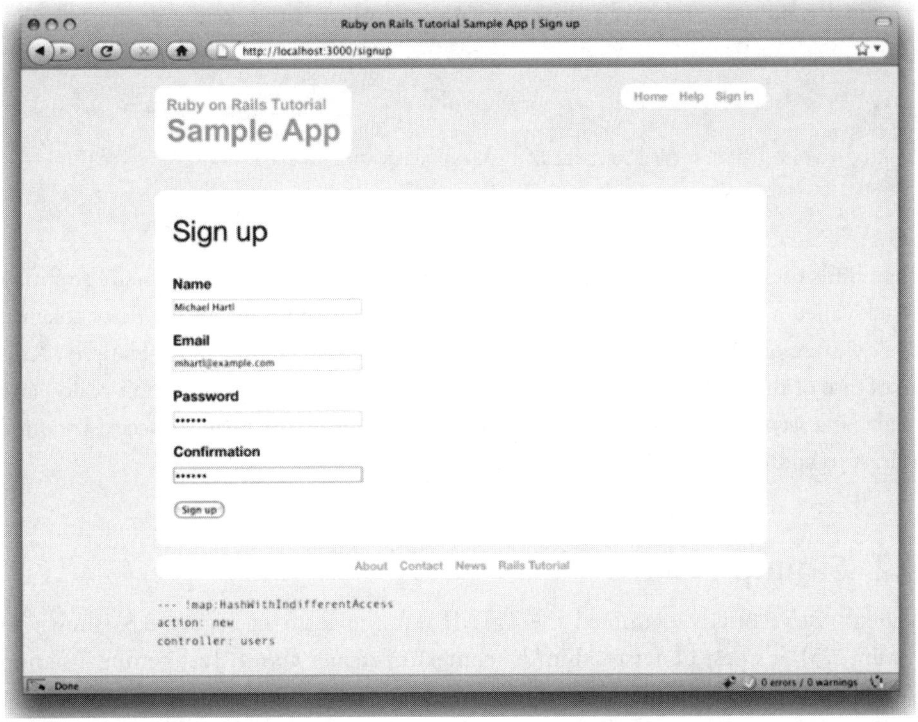

Figure 8.4 A filled-in form, showing the difference between **text** and **password** fields.

The second important element is the **form** tag itself. Rails creates the **form** tag using the **@user** object: because every Ruby object knows its own class (Section 4.4.1), Rails figures out that **@user** is of class **User**; moreover, since **@user** is a *new* user, Rails knows to construct a form with the **post** method, which is the proper verb for creating a new object (Box 3.1):

```
<form action="/users" class="new_user" id="new_user" method="post">
```

Here the **class** and **id** attributes are largely irrelevant; what's important is **action=-"/users"** and **method="post"**. Together, these constitute instructions to issue an HTML POST request to the /users URL. We'll see in the next two sections what effects this has.

Finally, note the rather obscure code for the "authenticity token":

```
<div style="margin:0;padding:0;display:inline">
<input name="authenticity_token" type="hidden"
       value="rB82sI7Qw5J9J1UMILG/VQL411vH5putR+JwlxLScMQ=" />
</div>
```

Here Rails uses a special unique value to thwart a particular kind of cross-site scripting attack called a *forgery*; see the Stack Overflow entry on the Rails authenticity token if you're interested in the details of how this works and why it's important. Happily, Rails takes care of the problem for you, and the input tag is **hidden** so you don't really have to give it a second thought, but it shows up when you view the form source so I wanted at least to address it.

8.2 Signup Failure

Though we've briefly examined the HTML for the form in Figure 8.3 (shown in Listing 8.5), it's best understood in the context of *signup failure*. Just getting a signup form that accepts an invalid submission and re-renders the signup page (as mocked up in Figure 8.5) is a significant accomplishment, and it's the goal of this section.

8.2.1 Testing Failure

Recall from Section 6.3.3 that adding **resources :users** to the **routes.rb** file (Listing 6.26) automatically ensures that our Rails application responds to the RESTful URLs from Table 6.2. In particular, it ensures that a POST request to /users is handled by the **create** action. Our strategy for the **create** action is to use the form submission to make a new user object using **User.new**, try (and fail) to save that user, and then render the signup page for possible resubmission. Our task is to write tests for this action, and then add **create** to the Users controller to get it to pass.

Let's get started by reviewing the code for the signup form:

```
<form action="/users" class="new_user" id="new_user" method="post">
```

As noted in Section 8.1.2, this HTML issues a POST request to the /users URL. In an analogy with the **get** method, which issues a GET request inside of tests, we use the **post**

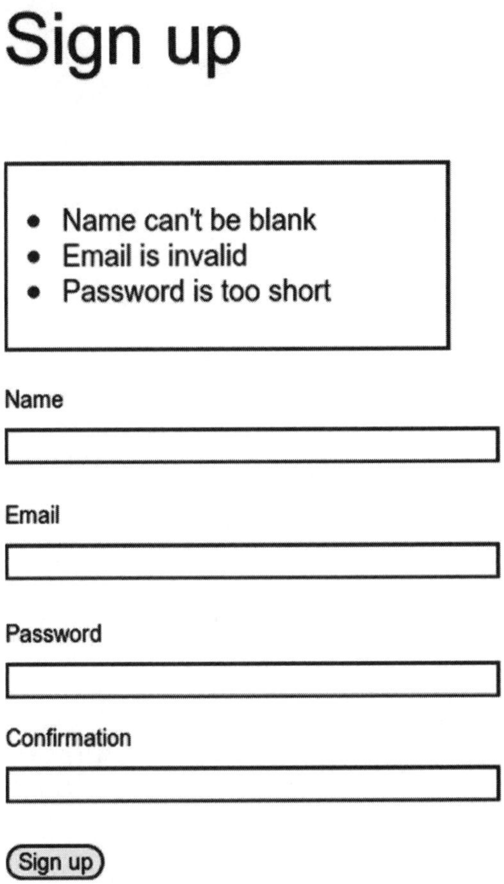

Sign up

- Name can't be blank
- Email is invalid
- Password is too short

Name

Email

Password

Confirmation

(Sign up)

Figure 8.5   A mockup of the signup failure page.

method to issue a POST request to the **create** action. As we'll see shortly, **create** takes in a hash corresponding to the object type being created; since this is a test for signup *failure*, we'll just pass an **@attr** hash with blank entries, as seen in Listing 8.6. This is essentially equivalent to visiting the signup page and clicking on the button without filling in any of the fields.

Listing 8.6   Tests for failed user signup.
spec/controllers/users_controller_spec.rb

```
require 'spec_helper'

describe UsersController do
```

```
render_views
.
.
.

describe "POST 'create'" do

  describe "failure" do

    before(:each) do
      @attr = { :name => "", :email => "", :password => "",
                :password_confirmation => "" }
    end

    it "should not create a user" do
      lambda do
        post :create, :user => @attr
      end.should_not change(User, :count)
    end

    it "should have the right title" do
      post :create, :user => @attr
      response.should have_selector("title", :content => "Sign up")
    end

    it "should render the 'new' page" do
      post :create, :user => @attr
      response.should render_template('new')
    end
  end
end
end
```

The final two tests are relatively straightforward: we make sure that the title is correct, and then we check that a failed signup attempt just re-renders the new user page (using the **render_template** RSpec method). The first test, on the other hand, is a little tricky.

The purpose of the test

```
it "should not create a user" do
  lambda do
    post :create, :user => @attr
  end.should_not change(User, :count)
end
```

is to verify that a failed **create** action doesn't create a user in the database. To do this, it introduces two new elements. First, we use the RSpec **change** method to return the number of users in the database:

```
change(User, :count)
```

This defers to the Active Record **count** method, which simply returns how many records of that type are in the database. For example, if you cleared the development database at the beginning of the chapter, this count should currently be **0**:

```
$ rails console
>> User.count
=> 0
```

The second new idea is to wrap the **post :create** step in a package using a Ruby construct called a **lambda**,[2] which allows us to check that it doesn't change the **User** count:

```
lambda do
  post :create, :user => @attr
end.should_not change(User, :count)
```

Although this **lambda** may seem strange at this point, there will be more examples in the tests to come, and the pattern will quickly become clear.

8.2.2 A Working Form

We can get the tests from Section 8.2.1 to pass with the code in Listing 8.7. This listing includes a second use of the **render** method, which we first saw in the context of partials (Section 5.1.3); as you can see, **render** works in controller actions as well. Note that we've taken this opportunity to introduce an **if-else** branching structure, which allows us to handle the cases of failure and success separately based on the value of **@user.save**.

---

2. The name comes from the lambda calculus, a mathematical system for representing functions and their operations.

Listing 8.7 A **create** action that can handle signup failure (but not success).
app/controllers/users_controller.rb

```
class UsersController < ApplicationController
  .
  .
  .
  def create
    @user = User.new(params[:user])
    if @user.save
      # Handle a successful save.
    else
      @title = "Sign up"
      render 'new'
    end
  end
end
```

The best way to understand how the code in Listing 8.7 works is to *submit* the form with some invalid signup data; the results appear in Figure 8.6.

To get a clearer picture of how Rails handles the submission, let's take a closer look at the **params** hash in the debug information at the bottom of Figure 8.6:

```
--- !map:ActiveSupport::HashWithIndifferentAccess
commit: Sign up
authenticity_token: rB82sI7Qw5J9J1UMILG/VQL411vH5puR+Jw1xL5cMQ=
action: create
controller: users
user: !map:ActiveSupport::HashWithIndifferentAccess
  name: Foo Bar
  password_confirmation: dude
  password: dude
  email: foo@invalid
```

We saw starting in Section 6.3.2 that the **params** hash contains information about each request; in the case of a URL like /users/1, the value of **params[:id]** is the **id** of the corresponding user (**1** in this example). In the case of posting to the signup form, **params** instead contains a hash of hashes, a construction we first saw in Section 4.3.3, which introduced the strategically named **params** variable in a console session. This debug information above shows that submitting the form results in a **user** hash with attributes corresponding to the submitted values, where the keys

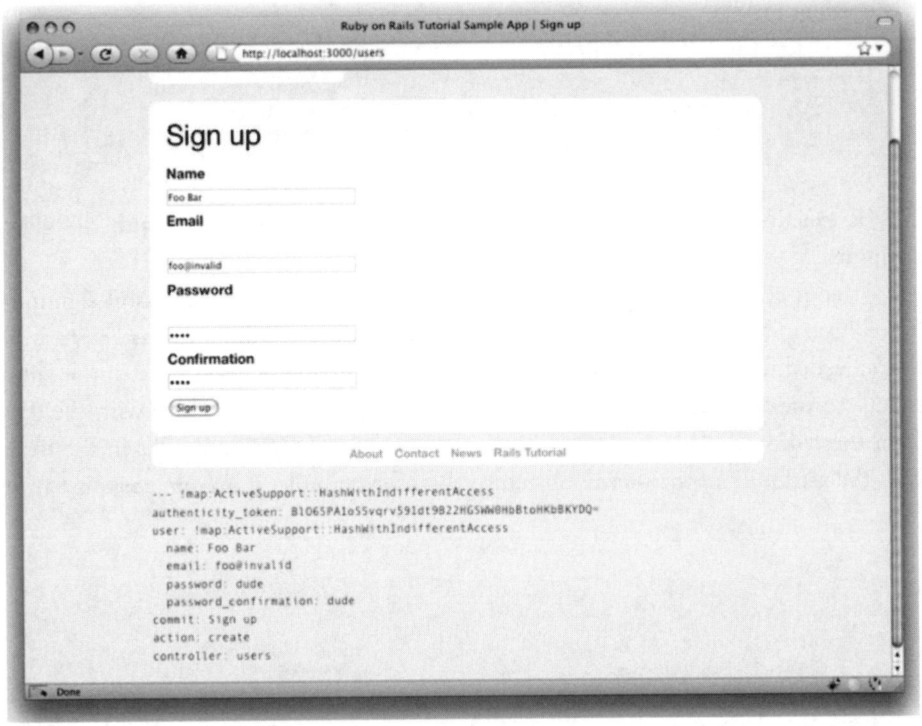

Figure 8.6 Signup failure with a **params** hash.

come from the **name** attributes of the **input** tags seen in Listing 8.2; for example, the value of

```
<input id="user_email" name="user[email]" size="30" type="text" />
```

with name **"user[email]"** is precisely the **email** attribute of the **user** hash.

Though the hash keys appear as strings in the debug output, internally Rails uses symbols, so that **params[:user]** is the hash of user attributes—in fact, exactly the attributes needed as an argument to **User.new**, as first seen in Section 4.4.5 and appearing in Listing 8.7. This means that the line

```
@user = User.new(params[:user])
```

is equivalent to

```
@user = User.new(:name => "Foo Bar", :email => "foo@invalid",
                 :password => "dude", :password_confirmation => "dude")
```

This is exactly the format needed to initialize a User model object with the given attributes.

Of course, instantiating such a variable has implications for successful signup—as we'll see in Section 8.3, once **@user** is defined properly, calling **@user.save** is all that's needed to complete the registration—but it has consequences even in the failed signup considered here. Note in Figure 8.6 that the fields are *pre-filled* with the data from the failed submission. This is because **form_for** automatically fills in the fields with the attributes of the **@user** object, so that, for example, if **@user.name** is **"Foo"** then

```
<%= form_for(@user) do |f| %>
  <div class="field">
    <%= f.label :name %><br />
    <%= f.text_field :name %>
  </div>
  .
  .
  .
```

will produce the HTML

```
<form action="/users" class="new_user" id="new_user" method="post">

  <div class="field">
    <label for="user_name">Name</label><br />
    <input id="user_name" name="user[name]" size="30" type="text" value="Foo"/>
  </div>
  .
  .
  .
```

Here the **value** of the **input** tag is **"Foo"**, so that's what appears in the text field.

8.2.3 Signup Error Messages

Though not strictly necessary, it's helpful to output error messages on failed signup to indicate the problems that prevented successful user registration. Rails provides just such messages based on the User model validations. For example, consider trying to save a user with an invalid email address and with a short password:

```
$ rails console
>> user = User.new(:name => "Foo Bar", :email => "foo@invalid",
?>                 :password => "dude", :password_confirmation => "dude")
>> user.save
=> false
>> user.errors.full_messages
=> ["Email is invalid", "Password is too short (minimum is 6 characters)"]
```

Here the **errors.full_messages** object (which we saw briefly in Section 6.2.1) contains an array of error messages.

As in the console session above, the failed save in Listing 8.7 generates a list of error messages associated with the **@user** object. To display the messages in the browser, we'll render an error-messages partial on the user **new** page (Listing 8.8).[3]

Listing 8.8 Code to display error messages on the signup form.
app/views/users/new.html.erb

```
<h1>Sign up</h1>

<%= form_for(@user) do |f| %>
  <%= render 'shared/error_messages' %>
  .
  .
  .
<% end %>
```

Notice here that we **render** a partial called **'shared/error_messages'**; this reflects a common Rails convention that puts partials we expect to be used from multiple controllers in a dedicated **shared/** directory. (We'll see this expectation fulfilled in

---

3. Before Rails 3, displaying error messages was done through a magical call to a special **error_messages** method on the form object **f**, as follows: <%= f.error_messages %>. Though often convenient, this magical method was hard to customize, so the Rails Core team decided to recommend using Embedded Ruby to display the errors by hand.

Section 10.1.1.) This means that we have to create this new directory along with the
_error_messages.html.erb partial file. The partial itself appears in Listing 8.9.

Listing 8.9 A partial for displaying form submission error messages.
app/views/shared/_error_messages.html.erb

```
<% if @user.errors.any? %>
  <div id="error_explanation">
    <h2><%= pluralize(@user.errors.count, "error") %>
        prohibited this user from being saved:</h2>
    <p>There were problems with the following fields:</p>
    <ul>
    <% @user.errors.full_messages.each do |msg| %>
      <li><%= msg %></li>
    <% end %>
    </ul>
  </div>
<% end %>
```

This partial introduces several new Rails and Ruby constructs, including two methods
for objects of class **Array**. Let's open up a console session to see how they work. The
first method is **count**, which simply returns the number of elements in the object:

```
$ rails console
>> a = [1, 2, 3]
=> [1, 2, 3]
>> a.count
=> 3
```

The other new method is **any?**, one of a pair of complementary methods:

```
>> [].empty?
=> true
>> [].any?
=> false
>> a.empty?
=> false
>> a.any?
=> true
```

We see here that the **empty?** method, which we first saw in Section 4.2.3 in the context
of strings, also works on arrays, returning **true** for an empty array and **false** otherwise.

The **any?** method is just the opposite of **empty?**, returning **true** if there are any elements in the array and **false** otherwise.

The other new idea is the **pluralize** text helper. It isn't available in the console, but we can include it explicitly through the **ActionView::Helpers::TextHelper** module:[4]

```
>> include ActionView::Helpers::TextHelper
=> Object
>> pluralize(1, "error")
=> "1 error"
>> pluralize(5, "error")
=> "5 errors"
>>
```

We see here that **pluralize** takes an integer argument and then returns the number with a properly pluralized version of its second argument. Underlying this method is a powerful *inflector* that knows how to pluralize a large number of words (including many with irregular plurals):

```
>> pluralize(2, "woman")
=> "2 women"
>> pluralize(3, "erratum")
=> "3 errata"
```

As a result, the code

```
<%= pluralize(@user.errors.count, "error") %>
```

returns **"1 error"** or **"2 errors"** (etc.) depending on how many errors there are.

Note that Listing 8.9 includes the CSS id **error_explanation** for use in styling the error messages. (Recall from Section 5.1.2 that CSS uses the pound sign **#** to style ids.) In addition, on error pages Rails automatically wraps the fields with errors in **div**s with the CSS class **field_with_errors**. These labels then allow us to style the error messages with the CSS shown in Listing 8.10. As a result, on failed submission the error messages appear as in Figure 8.7. Because the messages are generated by the model validations, they will automatically change if you ever change your mind about, say, the format of email addresses, or the minimum length on passwords.

---

4. I figured this out by looking up **pluralize** in the Rails API.

Listing 8.10 CSS for styling error messages.
`public/stylesheets/custom.css`

```css
.
.
.
.field_with_errors {
  margin-top: 10px;
  padding: 2px;
  background-color: red;
  display: table;
}

.field_with_errors label {
  color: #fff;
}

#error_explanation {
  width: 400px;
  border: 2px solid red;
  padding: 7px;
  padding-bottom: 12px;
  margin-bottom: 20px;
  background-color: #f0f0f0;
}

#error_explanation h2 {
  text-align: left;
  font-weight: bold;
  padding: 5px 5px 5px 15px;
  font-size: 12px;
  margin: -7px;
  background-color: #c00;
  color: #fff;
}

#error_explanation p {
  color: #333;
  margin-bottom: 0;
  padding: 5px;
}

#error_explanation ul li {
  font-size: 12px;
  list-style: square;
}
```

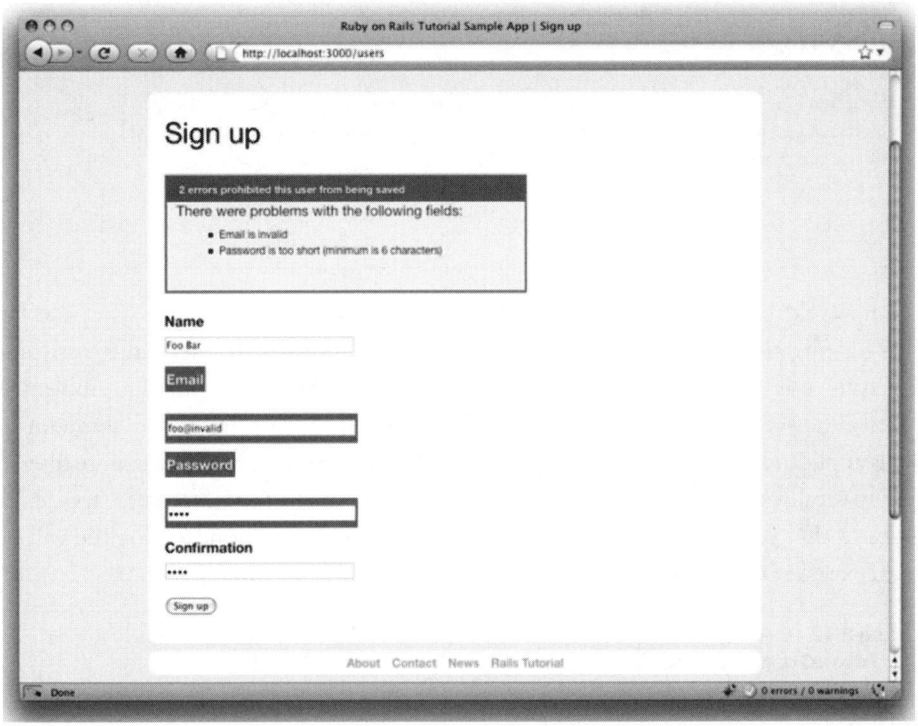

Figure 8.7   Failed signup with error messages.

8.2.4   Filtering Parameter Logging

Before moving on to successful signup, there's one loose end to tie off. You might have noticed that, even though we went to great pains to encrypt the password in Chapter 7, both the password and its confirmation appear as cleartext in the debug information. By itself this is no problem—recall from Listing 6.23 that this information only appears for applications running in **development** mode, so actual users would never see it—but it does hint at a potential problem: the passwords might also appear unencrypted in the *log file* that Rails uses to record information about the running application. Indeed, in previous versions of Rails, the development log file in this case would contain lines like those shown in Listing 8.11.

Listing 8.11   The pre–Rails 3 development log with visible passwords.
`log/development.log`

```
Parameters: {"commit"=>"Sign up", "action"=>"create",
"authenticity_token"=>"K1HchFF8uYE8ZaQKz5DVG9vF2KGoXJu4JGp/VE3NMjA=",
"controller"=>"users",
  "user"=>{"name"=>"Foo Bar", "password_confirmation"=>"dude",
          "password"=>"dude", "email"=>"foo@invalid"}}
```

It would be a terrible security breach to store unencrypted passwords in the log files—if anyone ever got a hold of the file, they would potentially obtain the passwords for every user on the system. (Of course, here the signup fails, but the problem is exactly the same for successful submissions.) Since this problem was so common in Rails applications, Rails 3 implements a new default: all **password** attributes are filtered automatically, as seen in Listing 8.12. We see that the string **"[FILTERED]"** appears in place of the password and password confirmation. (In production, the log file will be **log/production.log**, and the filtering will work the same way.)

Listing 8.12   The development log with filtered passwords.
`log/development.log`

```
Parameters: {"commit"=>"Sign up", "action"=>"create",
"authenticity_token"=>"K1HchFF8uYE8ZaQKz5DVG9vF2KGoXJu4JGp/VE3NMjA=",
"controller"=>"users",
  "user"=>{"name"=>"Foo Bar", "password_confirmation"=>"[FILTERED]",
          "password"=>"[FILTERED]", "email"=>"foo@invalid"}}
```

The password filtering itself is accomplished via a setting in the **application.rb** configuration file (Listing 8.13).

Listing 8.13   Filtering passwords by default.
`config/application.rb`

```
require File.expand_path('../boot', __FILE__)

require 'rails/all'

# If you have a Gemfile, require the gems listed there, including any gems
# you've limited to :test, :development, or :production.
Bundler.require(:default, Rails.env) if defined?(Bundler)

module SampleApp
```

```
class Application < Rails::Application
    .
    .
    .
    # Configure sensitive parameters which will be filtered from the log file.
    config.filter_parameters += [:password]
  end
end
```

If you ever write a Rails application with a secure parameter with a name *other* than **password**, you will need to add it to the array of filtered parameters. For example, if you included a secret code as part of the signup process, you might include a line like

```
<div class="field">
  <%= f.label :secret_code %><br />
  <%= f.text_field :secret_code %>
</div>
```

in the signup form. You would then need to add **:secret_code** to **application.rb** as follows:

```
config.filter_parameters += [:password, :secret_code]
```

8.3 Signup Success

Having handled invalid form submissions, now it's time to complete the signup form by actually saving a new user (if valid) to the database. First, we try to save the user; if the save succeeds, the user's information gets written to the database automatically, and we then *redirect* the browser to show the user's profile (together with a friendly greeting), as mocked up in Figure 8.8. If it fails, we simply fall back on the behavior developed in Section 8.2.

8.3.1 Testing Success

The tests for a successful signup follow the lead of the failed signup tests from Listing 8.6. Let's take a look at the result, shown in Listing 8.14.

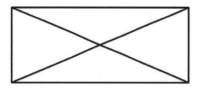

Welcome to the Sample App!

 Raoul Duke

Name   Raoul Duke
URL   /users/9

Figure 8.8   A mockup of successful signup.

Listing 8.14 Tests for signup success.
spec/controllers/users_controller_spec.rb

```
require 'spec_helper'

describe UsersController do
  render_views
  .
  .
  .
  describe "POST 'create'" do
    .
    .
    .
    describe "success" do
```

```
      before(:each) do
        @attr = { :name => "New User", :email => "user@example.com",
                  :password => "foobar", :password_confirmation => "foobar" }
      end

      it "should create a user" do
        lambda do
          post :create, :user => @attr
        end.should change(User, :count).by(1)
      end

      it "should redirect to the user show page" do
        post :create, :user => @attr
        response.should redirect_to(user_path(assigns(:user)))
      end
    end
  end
end
```

As with the signup failure tests (Listing 8.6), here we use **post :create** to hit the
create action with an HTTP POST request. As in the failed creation tests from
Listing 8.6, the first test wraps the user creation in a **lambda** and uses the **count** method
to verify that the database has changed appropriately:

```
it "should create a user" do
  lambda do
    post :create, :user => @attr
  end.should change(User, :count).by(1)
end
```

Here, instead of **should_not change(User, :count)** as in the case of a failed user
creation, we have **should change(User, :count).by(1)**, which asserts that the
lambda block should change the **User** count by 1.

The second test uses the **assigns** method first seen in Listing 7.17 to verify that
the **create** action redirects to the newly created user's **show** page:

```
it "should redirect to the user show page" do
  post :create, :user => @attr
  response.should redirect_to(user_path(assigns(:user)))
end
```

This is the kind of redirect that happens on nearly every successful form submission on the web, and with RSpec's helpful syntax you don't have to know anything about the underlying HTTP response code.[5] The URL itself is generated using the named route **user_path** shown in Table 7.1.

8.3.2 The Finished Signup Form

To get these tests to pass and thereby complete a working signup form, fill in the commented-out section in Listing 8.7 with a redirect, as shown in Listing 8.15.

Listing 8.15 The user **create** action with a save and a redirect.
app/controllers/users_controller.rb

```
class UsersController < ApplicationController
  .
  .
  .
  def create
    @user = User.new(params[:user])
    if @user.save
      redirect_to @user
    else
      @title = "Sign up"
      render 'new'
    end
  end
end
```

Note that we can omit the **user_path** in the redirect, writing simply **redirect_to @user** to redirect to the user show page, a convention we saw before with **link_to** in Listing 7.25. This syntax is nicely succinct, but unfortunately RSpec doesn't understand it, so we have to use the more verbose **user_path(@user)** in that case.

8.3.3 The Flash

Before submitting a valid registration in a browser, we're going to add a bit of polish common in web applications: a message that appears temporarily and then disappears upon page reload. (If this is unclear now, be patient; a concrete example appears shortly.) The

---

5. In case you're curious, the response code is 302, in contrast to the "permanent" 301 redirect discussed briefly in Box 3.2.

Rails way to accomplish this is to use a special variable called the *flash*, which operates like flash memory in that it stores its data temporarily. The **flash** variable is effectively a hash; you may even recall the console example in Section 4.3.3, where we saw how to iterate through a hash using a strategically named **flash** hash. To recap, try this console session:

```
$ rails console
>> flash = { :success => "It worked!", :error => "It failed. :-(" }
=> {:success=>"It worked!", :error => "It failed. :-("}
>> flash.each do |key, value|
?>   puts "#{key}"
?>   puts "#{value}"
>> end
success
It worked!
error
It failed. :-(
```

We can arrange to display the contents of the flash site-wide by including it in our application layout, as in Listing 8.16.

Listing 8.16 Adding the contents of the **flash** variable to the site layout.
app/views/layouts/application.html.erb

```
<!DOCTYPE html>
<html>
      .
      .
      .
      <%= render 'layouts/header' %>
      <section class="round">
        <% flash.each do |key, value| %>
          <div class="flash <%= key %>"><%= value %></div>
        <% end %>
        <%= yield %>
      </section>
      .
      .
      .
</html>
```

This code arranges to insert a **div** tag for each element in the flash, with a CSS class indicating the type of message. For example, if **flash[:success] = "Welcome to the Sample App!"**, then the code

```
<% flash.each do |key, value| %>
  <div class="flash <%= key %>"><%= value %></div>
<% end %>
```

will produce this HTML:[6]

```
<div class="flash success">Welcome to the Sample App!</div>
```

The reason we iterate through all possible key/value pairs is so that we can include other kinds of flash messages; for example, in Listing 9.8 we'll see **flash[:error]** used to indicate a failed signin attempt.[7]

Let's test for the right flash message by making sure the right message appears under the key **:success** (Listing 8.17).

Listing 8.17 A test for a flash message on successful user signup.
spec/controllers/users_controller_spec.rb

```
require 'spec_helper'

describe UsersController do
  render_views
  .
  .
  .
  describe "POST 'create'" do
    .
    .
    describe "success" do
      .
      .
      .
      it "should have a welcome message" do
        post :create, :user => @attr
        flash[:success].should =~ /welcome to the sample app/i
      end
    end
  end
end
```

---

6. Note that the key **:success** is a symbol, but Embedded Ruby automatically converts it to the string **"success"** before inserting it into the template.

7. Actually, we'll use the closely related **flash.now**, but we'll defer that subtlety until we need it.

This introduces the "equals-tilde" =~ operator for comparing strings to regular expressions. (We first saw regular expressions in the **email_regex** of Listing 6.17). Rather than testing for the full flash message, we just test to make sure that "welcome to the sample app" is present. (Note that we don't yet test for the appearance of the actual flash message's HTML; we'll fix this by testing for the actual **div** tag in Section 8.4.3.)

If you've programmed much before, it's likely that you're already familiar with regular expressions, but here's a quick **console** session in case you need an introduction:

```
>> "foo bar" =~ /Foo/     # Regex comparison is case-sensitive by default.
=> nil
>> "foo bar" =~ /foo/
=> 0
```

Here the console's return values may look odd: for no match, the regex comparison returns **nil**; for a match, it returns the *index* (position) in the string where the match starts.[8] Usually, though, the exact index doesn't matter, since the comparison is usually used in a boolean context: recall from Section 4.2.3 that **nil** is **false** in a boolean context and that anything else (even **0**) is true. Thus, we can write code like this:

```
>> success = "Welcome to the Sample App!"
=> "Welcome to the Sample App!"
>> "It's a match!" if success =~ /welcome to the sample app/
=> nil
```

Here there's no match because regular expressions are case-sensitive by default, but we can be more permissive in the match using **/.../i** to force a case-insensitive match:

```
>> "It's a match!" if success =~ /welcome to the sample app/i
=> "It's a match!"
```

Now that we understand how the flash test's regular expression comparison works, we can get the test to pass by assigning to **flash[:success]** in the **create** action as in Listing 8.18. The message uses different capitalization from the one in the test, but

---

8. The indices are zero-offset, as with arrays (Section 4.3.1), so a return value of **0** means the string matches the regular expression starting with the first character.

the test passes anyway because of the **i** at the end of the regular expression. This way we won't break the test if we write, e.g., **sample app** in place of **Sample App**.

Listing 8.18 Adding a flash message to user signup.
app/controllers/users_controller.rb

```ruby
class UsersController < ApplicationController
  .
  .
  .
  def create
    @user = User.new(params[:user])
    if @user.save
      flash[:success] = "Welcome to the Sample App!"
      redirect_to @user
    else
      @title = "Sign up"
      render 'new'
    end
  end
end
```

8.3.4 The First Signup

We can see the result of all this work by signing up our first user (under the name "Rails Tutorial" and email address "example@railstutorial.org"), which shows a friendly message upon successful signup, as seen in Figure 8.9. (The nice green styling for the **success** class comes included with the Blueprint CSS framework from Section 4.1.2.) Then, upon reloading the user show page, the flash message disappears as promised (Figure 8.10).

We can now check our database just to be double-sure that the new user was actually created:

```
$ rails console
>> user = User.first
=> #<User id: 1, name: "Rails Tutorial", email: "example@railstutorial.org",
created_at: "2010-02-17 03:07:53", updated_at: "2010-02-17 03:07:53",
encrypted_password: "48aa8f4444b71f3f713d87d051819b0d44cd89f4a963949f201...",
salt: "f52924ba502d4f92a634d4f9647622cccce26205176cceca2adc...">
```

Success!

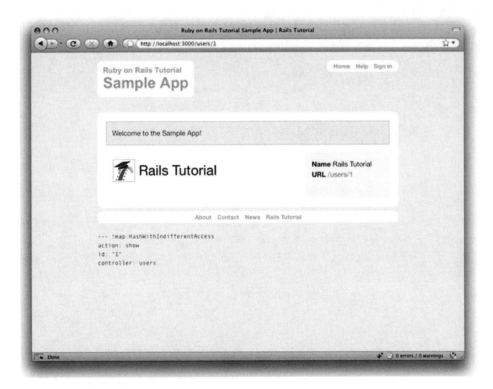

Figure 8.9   The results of a successful user signup, with flash message.

8.4   RSpec Integration Tests

In principle, we are done with user signup at this point, but you may have noticed that we haven't tested the structure of the signup form, nor have we tested that submissions actually work. Of course, we *have* checked these things by viewing the pages in our browser, but the whole point of automated testing is to make sure that once things work they stay that way. Making such tests is the goal of this section—and the results are pretty sweet.

One testing method would be to check the HTML structure of the form (using **render_views** and the **have_selector** method), and indeed this is a good way to test-drive views. (Section 8.6 has an exercise to this effect.) But I prefer not to test the detailed HTML structure of views—I don't see any reason why we should have to know that Rails implements user email submission using **name="user[email]"**, and indeed any test of that structure would break if a future Rails version changed this convention. Moreover, it would be nice to have a test for the entire signup process: visiting the signup

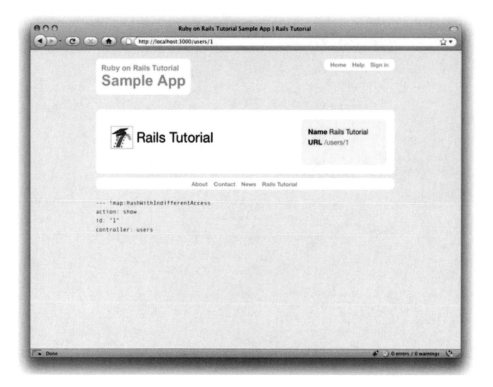

Figure 8.10   The flash-less profile page after a browser reload.

page, filling in the form values, clicking the button, and making sure (if the submission is valid) that a new user gets created in the (test) database.

Though it's not the only way (see Box 8.1), my preferred solution to this problem is to use an RSpec integration test, which we first used in Section 5.2.1 to test the custom routes (such as `/about` for the About page). In that section, we saw only a tiny fraction of the power of integration tests; starting in this section, we'll see just how amazing they can be.

Box 8.1   Integration alternatives

As we've seen in this and previous chapters, *Ruby on Rails Tutorial* uses RSpec for all its tests, including integration tests. In my view, there is no match for the simplicity and power of RSpec integration tests. There are a couple of viable alternatives, though. One is the Rails default, integration testing with `Test::Unit`. This is fine if you use `Test::Unit` elsewhere, but we're using RSpec in this tutorial, and I prefer not to mix RSpec and `Test::Unit` in a single project.

A second option is Cucumber, which works nicely with RSpec and allows the definition of plain-text stories describing application behavior. Many Rails programmers find Cucumber especially convenient when doing client work; since they can be read even by non-technical users, Cucumber tests, or "scenarios", can be shared with (and can sometimes even be written by) the client. Of course, using a testing framework that isn't pure Ruby has a downside, and I find that the plain-text stories can be a bit verbose and (cu)cumbersome. Since we don't have any client requirements in *Rails Tutorial*, and since I strongly prefer a pure-Ruby testing approach in any case, we'll stick to RSpec integration tests in this book. Nevertheless, I suggest taking a look at some Cucumber tutorials some time to see if it suits you.

8.4.1 Integration Tests with Style

We saw in Listing 5.13 that RSpec integration tests support controller-test–style constructions such as

```
get '/'
response.should have_selector('title', :content => "Home")
```

This is not the only kind of syntax supported, though; RSpec integration tests also support a highly expressive web-navigation syntax.[9] In this section, we'll see how to use this syntax to simulate filling out the signin form using code like

```
visit signin_path
fill_in "Name", :with => "Example User"
click_button
```

8.4.2 Users Signup Failure Should Not Make a New User

Now we're ready to make an integration test for signing up users. As we saw in Section 5.2.1, RSpec comes with a generator to make such integration specs; in the

---

9. As of this writing, this syntax is available thanks to Webrat, which appears as a gem dependency for `rspec-rails`, but Webrat was written before the widespread adoption of Rack and will eventually be supplanted by the Capybara project. Happily, Capybara is designed as a drop-in replacement for Webrat, so the syntax should remain the same.

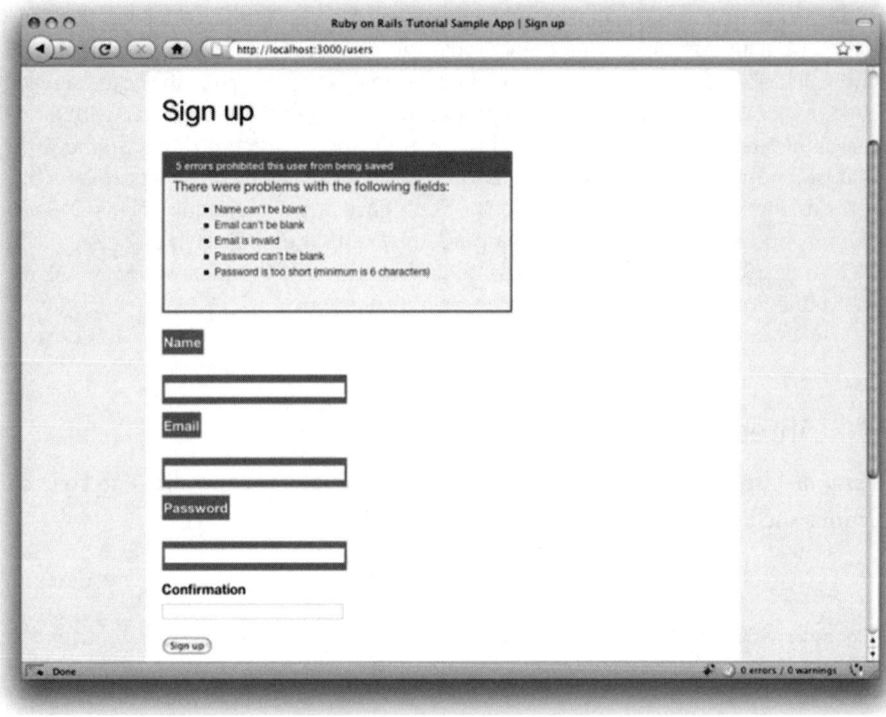

Figure 8.11   The result of visiting `/signup` and just clicking "Sign up".

present case, our integration tests will contain various actions taken by users, so we'll name the test **users** accordingly:

```
$ rails generate integration_test users
      invoke  rspec
      create    spec/requests/users_spec.rb
```

As in Section 5.2.1, the generator automatically appends a spec identifier, yielding **users_spec.rb**.[10]

We start with signup failure. A simple way to arrange a failing signup is to visit the signup URL and just click the button, resulting in a page as in Figure 8.11. Upon

---

10. Note the plural; this is *not* the User spec **user_spec.rb**, which is a model test, not an integration test.

failed submission, the response should render the **users/new** template. If you inspect the resulting HTML, you should see something like the markup in Listing 8.19. This means that we can test for the presence of error messages by looking for a **div** tag with the CSS id **"error_explanation"**. A test for these steps appears in Listing 8.20.

Listing 8.19 The error explanation **div** from the page in Figure 8.11.

```
<div class="error_explanation" id="error_explanation">
  <h2>5 errors prohibited this user from being saved</h2>
  <p>There were problems with the following fields:</p>
  <ul>
    <li>Name can't be blank</li>
    <li>Email can't be blank</li>
    <li>Email is invalid</li>
    <li>Password can't be blank</li>
    <li>Password is too short (minimum is 6 characters)</li>
  </ul>
</div>
```

Listing 8.20 Testing signup failure.
spec/requests/users_spec.rb

```
require 'spec_helper'

describe "Users" do

  describe "signup" do

    describe "failure" do

      it "should not make a new user" do
        visit signup_path
        fill_in "Name",         :with => ""
        fill_in "Email",        :with => ""
        fill_in "Password",     :with => ""
        fill_in "Confirmation", :with => ""
        click_button
        response.should render_template('users/new')
        response.should have_selector("div#error_explanation")
      end
    end
  end
end
```

Here **"div#error_explanation"** is CSS-inspired shorthand for

```
<div id="error_explanation">...</div>
```

Notice how natural the language is in Listing 8.20. The only problem is that it doesn't *quite* test what we want: we're not actually testing that a failed submission fails to create a new user. To do so, we need to wrap the test steps in a single package, and then check that it doesn't change the **User** count. As we saw in Listing 8.6 and Listing 8.14, this can be accomplished with a **lambda**. In those cases, the **lambda** block only contained a single line, but we see in Listing 8.21 that it can wrap multiple lines just as easily.

Listing 8.21 Testing signup failure with a **lambda**.
spec/requests/users_spec.rb

```
require 'spec_helper'

describe "Users" do

  describe "signup" do

    describe "failure" do

      it "should not make a new user" do
        lambda do
          visit signup_path
          fill_in "Name",         :with => ""
          fill_in "Email",        :with => ""
          fill_in "Password",     :with => ""
          fill_in "Confirmation", :with => ""
          click_button
          response.should render_template('users/new')
          response.should have_selector("div#error_explanation")
        end.should_not change(User, :count)
      end
    end
  end
end
```

As in Listing 8.6, this uses

```
should_not change(User, :count)
```

to verify that the code inside the **lambda** block doesn't change the value of **User.count**.

The integration test in Listing 8.21 ties together all the different parts of Rails, including models, views, controllers, routing, and helpers. It provides an end-to-end verification that our signup machinery is working, at least for failed submissions.

8.4.3 Users Signup Success Should Make a New User

We come now to the integration test for successful signup. In this case, we need to fill in the signup fields with valid user data. When we do, the result should be the user show page with a "flash success" **div** tag, and it should change the User count by 1. Listing 8.22 shows how to do it.

Listing 8.22 Testing signup success.
spec/requests/users_spec.rb

```
require 'spec_helper'

describe "Users" do

  describe "signup" do
    .
    .
    .
    describe "success" do

      it "should make a new user" do
        lambda do
          visit signup_path
          fill_in "Name",         :with => "Example User"
          fill_in "Email",        :with => "user@example.com"
          fill_in "Password",     :with => "foobar"
          fill_in "Confirmation", :with => "foobar"
          click_button
          response.should have_selector("div.flash.success",
                                        :content => "Welcome")
          response.should render_template('users/show')
        end.should change(User, :count).by(1)
      end
    end
  end
end
```

By the way, although it's not obvious from the RSpec documentation, you can use the CSS id of the text box instead of the label, so `fill_in :user_name` also works.[11] (This is especially nice for forms that don't use labels.)

I hope you agree that this web navigation syntax is incredibly natural and succinct. For example, to fill in a field with a value, we just use code like this:

```
fill_in "Name",          :with => "Example User"
fill_in "Email",         :with => "user@example.com"
fill_in "Password",      :with => "foobar"
fill_in "Confirmation",  :with => "foobar"
```

Here the first arguments to `fill_in` are the label values, i.e., exactly the text the user sees in the browser; there's no need to know anything about the underlying HTML structure generated by the Rails `form_for` helper.

Finally, we come to the coup de grâce—testing that successful signup actually creates a user in the database:

```
it "should make a new user" do
  lambda do
    .
    .
    .
  end.should change(User, :count).by(1)
```

As in Listing 8.21, we've wrapped the code for a successful signup in a `lambda` block. In this case, instead of making sure that the User count *doesn't* change, we verify that it increases by 1 due to a User record being created in the test database. The result is as follows:

```
$ rspec spec/requests/users_spec.rb
. .


Finished in 2.14 seconds
2 examples, 0 failures
```

---

11. You can use Firebug or your browser's "view source" if you need to figure out the id. Or you can note that Rails uses the name of the resource and the name of the attribute separated with an underscore, yielding `user_name`, `user_email`, etc.

With that, our signup integration tests are complete, and we can be confident that, if users don't join our site, it's not because the signup form is broken.

8.5 Conclusion

Being able to sign up users is a major milestone for our application. Though the sample app has yet to accomplish anything useful, we have laid an essential foundation for all future development. In the next two chapters, we will complete two more major milestones: first, in Chapter 9 we will complete our authentication machinery by allowing users to sign in and out of the application; second, in Chapter 10 we will allow all users to update their account information and will allow site administrators to delete users, while also adding page protection to enforce a site security model, thereby completing the full suite of the Users resource REST actions from Table 6.2.

As usual, if you're using Git, you should merge your changes into the **master** branch at this point:

```
$ git add .
$ git commit -am "User signup complete"
$ git checkout master
$ git merge signing-up
```

8.6 Exercises

1. Using the model in Listing 8.23, write tests to check for the presence of each field on the signup form. (Don't forget the **render_views** line, which is essential for this to work.)
2. Oftentimes signup forms will clear the password field for failed submissions, as shown in Figure 8.12. Modify the Users controller **create** action to replicate this behavior. *Hint:* Reset **@user.password**.
3. The flash HTML in Listing 8.16 is a particularly ugly combination of HTML and ERb. Verify by running the test suite that the cleaner code in Listing 8.24, which uses the Rails **content_tag** helper, also works.

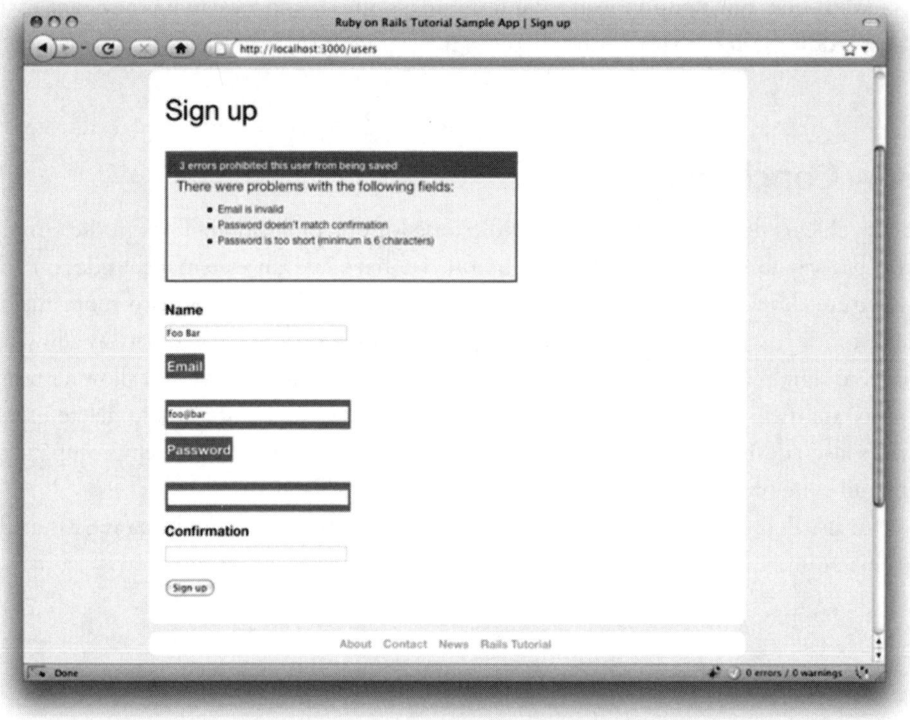

Figure 8.12   A failed signup form submission with the password field cleared.

Listing 8.23   A template for testing for each field on the signup form.
spec/controllers/users_controller_spec.rb

```
require 'spec_helper'

describe UsersController do
  render_views
   .
   .
  describe "GET 'new'" do
    .
    .
    it "should have a name field" do
      get :new
      response.should have_selector("input[name='user[name]'][type='text']")
```

```
        end

    it "should have an email field"

    it "should have a password field"

    it "should have a password confirmation field"
  end
  .
  .
  .
end
```

Listing 8.24 The **flash** ERb in the site layout using **content_tag**.
app/views/layouts/application.html.erb

```erb
<!DOCTYPE html>
<html>
    .
    .
    .
    <section class="round">
      <% flash.each do |key, value| %>
        <%= content_tag(:div, value, :class => "flash #{key}") %>
      <% end %>
      <%= yield %>
    </section>
    .
    .
    .
</html>
```

CHAPTER 9
Sign In, Sign Out

Now that new users can sign up for our site (Chapter 8), it's time to give registered users the ability to sign in and sign out. This will allow us to add customizations based on signin status and depending on the identity of the current user. For example, in this chapter we'll update the site header with signin/signout links and a profile link; in Chapter 11, we'll use the identity of a signed-in user to create microposts associated with that user, and in Chapter 12 we'll allow the current user to follow other users of the application (thereby receiving a feed of their microposts).

Having users sign in will also allow us to implement a security model, restricting access to particular pages based on the identity of the signed-in user. For instance, as we'll see in Chapter 10, only signed-in users will be able to access the page used to edit user information. The signin system will also make possible special privileges for administrative users, such as the ability (also in Chapter 10) to delete users from the database.

As in previous chapters, we'll do our work on a topic branch and merge in the changes at the end:

```
$ git checkout -b sign-in-out
```

9.1 Sessions

A *session* is a semi-permanent connection between two computers, such as a client computer running a web browser and a server running Rails. There are several different models for session behavior common on the web: "forgetting" the session on browser close, using an optional "remember me" checkbox for persistent sessions, and remembering sessions until the user explicitly signs out.[1] We'll opt for the final of these options: when users sign in, we will remember their signin status "forever",[2] clearing the session only when the user explicitly signs out.

It's convenient to model sessions as a RESTful resource: we'll have a signin page for **new** sessions, signing in will **create** a session, and signing out will **destroy** it. We will therefore need a Sessions controller with **new**, **create**, and **destroy** actions. Unlike the case of the Users controller, which uses a database back-end (via the User model) to persist data, the Sessions controller will use a *cookie*, which is a small piece of text placed on the user's browser. Much of the work involved in signin comes from building this cookie-based authentication machinery. In this section and the next, we'll prepare for this work by constructing a Sessions controller, a signin form, and the relevant controller actions. (Much of this work parallels user signup from Chapter 8.) We'll then complete user signin with the necessary cookie-manipulation code in Section 9.3.

9.1.1 Sessions Controller

The elements of signing in and out correspond to particular REST actions of the Sessions controller: the signin form is handled by the **new** action (covered in this section), actually signing in is handled by sending a POST request to the **create** action (Section 9.2 and Section 9.3), and signing out is handled by sending a DELETE request to the **destroy** action (Section 9.4). (Recall the association of HTTP verbs with REST actions from Table 6.2.) Since we know that we'll need a **new** action, we can create it when we generate the Sessions controller (just as with the Users controller in Listing 5.23):[3]

```
$ rails generate controller Sessions new
$ rm -rf spec/views
$ rm -rf spec/helpers
```

Now, as with the signup form in Section 8.1, we create a new file for the Sessions controller specs and add a couple of tests for the **new** action and corresponding view (Listing 9.1). (This pattern should start to look familiar by now.)

---

1. Another common model is to expire the session after a certain amount of time. This is especially appropriate on sites containing sensitive information, such as banking and financial trading accounts.

2. We'll see in Section 9.3.2 just how long "forever" is.

3. If given the **create** and **destroy** actions as well, the generate script would make *views* for those actions, which we don't need. Of course, we could delete the views, but I've elected to omit them from **generate** and instead define the actions by hand.

Listing 9.1 Tests for the **new** session action and view.
spec/controllers/sessions_controller_spec.rb

```
require 'spec_helper'

describe SessionsController do
  render_views

  describe "GET 'new'" do

    it "should be successful" do
      get :new
      response.should be_success
    end

    it "should have the right title" do
      get :new
      response.should have_selector("title", :content => "Sign in")
    end
  end
end
```

To get these tests to pass, we first need to add a route for the **new** action; while we're at it, we'll create all the actions needed throughout the chapter as well. We generally follow the example from Listing 6.26, but in this case we define only the particular actions we need, i.e., **new**, **create**, and **destroy**, and also add named routes for signin and signout (Listing 9.2).

Listing 9.2 Adding a resource to get the standard RESTful actions for sessions.
config/routes.rb

```
SampleApp::Application.routes.draw do
  resources :users
  resources :sessions, :only => [:new, :create, :destroy]

  match '/signup',  :to => 'users#new'
  match '/signin',  :to => 'sessions#new'
  match '/signout', :to => 'sessions#destroy'
  .
  .
  .
end
```

Table 9.1 RESTful routes provided by the sessions rules in Listing 9.2

HTTP Request	URL	Named route	Action	Purpose
GET	/signin	**signin_path**	**new**	page for a new session (signin)
POST	/sessions	**sessions_path**	**create**	create a new session
DELETE	/signout	**signout_path**	**destroy**	delete a session (sign out)

As you can see, the **resources** method can take an options hash, which in this case has key **:only** and value equal to an array of the actions the Sessions controller has to respond to. The resources defined in Listing 9.2 provide URLs and actions similar to those for users (Table 6.2), as shown in Table 9.1.

   We can get the second test in Listing 9.1 to pass by adding the proper title instance variable to the **new** action, as shown in Listing 9.3 (which also defines the **create** and **destroy** actions for future reference).

Listing 9.3 Adding the title for the signin page.
app/controllers/sessions_controller.rb

```ruby
class SessionsController < ApplicationController

  def new
    @title = "Sign in"
  end

  def create
  end

  def destroy
  end
end
```

With that, the tests in Listing 9.1 should be passing, and we're ready to make the actual signin form.

9.1.2 Signin Form

The signin form (or, equivalently, the new session form) is similar in appearance to the signup form, except with two fields (email and password) in place of four. A mockup appears in Figure 9.1.

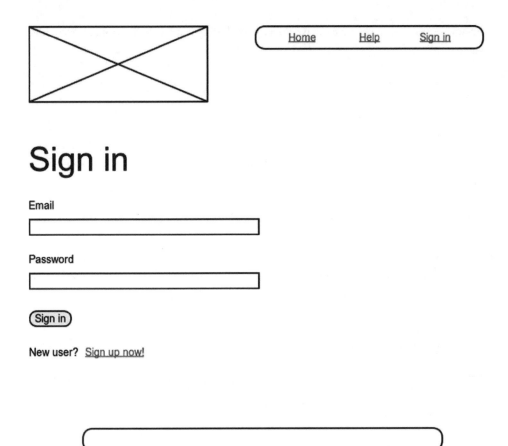

Figure 9.1 A mockup of the signin form.

Recall from Listing 8.2 that the signup form uses the **form_for** helper, taking as an argument the user instance variable **@user**:

```
<%= form_for(@user) do |f| %>
  .
  .
  .
<% end %>
```

The main difference between this and the new session form is that we have no Session model, and hence no analogue for the **@user** variable. This means that, in constructing the new session form, we have to give **form_for** slightly more information; in particular, whereas

```
form_for(@user)
```

allows Rails to infer that the **action** of the form should be to POST to the URL /users, in the case of sessions we need to indicate both the *name* of the resource and the appropriate URL:

```
form_for(:session, :url => sessions_path)
```

Since we're authenticating users with email address and password, we need a field for each one inside the form; the result appears in Listing 9.4.

Listing 9.4 Code for the signin form.
`app/views/sessions/new.html.erb`

```
<h1>Sign in</h1>

<%= form_for(:session, :url => sessions_path) do |f| %>
  <div class="field">
    <%= f.label :email %><br />
    <%= f.text_field :email %>
  </div>
  <div class="field">
    <%= f.label :password %><br />
    <%= f.password_field :password %>
  </div>
  <div class="actions">
    <%= f.submit "Sign in" %>
  </div>
<% end %>

<p>New user? <%= link_to "Sign up now!", signup_path %></p>
```

With the code in Listing 9.4, the signin form appears as in Figure 9.2.

Though you'll soon get out of the habit of looking at the HTML generated by Rails (instead trusting the helpers to do their job), for now let's take a look at it (Listing 9.5).

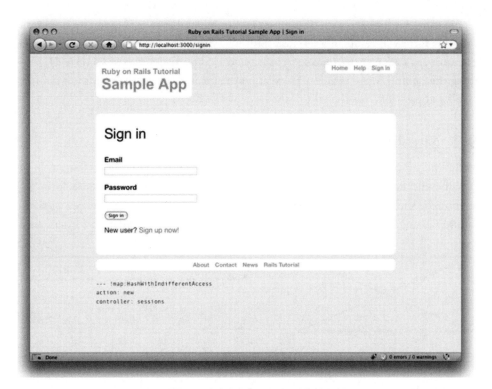

Figure 9.2   The signin form (/sessions/new).

Listing 9.5 HTML for the signin form produced by Listing 9.4.

```
<form action="/sessions" method="post">
  <div class="field">
    <label for="session_email">Email</label><br />
    <input id="session_email" name="session[email]" size="30" type="text" />

  </div>
  <div class="field">
    <label for="session_password">Password</label><br />
    <input id="session_password" name="session[password]" size="30"
           type="password" />
  </div>
  <div class="actions">
    <input id="session_submit" name="commit" type="submit" value="Sign in" />
  </div>
</form>
```

Comparing Listing 9.5 with Listing 8.5, you might be able to guess that submitting this form will result in a **params** hash where **params[:session][:email]** and **params[:session][:password]** correspond to the email and password fields. Handling this submission—and, in particular, authenticating users based on the submitted email and password—is the goal of the next two sections.

9.2 Signin Failure

As in the case of creating users (signup), the first step in creating sessions (signin) is to handle *invalid* input. We'll start by reviewing what happens when a form gets submitted, and then arrange for helpful error messages to appear in the case of signin failure (as mocked up in Figure 9.3.) Finally, we'll lay the foundation for successful

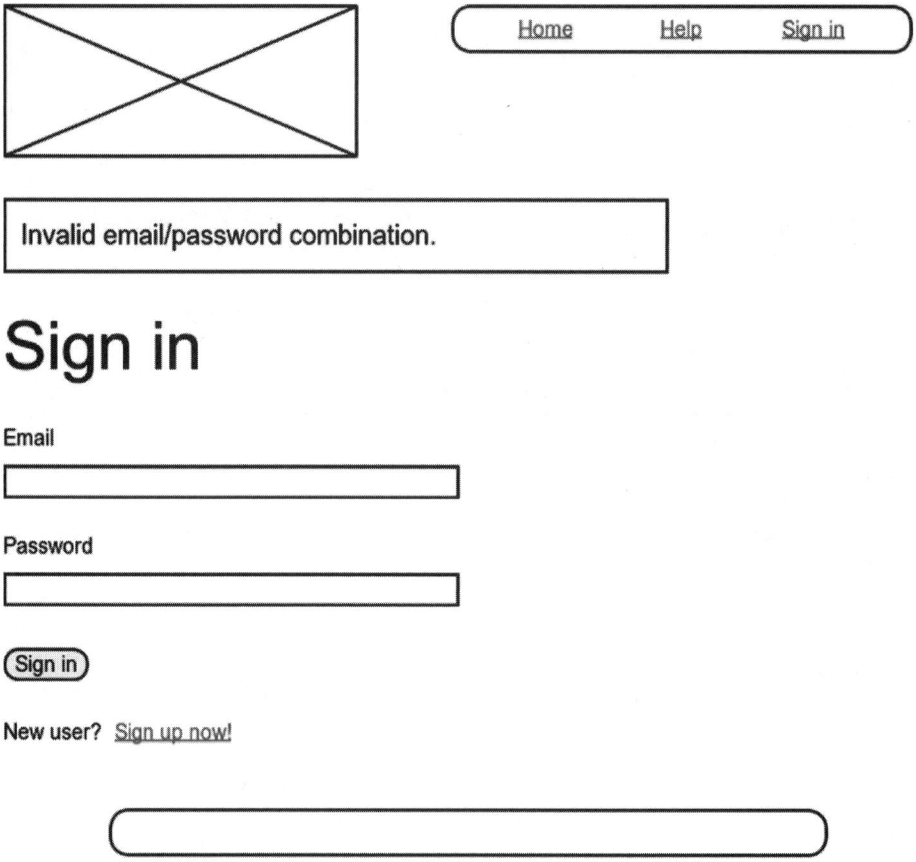

Figure 9.3   A mockup of signin failure.

signin (Section 9.3) by evaluating each signin submission based on the validity of its email/password combination.

9.2.1 Reviewing Form Submission

Let's start by defining a minimalist **create** action for the Sessions controller (Listing 9.6), which does nothing but render the **new** view. Submitting the /sessions/new form with blank fields then yields the result shown in Figure 9.4.

Listing 9.6 A preliminary version of the Sessions **create** action.
app/controllers/sessions_controller.rb

```
class SessionsController < ApplicationController
  .
  .
  .
  def create
    render 'new'
  end
  .
  .
  .
end
```

Carefully inspecting the debug information in Figure 9.4 shows that, as hinted at the end of Section 9.1.2, the submission results in a **params** hash containing the email and password under the key **:session**:

```
--- !map:ActiveSupport::HashWithIndifferentAccess
commit: Sign in
session: !ActiveSupport::HashWithIndifferentAccess
  password: ""
  email: ""
authenticity_token: B1065PA1oS5vqrv591dt9B22HGSWW0HbBtoHKbBKYDQ=
action: create
controller: sessions
```

As with the case of user signup (Figure 8.6) these parameters form a *nested* hash like the one we saw in Listing 4.5. In particular, **params** contains a nested hash of the form

```
{ :session => { :password => "", :email => "" } }
```

Figure 9.4   The initial failed signin, with **create** as in Listing 9.6.

This means that

```
params[:session]
```

is itself a hash:

```
{ :password => "", :email => "" }
```

As a result,

```
params[:session][:email]
```

is the submitted email address and

```
params[:session][:password]
```

is the submitted password.

In other words, inside the **create** action the **params** hash has all the information needed to authenticate users by email and password. Not coincidentally, we have already developed exactly the method needed: **User.authenticate** from Section 7.2.4 (Listing 7.12). Recalling that **authenticate** returns **nil** for an invalid authentication, our strategy for user signin can be summarized as follows:

```
def create
  user = User.authenticate(params[:session][:email],
                           params[:session][:password])
  if user.nil?
    # Create an error message and re-render the signin form.
  else
    # Sign the user in and redirect to the user's show page.
  end
end
```

9.2.2 Failed Signin (Test and Code)

In order to handle a failed signin attempt, first we need to determine that it's a failure. The tests follow the example from the analogous tests for user signup (Listing 8.6), as shown in Listing 9.7.

Listing 9.7 Tests for a failed signin attempt.
spec/controllers/sessions_controller_spec.rb

```
require 'spec_helper'

describe SessionsController do
  render_views
    .
    .
    .
  describe "POST 'create'" do

    describe "invalid signin" do
      before(:each) do
```

```
    @attr = { :email => "email@example.com", :password => "invalid" }
  end

  it "should re-render the new page" do
    post :create, :session => @attr
    response.should render_template('new')
  end

  it "should have the right title" do
    post :create, :session => @attr
    response.should have_selector("title", :content => "Sign in")
  end

  it "should have a flash.now message" do
    post :create, :session => @attr
    flash.now[:error].should =~ /invalid/i
  end
      end
    end
  end
end
```

The application code needed to get these tests to pass appears in Listing 9.8. As promised in Section 9.2.1, we extract the submitted email address and password from the **params** hash, and then pass them to the **User.authenticate** method. If the user is not authenticated (i.e., if it's **nil**), we set the title and re-render the signin form.[4] We'll handle the other branch of the if-else statement in Section 9.3; for now we'll just leave a descriptive comment.

Listing 9.8 Code for a failed signin attempt.
app/controllers/sessions_controller.rb

```
class SessionsController < ApplicationController
  .
  .
  .
  def create
    user = User.authenticate(params[:session][:email],
                             params[:session][:password])
    if user.nil?
      flash.now[:error] = "Invalid email/password combination."
```

---

4. If case you're wondering why we use **user** instead of **@user** in Listing 9.8, it's because this user variable is never needed in any view, so there is no reason to use an instance variable here. (Using **@user** still works, though.)

```
      @title = "Sign in"
      render 'new'
    else
      # Sign the user in and redirect to the user's show page.
    end
  end
  .
  .
  .
end
```

Recall from Section 8.4.2 that we displayed signup errors using the User model error messages. Since the session isn't an Active Record model, this strategy won't work here, so instead we've put a message in the flash (or, rather, in `flash.now`; see Box 9.1). Thanks to the flash message display in the site layout (Listing 8.16), the `flash[:error]` message automatically gets displayed; thanks to the Blueprint CSS, it automatically gets nice styling (Figure 9.5).

Figure 9.5   A failed signin (with a flash message).

Box 9.1   Flash Dot Now

There's a subtle difference between **flash** and **flash.now**. The **flash** variable is designed to be used before a *redirect*, and it persists on the resulting page for one request—that is, it appears once, and disappears when you click on another link. Unfortunately, this means that if we *don't* redirect, and instead simply render a page (as in Listing 9.8), the flash message persists for *two* requests: it appears on the rendered page but is still waiting for a "redirect" (i.e., a second request), and thus appears *again* if you click a link.

   To avoid this weird behavior, when **render**ing rather than **redirect**ing we use **flash.now** instead of **flash**. The **flash.now** object is specifically designed for displaying flash messages on rendered pages. If you ever find yourself wondering why a flash message is showing up where you don't expect it, chances are good that you need to replace **flash** with **flash.now**.

9.3   Signin Success

Having handled a failed signin, we now need to actually sign a user in. A hint of where we're going—the user profile page, with modified navigation links—is mocked up in Figure 9.6.[5] Getting there will require some of the most challenging Ruby programming so far in this tutorial, so hang in there through the end and be prepared for a little heavy lifting. Happily, the first step is easy—completing the Sessions controller **create** action is a snap. Unfortunately, it's also a cheat.

9.3.1   The Completed **create** Action

Filling in the area now occupied by the signin comment (Listing 9.8) is simple: upon successful signin, we sign the user in using the **sign_in** function, and then redirect to the profile page (Listing 9.9). We see now why this is a cheat: alas, **sign_in** doesn't currently exist. Writing it will occupy the rest of this section.

Listing 9.9   The completed Sessions controller **create** action (not yet working).
app/controllers/sessions_controller.rb

```
class SessionsController < ApplicationController
  .
  .
  .
  def create
```

---

5. Image from http://www.flickr.com/photos/hermanusbackpackers/3343254977/.

```
    user = User.authenticate(params[:session][:email],
                             params[:session][:password])
  if user.nil?
    flash.now[:error] = "Invalid email/password combination."
    @title = "Sign in"
    render 'new'
  else
    sign_in user
    redirect_to user
  end
end
  .
  .
  .

end
```

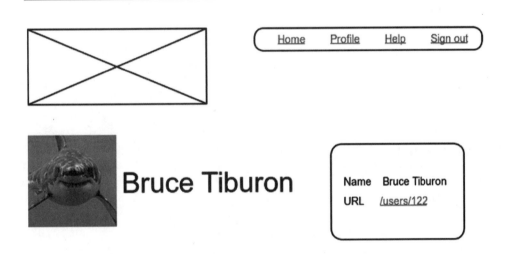

Figure 9.6 A mockup of the user profile after a successful signin (with updated nav links).

Even though we lack the **sign_in** function, we can still write the tests (Listing 9.10). (We'll fill in the body of the first test in Section 9.3.3.)

Listing 9.10 Pending tests for user signin (to be completed in Section 9.3.3).
spec/controllers/sessions_controller_spec.rb

```
describe SessionsController do
  .
  .
  .
  describe "POST 'create'" do
    .
    .
    .
    describe "with valid email and password" do

      before(:each) do
        @user = Factory(:user)
        @attr = { :email => @user.email, :password => @user.password }
      end

      it "should sign the user in" do
        post :create, :session => @attr
        # Fill in with tests for a signed-in user.
      end

      it "should redirect to the user show page" do
        post :create, :session => @attr
        response.should redirect_to(user_path(@user))
      end
    end
  end
end
```

These tests don't pass yet, but they're a good start.

9.3.2 Remember Me

We're now in a position to start implementing our signin model, namely, remembering user signin status "forever" and clearing the session only when the user explicitly signs out. The signin functions themselves will end up crossing the traditional Model-View-Controller lines; in particular, several signin functions will need to be available in both controllers and views. You may recall from Section 4.2.5 that Ruby provides a *module* facility for packaging functions together and including them in multiple places, and that's the plan for the authentication functions. We could make an entirely new module for authentication, but the Sessions controller already comes equipped with a module, namely, **SessionsHelper**. Moreover, helpers are automatically included in Rails views, so all we need to do to use the Sessions helper functions in controllers is to include the module into the Application controller (Listing 9.11).

Listing 9.11 Including the Sessions helper module into the Application controller.
app/controllers/application_controller.rb

```
class ApplicationController < ActionController::Base
  protect_from_forgery
  include SessionsHelper
end
```

By default, all the helpers are available in the **views** but not in the controllers. We need the methods from the Sessions helper in both places, so we have to include it explicitly.

Box 9.2   Sessions and Cookies

Because HTTP is a *stateless protocol*, web applications requiring user signin must implement a way to track each user's progress from page to page. One technique for maintaining the user signin status is to use a traditional Rails session (via the special **session** function) to store a *remember token* equal to the user's id:

```
session[:remember_token] = user.id
```

This **session** object makes the user id available from page to page by storing it in a cookie that expires upon browser close. On each page, the application can simply call

```
User.find_by_id(session[:remember_token])
```

to retrieve the user. Because of the way Rails handles sessions, this process is secure; if a malicious user tries to spoof the user id, Rails will detect a mismatch based on a special *session id* generated for each session.

   For our application's design choice, which involves *persistent* sessions—that is, signin status that lasts even after browser close—storing the user id is a security hole. As soon as we break the tie between the special session id and the stored user id, a malicious user could sign in as that user with a **remember_token** equal to the user's id. To fix this flaw, we generate a unique, secure remember token for each user based on the user's salt and id. Moreover, a *permanent* remember token would also represent a security hole—by inspecting the browser cookies, a malicious user could find the token and then use it to sign in from any other computer, any time. We solve this by adding a *timestamp* to the token, and reset the token every time the user signs into the application. This results in a persistent session essentially impervious to attack.

Now we're ready for the first signin element, the **sign_in** function itself. Our authentication method is to place a *remember token* as a cookie on the user's browser (Box 9.2), and then use the token to find the user record in the database as the user moves from page to page (implemented in Section 9.3.3). The result, Listing 9.12, pushes two things onto the stack: the **cookies** hash and **current_user**.[6] Let's start popping them off.

Listing 9.12 The complete (but not-yet-working) **sign_in** function.
app/helpers/sessions_helper.rb

```
module SessionsHelper

  def sign_in(user)
    cookies.permanent.signed[:remember_token] = [user.id, user.salt]
    self.current_user = user
  end
end
```

Listing 9.12 introduces the **cookies** utility supplied by Rails. We can use **cookies** as if it were a hash; each element in the cookie is itself a hash of two elements, a **value** and an optional **expires** date. For example, we could implement user signin by placing a cookie with value equal to the user's id that expires 20 years from now:

```
cookies[:remember_token] = { :value   => user.id,
                             :expires => 20.years.from_now.utc }
```

(This code uses one of the convenient Rails time helpers, as discussed in Box 9.3.) We could then retrieve the user with code like

```
User.find_by_id(cookies[:remember_token])
```

Of course, **cookies** isn't *really* a hash, since assigning to **cookies** actually *saves* a piece of text on the browser (as seen in Figure 9.7), but part of the beauty of Rails is that it lets you forget about that detail and concentrate on writing the application.

---

6. On some systems, you might need to use **self.current_user = user** to get the upcoming tests to pass.

Box 9.3   Cookies Expire 20.years.from_now

You may recall from Section 4.4.2 that Ruby lets you add methods to *any* class, even built-in ones. In that section, we added a **palindrome?** method to the **String** class (and discovered as a result that **"deified"** is a palindrome), and we also saw how Rails adds a **blank?** method to class **Object** (so that **""**.blank?, **" "**.blank?, and **nil.blank?** are all **true**). The cookie code in Listing 9.12 (which internally sets a cookie that expires **20.years.from_now**) shows yet another example of this practice, through one of Rails' *time helpers*, which are methods added to **Fixnum** (the base class for numbers):

```
$ rails console
>> 1.year.from_now
=> Sun, 13 Mar 2011 03:38:55 UTC +00:00
>> 10.weeks.ago
=> Sat, 02 Jan 2010 03:39:14 UTC +00:00
```

Rails adds other helpers, too:

```
>> 1.kilobyte
=> 1024
>> 5.megabytes
=> 5242880
```

These are useful for upload validations, making it easy to restrict, say, image uploads to **5.megabytes**.

Though it must be used with caution, the flexibility to add methods to built-in classes allows for extraordinarily natural additions to plain Ruby. Indeed, much of the elegance of Rails ultimately derives from the malleability of the underlying Ruby language.

Unfortunately, using the user id in this manner is insecure for the same reason discussed in Box 9.2: a malicious user could simulate a cookie with the given id, thereby allowing access to any user in the system. The traditional solution before Rails 3 was to create a secure remember token associated with the User model to be used in place of the user id (see, e.g., the Rails 2.3 version of *Rails Tutorial*).

This pattern became so common that Rails 3 now implements it for us using **cookies.permanent.signed**:

```
cookies.permanent.signed[:remember_token] = [user.id, user.salt]
```

Figure 9.7   A secure remember token.

The assignment value on the right-hand side is an array consisting of a unique identifier (i.e., the user's id) and a secure value used to create a digital signature to prevent the kind of attacks described in Section 7.2. In particular, since we went to the trouble of creating a secure salt in Section 7.2.3, we can re-use that value here to sign the remember token. Under the hood, using **permanent** causes Rails to set the expiration to **20.years.from_now**, and **signed** makes the cookie secure, so that the user's id is never exposed in the browser. (We'll see how to retrieve the user using the remember token in Section 9.3.3.)

The code above shows the importance of using **new_record?** in Listing 7.10 to save the salt only upon user creation. Otherwise, the salt would change each time the user was saved, preventing the retrieval of the session's user in Section 9.3.3.

9.3.3 Current User

In this section, we'll learn how to get and set the session's current user. Let's look again at the **sign_in** function to see where we are:

```
module SessionsHelper

  def sign_in(user)
    cookies.permanent.signed[:remember_token] = [user.id, user.salt]
    self.current_user = user
  end
end
```

Our focus now is the second line:

```
self.current_user = user
```

The purpose of this line is to create **current_user**, accessible in both controllers and views, which will allow constructions such as

```
<%= current_user.name %>
```

and

```
redirect_to current_user
```

The principal goal of this section is to define **current_user**.

To describe the behavior of the remaining signin machinery, we'll first fill in the test for signing a user in (Listing 9.13).

Listing 9.13 Filling in the test for signing the user in.
spec/controllers/sessions_controller_spec.rb

```
describe SessionsController do
  .
  .
  .
  describe "POST 'create'" do
```

```
    .
    .
    .
  describe "with valid email and password" do

    before(:each) do
      @user = Factory(:user)
      @attr = { :email => @user.email, :password => @user.password }
    end

    it "should sign the user in" do
      post :create, :session => @attr
      controller.current_user.should == @user
      controller.should be_signed_in
    end

    it "should redirect to the user show page" do
      post :create, :session => @attr
      response.should redirect_to(user_path(@user))
    end
  end
 end
end
```

The new test uses the **controller** variable (which is available inside Rails tests) to check that the **current_user** variable is set to the signed-in user, and that the user is signed in:

```
it "should sign the user in" do
  post :create, :session => @attr
  controller.current_user.should == @user
  controller.should be_signed_in
end
```

The second line may be a little confusing at this point, but you can guess based on the RSpec convention for boolean methods that

```
controller.should be_signed_in
```

is equivalent to

```
controller.signed_in?.should be_true
```

This is a hint that we will be defining a **signed_in?** method that returns **true** if a user is signed in and **false** otherwise. Moreover, the **signed_in?** method will be attached to the *controller*, not to a user, which is why we write **controller.signed_in?** instead of **current_user.signed_in?**. (If no user is signed in, how could we call **signed_in?** on it?)

To start writing the code for **current_user**, note that the line

```
self.current_user = user
```

is an *assignment*. Ruby has a special syntax for defining such an assignment function, shown in Listing 9.14.

Listing 9.14 Defining assignment to **current_user**.
app/helpers/sessions_helper.rb

```
module SessionsHelper

  def sign_in(user)
    .
    .
    .
  end

  def current_user=(user)
    @current_user = user
  end
end
```

This might look confusing, but it simply defines a method **current_user=** expressly designed to handle assignment to **current_user**. Its one argument is the right-hand side of the assignment, in this case the user to be signed in. The one-line method body just sets an instance variable **@current_user**, effectively storing the user for later use.

In ordinary Ruby, we could define a second method, **current_user**, designed to return the value of **@current_user** (Listing 9.15).

Listing 9.15 A tempting but useless definition for **current_user**.

```
module SessionsHelper

  def sign_in(user)
    .
    .
    .
```

```
    end

  def current_user=(user)
    @current_user = user
  end

  def current_user
    @current_user      # Useless! Don't use this line.
  end
end
```

If we did this, we would effectively replicate the functionality of **attr_accessor**, first
seen in Section 4.4.5 and used to make the virtual **password** attribute in Section 7.1.1.[7]
The problem is that it utterly fails to solve our problem: with the code in Listing 9.15,
the user's signin status would be forgotten: as soon as the user went to another
page—poof!—the session would end and the user would be automatically signed out.

To avoid this problem, we can find the session user corresponding to the cookie
created by the code in Listing 9.12, as shown in Listing 9.16.

Listing 9.16 Finding the current user by **remember_token**.
app/helpers/sessions_helper.rb

```
module SessionsHelper
  .
  .
  .
  def current_user
    @current_user ||= user_from_remember_token
  end

  private

    def user_from_remember_token
      User.authenticate_with_salt(*remember_token)
    end

    def remember_token
      cookies.signed[:remember_token] || [nil, nil]
    end
end
```

7. In fact, the two are exactly equivalent; **attr_accessor** is merely a convenient way to create just such
getter/setter methods automatically.

This code uses several more advanced features of Ruby, so let's take a moment to examine them.

First, Listing 9.16 uses the common but initially obscure **||=** ("or equals") assignment operator (Box 9.4). Its effect is to set the **@current_user** instance variable to the user corresponding to the remember token, but only if **@current_user** is undefined. In other words, the construction

```
@current_user ||= user_from_remember_token
```

calls the **user_from_remember_token** method the first time **current_user** is called, but on subsequent invocations returns **@current_user** without calling **user_from_remember_token**.[8]

> **Box 9.4   What the *$@! is ||= ?**
>
> The ||= construction is very Rubyish—that is, it is highly characteristic of the Ruby language—and hence important to learn if you plan on doing much Ruby programming. Though at first it may seem mysterious, *or equals* is easy to understand by analogy.
>
> We start by noting a common idiom for changing a currently defined variable. Many computer programs involve incrementing a variable, as in
>
> ```
> x = x + 1
> ```
>
> Most languages provide a syntactic shortcut for this operation; in Ruby (and in C, C++, Perl, Python, Java, etc.), it appears as follows:
>
> ```
> x += 1
> ```
>
> Analogous constructs exist for other operators as well:
>
> ```
> $ rails console
> >> x = 1
> => 1
> >> x += 1
> => 2
> >> x *= 3
> => 6
> >> x -= 7
> => -1
> ```

---

8. This optimization technique to avoid repeated function calls is known as memorization.

In each case, the pattern is that **x = x O y** and **x O= y** are equivalent for any operator **O**.

Another common Ruby pattern is assigning to a variable if it's **nil** but otherwise leaving it alone. Recalling the *or* operator **||** seen in Section 4.2.3, we can write this as follows:

```
>> @user
=> nil
>> @user = @user || "the user"
=> "the user"
>> @user = @user || "another user"
=> "the user"
```

Since **nil** is false in a boolean context, the first assignment is **nil || "the user"**, which evaluates to **"the user"**; similarly, the second assignment is **"the user" || "another user"**, which also evaluates to **"the user"**—since strings are **true** in a boolean context, the series of **||** expressions terminates after the first expression is evaluated. (This practice of evaluating **||** expressions from left to right and stopping on the first true value is known as *short-circuit evaluation*.)

Comparing the console sessions for the various operators, we see that **@user = @user || value** follows the **x = x O y** pattern with **||** in the place of **O**, which suggests the following equivalent construction:

```
>> @user ||= "the user"
=> "the user"
```

Voilà!

Listing 9.16 also uses the * operator, which allows us to use a two-element array as an argument to a method expecting two variables, as we can see in this console session:

```
$ rails console
>> def foo(bar, baz)
?>   bar + baz
?> end
=> nil
>> foo(1, 2)
=> 3
>> foo(*[2, 3])
=> 5
```

The reason this is needed in Listing 9.16 is that **cookies.signed[:remember_me]** returns an array of two elements—the user id and the salt—but (following usual Ruby conventions) we want the **authenticate_with_salt** method to take two arguments, so that it can be invoked with

```
User.authenticate_with_salt(id, salt)
```

(There's no fundamental reason that **authenticate_with_salt** couldn't take an array as an argument, but it wouldn't be idiomatically correct Ruby.)

Finally, in the **remember_token** helper method defined by Listing 9.16, we use the || operator to return an *array* of **nil** values if **cookies.signed[:remember_me]** itself is **nil**:

```
cookies.signed[:remember_token] || [nil, nil]
```

The reason for this code is that the support for signed cookies inside Rails tests is still immature, and a **nil** value for the cookie causes spurious test breakage. Returning **[nil, nil]** instead fixes the issue.[9]

The final step to getting the code in Listing 9.16 working is to define an **authenticate_with_salt** class method. This method, which is analogous to the original **authenticate** method defined in Listing 7.12, is shown in Listing 9.17.

Listing 9.17 Adding an **authenticate_with_salt** method to the User model.
app/models/user.rb

```
class User < ActiveRecord::Base
  .
  .
  .

  def self.authenticate(email, submitted_password)
    user = find_by_email(email)
    return nil  if user.nil?
    return user if user.has_password?(submitted_password)
  end

  def self.authenticate_with_salt(id, cookie_salt)
    user = find_by_id(id)
    (user && user.salt == cookie_salt) ? user : nil
```

---

9. This feels like the tail wagging the dog, but that's the price we pay for being on the cutting edge.

```
  end
      .
      .
      .
  end
```

Here **authenticate_with_salt** firsts finds the user by unique id, and then verifies that the salt stored in the cookie is the correct one for that user.

It's worth noting that this implementation of **authenticate_with_salt** is identical in function to the following code, which more closely parallels the **authenticate** method:

```
def self.authenticate_with_salt(id, cookie_salt)
  user = find_by_id(id)
  return nil  if user.nil?
  return user if user.salt == cookie_salt
end
```

In both cases, the method returns the user if **user** is not **nil** and the user salt matches the cookie's salt, and returns **nil** otherwise. On the other hand, code like

```
(user && user.salt == cookie_salt) ? user : nil
```

is common in idiomatically correct Ruby, so I thought it was a good idea to introduce it. This code uses the strange but useful *ternary operator* to compress an **if-else** construction into one line (Box 9.5).

Box 9.5   10 Types of People

There are 10 kinds of people in the world: Those who like the ternary operator, those who don't, and those who don't know about it. (If you happen to be in the third category, soon you won't be any longer.)

When you do a lot of programming, you quickly learn that one of the most common bits of control flow goes something like this:

```
if boolean?
  do_one_thing
else
  do_something_else
end
```

Ruby, like many other languages (including C/C++, Perl, PHP, and Java), allows you to replace this with a much more compact expression using the *ternary operator* (so called because it consists of three parts):

```
boolean? ? do_one_thing : do_something_else
```

You can also use the ternary operator to replace assignment:

```
if boolean?
  var = foo
else
  var = bar
end
```

becomes

```
var = boolean? ? foo : bar
```

The ternary operator is common in idiomatic Ruby, so it's a good idea to look for opportunities to use it.

At this point, the signin test is almost passing; the only thing remaining is to define the required **signed_in?** boolean method. Happily, it's easy with the use of the "not" operator **!**: a user is signed in if **current_user** is not **nil** (Listing 9.18).

Listing 9.18 The **signed_in?** helper method.
app/helpers/sessions_helper.rb

```
module SessionsHelper
  .
  .
  .
  def signed_in?
    !current_user.nil?
  end

  private
  .
  .
  .
end
```

Though it's already useful for the test, we'll put the **signed_in?** method to even better use in Section 9.4.3 and again in Chapter 10.

With that, all the tests should pass.

9.4 Signing Out

As discussed in Section 9.1, our authentication model is to keep users signed in until they sign out explicitly. In this section, we'll add this necessary signout capability. Once we're done, we'll add some integration tests to put our authentication machinery through its paces.

9.4.1 Destroying Sessions

So far, the Sessions controller actions have followed the RESTful convention of using **new** for a signin page and **create** to complete the signin. We'll continue this theme by using a **destroy** action to delete sessions, i.e., to sign out.

In order to test the signout action, we first need a way to sign in within a test. The easiest way to do this is to use the **controller** object we saw in Section 9.3.3 and use the **sign_in** helper to sign in the given user. In order to use the resulting **test_sign_in** function in all our tests, we need to put it in the spec helper file, as shown in Listing 9.19.[10]

Listing 9.19 A **test_sign_in** function to simulate user signin inside tests.
spec/spec_helper.rb

```
.
.
.
Rspec.configure do |config|
  .
  .
  .
  def test_sign_in(user)
    controller.sign_in(user)
  end
end
```

After running **test_sign_in**, the **current_user** will not be **nil**, so **signed_in?** will be **true**.

---

10. If you are using Spork, this will be located inside the **Spork.prefork** block.

With this spec helper in hand, the test for signout is straightforward: sign in as a (factory) user and then hit the **destroy** action and verify that the user gets signed out (Listing 9.20).

Listing 9.20 A test for destroying a session (user signout).
spec/controllers/sessions_controller_spec.rb

```
describe SessionsController do
  .
  .
  .
  describe "DELETE 'destroy'" do

    it "should sign a user out" do
      test_sign_in(Factory(:user))
      delete :destroy
      controller.should_not be_signed_in
      response.should redirect_to(root_path)
    end
  end
end
```

The only novel element here is the **delete** method, which issues an HTTP DELETE request (in analogy with the **get** and **post** methods seen in previous tests), as required by the REST conventions (Table 9.1).

As with user signin, which relied on the **sign_in** function, user signout just defers the hard work to a **sign_out** function (Listing 9.21).

Listing 9.21 Destroying a session (user signout).
app/controllers/sessions_controller.rb

```
class SessionsController < ApplicationController
  .
  .
  .
  def destroy
    sign_out
    redirect_to root_path
  end
end
```

As with the other authentication elements, we'll put **sign_out** in the Sessions helper module (Listing 9.22).

Listing 9.22 The **sign_out** method in the Sessions helper module.
app/helpers/sessions_helper.rb

```
module SessionsHelper

  def sign_in(user)
    cookies.permanent.signed[:remember_token] = [user.id, user.salt]
    self.current_user = user
  end
  .
  .
  .
  def sign_out
    cookies.delete(:remember_token)
    self.current_user = nil
  end

  private
    .
    .
    .
end
```

As you can see, the **sign_out** method effectively undoes the **sign_in** method by deleting the remember token and by setting the current user to **nil**.[11]

9.4.2 Signin Upon Signup

In principle, we are now done with authentication, but as currently constructed there are no links to the signin or signout actions. Moreover, newly registered users might be confused, as they are not signed in by default.

We'll fix the second problem first, starting with testing that a new user is automatically signed in (Listing 9.23).

Listing 9.23 Testing that newly signed-up users are also signed in.
spec/controllers/users_controller_spec.rb

```
require 'spec_helper'

describe UsersController do
```

---

11. You can learn about things like **cookies.delete** by reading the cookies entry in the Rails API. (Since Rails API links tend to go stale quickly, use your Google-fu to find a current version.)

```
  render_views
  .
  .
  .
  describe "POST 'create'" do
    .
    .
    .
    describe "success" do
      .
      .
      .
      it "should sign the user in" do
        post :create, :user => @attr
        controller.should be_signed_in
      end
      .
      .
      .
    end
  end
end
```

With the **sign_in** method from Section 9.3, getting this test to pass by actually signing in the user is easy: just add **sign_in @user** right after saving the user to the database (Listing 9.24).

Listing 9.24 Signing in the user upon signup.
app/controllers/users_controller.rb

```
class UsersController < ApplicationController
  .
  .
  def create
    @user = User.new(params[:user])
    if @user.save
      sign_in @user
      flash[:success] = "Welcome to the Sample App!"
      redirect_to @user
    else
      @title = "Sign up"
      render 'new'
    end
  end
```

9.4.3   Changing the Layout Links

We come finally to a practical application of all our signin/out work: we'll change the layout links based on signin status. In particular, as seen in the Figure 9.6 mockup, we'll arrange for the links change when users sign in or sign out, and we'll also add a profile link to the user show page for signed-in users.

We start with two integration tests: one to check that a **"Sign in"** link appears for non-signed-in users, and one to check that a **"Sign out"** link appears for signed-in users; both cases verify that the link goes to the proper URL. We'll put these tests in the layout links test we created in Section 5.2.1; the result appears in Listing 9.25.

Listing 9.25 Tests for the signin/signout links on the site layout.
spec/requests/layout_links_spec.rb

```ruby
describe "Layout links" do
  .
  .
  .
  describe "when not signed in" do
    it "should have a signin link" do
      visit root_path
      response.should have_selector("a", :href => signin_path,
                                         :content => "Sign in")
    end
  end

  describe "when signed in" do

    before(:each) do
      @user = Factory(:user)
      visit signin_path
      fill_in :email,    :with => @user.email
      fill_in :password, :with => @user.password
      click_button
    end

    it "should have a signout link" do
      visit root_path
      response.should have_selector("a", :href => signout_path,
                                         :content => "Sign out")
    end

    it "should have a profile link"
  end
end
```

Here the **before(:each)** block signs in by visiting the signin page and submitting a valid email/password pair.[12] We do this instead of using the **test_sign_in** function from Listing 9.19 because **test_sign_in** doesn't work inside integration tests for some reason. (See Section 9.6 for an exercise to make an **integration_sign_in** function for use in integration tests.)

The application code uses an if-then branching structure inside of Embedded Ruby, using the **signed_in?** method defined in Listing 9.18:

```
<% if signed_in? %>
<li><%= link_to "Sign out", signout_path, :method => :delete %></li>
<% else %>
<li><%= link_to "Sign in", signin_path %></li>
<% end %>
```

Notice that the signout link passes a hash argument indicating that it should submit with an HTTP DELETE request.[13] With this snippet added, the full header partial appears as in Listing 9.26.

Listing 9.26 Changing the layout links for signed-in users.
app/views/layouts/_header.html.erb

```
<header>
  <%= link_to logo, root_path %>
  <nav class="round">
    <ul>
      <li><%= link_to "Home", root_path %></li>
      <li><%= link_to "Help", help_path %></li>
      <% if signed_in? %>
      <li><%= link_to "Sign out", signout_path, :method => :delete %></li>
      <% else %>
      <li><%= link_to "Sign in", signin_path %></li>
      <% end %>
    </ul>
  </nav>
</header>
```

In Listing 9.26 we've used the **logo** helper from the Chapter 5 exercises (Section 5.5); in case you didn't work that exercise, the answer appears in Listing 9.27.

---

12. Note that we can use symbols in place of strings for the labels, e.g., **fill_in :email** instead of **fill_in "Email"**. We used the latter in Listing 8.22, but by now it shouldn't surprise you that Rails allows us to use symbols instead.

13. Web browsers can't actually issue DELETE requests; Rails fakes it with JavaScript.

Listing 9.27 A helper for the site logo.
app/helpers/application_helper.rb

```
module ApplicationHelper
  .
  .
  .
  def logo
    image_tag("logo.png", :alt => "Sample App", :class => "round")
  end
end
```

Finally, let's add a profile link. The test (Listing 9.28) and application code (Listing 9.29) are both straightforward. Notice that the profile link's URL is simply **current_user**,[14] which is our first use of that helpful method. (It won't be our last.)

Listing 9.28 A test for a profile link.
spec/requests/layout_links_spec.rb

```
describe "Layout links" do
  .
  .
  .
  describe "when signed in" do
    .
    .
    .
    it "should have a profile link" do
      visit root_path
      response.should have_selector("a", :href => user_path(@user),
                                         :content => "Profile")
    end
  end
end
```

Listing 9.29 Adding a profile link.
app/views/layouts/_header.html.erb

```
<header>
  <%= link_to logo, root_path %>
  <nav class="round">
```

---

14. Recall from Section 7.3.3 that we can link directly to a user object and allow Rails to figure out the appropriate URL.

```
  <ul>
    <li><%= link_to "Home", root_path %></li>
    <% if signed_in? %>
    <li><%= link_to "Profile", current_user %></li>
    <% end %>
    <li><%= link_to "Help", help_path %></li>
    <% if signed_in? %>
    <li><%= link_to "Sign out", signout_path, :method => :delete %></li>
    <% else %>
    <li><%= link_to "Sign in", signin_path %></li>
    <% end %>
  </ul>
  </nav>
</header>
```

With the code in this section, a signed-in user now sees both signout and profile links, as expected (Figure 9.8).

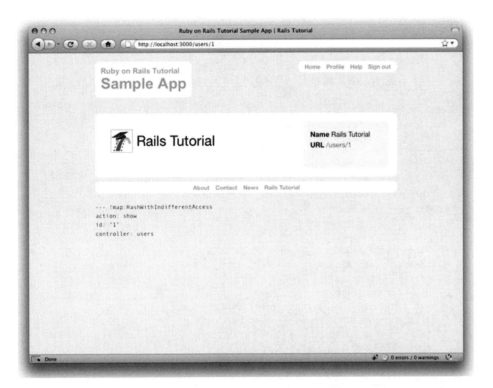

Figure 9.8   A signed-in user with signout and profile links.

9.4.4 Signin/Out Integration Tests

As a capstone to our hard work on authentication, we'll finish with integration tests for signin and signout (placed in the **users_spec.rb** file for convenience). RSpec integration testing is expressive enough that Listing 9.30 should need little explanation; I especially like the use of **click_link "Sign out"**, which not only simulates a browser clicking the signout link, but also raises an error if no such link exists—thereby testing the URL, the named route, the link text, and the changing of the layout links, all in one line. If that's not an *integration* test, I don't know what is.

Listing 9.30 An integration test for signing in and out.
spec/requests/users_spec.rb

```
require 'spec_helper'

describe "Users" do

  describe "signup" do
    .
    .
    .
  end

  describe "sign in/out" do

    describe "failure" do
      it "should not sign a user in" do
        visit signin_path
        fill_in :email,    :with => ""
        fill_in :password, :with => ""
        click_button
        response.should have_selector("div.flash.error", :content => "Invalid")
      end
    end

    describe "success" do
      it "should sign a user in and out" do
        user = Factory(:user)
        visit signin_path
        fill_in :email,    :with => user.email
        fill_in :password, :with => user.password
        click_button
        controller.should be_signed_in
        click_link "Sign out"
        controller.should_not be_signed_in
```

```
      end
    end
  end
end
```

9.5 Conclusion

We've covered a lot of ground in this chapter, transforming our promising but unformed application into a site capable of the full suite of registration and login behaviors. All that is needed to complete the authentication functionality is to restrict access to pages based on signin status and user identity. We'll accomplish this task en route to giving users the ability to edit their information and giving administrators the ability to remove users from the system.

Before moving on, merge your changes back into the master branch:

```
$ git add .
$ git commit -am "Done with sign in"
$ git checkout master
$ git merge sign-in-out
```

9.6 Exercises

The second and third exercises are more difficult than usual. Solving them will require some outside research (e.g., Rails API reading and Google searches), and they can be skipped without loss of continuity.

1. Several of the integration specs use the same code to sign a user in. Replace that code with the **integration_sign_in** function in Listing 9.31 and verify that the tests still pass.
2. Use **session** instead of **cookies** so that users are automatically signed out when they close their browsers.[15] *Hint:* Do a Google search on "Rails session".

---

15. Somewhat confusingly, we've used **cookies** to implement sessions, and **session** is implemented with cookies!

3. **(Advanced)** Some sites use secure HTTP (HTTPS) for their signin pages. Search online to learn how to use HTTPS in Rails, and then secure the Sessions controller **new** and **create** actions. *Extra challenge:* Write tests for the HTTPS functionality. (*Note:* I suggest doing this exercise only in development, which does not require obtaining an SSL certificate or setting up the SSL encryption machinery. Actually deploying an SSL-enabled site is *much* more difficult.)

Listing 9.31 A function to sign users in inside of integration tests.
spec/spec_helper.rb

```
.
.
.
Rspec.configure do |config|
  .
  .
  .
  def test_sign_in(user)
    controller.sign_in(user)
  end

  def integration_sign_in(user)
    visit signin_path
    fill_in :email,    :with => user.email
    fill_in :password, :with => user.password
    click_button
  end
end
```

CHAPTER 10

Updating, Showing, and Deleting Users

In this chapter, we will complete the REST actions for the Users resource (Table 6.2) by adding **edit**, **update**, **index**, and **destroy** actions. We'll start by giving users the ability to update their profiles, which will also provide a natural opportunity to enforce a security model (made possible by the authentication code in Chapter 9). Then we'll make a listing of all users (also requiring authentication), which will motivate the introduction of sample data and pagination. Finally, we'll add the ability to destroy users, wiping them clear from the database. Since we can't allow just any user to have such dangerous powers, we'll take care to create a privileged class of administrative users (admins) along the way.

To get started, let's start work on an **updating-users** topic branch:

```
$ git checkout -b updating-users
```

10.1 Updating Users

The pattern for editing user information closely parallels that for creating new users (Chapter 8). Instead of a **new** action rendering a view for new users, we have an **edit** action rendering a view to edit users; instead of **create** responding to a POST request, we have an **update** action responding to a PUT request (Box 3.1). The biggest difference is that, while anyone can sign up, only the current user should be able to update their information. This means that we need to enforce access control so that only authorized users can edit and update; the authentication machinery from Chapter 9 will allow us to use a *before filter* to ensure that this is the case.

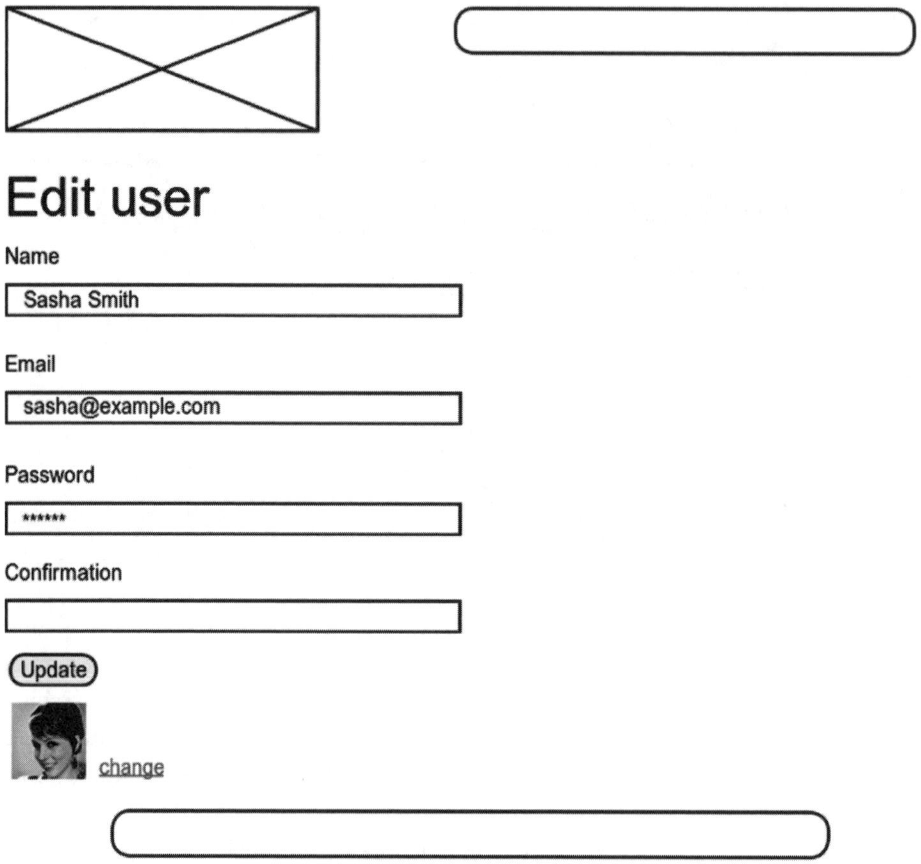

Edit user

Name

| Sasha Smith |

Email

| sasha@example.com |

Password

| ****** |

Confirmation

| |

(Update)

<u>change</u>

Figure 10.1   A mockup of the user edit page.

10.1.1   Edit Form

We start with tests for the edit form, whose mockup appears in Figure 10.1.[1] Two are analogous to tests we saw for the **new** user page (Listing 8.1), checking for the proper response and title; the third test makes sure that there is a link to edit the user's Gravatar image (Section 7.3.2). If you poke around the Gravatar site, you'll see that the page to add or edit images is (somewhat oddly) located at `http://gravatar.com/emails`, so we test the **edit** page for a link with that URL.[2] The result is shown in Listing 10.1.

---

1. Image from http://www.flickr.com/photos/sashawolff/4598355045/.

2. The Gravatar site actually redirects this to `http://en.gravatar.com/emails`, which is for English language users, but I've omitted the en part to account for the use of other languages.

Listing 10.1 Tests for the user **edit** action.
spec/controllers/users_controller_spec.rb

```ruby
require 'spec_helper'

describe UsersController do
  render_views
  .
  .
  .
  describe "GET 'edit'" do

    before(:each) do
      @user = Factory(:user)
      test_sign_in(@user)
    end

    it "should be successful" do
      get :edit, :id => @user
      response.should be_success
    end

    it "should have the right title" do
      get :edit, :id => @user
      response.should have_selector("title", :content => "Edit user")
    end

    it "should have a link to change the Gravatar" do
      get :edit, :id => @user
      gravatar_url = "http://gravatar.com/emails"
      response.should have_selector("a", :href => gravatar_url,
                                         :content => "change")
    end
  end
end
```

Here we've made sure to use **test_sign_in(@user)** to sign in as the user in anticipation of protecting the edit page from unauthorized access (Section 10.2). Otherwise, these tests would break as soon as we implemented our authentication code.

Note from Table 6.2 that the proper URL for a user's edit page is /users/1/edit (assuming the user's id is 1). Recall that the id of the user is available in the **params[:id]** variable, which means that we can find the user with the code in Listing 10.2. This uses **find** to find the relevant user in the database, and then sets the **@title** variable to the proper value.

Listing 10.2 The user **edit** action.
app/controllers/users_controller.rb

```ruby
class UsersController < ApplicationController
  .
  .
  .
  def edit
    @user = User.find(params[:id])
    @title = "Edit user"
  end
end
```

Getting the tests to pass requires making the actual edit view, shown in Listing 10.3. Note how closely this resembles the new user view from Listing 8.2; the large overlap suggests factoring the repeated code into a partial, which is left as an exercise (Section 10.6).

Listing 10.3 The user edit view.
app/views/users/edit.html.erb

```erb
<h1>Edit user</h1>

<%= form_for(@user) do |f| %>
  <%= render 'shared/error_messages', :object => f.object %>
  <div class="field">
    <%= f.label :name %><br />
    <%= f.text_field :name %>
  </div>
  <div class="field">
    <%= f.label :email %><br />
    <%= f.text_field :email %>
  </div>
  <div class="field">
    <%= f.label :password %><br />
    <%= f.password_field :password %>
  </div>
  <div class="field">
    <%= f.label :password_confirmation, "Confirmation" %><br />
    <%= f.password_field :password_confirmation %>
  </div>
  <div class="actions">
    <%= f.submit "Update" %>
  </div>
<% end %>
```

```
<div>
  <%= gravatar_for @user %>
  <a href="http://gravatar.com/emails">change</a>
</div>
```

Here we have reused the shared **error_messages** partial introduced in Section 8.2.3.

You may recall from Listing 8.8 that the error-messages partial references the **@user** variable explicitly. In the present case, we *do* happen to have an **@user** variable, but in order to make this a truly shared partial we should not depend on this fact. The solution is to pass the object corresponding to the form variable **f** as a parameter to the partial:

```
<%= render 'shared/error_messages', :object => f.object %>
```

This creates a variable called **object** in the partial, which we can then use to generate the error messages, as shown in Listing 10.4. (Note the fancy chain of methods to get a nice version of the object name; see the Rails API entry on, say, **humanize**, to get an idea of the range of Rails utilities available.)

Listing 10.4 Updating the error-messages partial from Listing 8.9 to work with other objects.
app/views/shared/_error_messages.html.erb

```
<% if object.errors.any? %>
  <div id="error_explanation">
    <h2><%= pluralize(object.errors.count, "error") %>
        prohibited this <%= object.class.to_s.underscore.humanize.downcase %>
        from being saved:</h2>
    <p>There were problems with the following fields:</p>
    <ul>
    <% object.errors.full_messages.each do |msg| %>
      <li><%= msg %></li>
    <% end %>
    </ul>
  </div>
<% end %>
```

While we're at it, we'll update the signup form with the more general code (Listing 10.5).

Listing 10.5 Updating the rendering of user signup errors.
`app/views/users/new.html.erb`

```erb
<h1>Sign up</h1>

<%= form_for(@user) do |f| %>
  <%= render 'shared/error_messages', :object => f.object %>
  .
  .
  .
<% end %>
```

We'll also add a link to the site navigation for the user edit page (which we'll call "Settings"), as mocked up in Figure 10.2[3] and shown in Listing 10.6.

Listing 10.6 Adding a Settings link.
`app/views/layouts/_header.html.erb`

```erb
<header>
  <%= link_to logo, root_path %>
  <nav class="round">
    <ul>
      <li><%= link_to "Home", root_path %></li>
      <% if signed_in? %>
      <li><%= link_to "Profile", current_user %></li>
      <li><%= link_to "Settings", edit_user_path(current_user) %></li>
      <% end %>
      .
      .
      .
    </ul>
  </nav>
</header>
```

Here we use the named route `edit_user_path` from Table 6.2, together with the handy `current_user` helper method defined in Listing 9.16.

With the `@user` instance variable from Listing 10.2, the tests from Listing 10.1 pass. As seen in Figure 10.3, the **new** page renders, though it doesn't yet work.

Looking at the HTML source for Figure 10.3, we see a form tag as expected (Listing 10.7).

---

3. Image from http://www.flickr.com/photos/sashawolff/4598355045/.

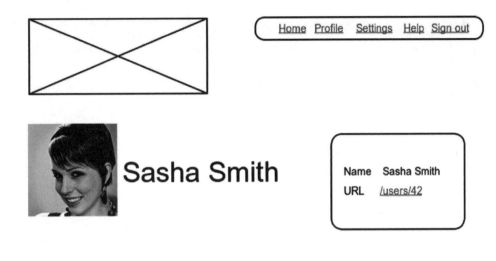

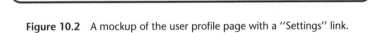

Figure 10.2   A mockup of the user profile page with a "Settings" link.

Listing 10.7 HTML for the edit form defined in Listing 10.3 and shown in Figure 10.3.

```
<form action="/users/1" class="edit_user" id="edit_user_1" method="post">
  <input name="_method" type="hidden" value="put" />
  .
  .
  .
</form>
```

Note here the hidden input field

```
<input name="_method" type="hidden" value="put" />
```

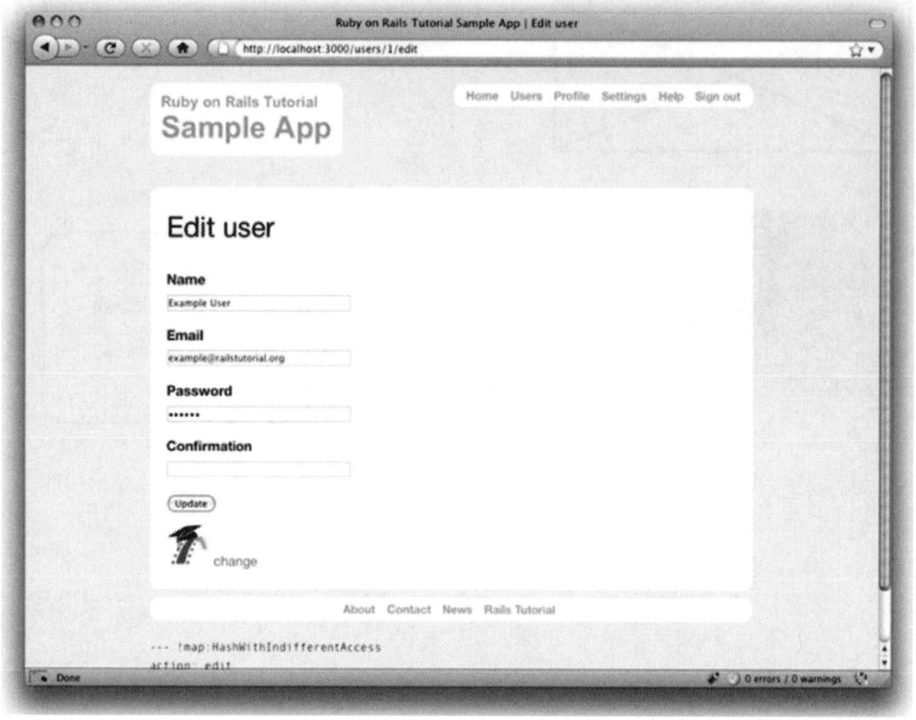

Figure 10.3   Editing user settings (`/users/1/edit`).

Since web browsers can't natively send PUT requests (as required by the REST conventions from Table 6.2), Rails fakes it with a POST request and a hidden **input** field.[4]

There's another subtlety to address here: the code **form_for(@user)** in Listing 10.3 is *exactly* the same as the code in Listing 8.2—so how does Rails know to use a POST request for new users and a PUT for editing users? The answer is that it is possible to tell whether a user is new or already exists in the database via the **new_record?** boolean method (which we saw briefly in Listing 7.10):

```
$ rails console
>> User.new.new_record?
=> true
>> User.first.new_record?
=> false
```

---

4. Don't be worried about how this works; the details are of interest to developers of the Rails framework itself, but by design are not important for Rails application developers.

When constructing a form using **form_for(@user)**, Rails uses POST if **@user.new_-record?** is **true** and PUT if it is **false**.

10.1.2   Enabling Edits

Although the edit form doesn't yet work, we've outsourced image upload to Gravatar, so it works straightaway by clicking on the "change" link from Figure 10.3, as shown in Figure 10.4. Let's get the rest of the user edit functionality working as well.

The tests for the **update** action are similar to those for **create**. In particular, we test both update failure and update success (Listing 10.8). (This is a lot of code; see if you can work through it by referring back to the tests in Chapter 8.)

Figure 10.4   The Gravatar image-cropping interface, with a picture of some dude.

Listing 10.8 Tests for the user **update** action.
`spec/controllers/users_controller_spec.rb`

```ruby
describe UsersController do
  render_views
  .
  .
  .
  describe "PUT 'update'" do

    before(:each) do
      @user = Factory(:user)
      test_sign_in(@user)
    end

    describe "failure" do

      before(:each) do
        @attr = { :email => "", :name => "", :password => "",
                  :password_confirmation => "" }
      end

      it "should render the 'edit' page" do
        put :update, :id => @user, :user => @attr
        response.should render_template('edit')
      end

      it "should have the right title" do
        put :update, :id => @user, :user => @attr
        response.should have_selector("title", :content => "Edit user")
      end
    end

    describe "success" do

      before(:each) do
        @attr = { :name => "New Name", :email => "user@example.org",
                  :password => "barbaz", :password_confirmation => "barbaz" }
      end

      it "should change the user's attributes" do
        put :update, :id => @user, :user => @attr
        @user.reload
        @user.name.should  == @attr[:name]
        @user.email.should == @attr[:email]
      end

      it "should redirect to the user show page" do
        put :update, :id => @user, :user => @attr
```

```
        response.should redirect_to(user_path(@user))
      end

      it "should have a flash message" do
        put :update, :id => @user, :user => @attr
        flash[:success].should =~ /updated/
      end
    end
  end
end
```

The only novelty here is the **reload** method, which appears in the test for changing the user's attributes:

```
it "should change the user's attributes" do
  @user.reload
  @user.name.should  == @attr[:name]
  @user.email.should == @attr[:email]
end
```

This code reloads the **@user** variable from the (test) database using **@user.reload**, and then verifies that the user's new name and email match the attributes in the **@attr** hash.

The **update** action needed to get the tests in Listing 10.8 to pass is similar to the final form of the **create** action (Listing 9.24), as seen in Listing 10.9.

Listing 10.9 The user **update** action.
app/controllers/users_controller.rb

```
class UsersController < ApplicationController
  .
  .
  .
  def update
    @user = User.find(params[:id])
    if @user.update_attributes(params[:user])
      flash[:success] = "Profile updated."
      redirect_to @user
    else
      @title = "Edit user"
      render 'edit'
    end
  end
end
```

With that, the user edit page should be working. As currently constructed, every edit requires the user to reconfirm the password (as implied by the empty confirmation text box in Figure 10.3), which makes updates more secure but is a minor annoyance.

10.2 Protecting Pages

Although the edit and update actions from Section 10.1 are functionally complete, they suffer from a ridiculous security flaw: they allow anyone (even non-signed-in users) to access either action, and any signed-in user can update the information for any other user.[5] In this section, we'll implement a security model that requires users to be signed in and prevents them from updating any information other than their own. Users who aren't signed in and who try to access protected pages will be forwarded to the signin page with a helpful message, as mocked up in Figure 10.5.

10.2.1 Requiring Signed-In Users

Since the security restrictions for the **edit** and **update** actions are identical, we'll handle them in a single RSpec **describe** block. Starting with the sign-in requirement, our initial tests verify that non-signed-in users attempting to access either action are simply redirected to the signin page, as seen in Listing 10.10.

Listing 10.10 The first tests for authentication.
spec/controllers/users_controller_spec.rb

```
describe UsersController do
  render_views
    .
    .
    .
  describe "authentication of edit/update pages" do

    before(:each) do
      @user = Factory(:user)
    end

    describe "for non-signed-in users" do

      it "should deny access to 'edit'" do
        get :edit, :id => @user
```

---

5. To be fair, they would need the user's password, but if we ever made the password unnecessary (as planned for the screencasts) it would open up a *huge* security hole.

```
            response.should redirect_to(signin_path)
        end

        it "should deny access to 'update'" do
          put :update, :id => @user, :user => {}
          response.should redirect_to(signin_path)
        end
      end
    end
  end
end
```

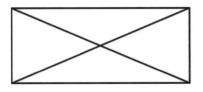

Figure 10.5   A mockup of the result of visiting a protected page.

The application code gets these tests to pass using a *before filter*, which arranges for a particular method to be called before the given actions. In this case, we define an **authenticate** method and invoke it using **before_filter :authenticate**, as shown in Listing 10.11.

Listing 10.11 Adding an **authenticate** before filter.
app/controllers/users_controller.rb

```
class UsersController < ApplicationController
  before_filter :authenticate, :only => [:edit, :update]
  .
  .
  .
  private

    def authenticate
      deny_access unless signed_in?
    end
end
```

By default, before filters apply to *every* action in a controller, so here we restrict the filter to act only on the **:edit** and **:update** actions by passing the **:only** options hash.

This code won't work yet, because **deny_access** hasn't been defined. Since access denial is part of authentication, we'll put it in the Sessions helper from Chapter 9. All **deny_access** does is put a message in **flash[:notice]** and then redirect to the signin page (Listing 10.12).

Listing 10.12 The **deny_access** method for user authentication.
app/helpers/sessions_helper.rb

```
module SessionsHelper
  .
  .
  .
  def deny_access
    redirect_to signin_path, :notice => "Please sign in to access this page."
  end
end
```

Note here that Listing 10.12 uses a shortcut for setting **flash[:notice]** by passing an options hash to the *redirect_to* function. The code in Listing 10.12 is equivalent to the more verbose

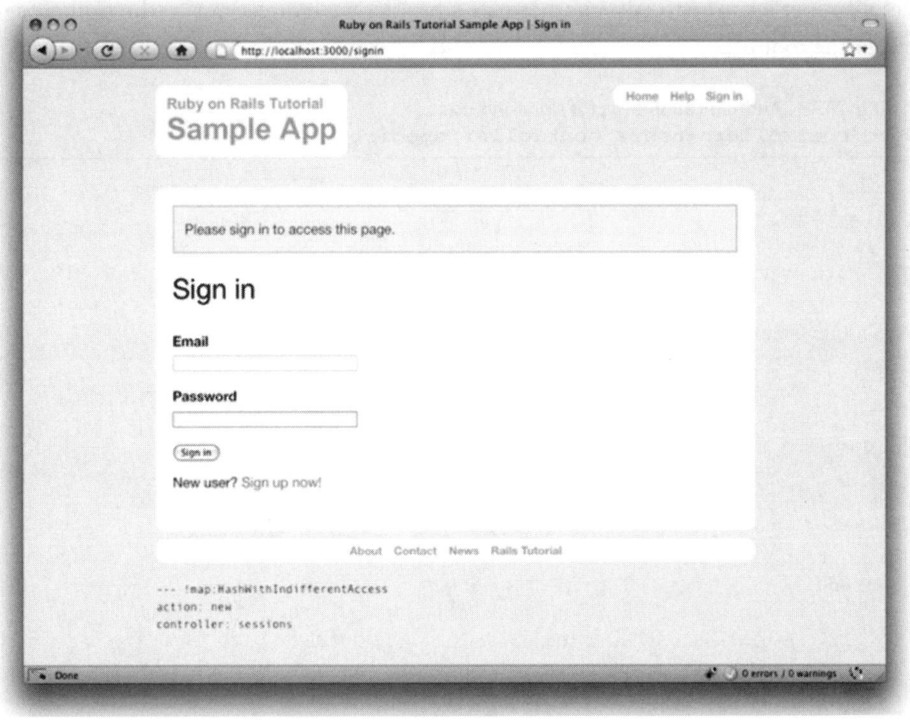

Figure 10.6   The signin form after trying to access a protected page.

```
flash[:notice] = "Please sign in to access this page."
redirect_to signin_path
```

(The same construction works for the `:error` key, but not for `:success`.)

Together with `:success` and `:error`, the `:notice` key completes our triumvirate of `flash` styles, all of which are supported natively by Blueprint CSS. By signing out and attempting to access the user edit page `/users/1/edit`, we can see the resulting yellow `"notice"` box, as seen in Figure 10.6.

10.2.2   Requiring the Right User

Of course, requiring users to sign in isn't quite enough; users should only be allowed to edit their *own* information. We can test for this by first signing in as an incorrect user and then hitting the `edit` and `update` actions (Listing 10.13). Note that, since users should never even *try* to edit another user's profile, we redirect not to the signin page but to the root url.

Listing 10.13 Authentication tests for signed-in users.
spec/controllers/users_controller_spec.rb

```
describe UsersController do
  render_views
    .
    .
    .
  describe "authentication of edit/update pages" do
      .
      .
      .
    describe "for signed-in users" do

      before(:each) do
        wrong_user = Factory(:user, :email => "user@example.net")
        test_sign_in(wrong_user)
      end

      it "should require matching users for 'edit'" do
        get :edit, :id => @user
        response.should redirect_to(root_path)
      end

      it "should require matching users for 'update'" do
        put :update, :id => @user, :user => {}
        response.should redirect_to(root_path)
      end
    end
  end
end
```

The application code is simple: we add a second before filter to call the **correct_user** method (which we have to write), as shown in Listing 10.14.

Listing 10.14 A **correct_user** before filter to protect the edit/update pages.
app/controllers/users_controller.rb

```
class UsersController < ApplicationController
  before_filter :authenticate, :only => [:edit, :update]
  before_filter :correct_user, :only => [:edit, :update]
    .
    .
    .
```

```
def edit
  @title = "Edit user"
end
  .
  .
  .

private

  def authenticate
    deny_access unless signed_in?
  end

  def correct_user
    @user = User.find(params[:id])
    redirect_to(root_path) unless current_user?(@user)
  end
end
```

This uses the **current_user?** method, which (as with **deny_access**) we define in the Sessions helper (Listing 10.15).

Listing 10.15 The **current_user?** method.
app/helpers/sessions_helper.rb

```
module SessionsHelper
  .
  .
  .
  def current_user?(user)
    user == current_user
  end
  def deny_access
    redirect_to signin_path, :notice => "Please sign in to access this page."
  end
  private
  .
  .
  .
end
```

Listing 10.14 also shows the updated **edit** action. Before, in Listing 10.2, we had

```
def edit
  @user = User.find(params[:id])
  @title = "Edit user"
end
```

but now that the **correct_user** before filter defines **@user** we can omit it from the **edit** action (and from the **update** action as well).

10.2.3 Friendly Forwarding

Our page protection is complete as written, but there is one minor blemish: when users try to access a protected page, they are currently redirected to their profile pages regardless of where they were trying to go. In other words, if a non-logged-in user tries to visit the edit page, after signing in the user will be redirected to /users/1 instead of /users/1/edit. It would be much friendlier to redirect them to their intended destination instead.

The sequence of attempted page visitation, signin, and redirect to destination page is a perfect job for an integration test, so let's make one for friendly forwarding:

```
$ rails generate integration_test friendly_forwarding
```

The code then appears as in Listing 10.16.

Listing 10.16 An integration test for friendly forwarding.
spec/requests/friendly_forwardings_spec.rb

```
require 'spec_helper'

describe "FriendlyForwardings" do

  it "should forward to the requested page after signin" do
    user = Factory(:user)
    visit edit_user_path(user)
    # The test automatically follows the redirect to the signin page.
    fill_in :email,    :with => user.email
    fill_in :password, :with => user.password
    click_button
    # The test follows the redirect again, this time to users/edit.
    response.should render_template('users/edit')
  end
end
```

(As indicated by the comments, the integration test *follows* redirects, so testing that the response **should redirect_to** some URL won't work. I learned this the hard way.)

Now for the implementation.[6] In order to forward users to their intended destination, we need to store the location of the requested page somewhere, and then redirect there instead. The storage mechanism is the **session** facility provided by Rails, which you can think of as being like an instance of the **cookies** variable from Section 9.3.2 that automatically expires upon browser close.[7] We also use the **request** object to get the **request_uri**, i.e., the URL of the requested page. The resulting application code appears in Listing 10.17.

Listing 10.17   Code to implement friendly forwarding.
app/helpers/sessions_helper.rb

```ruby
module SessionsHelper
  .
  .
  .
  def deny_access
    store_location
    redirect_to signin_path, :notice => "Please sign in to access this page."
  end
  def redirect_back_or(default)
    redirect_to(session[:return_to] || default)
    clear_return_to
  end
  private
    .
    .
    .
    def store_location
      session[:return_to] = request.fullpath
    end
    def clear_return_to
      session[:return_to] = nil
    end
end
```

Here we've added a line to the **deny_access** method, first storing the full path of the request with **store_location** and then proceeding as before. The **store_location** method puts the requested URL in the **session** variable under the key **:return_to**. (We've made both **store_location** and **clear_return_to** private methods since they are never needed outside the Sessions helper.)

---

6. The code in this section is adapted from the Clearance gem by thoughtbot.

7. Indeed, as noted in Section 9.6, **session** is implemented in just this way.

We've also defined the **redirect_back_or** method to redirect to the requested URL if it exists, or some default URL otherwise. This method is needed in the Sessions controller **create** action to redirect after successful signin (Listing 10.18).

Listing 10.18 The Sessions **create** action with friendly forwarding.
app/controllers/sessions_controller.rb

```
class SessionsController < ApplicationController
  .
  .
  .
  def create
    user = User.authenticate(params[:session][:email],
                             params[:session][:password])
    if user.nil?
      flash.now[:error] = "Invalid email/password combination."
      @title = "Sign in"
      render 'new'
    else
      sign_in user
      redirect_back_or user
    end
  end
  .
  .
  .
end
```

With that, the friendly forwarding integration test in Listing 10.16 should pass, and the basic user authentication and page protection implementation is complete.

10.3 Showing Users

In this section, we'll add the penultimate user action, the **index** action, which is designed to display *all* the users, not just one. Along the way, we'll learn about populating the database with sample users and *paginating* the user output so that the index page can scale up to display a potentially large number of users. A mockup of the result—users, pagination links, and a "Users" navigation link—appears in Figure 10.7.[8] In Section 10.4, we'll add an administrative interface to the user index so that (presumably troublesome) users can be destroyed.

---

8. Baby photo from http://www.flickr.com/photos/glasgows/338937124/.

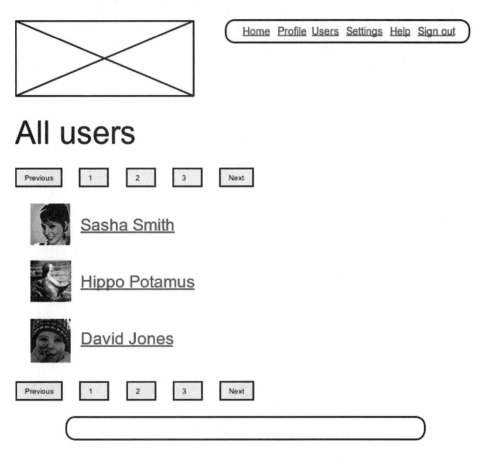

Figure 10.7   A mockup of the user index, with pagination and a "Users" nav link.

10.3.1   User Index

Although we'll keep individual user **show** pages visible to all site visitors, the user **index** will be restricted to signed-in users so that there's a limit to how much unregistered users can see by default. Our **index** tests check for this, and also verify that for signed-in users all the site's users are listed (Listing 10.19).

Listing 10.19   Tests for the user index page.
spec/controllers/users_controller_spec.rb

```
require 'spec_helper'

describe UsersController do
```

```ruby
render_views

describe "GET 'index'" do

  describe "for non-signed-in users" do
    it "should deny access" do
      get :index
      response.should redirect_to(signin_path)
      flash[:notice].should =~ /sign in/i
    end
  end

  describe "for signed-in users" do

    before(:each) do
      @user = test_sign_in(Factory(:user))
      second = Factory(:user, :email => "another@example.com")
      third  = Factory(:user, :email => "another@example.net")

      @users = [@user, second, third]
    end

    it "should be successful" do
      get :index
      response.should be_success
    end

    it "should have the right title" do
      get :index
      response.should have_selector("title", :content => "All users")
    end

    it "should have an element for each user" do
      get :index
      @users.each do |user|
        response.should have_selector("li", :content => user.name)
      end
    end
  end
end
  .
  .
  .
end
```

As you can see, the method for checking the index page is to make three factory users (signing in as the first one) and then verify that the index page has a list element (**li**) tag for the name of each one.

As expected, the application code uses **User.all** to make an **@users** instance variable in the **index** action of the Users controller (Listing 10.20).

Listing 10.20 The user **index** action.
app/controllers/users_controller.rb

```
class UsersController < ApplicationController
  before_filter :authenticate, :only => [:index, :edit, :update]
  .
  .
  .
  def index
    @title = "All users"
    @users = User.all
  end

  def show
    @user = User.find(params[:id])
    @title = @user.name
  end
  .
  .
  .
end
```

Note that we have added **:index** to the list of controllers protected by the **authenticate** before filter, thereby getting the first test from Listing 10.19 to pass.

To make the actual page, we need to make a view that iterates through the users and wraps each one in an **li** tag. We do this with the **each** method, displaying each user's Gravatar and name, while wrapping the whole thing in an unordered list (**ul**) tag (Listing 10.21).

Listing 10.21 The user index view.
app/views/users/index.html.erb

```
<h1>All users</h1>

<ul class="users">
  <% @users.each do |user| %>
    <li>
      <%= gravatar_for user, :size => 30 %>
      <%= link_to user.name, user %>
    </li>
  <% end %>
</ul>
```

We'll then add a little CSS for style (Listing 10.22).

Listing 10.22 CSS for the user index.
`public/stylesheets/custom.css`

```
.
.
.
ul.users {
  margin-top: 1em;
}

.users li {
  list-style: none;
}
```

Finally, we'll add a "Users" link to the site's navigation header (Listing 10.23). This puts to use the **users_path** named route from Table 6.2.

Listing 10.23 A layout link to the user index.
`app/views/layouts/_header.html.erb`

```erb
<header>
  <%= link_to logo, root_path %>
  <nav class="round">
    <ul>
      <li><%= link_to "Home", root_path %></li>
      <% if signed_in? %>
      <li><%= link_to "Users", users_path %></li>
      <li><%= link_to "Profile", current_user %></li>
      <li><%= link_to "Settings", edit_user_path(current_user) %></li>
      <% end %>
        .
        .
        .
    </ul>
  </nav>
</header>
```

With that, the user index is fully functional (with all tests passing), but it is a bit... lonely (Figure 10.8).

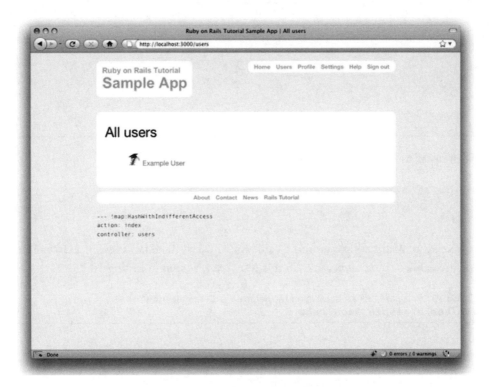

Figure 10.8   The user index page /users with only one user.

10.3.2 Sample Users

In this section, we'll give our lonely sample user some company. Of course, to create enough users to make a decent user index, we *could* use our web browser to visit the signup page and make the new users one by one, but a far better solution is to use Ruby (and Rake) to make the users for us.

First, we'll add the Faker gem to the **Gemfile**, which will allow us to make sample users with semi-realistic names and email addresses (Listing 10.24).

Listing 10.24   Adding the Faker gem to the **Gemfile**.

```
source 'http://rubygems.org'
   .
   .
   .
group :development do
```

```
  gem 'rspec-rails', '2.0.1'
  gem 'annotate-models', '1.0.4'
  gem 'faker', '0.3.1'
end
   .
   .
   .
```

Then install as usual:

```
$ bundle install
```

Next, we'll add a Rake task to create sample users. Rake tasks live in **lib/tasks**, and are defined using *namespaces* (in this case, **:db**), as seen in Listing 10.25.

Listing 10.25 A Rake task for populating the database with sample users.
lib/tasks/sample_data.rake

```
require 'faker'

namespace :db do
  desc "Fill database with sample data"
  task :populate => :environment do
    Rake::Task['db:reset'].invoke
    User.create!(:name => "Example User",
                 :email => "example@railstutorial.org",
                 :password => "foobar",
                 :password_confirmation => "foobar")
    99.times do |n|
      name  = Faker::Name.name
      email = "example-#{n+1}@railstutorial.org"
      password  = "password"
      User.create!(:name => name,
                   :email => email,
                   :password => password,
                   :password_confirmation => password)
    end
  end
end
```

This defines a task **db:populate** that resets the development database using **db:reset** (using slightly weird syntax you shouldn't worry about too much), creates an example user with name and email address replicating our previous one, and then makes 99 more. The line

```
task :populate => :environment do
```

ensures that the Rake task has access to the local Rails environment, including the User model (and hence **User.create!**).

With the **:db** namespace as in Listing 10.25, we can invoke the Rake task as follows:

```
$ rake db:populate
```

After running the Rake task, our application has 100 sample users, as seen in Figure 10.9. (I've taken the liberty of associating the first few sample addresses with photos so that they're not all the default Gravatar image.)

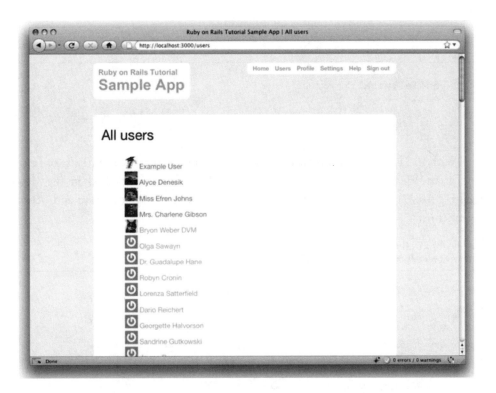

Figure 10.9 The user index page /users with 100 sample users.

10.3.3 Pagination

Having solved the problem of too few sample users, we now encounter the opposite problem: having too many users on a page. Right now there are a hundred, which is already a reasonably large number, and on a real site it could be thousands. The solution is to *paginate* the users, so that (for example) only 30 show up on a page at any one time.

There are several pagination methods in Rails; we'll use one of the simplest and most robust, called `will_paginate`. To use it, we need to update the **Gemfile** as usual (Listing 10.26).

Listing 10.26 Including `will_paginate` in the Gemfile.

```
source 'http://rubygems.org'

gem 'rails', '3.0.0'
gem 'sqlite3-ruby', '1.2.5', :require => 'sqlite3'
gem 'gravatar_image_tag', '0.1.0'
gem 'will_paginate', '3.0.pre2'
.
.
.
```

Then **bundle install**:

```
$ bundle install
```

With `will_paginate` installed, we are now ready to paginate the results of finding users. We'll start by adding the special **will_paginate** method in the view (Listing 10.27); we'll see in a moment why the code appears both above and below the user list.

Listing 10.27 The user index with pagination.
app/views/users/index.html.erb

```erb
<h1>All users</h1>

<%= will_paginate %>

<ul class="users">
  <% @users.each do |user| %>
    <li>
      <%= gravatar_for user, :size => 30 %>
      <%= link_to user.name, user %>
    </li>
```

```
  <% end %>
</ul>

<%= will_paginate %>
```

The **will_paginate** method is a little magical; inside a **users** view, it automatically looks for an **@users** object, and then displays pagination links to access other pages. The view in Listing 10.27 doesn't work yet, though, because currently **@users** contains the results of **User.all** (Listing 10.20), which is of class Array, whereas **will_paginate** expects an object of class **WillPaginate::Collection**. Happily, this is just the kind of object returned by the **paginate** method supplied by the will_paginate gem:

```
$ rails console
>> User.all.class
=> Array
>> User.paginate(:page => 1).class
=> WillPaginate::Collection
```

Note that **paginate** takes a hash argument with key **:page** and value equal to the page requested. **User.paginate** pulls the users out of the database one chunk at a time (30 by default), based on the **:page** parameter. So, for example, page 1 is users 1–30, page 2 is users 31–60, etc.

We can paginate the users in the sample application by using **paginate** in place of **all** in the **index** action (Listing 10.28). Here the **:page** parameter comes from **params[:page]**, which is generated automatically by **will_paginate**.

Listing 10.28 Paginating the users in the **index** action.
app/controllers/users_controller.rb

```
class UsersController < ApplicationController
  before_filter :authenticate, :only => [:index, :edit, :update]
  .
  .
  .
  def index
    @title = "All users"
    @users = User.paginate(:page => params[:page])
  end
  .
  .
  .
end
```

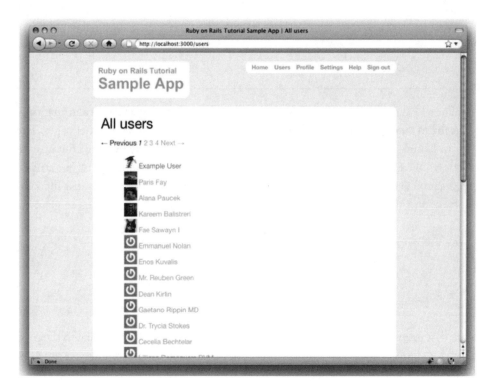

Figure 10.10   The user index page /users with pagination.

The user index page should now be working, appearing as in Figure 10.10; because we included `will_paginate` both above and below the user list, the pagination links appear in both places.

If you now click on either the 2 link or Next link, you'll get the second page of results, as shown in Figure 10.11.

Testing Pagination

Testing pagination requires detailed knowledge of how `will_paginate` works, so we did the implementation first, but it's still a good idea to test it. To do this, we need to invoke pagination in a test, which means making more than 30 (factory) users.

As before, we'll use Factory Girl to simulate users, but immediately we have a problem: user email addresses must be unique, which would appear to require creating more than 30 users by hand—a terribly cumbersome job. Fortunately, Factory Girl anticipates this issue, and provides *sequences* to solve it, as shown in Listing 10.29.

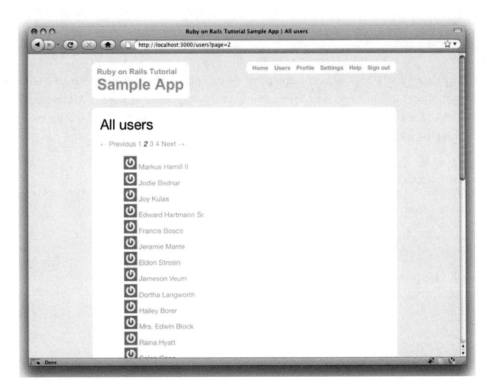

Figure 10.11 Page 2 of the user index (/users?page=2).

Listing 10.29 Defining a Factory Girl sequence.
spec/factories.rb

```
Factory.define :user do |user|
  user.name                  "Michael Hartl"
  user.email                 "mhartl@example.com"
  user.password              "foobar"
  user.password_confirmation "foobar"
end

Factory.sequence :email do |n|
  "person-#{n}@example.com"
end
```

This arranges to return email addresses like **person-1@example.com**, **person-2@example.com**, etc., which we invoke using the **next** method:

```
Factory(:user, :email => Factory.next(:email))
```

Applying the idea of factory sequences, we can make 31 users (the original **@user**
plus 30 more) inside a test, and then verify that the response has the HTML expected
from `will_paginate` (which you should be able to determine using Firebug or by
viewing the page source). The result appears in Listing 10.30.

Listing 10.30 A test for pagination.
spec/controllers/users_controller_spec.rb

```
require 'spec_helper'

describe "UsersController" do
  render_views

  describe "GET 'index'" do
    .
    .
    .
    describe "for signed-in users" do

      before(:each) do
        .
        .
        .
        @users = [@user, second, third]
        30.times do
          @users << Factory(:user, :email => Factory.next(:email))
        end
      end
      .
      .
      .
      it "should have an element for each user" do
        get :index
        @users[0..2].each do |user|
          response.should have_selector("li", :content => user.name)
        end
      end

      it "should paginate users" do
        get :index
        response.should have_selector("div.pagination")
        response.should have_selector("span.disabled", :content => "Previous")
        response.should have_selector("a", :href => "/users?page=2",
                                           :content => "2")
```

```
        response.should have_selector("a", :href => "/users?page=2",
                                           :content => "Next")

    end
  end
 end
 .
 .
 .
end
```

This code ensures that the tests invoke pagination by adding 30^9 users to the **@users** variable using the **Array** push notation **<<**, which appends an element to an existing array:

```
$ rails console
>> a = [1, 2, 5]
=> [1, 2, 5]
>> a << 17
=> [1, 2, 5, 17]
>> a << 42 << 1337
=> [1, 2, 5, 17, 42, 1337]
```

We see from the last example that occurrences of **<<** can be chained. In the test itself, note the compact notation **have_selector("div.pagination")**, which borrows the class convention from CSS (first seen in Listing 5.3) to check for a **div** tag with class **pagination**. Also note that, since there are now 33 users, we've updated the user element test to use only the first three elements (**[0..2]**) of the **@users** array, which is what we had before in Listing 10.19:

```
@users[0..2].each do |user|
  response.should have_selector("li", :content => user.name)
end
```

With that, our pagination code is well-tested, and there's only one minor detail left, as we'll see in the next section.

---

9. Technically, we only need to create 28 additional factory users since we already have three, but I find the meaning clearer if we create 30 instead.

10.3.4 Partial Refactoring

The paginated user index is now complete, but there's one improvement I can't resist including: Rails has some incredibly slick tools for making compact views, and in this section we'll refactor the index page to use them. Because our code is well-tested, we can refactor with confidence, assured that we are unlikely to break our site's functionality.

The first step in our refactoring is to replace the user **li** from Listing 10.27 with a **render** call (Listing 10.31).

Listing 10.31 The first refactoring attempt at the index view.
app/views/users/index.html.erb

```
<h1>All users</h1>

<%= will_paginate %>

<ul class="users">
  <% @users.each do |user| %>
    <%= render user %>
  <% end %>
</ul>

<%= will_paginate %>
```

Here we call **render** not on a string with the name of a partial, but rather on a **user** variable of class **User**;[10] in this context, Rails automatically looks for a partial called **_user.html.erb**, which we must create (Listing 10.32).

Listing 10.32 A partial to render a single user.
app/views/users/_user.html.erb

```
<li>
  <%= gravatar_for user, :size => 30 %>
  <%= link_to user.name, user %>
</li>
```

This is a definite improvement, but we can do even better: we can call **render** *directly* on the **@users** variable (Listing 10.33).

---

10. The name **user** is immaterial—we could have written **@users.each do |foobar|** and then used **render foobar**. The key is the *class* of the object—in this case, User.

Listing 10.33   The fully refactored user index.
app/views/users/index.html.erb

```
<h1>All users</h1>

<%= will_paginate %>

<ul class="users">
  <%= render @users %>
</ul>

<%= will_paginate %>
```

Here Rails infers that **@users** is an list of **User** objects; moreover, when called with a collection of users, Rails automatically iterates through them and renders each one with the **_user.html.erb** partial. The result is the impressively compact code in Listing 10.33.

10.4   Destroying Users

Now that the user index is complete, there's only one canonical REST action left: **destroy**. In this section, we'll add links to delete users, as mocked up in Figure 10.12, and define the **destroy** action necessary to accomplish the deletion. But first, we'll create the class of administrative users authorized to do so.

10.4.1   Administrative Users

We will identify privileged administrative users with a boolean **admin** attribute in the User model, which will lead to an **admin?** method to test for admin status. We can write tests for this attribute as in Listing 10.34.

Listing 10.34   Tests for an **admin** attribute.
spec/models/user_spec.rb

```
  .
  .
  .
  describe "admin attribute" do

    before(:each) do
      @user = User.create!(@attr)
    end
```

```ruby
    it "should respond to admin" do
      @user.should respond_to(:admin)
    end

    it "should not be an admin by default" do
      @user.should_not be_admin
    end

    it "should be convertible to an admin" do
      @user.toggle!(:admin)
      @user.should be_admin
    end
  end
end
```

All users

Figure 10.12   A mockup of the user index with delete links.

Here we've used the **toggle!** method to flip the **admin** attribute from **false** to **true**. Also note that the line

```
@user.should be_admin
```

implies (via the RSpec boolean convention) that the user should have an **admin?** boolean method.

We add the **admin** attribute with a migration as usual, indicating the **boolean** type on the command line:

```
$ rails generate migration add_admin_to_users admin:boolean
```

The migration simply adds the **admin** column to the **users** table (Listing 10.35), yielding the data model in Figure 10.13.

Listing 10.35 The migration to add a boolean **admin** attribute to users.
db/migrate/<timestamp>_add_admin_to_users.rb

```
class AddAdminToUsers < ActiveRecord::Migration
  def self.up
    add_column :users, :admin, :boolean, :default => false
  end

  def self.down
    remove_column :users, :admin
  end
end
```

users	
id	integer
name	string
email	string
encrypted_password	string
salt	string
remember_token	string
admin	boolean
created_at	datetime
updated_at	datetime

Figure 10.13   The User model with an added **admin** boolean attribute.

Note that we've added the argument **:default => false** to **add_column** in
Listing 10.35, which means that users will *not* be administrators by default. (Without
the **:default => false** argument, **admin** will be **nil** by default, which is still **false**,
so this step is not strictly necessary. It is more explicit, though, and communicates our
intentions more clearly both to Rails and to readers of our code.)

Finally, we migrate the development database and prepare the test database:

```
$ rake db:migrate
$ rake db:test:prepare
```

As expected, Rails figures out the boolean nature of the **admin** attribute and automatically adds the question-mark method **admin?**:[11]

```
$ rails console
>> user = User.first
>> user.admin?
=> false
>> user.password = "foobar"
>> user.toggle!(:admin)
=> true
>> user.admin?
=> true
```

As a final step, let's update our sample data populator to make the first user an admin
(Listing 10.36).

Listing 10.36 The sample data populator code with an admin user.
lib/tasks/sample_data.rake

```
require 'faker'

namespace :db do
  desc "Fill database with sample data"
  task :populate => :environment do
    Rake::Task['db:reset'].invoke
    admin = User.create!(:name => "Example User",
```

---

11. The **toggle!** method invokes the Active Record callbacks but not the validations, so we have to set the
password attribute (but not the confirmation) in order to have a non-blank password in the **encrypt_password**
callback.

```
                            :email => "example@railstutorial.org",
                            :password => "foobar",
                            :password_confirmation => "foobar")
    admin.toggle!(:admin)
    .
    .
    .
  end
end
```

Finally, re-run the populator to reset the database and then rebuild it from scratch:

```
$ rake db:populate
```

Revisiting `attr_accessible`

You might have noticed that Listing 10.36 makes the user an admin with **toggle!(:admin)**, but why not just add **:admin => true** to the initialization hash? The answer is, it won't work, and this is by design: only **attr_accessible** attributes can be assigned through mass assignment, and the **admin** attribute isn't accessible. Listing 10.37 reproduces the most recent list of **attr_accessible** attributes—note that **:admin** is *not* on the list.

Listing 10.37 The **attr_accessible** attributes for the User model *without* an **:admin** attribute. **app/models/user.rb**

```
class User < ActiveRecord::Base
  attr_accessor :password
  attr_accessible :name, :email, :password, :password_confirmation
  .
  .
  .
end
```

Explicitly defining accessible attributes is crucial for good site security. If we omitted the **attr_accessible** list in the User model (or foolishly added **:admin** to the list), a malicious user could send a PUT request as follows:[12]

---

12. Command-line tools such as curl (seen in Box 3.2) can issue PUT requests of this form.

```
put /users/17?admin=1
```

This request would make user 17 an admin, which could be a potentially serious security breach, to say the least. Because of this danger, it is a good practice to define
attr_accessible for every model.

10.4.2 The **destroy** Action

The final step needed to complete the Users resource is to add delete links and a
destroy action. We'll start by adding a delete link for each user on the user index
page (Listing 10.38).

Listing 10.38 User delete links (viewable only by admins).
app/views/users/_user.html.erb

```
<li>
  <%= gravatar_for user, :size => 30 %>
  <%= link_to user.name, user %>
  <% if current_user.admin? %>
  | <%= link_to "delete", user, :method => :delete, :confirm => "You sure?",
                                :title => "Delete #{user.name}" %>
  <% end %>
</li>
```

Note the **:method => :delete** argument, which arranges for the link to issue the
necessary DELETE request. We've also wrapped each link inside an **if** statement so that
only admins can see them. The result for our admin user appears in Figure 10.14.

Web browsers can't send DELETE requests natively, so Rails fakes them with
JavaScript.[13] To get the delete links to work, we therefore have to include the default
Rails JavaScript libraries, which we do by adding the line

```
<%= javascript_include_tag :defaults %>
```

to the site layout. The result is shown in Listing 10.39.

---

13. This means that the delete links won't work if the user has JavaScript disabled. If you must support non-
JavaScript-enabled browsers you can fake a DELETE request using a form and a POST request, which works even
without JavaScript; see the Railscast on Destroy Without JavaScript for details.

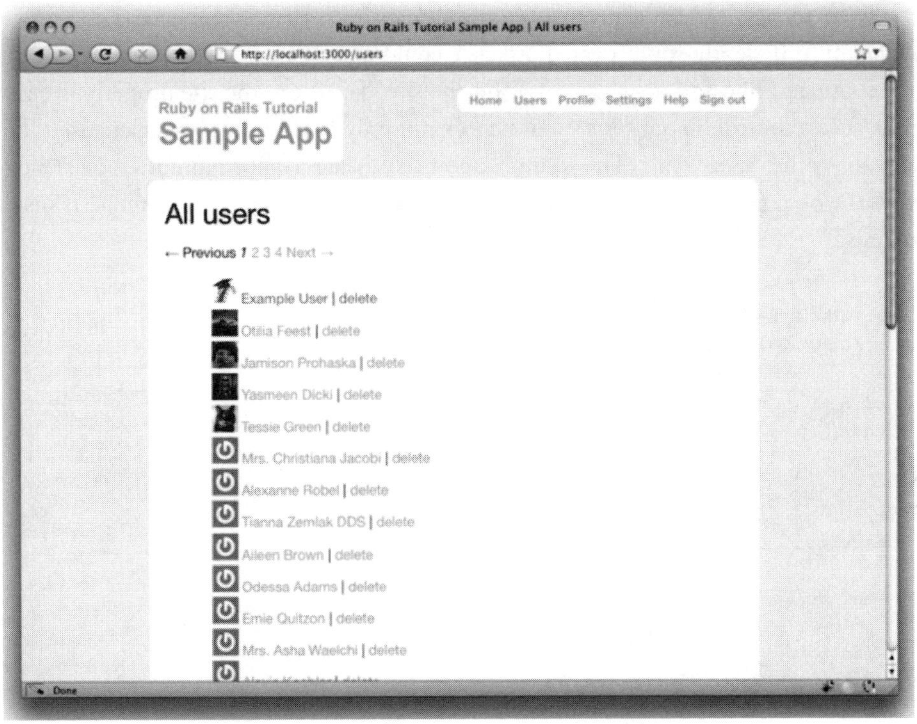

Figure 10.14 The user index /users with delete links.

Listing 10.39 Adding the default JavaScript libraries to the sample app.
`app/views/layouts/application.html.erb`

```
<!DOCTYPE html>
<html>
  <head>
    <title><%= title %></title>
    <%= csrf_meta_tag %>
    <%= render 'layouts/stylesheets' %>
    <%= javascript_include_tag :defaults %>
  </head>
  <body>
    .
    .
    .
  </body>
</html>
```

Even though only admins can see the delete links, there's still a terrible security hole: any sufficiently sophisticated attacker could simply issue DELETE requests from the command line and delete any user on the site. To secure the site properly, we also need access control, so our tests should check not only that admins *can* delete users, but also that other users *can't*. The results appear in Listing 10.40. Note that, in analogy with the **get**, **post**, and **put** methods, we use **delete** to issue DELETE requests inside of tests.

Listing 10.40 Tests for destroying users.
spec/controllers/users_controller_spec.rb

```ruby
describe UsersController do
  render_views
  .
  .
  .
  describe "DELETE 'destroy'" do

    before(:each) do
      @user = Factory(:user)
    end

    describe "as a non-signed-in user" do
      it "should deny access" do
        delete :destroy, :id => @user
        response.should redirect_to(signin_path)
      end
    end

    describe "as a non-admin user" do
      it "should protect the page" do
        test_sign_in(@user)
        delete :destroy, :id => @user
        response.should redirect_to(root_path)
      end
    end

    describe "as an admin user" do

      before(:each) do
        admin = Factory(:user, :email => "admin@example.com", :admin => true)
        test_sign_in(admin)
      end

      it "should destroy the user" do
```

```
      lambda do
        delete :destroy, :id => @user
      end.should change(User, :count).by(-1)
    end

    it "should redirect to the users page" do
      delete :destroy, :id => @user
      response.should redirect_to(users_path)
    end
  end
 end
end
```

(You might notice that we've set an admin user using **:admin => true**; user factories are not bound by the rules of **attr_accessible** parameters.) Note here that the **change** method can take a negative value, which means that, just as we verified user creation by testing for a change of +1 (Listing 8.14), we can verify user destruction by testing for a change of -1:

```
lambda do
  delete :destroy, :id => @user
end.should change(User, :count).by(-1)
```

As you might suspect by now, the implementation uses a before filter, this time to restrict access to the **destroy** action to admins. The **destroy** action itself finds the user, destroys it, and then redirects to user index (Listing 10.41).

Listing 10.41 A before filter restricting the **destroy** action to admins.
app/controllers/users_controller.rb

```
class UsersController < ApplicationController
  before_filter :authenticate, :only => [:index, :edit, :update, :destroy]
  before_filter :correct_user, :only => [:edit, :update]
  before_filter :admin_user,   :only => :destroy
  .
  .
  .
  def destroy
    User.find(params[:id]).destroy
    flash[:success] = "User destroyed."
```

```
      redirect_to users_path
  end

  private
    .
    .
    .
    def admin_user
      redirect_to(root_path) unless current_user.admin?
    end
end
```

Note that the **destroy** action uses *method chaining* (seen briefly in Section 4.2.3) in the line

```
User.find(params[:id]).destroy
```

which saves a line of code.

At this point, all the tests should be passing, and the Users resource—with its controller, model, and views—is functionally complete.

10.5 Conclusion

We've come a long way since introducing the Users controller way back in Section 5.3. Those users couldn't even sign up; now users can sign up, sign in, sign out, view their profiles, edit their settings, and see an index of all users—and some can even destroy other users.

The rest of this book builds on the foundation of the Users resource (and associated authentication system) to make a site with Twitter-like microposts (Chapter 11) and user following (Chapter 12). These chapters will introduce some of the most powerful features of Rails, including data modeling with **has_many** and **has_many :through**.

Before moving on, be sure to merge all the changes into the master branch:

```
$ git add .
$ git commit -am "Done with user edit/update, index, and destroy actions"
$ git checkout master
$ git merge updating-users
```

It's also worth noting that this chapter saw the last of the necessary gem installations. For reference, the final **Gemfile** is shown in Listing 10.42.

Listing 10.42 The final **Gemfile** for the sample application.

```
source 'http://rubygems.org'

gem 'rails', '3.0.0'
gem 'sqlite3-ruby', '1.2.5', :require => 'sqlite3'
gem 'gravatar_image_tag', '0.1.0'
gem 'will_paginate', '3.0.pre2'

group :development do
  gem 'rspec-rails', '2.0.1'
  gem 'annotate-models', '1.0.4'
  gem 'faker', '0.3.1'
end

group :test do
  gem 'rspec', '2.0.1'
  gem 'webrat', '0.7.1'
  gem 'spork', '0.8.4'
  gem 'factory_girl_rails', '1.0'
end
```

10.6 Exercises

1. Arrange for the Gravatar "change" link in Listing 10.3 to open in a new window (or tab). *Hint:* Search the web; you should find one particularly robust method involving something called **_blank**.

2. Remove the duplicated form code by refactoring the **new.html.erb** and **edit.html.erb** views to use the partial in Listing 10.43. Note that you will have to pass the form variable **f** explicitly as a local variable, as shown in Listing 10.44.

3. Signed-in users have no reason to access the **new** and **create** actions in the Users controller. Arrange for such users to be redirected to the root url if they do try to hit those pages.

4. Add tests to check that the delete links in Listing 10.38 appear for admins but not for normal users.

5. Modify the **destroy** action to prevent admin users from destroying themselves. (Write a test first.)

Listing 10.43 A partial for the new and edit form fields.
`app/views/users/_fields.html.erb`

```erb
<%= render 'shared/error_messages', :object => f.object %>
<div class="field">
  <%= f.label :name %><br />
  <%= f.text_field :name %>
</div>
<div class="field">
  <%= f.label :email %><br />
  <%= f.text_field :email %>
</div>
<div class="field">
  <%= f.label :password %><br />
  <%= f.password_field :password %>
</div>
<div class="field">
  <%= f.label :password_confirmation, "Confirmation" %><br />
  <%= f.password_field :password_confirmation %>
</div>
```

Listing 10.44 The new user view with partial.
`app/views/users/new.html.erb`

```erb
<h1>Sign up</h1>

<%= form_for(@user) do |f| %>
  <%= render 'fields', :f => f %>
  <div class="actions">
    <%= f.submit "Sign up" %>
  </div>
<% end %>
```

CHAPTER 11

User Microposts

Chapter 10 saw the completion of the REST actions for the Users resource, so the time has finally come to add a second resource: user *microposts*.[1] These are short messages associated with a particular user, first seen in larval form in Chapter 2. In this chapter, we will make a full-strength version of the sketch from Section 2.3 by constructing the Micropost data model, associating it with the User model using the **has_many** and **belongs_to** methods, and then making the forms and partials needed to manipulate and display the results. In Chapter 12, we will complete our tiny Twitter clone by adding the notion of *following* users in order to receive a *feed* of their microposts.

If you're using Git for version control, I suggest making a topic branch as usual:

```
$ git checkout -b user-microposts
```

11.1 A Micropost Model

We begin the Microposts resource by creating a Micropost model, which captures the essential characteristics of microposts. What follows builds on the work from Section 2.3; as with the model in that section, our new Micropost model will include data validations and an association with the User model. Unlike that model, the present Micropost model will be fully tested, and will also have a default *ordering* and automatic *destruction* if its parent user is destroyed.

---

1. Technically, we treated sessions as a resource in Chapter 9, but they are not saved to the database the way users and microposts are.

11.1.1   The Basic Model

The Micropost model needs only two attributes: a **content** attribute to hold the micropost's content,[2] and a **user_id** to associate a micropost with a particular user. As with the case of the User model (Listing 6.1), we generate it using **generate model**:

```
$ rails generate model Micropost content:string user_id:integer
```

This produces a migration to create a **microposts** table in the database (Listing 11.1); compare it to the analogous migration for the **users** table from Listing 6.2.

Listing 11.1   The Micropost migration. (Note the index on **user_id**.)
db/migrate/<timestamp>_create_microposts.rb

```
class CreateMicroposts < ActiveRecord::Migration
  def self.up
    create_table :microposts do |t|
      t.string :content
      t.integer :user_id

      t.timestamps
    end
    add_index :microposts, :user_id
  end

  def self.down
    drop_table :microposts
  end
end
```

Note that, since we expect to retrieve all the microposts associated with a given user id, Listing 11.1 adds an index (Box 6.2) on the **user_id** column:

```
add_index :microposts, :user_id
```

Note also the **t.timestamps** line, which (as mentioned in Section 6.1.1) adds the magic **created_at** and **updated_at** columns. We'll put the **created_at** column to work in Section 11.1.3 and Section 11.2.1.

---

2. The **content** attribute will be a **string**, but, as noted briefly in Section 2.1.2, for longer text fields you should use the **text** data type.

microposts	
id	integer
content	string
user_id	integer
created_at	datetime
updated_at	datetime

Figure 11.1   The Micropost data model.

We can run the microposts migration as usual (taking care to prepare the test database since the data model has changed):

```
$ rake db:migrate
$ rake db:test:prepare
```

The result is a Micropost model with the structure shown in Figure 11.1.

Accessible Attribute

Before fleshing out the Micropost model, it's important first to use **attr_accessible** to indicate the attributes editable through the web. As discussed in Section 6.1.2 and Section 10.4.1.1, failing to define accessible attributes means that anyone could change any aspect of a micropost object simply by using a command-line client to issue malicious requests. For example, a malicious user could change the **user_id** attributes on microposts, thereby associating microposts with the wrong users.

In the case of the Micropost model, there is only *one* attribute that needs to be editable through the web, namely, the **content** attribute (Listing 11.2).

Listing 11.2   Making the **content** attribute (and *only* the **content** attribute) accessible.
app/models/micropost.rb

```
class Micropost < ActiveRecord::Base
  attr_accessible :content
end
```

Since **user_id** *isn't* listed as an **attr_accessible** parameter, it can't be edited through the web, because a **user_id** parameter in a mass assignment such as

```
Micropost.new(:content => "foo bar", :user_id => 17)
```

will simply be ignored.

The **attr_accessible** declaration in Listing 11.2 is necessary for site security, but it introduces a problem in the default Micropost model spec (Listing 11.3).

Listing 11.3 The initial Micropost spec.
spec/models/micropost_spec.rb

```
require 'spec_helper'

describe Micropost do

  before(:each) do
    @attr = {
      :content => "value for content",
      :user_id => 1
    }
  end

  it "should create a new instance given valid attributes" do
    Micropost.create!(@attr)
  end
end
```

This test currently passes, but there's something fishy about it. (See if you can figure out what before proceeding.)

The problem is that the **before(:each)** block in Listing 11.3 assigns the user id through mass assignment, which is exactly what **attr_accessible** is designed to prevent; in particular, as noted above, the **:user_id => 1** part of the initialization hash is simply ignored. The solution is to avoid using **Micropost.new** directly; instead, we will create the new micropost through its *association* with the User model, which sets the user id automatically. Accomplishing this is the task of the next section.

11.1.2 User/Micropost Associations

The goal of this section is to establish an *association* between the Micropost model and the User model—a relationship seen briefly in Section 2.3.3 and shown schematically in Figure 11.2 and Figure 11.3. Along the way, we'll write tests for the Micropost model that, unlike Listing 11.3, are compatible with the use of **attr_accessible** in Listing 11.2.

We start with tests for the Micropost model association. First, we want to replicate the **Micropost.create!** test shown in Listing 11.3 without the invalid mass assignment. Second, we see from Figure 11.2 that a **micropost** object should have a **user** method.

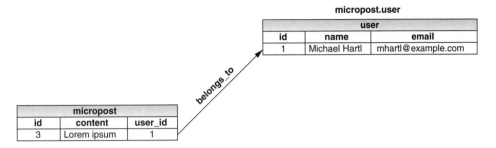

Figure 11.2   The **belongs_to** relationship between a micropost and its user.

Finally, **micropost.user** should be the user corresponding to the micropost's **user_id**. We can express these requirements in RSpec with the code in Listing 11.4.

Listing 11.4   Tests for the micropost's user association.
spec/models/micropost_spec.rb

```
require 'spec_helper'

describe Micropost do

  before(:each) do
    @user = Factory(:user)
    @attr = { :content => "value for content" }
  end

  it "should create a new instance given valid attributes" do
    @user.microposts.create!(@attr)
  end

  describe "user associations" do

    before(:each) do
      @micropost = @user.microposts.create(@attr)
    end

    it "should have a user attribute" do
      @micropost.should respond_to(:user)
    end

    it "should have the right associated user" do
      @micropost.user_id.should == @user.id
      @micropost.user.should == @user
    end
  end
end
```

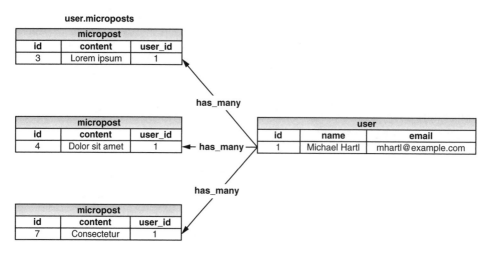

Figure 11.3   The **has_many** relationship between a user and its microposts.

Note that, rather than using **Micropost.create** or **Micropost.create!** to create a micropost, Listing 11.4 uses

```
@user.microposts.create(@attr)
```

and

```
@user.microposts.create!(@attr)
```

This pattern is the canonical way to create a micropost through its association with users. (We use a factory user because these tests are for the Micropost model, not the User model.) When created in this way, the micropost object *automatically* has its **user_id** set to the right value, which fixes the issue noted in Section 2. In particular, the code

```
before(:each) do
  @attr = {
    :content => "value for content",
    :user_id => 1
  }
end
```

```
it "should create a new instance given valid attributes" do
  Micropost.create!(@attr)
end
```

from Listing 11.3 is defective because **:user_id => 1** does nothing when **user_id** is not one of the Micropost model's accessible attributes. By going through the user association, on the other hand, the code

```
it "should create a new instance given valid attributes" do
  @user.microposts.create!(@attr)
end
```

from Listing 11.4 has the right **user_id** by construction.

These special **create** methods won't work yet; they require the proper **has_many** association in the User model. We'll defer the more detailed tests for this association to Section 11.1.3; for now, we'll simply test for the presence of a **microposts** attribute (Listing 11.5).

Listing 11.5 A test for the user's **microposts** attribute.
spec/models/user_spec.rb

```
require 'spec_helper'

describe User do
  .
  .
  .
  describe "micropost associations" do

    before(:each) do
      @user = User.create(@attr)
    end

    it "should have a microposts attribute" do
      @user.should respond_to(:microposts)
    end
  end
end
```

We can get the tests in both Listing 11.4 and Listing 11.5 to pass using the **belongs_to/has_many** association illustrated in Figure 11.2 and Figure 11.3, as shown in Listing 11.6 and Listing 11.7.

Listing 11.6 A micropost **belongs_to** a user.
app/models/micropost.rb

```
class Micropost < ActiveRecord::Base
  attr_accessible :content

  belongs_to :user
end
```

Listing 11.7 A user **has_many** microposts.
app/models/user.rb

```
class User < ActiveRecord::Base
  attr_accessor :password
  attr_accessible :name, :email, :password, :password_confirmation

  has_many :microposts
  .
  .
  .
end
```

Using this **belongs_to/has_many** association, Rails constructs the methods shown in Table 11.1. You should compare the entries in Table 11.1 with the code in Listing 11.4 and Listing 11.5 to satisfy yourself that you understand the basic nature of the associations. (There is one method in Table 11.1 we haven't used so far, the **build** method; it will be put to good use in Section 11.1.4 and especially in Section 11.3.2.)

Table 11.1 A summary of user/micropost association methods

Method	Purpose
`micropost.user`	Return the User object associated with the micropost.
`user.microposts`	Return an array of the user's microposts.
`user.microposts.create(arg)`	Create a micropost (`user_id = user.id`).
`user.microposts.create!(arg)`	Create a micropost (exception on failure).
`user.microposts.build(arg)`	Return a new Micropost object (`user_id = user.id`).

11.1.3   Micropost Refinements

The test in Listing 11.5 of the **has_many** association doesn't test for much—it merely verifies the *existence* of a **microposts** attribute. In this section, we'll add *ordering* and *dependency* to microposts, while also testing that the **user.microposts** method actually returns an array of microposts

We will need to construct some microposts in the User model spec, which means that we should make a micropost factory at this point. To do this, we need a way to make an association in Factory Girl. Happily, this is easy—we just use the Factory Girl method **micropost.association**, as seen in Listing 11.8.[3]

Listing 11.8   The complete factory file, including a new factory for microposts.
spec/factories.rb

```
# By using the symbol ':user', we get Factory Girl to simulate the User model.
Factory.define :user do |user|
  user.name                  "Michael Hartl"
  user.email                 "mhartl@example.com"
  user.password              "foobar"
  user.password_confirmation "foobar"
end

Factory.sequence :email do |n|
  "person-#{n}@example.com"
end

Factory.define :micropost do |micropost|
  micropost.content "Foo bar"
  micropost.association :user
end
```

Default Scope

We can put the micropost factory to work in a test for the ordering of microposts. By default, using **user.microposts** to pull a user's microposts from the database makes no guarantees about the order of the posts, but (following the convention of blogs and Twitter) we want the microposts to come out in reverse order of when they were created, i.e., most recent first. To test this ordering, we first create a couple of microposts as follows:

---

3. For more on Factory Girl associations, including the many options available, see the Factory Girl documentation.

```
@mp1 = Factory(:micropost, :user => @user, :created_at => 1.day.ago)
@mp2 = Factory(:micropost, :user => @user, :created_at => 1.hour.ago)
```

Here we indicate that the second post was created more recently, **1.hour.ago**, with the first post created **1.day.ago**. Note how convenient the use of Factory Girl is: not only can we assign the user using mass assignment (since factories bypass **attr_accessible**), we can also set **created_at** manually, which Active Record won't allow us to do.[4]

Most database adapters (including the one for SQLite) return the microposts in order of their ids, so we can arrange for an initial test that almost certainly fails using the code in Listing 11.9.

Listing 11.9 Testing the order of a user's microposts.
spec/models/user_spec.rb

```
require 'spec_helper'

describe User do
    .
    .
    .
  describe "micropost associations" do

    before(:each) do
      @user = User.create(@attr)
      @mp1 = Factory(:micropost, :user => @user, :created_at => 1.day.ago)
      @mp2 = Factory(:micropost, :user => @user, :created_at => 1.hour.ago)
    end

    it "should have a microposts attribute" do
      @user.should respond_to(:microposts)
    end

    it "should have the right microposts in the right order" do
      @user.microposts.should == [@mp2, @mp1]
    end
  end
end
```

The key line here is

---

4. Recall that **created_at** and **updated_at** are "magic" columns, so any explicit initialization values are overwritten by the magic.

```
@user.microposts.should == [@mp2, @mp1]
```

indicating that the posts should be ordered newest first. This should fail because by default the posts will be ordered by id, i.e., **[@mp1, @mp2]**. This test also verifies the basic correctness of the **has_many** association itself, by checking (as indicated in Table 11.1) that **user.microposts** is an array of microposts.

To get the ordering test to pass, we use a Rails facility called **default_scope** with an **:order** parameter, as shown in Listing 11.10. (This is our first example of the notion of *scope*. We will learn about scope in a more general context in Chapter 12.)

Listing 11.10 Ordering the microposts with **default_scope**.
app/models/micropost.rb

```
class Micropost < ActiveRecord::Base
  .
  .
  .
  default_scope :order => 'microposts.created_at DESC'
end
```

The order here is **'microposts.created_at DESC'**, where **DESC** is SQL for "descending", i.e., in descending order from newest to oldest.

Dependent: Destroy

Apart from proper ordering, there is a second refinement we'd like to add to microposts. Recall from Section 10.4 that site administrators have the power to *destroy* users. It stands to reason that if a user is destroyed, the user's microposts should be destroyed as well. We can test for this by first destroying a micropost's user and then verifying that the associated microposts are no longer in the database (Listing 11.11).

Listing 11.11 Testing that microposts are destroyed when users are.
spec/models/user_spec.rb

```
describe User do
  .
  .
  .
  describe "micropost associations" do

    before(:each) do
      @user = User.create(@attr)
```

```
      @mp1 = Factory(:micropost, :user => @user, :created_at => 1.day.ago)
      @mp2 = Factory(:micropost, :user => @user, :created_at => 1.hour.ago)
    end
    .
    .
    .
    it "should destroy associated microposts" do
      @user.destroy
      [@mp1, @mp2].each do |micropost|
        Micropost.find_by_id(micropost.id).should be_nil
      end
    end
  end
  .
  .
  .
end
```

Here we have used **Micropost.find_by_id**, which returns **nil** if the record is not found, whereas **Micropost.find** raises an exception on failure, which is a bit harder to test for. (In case you're curious,

```
lambda do
  Micropost.find(micropost.id)
end.should raise_error(ActiveRecord::RecordNotFound)
```

does the trick in this case.)

The application code to get Listing 11.11 to pass is less than one line; in fact, it's just an option to the **has_many** association method, as shown in Listing 11.12.

Listing 11.12 Ensuring that a user's microposts are destroyed along with the user.
app/models/user.rb

```
class User < ActiveRecord::Base
  .
  .
  .
  has_many :microposts, :dependent => :destroy
  .
  .
  .
end
```

With that, the final form of the user/micropost association is in place.

11.1.4 Micropost Validations

Before leaving the Micropost model, we'll tie off a couple of loose ends by adding validations (following the example from Section 2.3.2). Both the **user_id** and **content** attributes are required, and **content** is further constrained to be shorter than 140 characters, which we test for using the code in Listing 11.13.

Listing 11.13 Tests for the Micropost model validations.
spec/models/micropost_spec.rb

```
require 'spec_helper'

describe Micropost do

  before(:each) do
    @user = Factory(:user)
    @attr = { :content => "value for content" }
  end
  .
  .
  .
  describe "validations" do

    it "should require a user id" do
      Micropost.new(@attr).should_not be_valid
    end

    it "should require nonblank content" do
      @user.microposts.build(:content => "  ").should_not be_valid
    end

    it "should reject long content" do
      @user.microposts.build(:content => "a" * 141).should_not be_valid
    end
  end
end
```

These generally follow the examples from the User model validation tests from Section 6.2. (The analogous tests were broken into multiple lines in that section, but you should be comfortable enough reading RSpec code by now to digest the more compact formulation above.)

As in Section 6.2, the code in Listing 11.13 uses string multiplication to test the micropost length validation:

```
$ rails console
>> "a" * 10
=> "aaaaaaaaaa"
>> "a" * 141
=> "aaaaaaaaaaaaaaaaaaaaaaaaaaaaaaaaaaaaaaaaaaaaaaaaaaaaaaaaaaaaaaaaaaaaaaaaaaaa
aaaaaaaaaaaaaaaaaaaaaaaaaaaaaaaaaaaaaaaaaaaaaaaaaaaaaaaaaaaaaaaaaaaaa"
```

In contrast, instead of using the default **new** constructor as in

```
User.new(...)
```

the code in Listing 11.13 uses the **build** method:

```
@user.microposts.build
```

Recall from Table 11.1 that this is essentially equivalent to **Micropost.new**, except that it automatically sets the micropost's **user_id** to **@user.id**.

The validations themselves are straightforward analogues of the User model validations, as seen in Listing 11.14.

Listing 11.14 The Micropost model validations.
app/models/micropost.rb

```
class Micropost < ActiveRecord::Base
  attr_accessible :content

  belongs_to :user

  validates :content, :presence => true, :length => { :maximum => 140 }
  validates :user_id, :presence => true

  default_scope :order => 'microposts.created_at DESC'
end
```

This completes the data modeling for users and microposts. It's time now to build the web interface.

11.2 Showing Microposts

Although we don't yet have a way to create microposts through the web—that comes in Section 11.3.2—that won't stop us from displaying them (and testing that display). Following Twitter's lead, we'll plan to display a user's microposts not on a separate microposts **index** page, but rather directly on the user **show** page itself, as mocked up in Figure 11.4. We'll start with fairly simple ERb templates for adding a micropost display to the user profile, and then we'll add microposts to the sample data populator from Section 10.3.2 so that we have something to display.

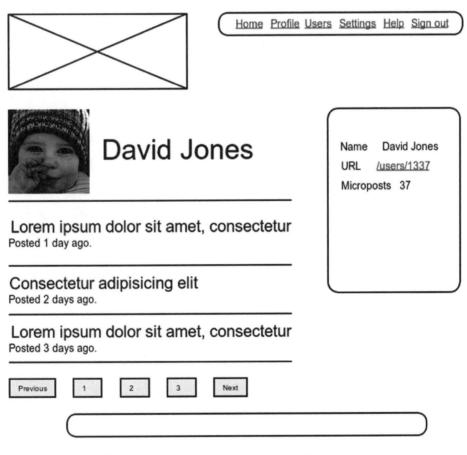

Figure 11.4 A mockup of a profile page with microposts.

As with the discussion of the signin machinery in Section 9.3.2, Section 11.2.1 will often push several elements onto the stack at a time, and then pop them off one by one. If you start getting bogged down, be patient; there's some nice payoff in Section 11.2.2.

11.2.1 Augmenting the User Show Page

We begin with a test for displaying the user's microposts. We work in the Users controller spec, since it is the Users controller that contains the user **show** action. Our strategy is to create a couple of factory microposts associated with the user, and then verify that the show page has a **span** tag with CSS class **"content"** containing each post's content. The resulting RSpec example appears in Listing 11.15.

Listing 11.15 A test for showing microposts on the user **show** page.
spec/controllers/users_controller_spec.rb

```
require 'spec_helper'

describe UsersController do
  render_views
  .
  .
  .
  describe "GET 'show'" do

    before(:each) do
      @user = Factory(:user)
    end
    .
    .
    .
    it "should show the user's microposts" do
      mp1 = Factory(:micropost, :user => @user, :content => "Foo bar")
      mp2 = Factory(:micropost, :user => @user, :content => "Baz quux")
      get :show, :id => @user
      response.should have_selector("span.content", :content => mp1.content)
      response.should have_selector("span.content", :content => mp2.content)
    end
  end
  .
  .
  .
end
```

Although these tests won't pass until Listing 11.17, we'll get started on the application code by inserting a table of microposts into the user profile page, as shown in Listing 11.16.[5]

Listing 11.16 Adding microposts to the user **show** page.
`app/views/users/show.html.erb`

```
<table class="profile">
  <tr>
    <td class="main">
      .
      .
      .
      <% unless @user.microposts.empty? %>
        <table class="microposts" summary="User microposts">
          <%= render @microposts %>
        </table>
        <%= will_paginate @microposts %>
      <% end %>
    </td>
    <td class="sidebar round">
      <strong>Name</strong> <%= @user.name %><br />
      <strong>URL</strong> <%= link_to user_path(@user), @user %><br />
      <strong>Microposts</strong> <%= @user.microposts.count %>
    </td>
  </tr>
</table>
```

We'll deal with the microposts **table** momentarily, but there are several other things to note first. One new idea is the use of **empty?** in the line

```
@user.microposts.empty?
```

This applies the **empty?** method, seen before in the context of strings (e.g., Section 4.2.3), to an array:

---

5. In the sense of semantic markup, it would probably be better to use an *ordered list*, but in that case the vertical alignment of text and images is much more difficult than with tables. See the exercise in Section 11.5 if you insist on struggling with the semantic version.

```
$ rails console
>> [1, 2].empty?
=> false
>> [].empty?
=> true
```

By using the conditional **unless** clause,

```
<% unless @user.microposts.empty? %>
```

we make sure that an empty table won't be displayed when the user has no microposts.

You'll also note from Listing 11.16 that we've preemptively added pagination for microposts through

```
<%= will_paginate @microposts %>
```

If you compare this with the analogous line on the user index page, Listing 10.27, you'll see that before we had just

```
<%= will_paginate %>
```

This worked because, in the context of the Users controller, **will_paginate** *assumes* the existence of an instance variable called **@users** (which, as we saw in Section 10.3.3, should be of class **WillPaginate::Collection**). In the present case, since we are still in the Users controller but want to paginate *microposts* instead, we pass an explicit **@microposts** variable to **will_paginate**. Of course, this means that we will have to define such a variable in the user **show** action (Listing 11.18).

Finally, note that we have taken this opportunity to add a count of the current number of microposts to the profile sidebar:

```
<td class="sidebar round">
  <strong>Name</strong> <%= @user.name %><br />
  <strong>URL</strong> <%= link_to user_path(@user), @user %><br />
  <strong>Microposts</strong> <%= @user.microposts.count %>
</td>
```

Here **@user.microposts.count** is the analogue of the **User.count** method, except
that it counts the microposts belonging to a given user through the user/micropost
association.[6]

Now for the microposts **table** itself:

```
<table class="microposts" summary="User microposts">
  <%= render @microposts %>
</table>
```

This code is responsible for generating the table of microposts, but you can see that it
just defers the heavy lifting to a micropost partial. We saw in Section 10.3.4 that the
code

```
<%= render @users %>
```

automatically renders each of the users in the **@users** variable using the
_user.html.erb partial. Similarly, the code

```
<%= render @microposts %>
```

does exactly the same thing for microposts. This means that we must define a
_micropost.html.erb partial (along with a **micropost** views directory), as shown
in Listing 11.17.

Listing 11.17 A partial for showing a single micropost.
app/views/microposts/_micropost.html.erb

```
<tr>
  <td class="micropost">
    <span class="content"><%= micropost.content %></span>
    <span class="timestamp">
      Posted <%= time_ago_in_words(micropost.created_at) %> ago.
    </span>
  </td>
</tr>
```

---

6. In case you're wondering, the association **count** method is smart, and performs the count directly in the
database. In particular, it does *not* pull all the microposts out of the database and then call **length** on the resulting
array, as this would become terribly inefficient as the number of microposts grew. Instead, it asks the database
to count the microposts with the given **user_id**. By the way, in the unlikely event that finding the count is
still a bottleneck in your application, you can make it even faster with a *counter cache.*

This uses the awesome **time_ago_in_words** helper method, whose effect we will see in Section 11.2.2.

Thus far, despite defining all the relevant ERb templates, the test in Listing 11.15 should have been failing for want of an **@microposts** variable. We can get it to pass with Listing 11.18.

Listing 11.18 Adding an **@microposts** instance variable to the user **show** action.
app/controllers/users_controller.rb

```
class UsersController < ApplicationController
  .
  .
  .
  def show
    @user = User.find(params[:id])
    @microposts = @user.microposts.paginate(:page => params[:page])
    @title = @user.name
  end
end
```

Notice here how clever **paginate** is—it even works with the microposts association, converting the array into a **WillPaginate::Collection** object on the fly.

Upon adding the CSS from Listing 11.19 to our **custom.css** stylesheet,[7] we can get a look at our new user profile page in Figure 11.5. It's rather... disappointing. Of course, this is because there are not currently any microposts. It's time to change that.

Listing 11.19 The CSS for microposts (includes all the CSS for this chapter).
public/stylesheets/custom.css

```
.
.
.
h1.micropost {
  margin-bottom: 0.3em;
}

table.microposts {
  margin-top: 1em;
}
```

---

7. For convenience, Listing 11.19 actually has *all* the CSS needed for this chapter.

```
table.microposts tr {
  height: 70px;
}

table.microposts tr td.gravatar {
  border-top: 1px solid #ccc;
  vertical-align: top;
  width: 50px;
}

table.microposts tr td.micropost {
  border-top: 1px solid #ccc;
  vertical-align: top;
  padding-top: 10px;
}

table.microposts tr td.micropost span.timestamp {
  display: block;
  font-size: 85%;
  color: #666;
}

div.user_info img {
  padding-right: 0.1em;
}

div.user_info a {
  text-decoration: none;
}

div.user_info span.user_name {
  position: absolute;
}

div.user_info span.microposts {
  font-size: 80%;
}

form.new_micropost {
  margin-bottom: 2em;
}

form.new_micropost textarea {
  height: 4em;
  margin-bottom: 0;
}
```

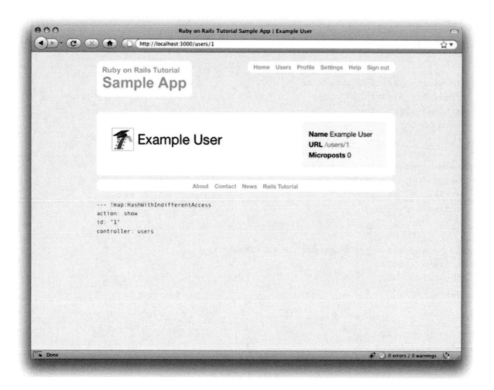

Figure 11.5   The user profile page with code for microposts—but no microposts.

11.2.2 Sample Microposts

With all the work making templates for user microposts in Section 11.2.1, the ending was rather anticlimactic. We can rectify this sad situation by adding microposts to the sample populator from Section 10.3.2. Adding sample microposts for *all* the users actually takes a rather long time, so first we'll select just the first six users[8] using the `:limit` option to the `User.all` method:[9]

```
User.all(:limit => 6)
```

---

8. (i.e., the five users with custom Gravatars, and one with the default Gravatar)

9. Tail your `log/development.log` file if you're curious about the SQL this method generates.

We then make 50 microposts for each user (plenty to overflow the pagination limit of 30), generating sample content for each micropost using the Faker gem's handy `Lorem.sentence` method. (**`Faker::Lorem.sentence`** returns *lorem ipsum* text; as noted in Chapter 6, *lorem ipsum* has a fascinating back story.) The result is the new sample data populator shown in Listing 11.20.

Listing 11.20 Adding microposts to the sample data.
`lib/tasks/sample_data.rake`

```
require 'faker'

namespace :db do
  desc "Fill database with sample data"
  task :populate => :environment do
    .
    .
    .
    User.all(:limit => 6).each do |user|
      50.times do
        user.microposts.create!(:content => Faker::Lorem.sentence(5))
      end
    end
  end
end
```

Of course, to generate the new sample data we have to run the **`db:populate`** Rake task:

```
$ rake db:populate
```

With that, we are in a position to enjoy the fruits of our Section 11.2.1 labors by displaying information for each micropost.[10] Figure 11.6 shows the user profile page for the first (signed-in) user, while Figure 11.7 shows the profile for a second user. Finally, Figure 11.8 shows the *second* page of microposts for the first user, along with the pagination links at the bottom of the display. In all three cases, observe that each micropost display indicates the time since it was created (e.g., "Posted 1 minute ago."); this is the work of the **`time_ago_in_words`** method from Listing 11.17. If you wait a couple minutes and reload the pages, you'll see how the text gets automatically updated based on the new time.

---

10. By design, the Faker gem's *lorem ipsum* text is randomized, so the contents of your sample microposts will differ.

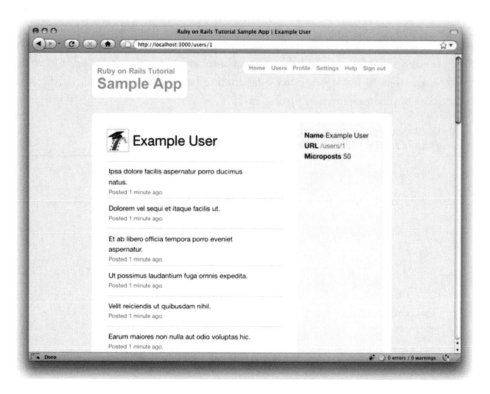

Figure 11.6   The user profile (`/users/1`) with microposts.

11.3 Manipulating Microposts

Having finished both the data modeling and display templates for microposts, we now turn our attention to the interface for creating them through the web. The result will be our third example of using an HTML form to create a resource—in this case, a Microposts resource.[11] In this section, we'll also see the first hint of a *status feed*—a notion brought to full fruition in Chapter 12. Finally, as with users, we'll make it possible to destroy microposts through the web.

There is one break with past convention worth noting: the interface to the Microposts resource will run principally through the Users and Pages controllers, rather than relying on a controller of its own. This means that the routes for the Microposts resource are unusually simple, as seen in Listing 11.21. The code in Listing 11.21 leads in turn to the

---

11. The other two resources are Users in Section 8.1 and Sessions in Section 9.1.

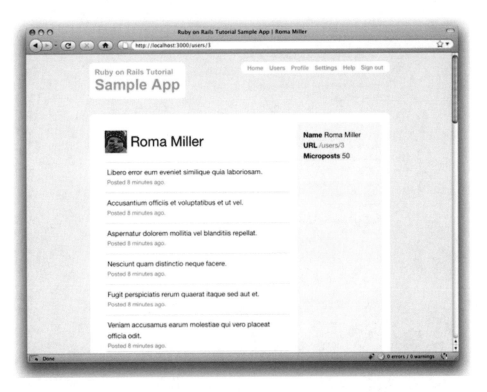

Figure 11.7   The profile of a different user, also with microposts (/users/3).

RESTful routes show in Table 11.2, which is a small subset of the full set of routes seen in Table 2.3. Of course, this simplicity is a sign of being *more* advanced, not less—we've come a long way since our reliance on scaffolding in Chapter 2, and we no longer need most of its complexity.

Listing 11.21   Routes for the Microposts resource.
config/routes.rb

```
SampleApp::Application.routes.draw do
  resources :users
  resources :sessions,    :only => [:new, :create, :destroy]
  resources :microposts, :only => [:create, :destroy]
  .
  .
  .
end
```

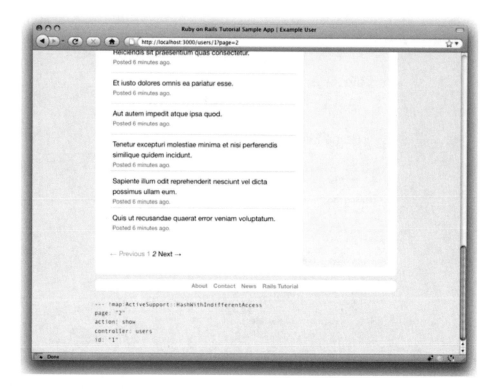

Figure 11.8   A second profile of microposts, with pagination links (`/users/1?page=2`).

11.3.1   Access Control

We begin our development of the Microposts resource with some access control in the Microposts controller. The idea is simple: both the **create** and **destroy** actions should require users to be signed in. The RSpec code to test for this appears in Listing 11.22, which will require creating the Microposts controller spec file. (We'll test for and add a third protection—ensuring that only a micropost's user can destroy it—in Section 11.3.4.)

Table 11.2   RESTful routes provided by the Microposts resource in Listing 11.21

HTTP Request	URL	Action	Purpose
POST	/microposts	**create**	create a new micropost
DELETE	/microposts/1	**destroy**	delete micropost with id **1**

Listing 11.22 Access control tests for the Microposts controller.
`spec/controllers/microposts_controller_spec.rb`

```ruby
require 'spec_helper'

describe MicropostsController do
  render_views

  describe "access control" do

    it "should deny access to 'create'" do
      post :create
      response.should redirect_to(signin_path)
    end

    it "should deny access to 'destroy'" do
      delete :destroy, :id => 1
      response.should redirect_to(signin_path)
    end
  end
end
```

Writing the application code needed to get the tests in Listing 11.22 to pass requires a little refactoring first. Recall from Section 10.2.1 that we enforced the signin requirement using a before filter that called the **authenticate** method (Listing 10.11). At the time, we only needed **authenticate** in the Users controller, but now we find that we need it in the Microposts controller as well, so we'll move **authenticate** into the Sessions helper, as shown in Listing 11.23.[12]

Listing 11.23 Moving the **authenticate** method into the Sessions helper.
`app/helpers/sessions_helper.rb`

```ruby
module SessionsHelper
  .
  .
  .
  def authenticate
    deny_access unless signed_in?
  end
```

---

12. We noted in Section 9.3.2 that helper methods are available only in *views* by default, but we arranged for the Sessions helper methods to be available in the controllers as well by adding **include SessionsHelper** to the Application controller (Listing 9.11).

```
def deny_access
  store_location
  redirect_to signin_path, :notice => "Please sign in to access this page."
end
  .
  .
  .

end
```

(To avoid code repetition, you should also remove **authenticate** from the Users controller at this time.)

With the code in Listing 11.23, the **authenticate** method is now available in the Microposts controller, which means that we can restrict access to the **create** and **destroy** actions with the before filter shown in Listing 11.24. (Since we didn't generate it at the command line, you will have to create the Microposts controller file by hand.)

Listing 11.24 Adding authentication to the Microposts controller actions.
`app/controllers/microposts_controller.rb`

```
class MicropostsController < ApplicationController
  before_filter :authenticate

  def create
  end

  def destroy
  end
end
```

Note that we haven't restricted the actions the before filter applies to, since presently it applies to them both. If we were to add, say, an **index** action accessible even to non-signed-in users, we would need to specify the protected actions explicitly:

```
class MicropostsController < ApplicationController
  before_filter :authenticate, :only => [:create, :destroy]

  def create
  end

  def destroy
  end
end
```

11.3.2 Creating Microposts

In Chapter 8, we implemented user signup by making an HTML form that issued an HTTP POST request to the **create** action in the Users controller. The implementation of micropost creation is similar; the main difference is that, rather than using a separate page at /microposts/new, we will (following Twitter's convention) put the form on the Home page itself (i.e., the root path /), as mocked up in Figure 11.9.

When we last left the Home page, it appeared as in Figure 5.7—that is, it had a big, fat "Sign up now!" button in the middle. Since a micropost creation form only makes sense in the context of a particular signed-in user, one goal of this section will be to serve different versions of the Home page depending on a visitor's signin status. We'll implement this in Listing 11.27, but for now the only implication is that the tests for the

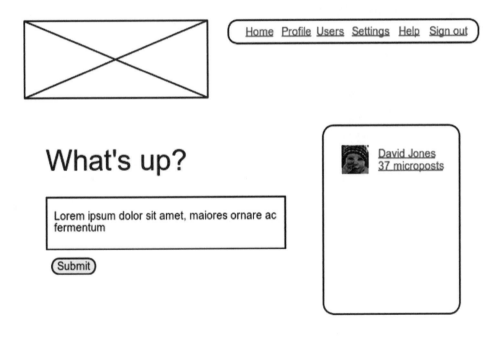

Figure 11.9 A mockup of the Home page with a form for creating microposts.

Microposts controller **create** action should sign a (factory) user in before attempting to make a post.

With that caveat in mind, the micropost creation tests parallel those for user creation from Listing 8.6 and Listing 8.14; the result appears in Listing 11.25.

Listing 11.25 Tests for the Microposts controller **create** action.
spec/controllers/microposts_controller_spec.rb

```
require 'spec_helper'

describe MicropostsController do
  .
  .
  .
  describe "POST 'create'" do

    before(:each) do
      @user = test_sign_in(Factory(:user))
    end

    describe "failure" do

      before(:each) do
        @attr = { :content => "" }
      end

      it "should not create a micropost" do
        lambda do
          post :create, :micropost => @attr
        end.should_not change(Micropost, :count)
      end

      it "should render the home page" do
        post :create, :micropost => @attr
        response.should render_template('pages/home')
      end
    end

    describe "success" do

      before(:each) do
        @attr = { :content => "Lorem ipsum" }
      end

      it "should create a micropost" do
        lambda do
          post :create, :micropost => @attr
```

```
        end.should change(Micropost, :count).by(1)
      end

      it "should redirect to the home page" do
        post :create, :micropost => @attr
        response.should redirect_to(root_path)
      end

      it "should have a flash message" do
        post :create, :micropost => @attr
        flash[:success].should =~ /micropost created/i
      end
    end
  end
end
```

The **create** action for microposts is similar to its user analogue (Listing 8.15); the principal difference lies in using the user/micropost association to **build** the new micropost, as seen in Listing 11.26.

Listing 11.26 The Microposts controller **create** action.
app/controllers/microposts_controller.rb

```
class MicropostsController < ApplicationController
  .
  .
  .
  def create
    @micropost = current_user.microposts.build(params[:micropost])
    if @micropost.save
      flash[:success] = "Micropost created!"
      redirect_to root_path
    else
      render 'pages/home'
    end
  end
  .
  .
  .
end
```

At this point, the tests in Listing 11.25 should all be passing, but of course we still don't have a form to create microposts. We can rectify this with Listing 11.27, which serves up different HTML based on whether the site visitor is signed in or not.

Listing 11.27 Adding microposts creation to the Home page (/).
`app/views/pages/home.html.erb`

```erb
<% if signed_in? %>
  <table class="front" summary="For signed-in users">
    <tr>
      <td class="main">
        <h1 class="micropost">What's up?</h1>
        <%= render 'shared/micropost_form' %>
      </td>
      <td class="sidebar round">
        <%= render 'shared/user_info' %>
      </td>
    </tr>
  </table>
<% else %>
  <h1>Sample App</h1>

  <p>
    This is the home page for the
    <a href="http://railstutorial.org/">Ruby on Rails Tutorial</a>
    sample application.
  </p>

  <%= link_to "Sign up now!", signup_path, :class => "signup_button round" %>
<% end %>
```

Having so much code in each branch of the **if-else** conditional is a bit messy, and
cleaning it up using partials is left as an exercise (Section 11.5). Filling in the necessary
partials from Listing 11.27 isn't an exercise, though; we fill in the micropost form partial
in Listing 11.28 and the new Home page sidebar in Listing 11.29.

Listing 11.28 The form partial for creating microposts.
`app/views/shared/_micropost_form.html.erb`

```erb
<%= form_for @micropost do |f| %>
  <%= render 'shared/error_messages', :object => f.object %>
  <div class="field">
    <%= f.text_area :content %>
  </div>
  <div class="actions">
    <%= f.submit "Submit" %>
  </div>
<% end %>
```

Listing 11.29 The partial for the user info sidebar.
app/views/shared/_user_info.html.erb

```
<div class="user_info">
  <a href="<%= user_path(current_user) %>">
    <%= gravatar_for current_user, :size => 30 %>
    <span class="user_name">
      <%= current_user.name %>
    </span>
    <span class="microposts">
      <%= pluralize(current_user.microposts.count, "micropost") %>
    </span>
  </a>
</div>
```

Note that, as in the profile sidebar (Listing 11.16), the user info in Listing 11.29 displays the total number of microposts for the user. There's a slight difference in the display, though; in the profile sidebar, **Microposts** is a label, and showing **Microposts** 1 makes perfect sense. In the present case, though, saying "1 microposts" is ungrammatical, so we arrange to display "1 micropost" (but "2 microposts") using the convenient **pluralize** helper method.

The form defined in Listing 11.28 is an exact analogue of the signup form in Listing 8.2, which means that it needs an **@micropost** instance variable. This is supplied in Listing 11.30—but only when the user is signed in.

Listing 11.30 Adding a micropost instance variable to the **home** action.
app/controllers/pages_controller.rb

```
class PagesController < ApplicationController

  def home
    @title = "Home"
    @micropost = Micropost.new if signed_in?
  end
  .
  .
  .
end
```

Now the HTML should render properly, showing the form as in Figure 11.10, and a form with a submission error as in Figure 11.11. You are invited at this point to create

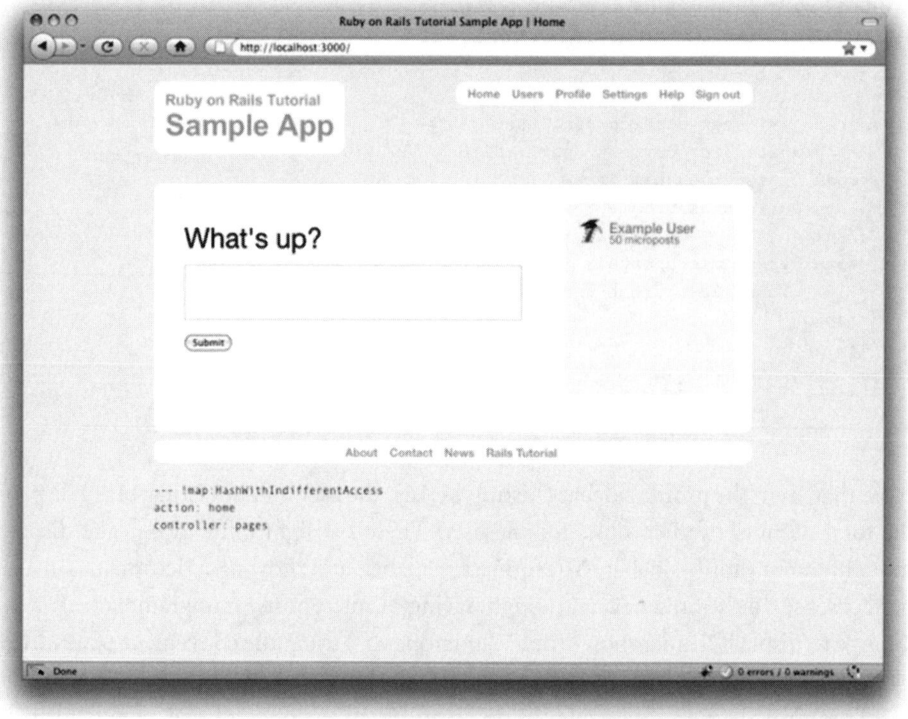

Figure 11.10   The Home page (/) with a new micropost form.

a new post for yourself and verify that everything is working—but you should probably wait until after Section 11.3.3.

11.3.3   A Proto-feed

The comment at the end of Section 11.3.2 alluded to a problem: the current Home page doesn't display any microposts. If you like, you can verify that the form shown in Figure 11.10 is working by submitting a valid entry and then navigating to the profile page to see the post, but that's rather cumbersome. It would be far better to have a *feed* of microposts that includes the user's own posts, as mocked up in Figure 11.12. (In Chapter 12, we'll generalize this feed to include the microposts of users being *followed* by the current user.)

Since each user should have a feed, we are led naturally to a **feed** method in the User model. Eventually, we will test that the feed returns the microposts of the users being followed, but for now we'll just test that the **feed** method *includes* the current user's

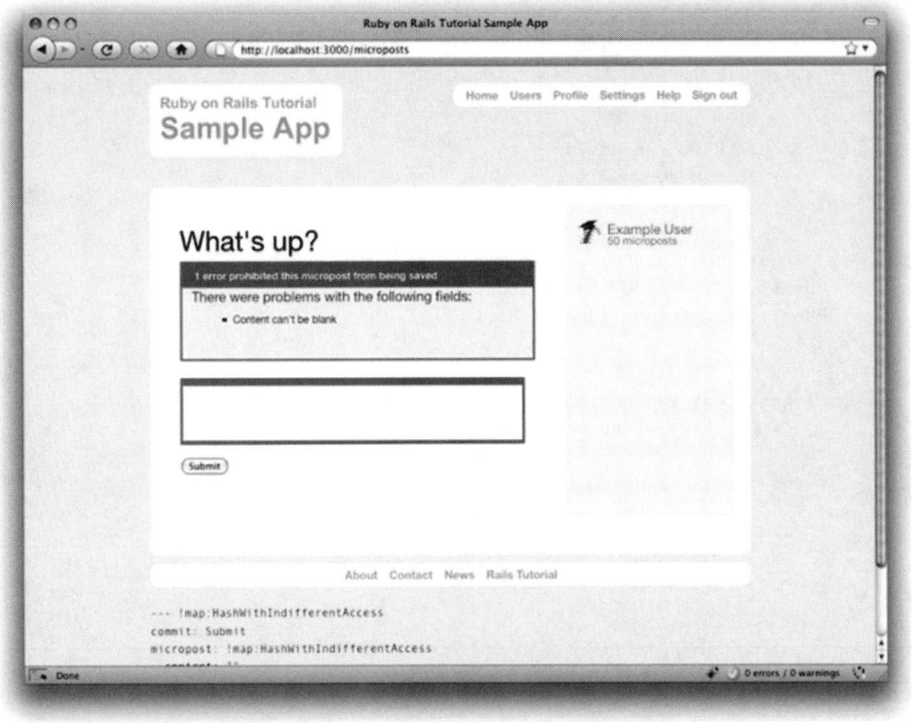

Figure 11.11 The home page with form errors.

microposts but *excludes* the posts of a different user. We can express these requirements in code with Listing 11.31.

Listing 11.31 Tests for the (proto-)status feed.
spec/models/user_spec.rb

```
require 'spec_helper'

describe User do
  .
  .
  .
  describe "micropost associations" do

    before(:each) do
      @user = User.create(@attr)
      @mp1 = Factory(:micropost, :user => @user, :created_at => 1.day.ago)
      @mp2 = Factory(:micropost, :user => @user, :created_at => 1.hour.ago)
    end
```

```
        .
        .
        .
    describe "status feed" do

      it "should have a feed" do
        @user.should respond_to(:feed)
      end

      it "should include the user's microposts" do
        @user.feed.include?(@mp1).should be_true
        @user.feed.include?(@mp2).should be_true
      end

      it "should not include a different user's microposts" do
        mp3 = Factory(:micropost,
                      :user => Factory(:user, :email => Factory.next(:email)))
        @user.feed.include?(mp3).should be_false
      end
    end
  end
end
```

These tests introduce the array **include?** method, which simply checks if an array
includes the given element:[13]

```
$ rails console
>> a = [1, "foo", :bar]
>> a.include?("foo")
=> true
>> a.include?(:bar)
=> true
>> a.include?("baz")
=> false
```

We can arrange for an appropriate micropost **feed** by selecting all the microposts
with **user_id** equal to the current user's id, which we accomplish using the **where**
method on the **Micropost** model, as shown in Listing 11.32.[14]

---

13. Learning about methods such as **include?** is one reason why, as noted in Section 1.1.1, I recommend
reading a pure Ruby book after finishing this one.

14. See the Rails Guide on the Active Record Query Interface for more on **where** and the like.

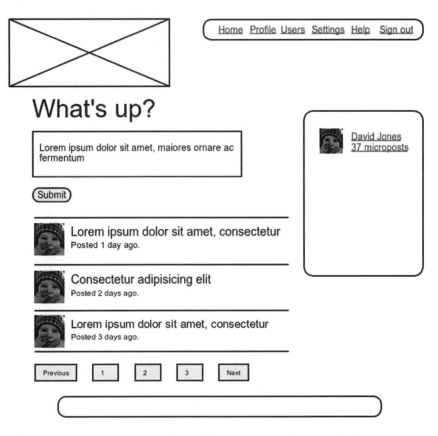

Figure 11.12   A mockup of the Home page with a proto-feed.

Listing 11.32   A preliminary implementation for the micropost status feed.
app/models/user.rb

```ruby
class User < ActiveRecord::Base
  .
  .
  .
  def feed
    # This is preliminary. See Chapter 12 for the full implementation.
    Micropost.where("user_id = ?", id)
  end
  .
  .
  .
end
```

The question mark in

```
Micropost.where("user_id = ?", id)
```

ensures that **id** is properly *escaped* before being included in the underlying SQL query, thereby avoiding a serious security hole called *SQL injection*. (The **id** attribute here is just an integer, so there is no danger in this case, but *always* escaping variables injected into SQL statements is a good habit to cultivate.)

Alert readers might note at this point that the code in Listing 11.32 is essentially equivalent to writing

```
def feed
  microposts
end
```

We've used the code in Listing 11.32 instead because it generalizes much more naturally to the full status feed needed in Chapter 12.

To use the feed in the sample application, we add an **@feed_items** instance variable for the current user's (paginated) feed, as in Listing 11.33, and then add a feed partial (Listing 11.34) to the Home page (Listing 11.36).

Listing 11.33 Adding a feed instance variable to the **home** action.
app/controllers/pages_controller.rb

```
class PagesController < ApplicationController

  def home
    @title = "Home"
    if signed_in?
      @micropost = Micropost.new
      @feed_items = current_user.feed.paginate(:page => params[:page])
    end
  end
  .
  .
  .
end
```

Listing 11.34   The status feed partial.
app/views/shared/_feed.html.erb

```
<% unless @feed_items.empty? %>
  <table class="microposts" summary="User microposts">
    <%= render :partial => 'shared/feed_item', :collection => @feed_items %>
  </table>
  <%= will_paginate @feed_items %>
<% end %>
```

The status feed partial defers the feed item rendering to a feed item partial using the code

```
<%= render :partial => 'shared/feed_item', :collection => @feed_items %>
```

Here we pass a **:collection** parameter with the feed items, which causes **render** to use the given partial (**'feed_item'** in this case) to render each item in the collection. (We have omitted the **:partial** parameter in previous renderings, writing, e.g., **render 'shared/micropost'**, but with a **:collection** parameter that syntax doesn't work.) The feed item partial itself appears in Listing 11.35; note the addition of a delete link to the feed item partial, following the example from Listing 10.38.

Listing 11.35   A partial for a single feed item.
app/views/shared/_feed_item.html.erb

```
<tr>
  <td class="gravatar">
    <%= link_to gravatar_for(feed_item.user), feed_item.user %>
  </td>
  <td class="micropost">
    <span class="user">
      <%= link_to feed_item.user.name, feed_item.user %>
    </span>
    <span class="content"><%= feed_item.content %></span>
    <span class="timestamp">
      Posted <%= time_ago_in_words(feed_item.created_at) %> ago.
    </span>
  </td>
  <% if current_user?(feed_item.user) %>
  <td>
```

```
        <%= link_to "delete", feed_item, :method => :delete,
                                          :confirm => "You sure?",
                                          :title => feed_item.content %>
    </td>
    <% end %>
</tr>
```

We can then add the feed to the Home page by rendering the feed partial as usual (Listing 11.36). The result is a display of the feed on the Home page, as required (Figure 11.13).

Listing 11.36 Adding a status feed to the Home page.
app/views/pages/home.html.erb

```
<% if signed_in? %>
  <table class="front" summary="For signed-in users">
    <tr>
      <td class="main">
        <h1 class="micropost">What's up?</h1>
        <%= render 'shared/micropost_form' %>
        <%= render 'shared/feed' %>
      </td>
      .
      .
      .
    </tr>
  </table>

<% else %>
  .
  .
  .
<% end %>
```

At this point, creating a new micropost works as expected, as seen in Figure 11.14. (We'll write an integration test to this effect in Section 11.3.5.) There is one subtlety, though: on *failed* micropost submission, the Home page expects an **@feed_items** instance variable, so failed submissions currently break (as you should be able to verify by running your test suite). The easiest solution is to suppress the feed entirely by assigning it an empty array, as shown in Listing 11.37.[15]

---

15. Unfortunately, returning a paginated feed doesn't work in this case. Implement it and click on a pagination link to see why. (The screencasts will cover this issue in more depth.)

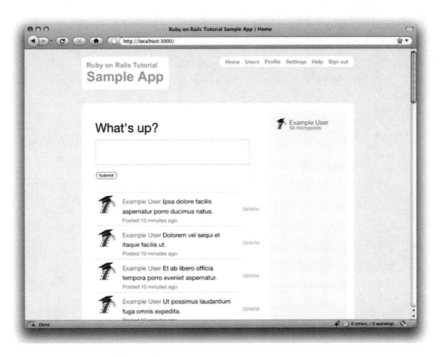

Figure 11.13   The Home page (/) with a proto-feed.

Listing 11.37   Adding an (empty) **@feed_items** instance variable to the **create** action.
app/controllers/microposts_controller.rb

```ruby
class MicropostsController < ApplicationController
  .
  .
  .
  def create
    @micropost = current_user.microposts.build(params[:micropost])
    if @micropost.save
      flash[:success] = "Micropost created!"
      redirect_to root_path
    else
      @feed_items = []
      render 'pages/home'
    end
  end
  .
  .
  .
end
```

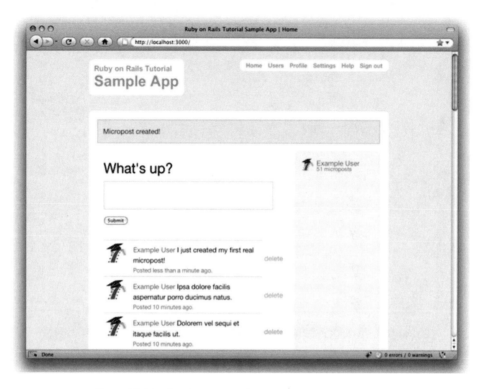

Figure 11.14   The Home page after creating a new micropost.

11.3.4 Destroying Microposts

The last piece of functionality to add to the Microposts resource is the ability to destroy posts. As with user deletion (Section 10.4.2), we accomplish this with "delete" links, as mocked up in Figure 11.15. Unlike that case, which restricted user destruction to admin users, the delete links will work only for microposts created by the current user.

Our first step is to add a delete link to the micropost partial as in Listing 11.35. The result appears in Listing 11.38.

Listing 11.38   A partial for showing a single micropost.
app/views/microposts/_micropost.html.erb

```erb
<tr>
  <td class="micropost">
    <span class="content"><%= micropost.content %></span>
    <span class="timestamp">
      Posted <%= time_ago_in_words(micropost.created_at) %> ago.
```

```
    </span>
  </td>
  <% if current_user?(micropost.user) %>
  <td>
    <%= link_to "delete", micropost, :method => :delete,
                                     :confirm => "You sure?",
                                     :title => micropost.content %>
  </td>
  <% end %>
</tr>
```

Note: As of the latest version of Rails 3.0, I and several other readers sometimes encounter a strange bug, whereby the **micropost.user** association isn't made properly. The result

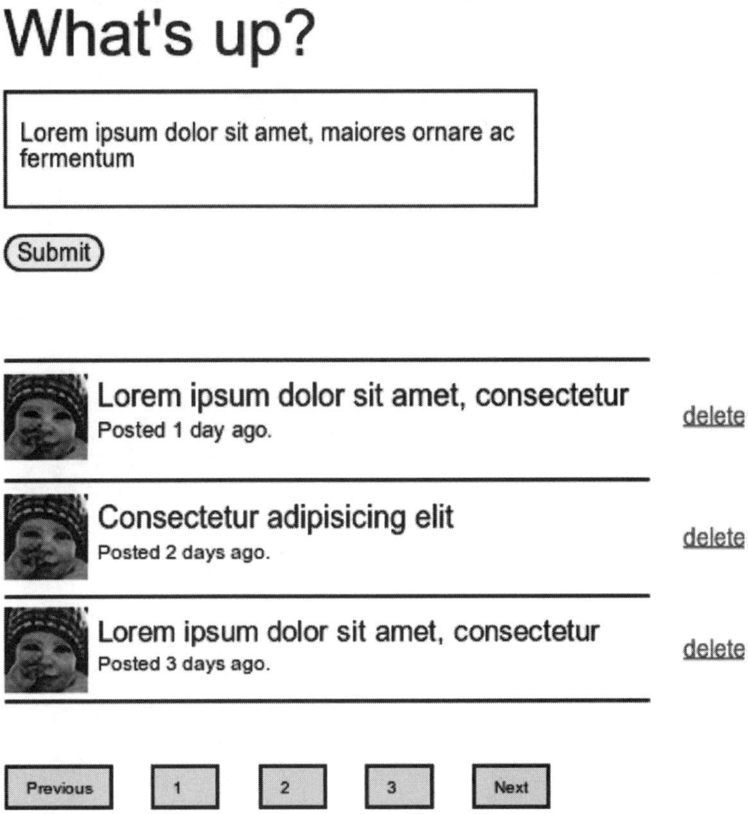

What's up?

Lorem ipsum dolor sit amet, maiores ornare ac fermentum

(Submit)

Lorem ipsum dolor sit amet, consectetur
Posted 1 day ago.

delete

Consectetur adipisicing elit
Posted 2 days ago.

delete

Lorem ipsum dolor sit amet, consectetur
Posted 3 days ago.

delete

Previous | 1 | 2 | 3 | Next

Figure 11.15 A mockup of the proto-feed with micropost delete links.

is that calling **`micropost.user`** raises a **`NoMethodError`** exception. Until this Rails bug is fixed, as a workaround you can replace the line

```
<% if current_user?(micropost.user) %>
```

with the lines

```
<% user = micropost.user rescue User.find(micropost.user_id) %>
<% if current_user?(user) %>
```

When the call to **`micropost.user`** raises an exception, this code finds the user based on the micropost's **`user_id`**.

The tests for the **`destroy`** action are straightforward generalizations of the similar tests for destroying users (Listing 10.40), as seen in Listing 11.39.

Listing 11.39 Tests for the Microposts controller **`destroy`** action.
`spec/controllers/microposts_controller_spec.rb`

```
describe MicropostsController do
  .
  .
  .
  describe "DELETE 'destroy'" do

    describe "for an unauthorized user" do

      before(:each) do
        @user = Factory(:user)
        wrong_user = Factory(:user, :email => Factory.next(:email))
        test_sign_in(wrong_user)
        @micropost = Factory(:micropost, :user => @user)
      end

      it "should deny access" do
        delete :destroy, :id => @micropost
        response.should redirect_to(root_path)
      end
    end

    describe "for an authorized user" do

      before(:each) do
        @user = test_sign_in(Factory(:user))
```

```
      @micropost = Factory(:micropost, :user => @user)
    end

    it "should destroy the micropost" do
      lambda do
        delete :destroy, :id => @micropost
      end.should change(Micropost, :count).by(-1)
    end
  end
end
```

The application code is also analogous to the user case in Listing 10.41; the main difference is that, rather than using an **admin_user** before filter, in the case of microposts we have an **authorized_user** before filter to check that the current user is the micropost's user. The code appears in Listing 11.40, and the result of destroying the second-most-recent post appears in Figure 11.16.

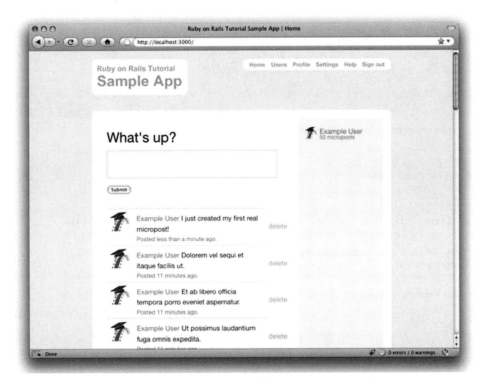

Figure 11.16   The user home page after deleting the second-most-recent micropost.

Listing 11.40 The Microposts controller **destroy** action.
`app/controllers/microposts_controller.rb`

```ruby
class MicropostsController < ApplicationController
  before_filter :authenticate, :only => [:create, :destroy]
  before_filter :authorized_user, :only => :destroy
  .
  .
  .
  def destroy
    @micropost.destroy
    redirect_back_or root_path
  end

  private

    def authorized_user
      @micropost = Micropost.find(params[:id])
      redirect_to root_path unless current_user?(@micropost.user)
    end
end
```

11.3.5 Testing the New Home Page

Before leaving micropost creation and destruction, we'll write some RSpec integration specs to test that our forms are working properly. As in the case of users (Section 8.4), we start by generating a microposts integration spec:

```
$ rails generate integration_test microposts
```

Tests for failed and successful micropost creation appear in Listing 11.41.

Listing 11.41 An integration test for the microposts on the **home** page.
`spec/requests/microposts_spec.rb`

```ruby
require 'spec_helper'

describe "Microposts" do

  before(:each) do
    user = Factory(:user)
    visit signin_path
    fill_in :email,    :with => user.email
```

```
      fill_in :password, :with => user.password
      click_button
  end

  describe "creation" do

    describe "failure" do

      it "should not make a new micropost" do
        lambda do
          visit root_path
          fill_in :micropost_content, :with => ""
          click_button
          response.should render_template('pages/home')
          response.should have_selector("div#error_explanation")
        end.should_not change(Micropost, :count)
      end
    end

    describe "success" do

      it "should make a new micropost" do
        content = "Lorem ipsum dolor sit amet"
        lambda do
          visit root_path
          fill_in :micropost_content, :with => content
          click_button
          response.should have_selector("span.content", :content => content)
        end.should change(Micropost, :count).by(1)
      end
    end
  end
end
```

Having finished testing the micropost functionality, we are now ready to move on to the final feature of our sample application: user following.

11.4 Conclusion

With the addition of the Microposts resource, we are nearly finished with our sample application. All that remains is to add a social layer by letting users follow each other. We'll learn how to model such user relationships, and see the implications for the status feed, in Chapter 12.

Before proceeding, be sure to commit and merge your changes if you're using Git for version control:

```
$ git add .
$ git commit -m "Added user microposts"
$ git checkout master
$ git merge user-microposts
```

You can also push the app up to Heroku at this point. Because the data model has changed through the addition of the **microposts** table, you will also need to migrate the production database:

```
$ git push heroku
$ heroku rake db:migrate
```

11.5 Exercises

We've covered enough material now that there is a combinatorial explosion of possible extensions to the application. Here are just a few of the many possibilities:

1. **(Challenging)** Add a JavaScript display to the Home page to count down from 140 characters.
2. Add tests for the sidebar micropost counts (including proper pluralization).
3. **(Mainly for designers)** Modify the microposts listing to use an ordered list instead of a table. (*Note:* this is how Twitter displays its status updates.) Then add the appropriate CSS to make the resulting feed not look like crap.
4. Add tests for micropost pagination.
5. Refactor the Home page to use separate partials for the two branches of the **if-else** statement.
6. Write a test to make sure delete links do not appear for microposts not created by the current user.
7. Add a nested route so that /users/1/microposts shows all the microposts for user 1. (You will also have to add a Microposts controller **index** action and corresponding view.)
8. Very long words currently break our layout, as shown in Figure 11.17. Fix this problem using the **wrap** helper defined in Listing 11.42. (Note the use of the **raw** method to prevent Rails from escaping the resulting HTML.)

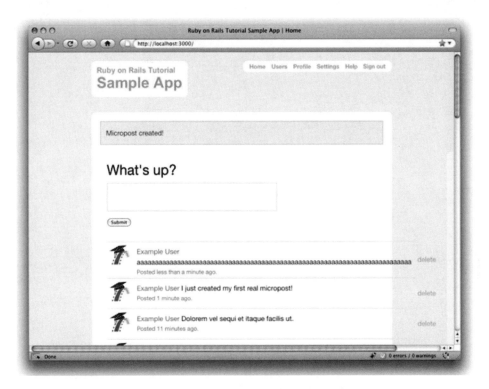

Figure 11.17 The (broken) site layout with a particularly long word.

Listing 11.42 A helper to wrap long words.
app/helpers/microposts_helper.rb

```ruby
module MicropostsHelper

  def wrap(content)
    raw(content.split.map{ |s| wrap_long_string(s) }.join(' '))
  end

  private

    def wrap_long_string(text, max_width = 30)
      zero_width_space = "&#8203;"
      regex = /.{1,#{max_width}}/
      (text.length < max_width) ? text :
                                  text.scan(regex).join(zero_width_space)
    end
end
```

CHAPTER 12

Following Users

In this chapter, we will complete the core sample application by adding a social layer that allows users to follow (and unfollow) other users, resulting in each user's Home page displaying a status feed of the followed users' microposts. We will also make views to display both a user's followers and the users each user is following. We will learn how to model user following in Section 12.1, and then make the web interface in Section 12.2 (including an introduction to Ajax). Finally, we'll end by developing a fully functional status feed in Section 12.3.

This final chapter contains some of the most challenging material in the tutorial, including a complicated data model and some Ruby/SQL trickery to make the status feed. Through these examples, you will see how Rails can handle even rather intricate data models, which should serve you well as you go on to develop your own applications with their own specific requirements. To help with the transition from tutorial to independent development, Section 12.4 contains suggested extensions to the core sample application, along with pointers to more advanced resources.

As usual, Git users should create a new topic branch:

```
$ git checkout -b following-users
```

Because the material in this chapter is particularly challenging, before writing any code we'll pause for a moment and take a tour of user following. As in previous chapters, at this early stage we'll represent pages using mockups.[1] The full page flow runs as

---

1. The photographs in the mockup tour are from http://www.flickr.com/photos/john_lustig/2518452221/ and http://www.flickr.com/photos/30775272@N05/2884963755/.

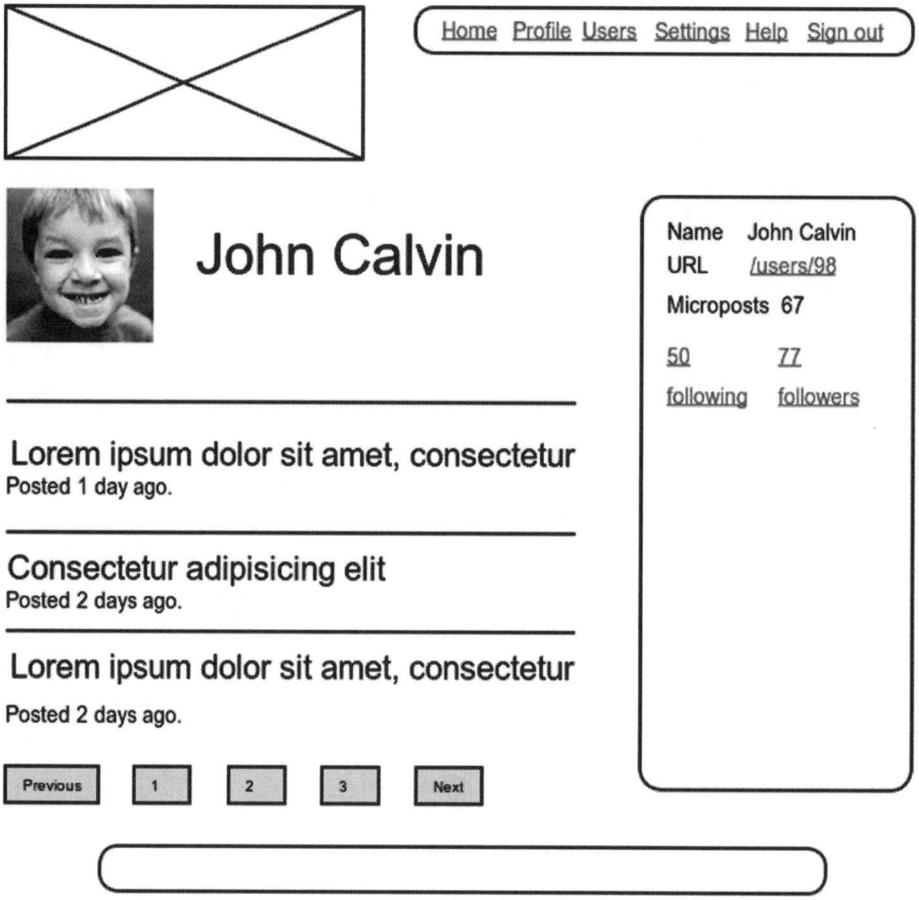

Figure 12.1   A mockup of the current user's profile.

follows: a user (John Calvin) starts at his profile page (Figure 12.1) and navigates to the Users page (Figure 12.2) to select a user to follow. Calvin navigates to the profile of a second user, Thomas Hobbes (Figure 12.3), clicking on the "Follow" button to follow that user. This changes the "Follow" button to "Unfollow", and increments Hobbes's "followers" count by one (Figure 12.4). Navigating to his home page, Calvin now sees an incremented "following" count and finds Hobbes's microposts in his status feed (Figure 12.5). The rest of this chapter is dedicated to making this page flow actually work.

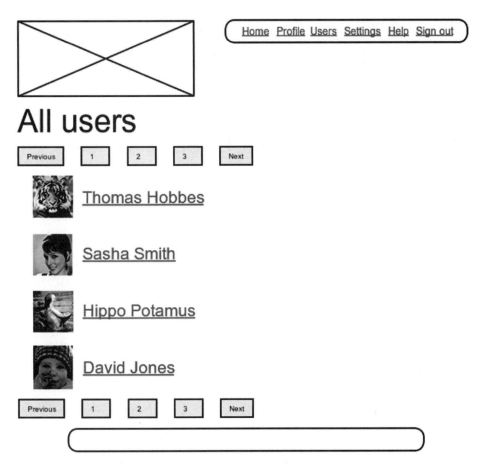

Figure 12.2   A mockup of finding a user to follow.

12.1 The Relationship Model

Our first step in implementing user following and followers is to construct a data model, which is not as straightforward as it seems. Naïvely, it seems that a **has_many** relationship should do: a user **has_many** following and **has_many** followers. As we will see, there is a problem with this approach, and we'll learn how to fix it using **has_many :through**. It's likely that many of the ideas in this section won't seem obvious at first, and it may take a while for the rather complicated data model to sink in. If you find yourself getting confused, try pushing forward to the end; then, read the section a second time through to see if things are clearer.

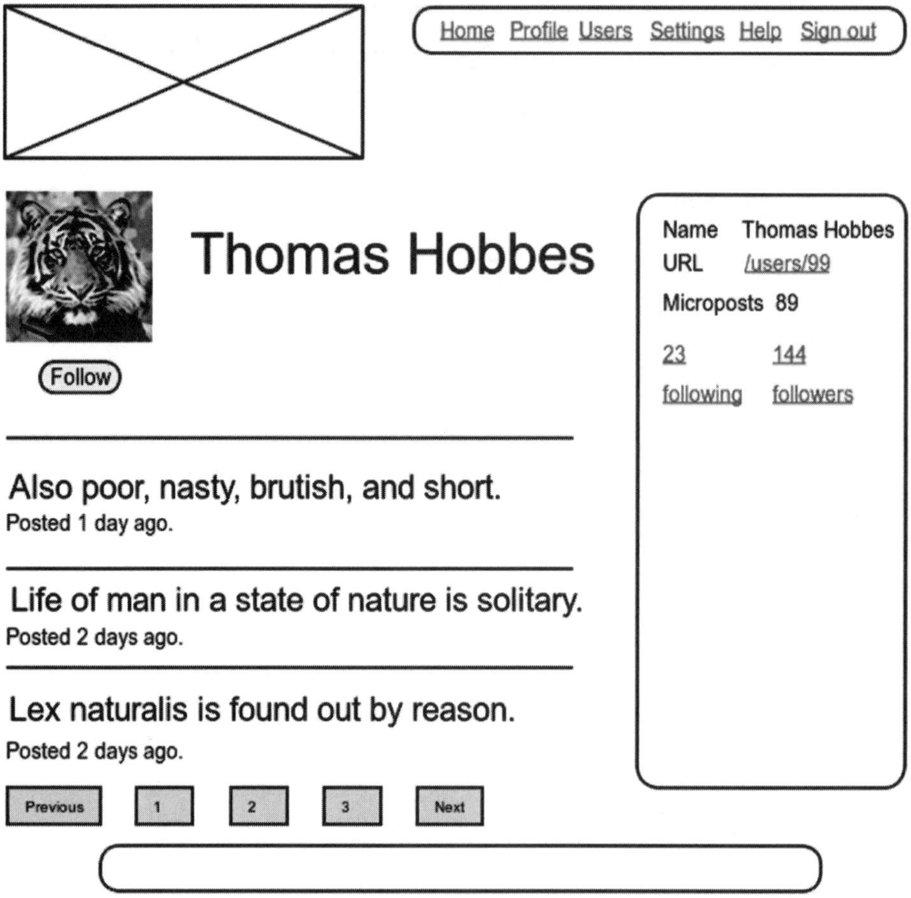

Figure 12.3   A mockup of the profile of another user, with a follow button.

12.1.1   A Problem with the Data Model (and a Solution)

As a first step toward constructing a data model for user following, let's examine a typical case. For instance, consider a user who follows a second user: we could say that, e.g., Calvin is following Hobbes, and Hobbes is followed by Calvin, so that Calvin is the *follower* and Hobbes is *followed*. Using Rails' default pluralization convention, the set of all such followed users would be called the *followeds*, but that is ungrammatical and clumsy; instead, we will override the default and call them *following*, so that `user.following` will contain an array of the users being followed. Similarly, the set of all users following

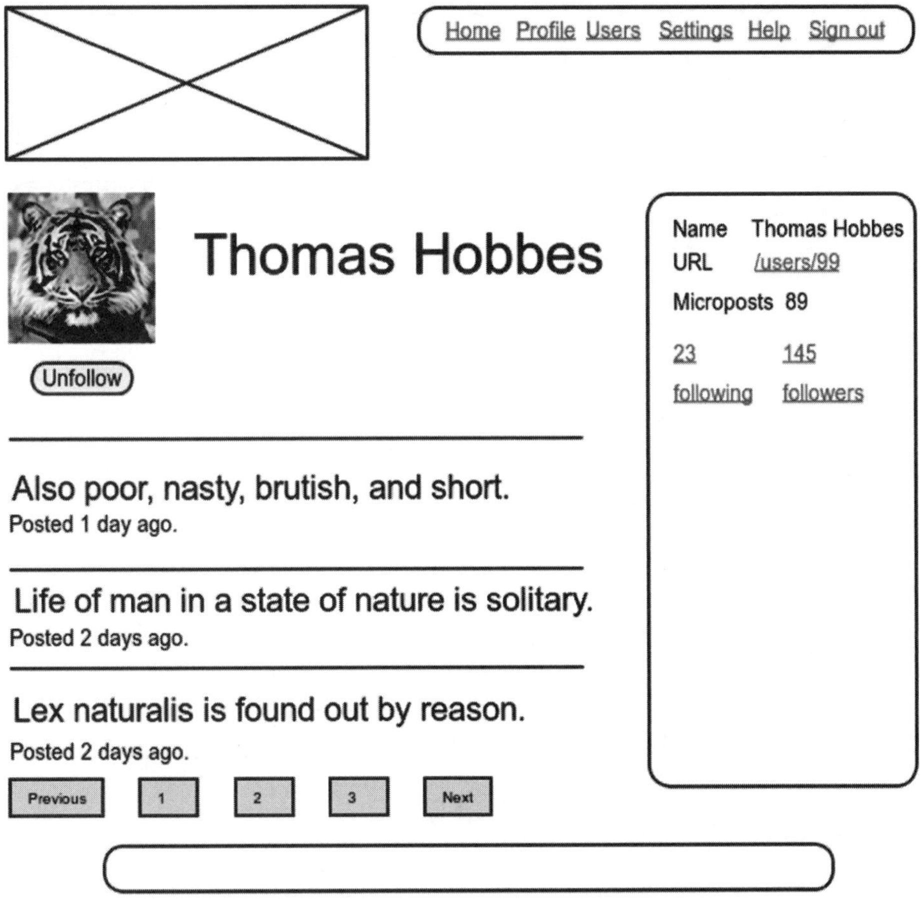

Figure 12.4   A profile mockup with an unfollow button and incremented followers count.

a given user is that user's *followers*, and `user.followers` will be an array of those users.

This suggests modeling the *following* users as in Figure 12.6, with a `following` table and a `has_many` association. Since `user.following` should be an array of users, each row of the `following` table would need to be a user, as identified by the `followed_id`, together with the `follower_id` to establish the association.[2] In addition, since each row is a user, we would need to include the user's other attributes, including the name, password, etc.

---

2. For simplicity, Figure 12.6 suppresses the `following` table's `id` column.

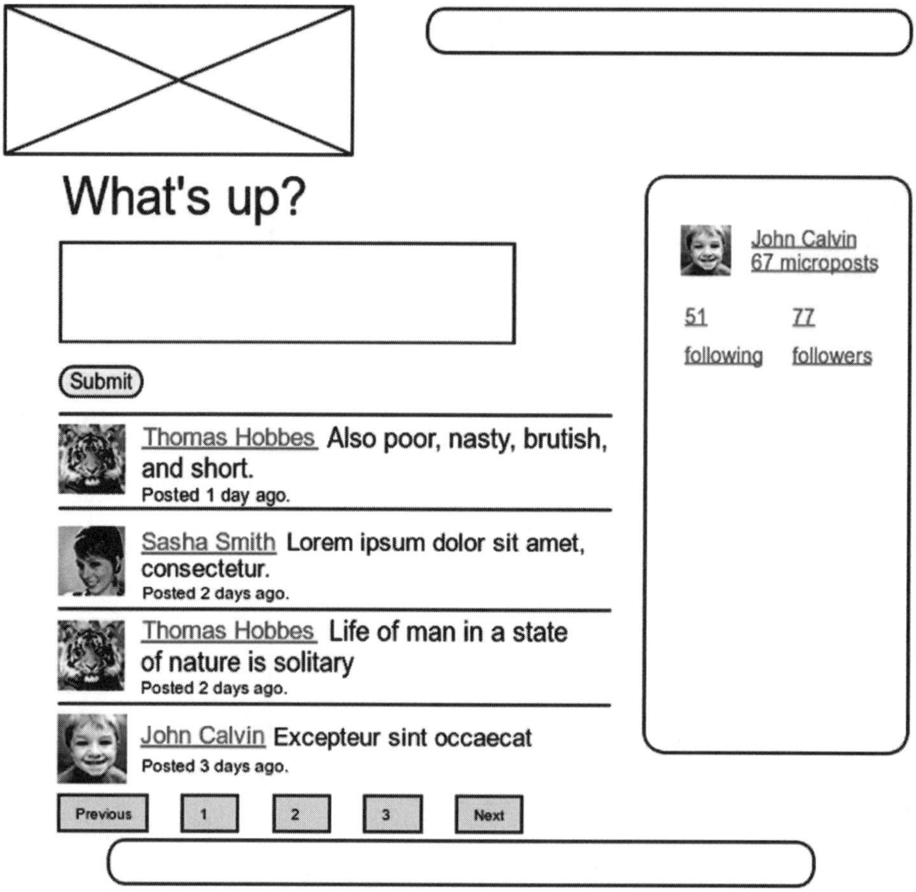

What's up?

(Submit)

Thomas Hobbes Also poor, nasty, brutish, and short.
Posted 1 day ago.

Sasha Smith Lorem ipsum dolor sit amet, consectetur.
Posted 2 days ago.

Thomas Hobbes Life of man in a state of nature is solitary
Posted 2 days ago.

John Calvin Excepteur sint occaecat
Posted 3 days ago.

Previous   1   2   3   Next

John Calvin
67 microposts

51   77
following   followers

Figure 12.5   A Home page mockup, with status feed and incremented following count.

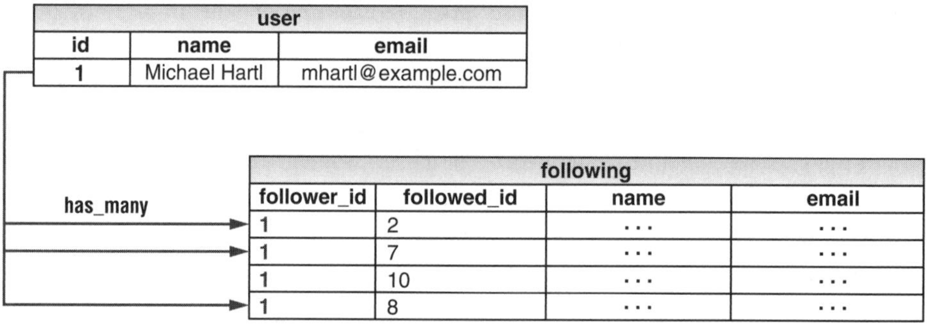

user		
id	name	email
1	Michael Hartl	mhartl@example.com

has_many

following			
follower_id	followed_id	name	email
1	2	. . .	. . .
1	7	. . .	. . .
1	10	. . .	. . .
1	8	. . .	. . .

Figure 12.6   A naïve implementation of user following.

The problem with the data model in Figure 12.6 is that it is terribly redundant: each row contains not only each followed user's id, but all their other information as well—all of which is *already* in the **users** table. Even worse, to model user *followers* we would need a separate **followers** table. Finally, this data model is a maintainability nightmare, since each time a user changed (say) his name, we would need to update not just the user's record in the **users** table but also *every row containing that user* in both the **following** and **followers** tables.

The problem here is that we are missing an underlying abstraction. One way to find the proper abstraction is to consider how we might implement *following* in a web application. Recall from Section 6.3.3 that the REST architecture involves *resources* that are created and destroyed. This leads us to ask two questions: When a user follows another user, what is being created? When a user *un*follows another user, what is being destroyed?

Upon reflection, we see that in these cases the application should either create or destroy a *relationship* (or *connection*[3]) between two users. A user then **has_many :relationships**, and has many **following** (or **followers**) *through* those relationships. Indeed, Figure 12.6 already contains most of the implementation: since each followed user is uniquely identified by **followed_id**, we could convert **following** to a **relationships** table, omit the user details, and use **followed_id** to retrieve the followed user from the **users** table. Moreover, by considering *reverse* relationships, we could use the **follower_id** column to extract an array of user's followers.

To make a **following** array of users, it would be possible to pull out an array of **followed_id** attributes and then find the user for each one. As you might expect, though, Rails has a way to make this procedure more convenient; the relevant technique is known as **has_many :through**.[4] As we will see in Section 12.1.4, Rails allows us to say that a user is following many users *through* the relationships table, using the succinct code

```
has_many :following, :through => :relationships, :source => "followed_id"
```

This code automatically populates **user.following** with an array of followed users. A diagram of the data model appears in Figure 12.7.

---

3. Unfortunately, Rails uses **connection** for a database connection, so introducing a Connection model leads to some rather subtle bugs. (I learned this the hard way when developing Insoshi.)

4. Indeed, this construction is so characteristic of Rails that well-known Rails programmer Josh Susser used it as the name of his geek blog.

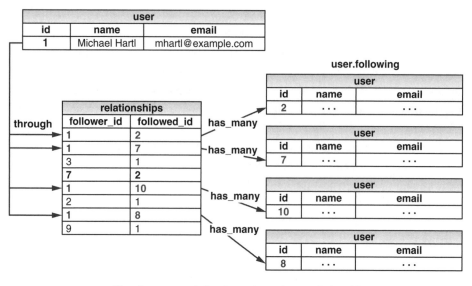

User has_many :following, :through => :relationships,
:source => "followed_id"

Figure 12.7 A model of user following through an intermediate Relationship model.

To get started with the implementation, we first generate a Relationship model as follows:

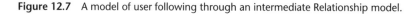

```
$ rails generate model Relationship follower_id:integer followed_id:integer
```

Since we will be finding relationships by **follower_id** and by **followed_id**, we should add an index on each column for efficiency, as shown in Listing 12.1.

Listing 12.1 Adding indices on the **follower_id** and **followed_id** columns.
db/migrate/<timestamp>_create_relationships.rb

```
class CreateRelationships < ActiveRecord::Migration
  def self.up
    create_table :relationships do |t|
      t.integer :follower_id
      t.integer :followed_id

      t.timestamps
    end
```

```
    add_index :relationships, :follower_id
    add_index :relationships, :followed_id
  end

  def self.down
    drop_table :relationships
  end
end
```

We then migrate the database and prepare the test database as usual:

```
$ rake db:migrate
$ rake db:test:prepare
```

The result is the Relationship data model shown in Figure 12.8.

As with any new model, before moving on, we should define the model's accessible attributes. In the case of the Relationship model, the **followed_id** should be accessible, since users will create relationships through the web, but the **follower_id** attribute should not be accessible; otherwise, malicious users could force other users to follow them. The result appears in Listing 12.2.

Listing 12.2 Making a relationship's **followed_id** (but *not* **follower_id**) accessible.
app/models/relationship.rb

```
class Relationship < ActiveRecord::Base
  attr_accessible :followed_id
end
```

relationships	
id	integer
follower_id	integer
followed_id	integer
created_at	datetime
updated_at	datetime

Figure 12.8   The Relationship data model.

12.1.2 User/Relationship Associations

Before implementing following and followers, we first need to establish the association between users and relationships. A user **has_many** relationships, and—since relationships involve *two* users—a relationship **belongs_to** both a follower and a followed user.

As with microposts in Section 11.1.2, we will create new relationships using the user association, with code such as

```
user.relationships.create(:followed_id => ...)
```

We start with a test, shown in Listing 12.3, which builds an **@relationships** instance variable (used below) and makes sure that it can be saved using **save!**. As with **create!**, the **save!** method raises an exception if the save fails; compare this to the use of **create!** in Listing 11.4.

Listing 12.3 Testing Relationship creation with **save!**.
spec/models/relationship_spec.rb

```
require 'spec_helper'

describe Relationship do

  before(:each) do
    @follower = Factory(:user)
    @followed = Factory(:user, :email => Factory.next(:email))

    @relationship = @follower.relationships.build(:followed_id => @followed.id)
  end

  it "should create a new instance given valid attributes" do
    @relationship.save!
  end
end
```

We should also test the User model for a **relationships** attribute, as shown in Listing 12.4.

Listing 12.4 Testing for the **user.relationships** attribute.
spec/models/user_spec.rb

```
describe User do
  .
  .
  .
```

```
describe "relationships" do

  before(:each) do
    @user = User.create!(@attr)
    @followed = Factory(:user)
  end

  it "should have a relationships method" do
    @user.should respond_to(:relationships)
  end
end
end
```

At this point you might expect application code as in Section 11.1.2, and it's similar, but there is one critical difference: in the case of the Micropost model, we could say

```
class Micropost < ActiveRecord::Base
  belongs_to :user
  .
  .
  .
end
```

and

```
class User < ActiveRecord::Base
  has_many :microposts
  .
  .
  .
end
```

because the **microposts** table has a **user_id** attribute to identify the user (Section 11.1.1). An id used in this manner to connect two database tables is known as a *foreign key*, and when the foreign key for a User model object is **user_id**, Rails can infer the association automatically: by default, Rails expects a foreign key of the form **<class>_id**, where **<class>** is the lower-case version of the class name.[5] In the present

---

5. Technically, Rails uses the **underscore** method to convert the class name to an id. For example, **"FooBar".underscore** is **foo_bar**, so the foreign key for a **FooBar** object would be **foo_bar_id**. (Incidentally, the inverse of **underscore** is **camelize**, which converts **camel_case** to **CamelCase**.)

case, although we are still dealing with users, they are now identified with the foreign key **follower_id**, so we have to tell that to Rails, as shown in Listing 12.5.[6]

Listing 12.5 Implementing the user/relationships **has_many** association.
app/models/user.rb

```
class User < ActiveRecord::Base
  .
  .
  .
  has_many :microposts, :dependent => :destroy
  has_many :relationships, :foreign_key => "follower_id",
                           :dependent => :destroy
  .
  .
  .
end
```

(Since destroying a user should also destroy that user's relationships, we've gone ahead and added **:dependent => :destroy** to the association; writing a test for this is left as an exercise (Section 12.5).) At this point, the association tests in Listing 12.3 and Listing 12.4 should pass.

As with the Micropost model, the Relationship model has a **belongs_to** relationship with users; in this case, a relationship object belongs to both a **follower** and a **followed** user, which we test for in Listing 12.6.

Listing 12.6 Testing the user/relationships **belongs_to** association.
spec/models/relationship_spec.rb

```
describe Relationship do
  .
  .
  .
  describe "follow methods" do

    before(:each) do
      @relationship.save
    end
```

---

6. If you've noticed that **followed_id** also identifies a user, and are concerned about the asymmetric treatment of followed and follower, you're ahead of the game. We'll deal with this issue in Section 12.1.5.

```
    it "should have a follower attribute" do
      @relationship.should respond_to(:follower)
    end

    it "should have the right follower" do
      @relationship.follower.should == @follower
    end

    it "should have a followed attribute" do
      @relationship.should respond_to(:followed)
    end

    it "should have the right followed user" do
      @relationship.followed.should == @followed
    end
  end
end
```

To write the application code, we define the **belongs_to** relationship as usual. Rails infers the names of the foreign keys from the corresponding symbols (i.e., **follower_id** from **:follower**, and **followed_id** from **:followed**), but since there is neither a Followed nor a Follower model we need to supply the class name **User**. The result is shown in Listing 12.7.

Listing 12.7 Adding the **belongs_to** associations to the Relationship model.
app/models/relationship.rb

```
class Relationship < ActiveRecord::Base
  attr_accessible :followed_id

  belongs_to :follower, :class_name => "User"
  belongs_to :followed, :class_name => "User"
end
```

The **followed** association isn't actually needed until Section 12.1.5, but the parallel follower/followed structure is clearer if we implement them both at the same time.

12.1.3 Validations

Before moving on, we'll add a couple of Relationship model validations for completeness. The tests (Listing 12.8) and application code (Listing 12.9) are straightforward.

Listing 12.8 Testing the Relationship model validations.
`spec/models/relationship_spec.rb`

```
describe Relationship do
  .
  .
  .
  describe "validations" do

    it "should require a follower_id" do
      @relationship.follower_id = nil
      @relationship.should_not be_valid
    end

    it "should require a followed_id" do
      @relationship.followed_id = nil
      @relationship.should_not be_valid
    end
  end
end
```

Listing 12.9 Adding the Relationship model validations.
`app/models/relationship.rb`

```
class Relationship < ActiveRecord::Base
  attr_accessible :followed_id

  belongs_to :follower, :class_name => "User"
  belongs_to :followed, :class_name => "User"

  validates :follower_id, :presence => true
  validates :followed_id, :presence => true
end
```

12.1.4 Following

We come now to the heart of the Relationship associations: **following** and **followers**. We start with **following**, as shown Listing 12.10.

Listing 12.10 A test for the **user.following** attribute.
`spec/models/user_spec.rb`

```
describe User do
  .
  .
```

```
  .
  describe "relationships" do

    before(:each) do
      @user = User.create!(@attr)
      @followed = Factory(:user)
    end

    it "should have a relationships method" do
      @user.should respond_to(:relationships)
    end

    it "should have a following method" do
      @user.should respond_to(:following)
    end
  end
end
```

The implementation uses **has_many :through** for the first time: a user has many
following *through* relationships, as illustrated in Figure 12.7. By default, in a **has_many**
:through association Rails looks for a foreign key corresponding to the singular version
of the association; in other words, code like

```
has_many :followeds, :through => :relationships
```

would assemble an array using the **followed_id** in the **relationships** table. But,
as noted in Section 12.1.1, **user.followeds** is rather awkward; far more natural is to
treat "following" as a plural of "followed", and write instead **user.following** for the
array of followed users. Naturally, Rails allows us to override the default, in this case
using the **:source** parameter (Listing 12.11), which explicitly tells Rails that the source
of the **following** array is the set of **followed** ids.

Listing 12.11 Adding the User model **following** association with **has_many :through**.
app/models/user.rb

```
class User < ActiveRecord::Base
  .
  .
  .
  has_many :microposts, :dependent => :destroy
  has_many :relationships, :foreign_key => "follower_id",
                           :dependent => :destroy
```

```
has_many :following, :through => :relationships, :source => :followed
  .
  .
  .
end
```

To create a following relationship, we'll introduce a **follow!** utility method so that we can write **user.follow!(other_user)**.[7] We'll also add an associated **following?** boolean method to test if one user is following another.[8] The tests in Listing 12.12 show how we expect these methods to be used in practice.

Listing 12.12 Tests for some following utility methods.
spec/models/user_spec.rb

```
describe User do
  .
  .
  .
  describe "relationships" do
    .
    .
    .
    it "should have a following? method" do
      @user.should respond_to(:following?)
    end

    it "should have a follow! method" do
      @user.should respond_to(:follow!)
    end

    it "should follow another user" do
      @user.follow!(@followed)
      @user.should be_following(@followed)
    end

    it "should include the followed user in the following array" do
      @user.follow!(@followed)
```

---

7. This **follow!** method should always work, so (following the model of **create!** and **save!**) we indicate with an exclamation point that an exception will be raised on failure.

8. Once you have a lot of experience modeling a particular domain, you can often guess such utility methods in advance, and even when you can't you'll often find yourself writing them to make the tests cleaner. In this case, though, it's OK if you wouldn't have guessed them. Software development is usually an iterative process—you write code until it starts getting ugly, and then you refactor it—but for brevity the tutorial presentation is streamlined a bit.

```
      @user.following.should include(@followed)
    end
  end
end
```

Note that we have replaced the **include?** method seen in Listing 11.31 with **should include**, effectively transforming

```
@user.following.include?(@followed).should be_true
```

into the clearer and more succinct

```
@user.following.should include(@followed)
```

This example shows just how flexible the RSpec boolean convention is; even though **include** is already a Ruby keyword (used to include a module, as seen in, e.g., Listing 9.11), in this context RSpec correctly guesses that we want to test array inclusion.

In the application code, the **following?** method takes in a user, called **followed**, and checks to see if a follower with that id exists in the database; the **follow!** method calls **create!** through the **relationships** association to create the following relationship. The results appear in Listing 12.13.[9]

Listing 12.13 The **following?** and **follow!** utility methods.
app/models/user.rb

```
class User < ActiveRecord::Base
  .
  .
  .
  def self.authenticate_with_salt(id, stored_salt)
    .
    .
    .
  end

  def following?(followed)
    relationships.find_by_followed_id(followed)
  end
```

---

9. The **authenticate_with_salt** method is included simply to orient you within the User model file.

```
def follow!(followed)
  relationships.create!(:followed_id => followed.id)
end
  .
  .
  .
end
```

Note that in Listing 12.13 we have omitted the user itself, writing just

```
relationships.create!(...)
```

instead of the equivalent code

```
self.relationships.create!(...)
```

Whether to include the explicit **self** is largely a matter of taste.

Of course, users should be able to unfollow other users as well as follow them, which leads to the somewhat predictable **unfollow!** method, as shown in Listing 12.14.[10]

Listing 12.14 A test for unfollowing a user.
spec/models/user_spec.rb

```
describe User do
  .
  .
  .
  describe "relationships" do
    .
    .
    .
    it "should have an unfollow! method" do
      @followed.should respond_to(:unfollow!)
    end

    it "should unfollow a user" do
      @user.follow!(@followed)
```

---

10. The **unfollow!** method *doesn't* raise an exception on failure—in fact, I don't even know how Rails indicates a failed destroy—but we use an exclamation point to maintain the **follow!**/**unfollow!** symmetry.

```
      @user.unfollow!(@followed)
      @user.should_not be_following(@followed)
    end
  end
end
```

The code for **unfollow!** is straightforward: just find the relationship by followed id and destroy it (Listing 12.15).[11]

Listing 12.15 Unfollowing a user by destroying a user relationship.
app/models/user.rb

```
class User < ActiveRecord::Base
  .
  .
  .
  def following?(followed)
    relationships.find_by_followed_id(followed)
  end

  def follow!(followed)
    relationships.create!(:followed_id => followed.id)
  end

  def unfollow!(followed)
    relationships.find_by_followed_id(followed).destroy
  end
  .
  .
  .
end
```

12.1.5 Followers

The final piece of the relationships puzzle is to add a **user.followers** method to go with **user.following**. You may have noticed from Figure 12.7 that all the information needed to extract an array of followers is already present in the **relationships** table. Indeed, the technique is exactly the same as for user following, with the roles of

---

11. You might notice that sometimes we access **id** explicitly, as in **followed.id**, and sometimes we just use **followed**. I am ashamed to admit that my usual algorithm for telling when to leave it off is to see if it works without **.id**, and then add **.id** if it breaks.

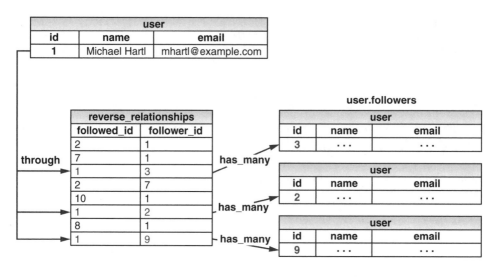

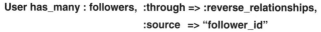

User has_many : followers, :through => :reverse_relationships,
:source => "follower_id"

Figure 12.9   A model for user followers using a reverse Relationship model. (full size)

`follower_id` and `followed_id` reversed. This suggests that, if we could some-how arrange for a `reverse_relationships` table with those two columns reversed (Figure 12.9), we could implement `user.followers` with little effort.

We begin with the tests, having faith that the magic of Rails will come to the rescue (Listing 12.16).

Listing 12.16 Testing for reverse relationships.
spec/models/user_spec.rb

```
describe User do
  .
  .
  .
  describe "relationships" do
    .
    .
    .
    it "should have a reverse_relationships method" do
      @user.should respond_to(:reverse_relationships)
    end

    it "should have a followers method" do
```

```
      @user.should respond_to(:followers)
    end

    it "should include the follower in the followers array" do
      @user.follow!(@followed)
      @followed.followers.should include(@user)
    end
  end
end
```

As you probably suspect, we will not be making a whole database table just to hold reverse relationships. Instead, we will exploit the underlying symmetry between followers and following to simulate a **reverse_relationships** table by passing **followed_id** as the primary key. In other words, where the **relationships** association uses the **follower_id** foreign key,

```
has_many :relationships, :foreign_key => "follower_id"
```

the **reverse_relationships** association uses **followed_id**:

```
has_many :reverse_relationships, :foreign_key => "followed_id"
```

The **followers** association then gets built through the reverse relationships, as shown in Listing 12.17.

Listing 12.17 Implementing **user.followers** using reverse relationships.
app/models/user.rb

```
class User < ActiveRecord::Base
  .
  .
  .
  has_many :reverse_relationships, :foreign_key => "followed_id",
                                   :class_name => "Relationship",
                                   :dependent => :destroy
  has_many :followers, :through => :reverse_relationships, :source => :follower
  .
  .
  .
end
```

(As with Listing 12.5, the test for **dependent :destroy** is left as an exercise (Section 12.5).) Note that we actually have to include the *class* name for this association, i.e.,

```
has_many :reverse_relationships, :foreign_key => "followed_id",
                                 :class_name => "Relationship"
```

because otherwise Rails will look for a **ReverseRelationship** class, which doesn't exist.

It's also worth noting that we could actually omit the **:source** key in this case, using simply

```
has_many :followers, :through => :reverse_relationships
```

since Rails will automatically look for the foreign key **follower_id** in this case. I've kept the **:source** key to emphasize the parallel structure with the **has_many :following** association, but you are free to leave it out.

With the code in Listing 12.17, the following/follower associations are complete, and all the tests should pass. This section has placed rather heavy demands on your data modeling skills, and it's fine if it takes a while to soak in. In fact, one of the best ways to understand the associations is to use them in the web interface, as seen in the next section.

12.2 A Web Interface for Following and Followers

In the introduction to this chapter, we saw a preview of the page flow for user following. In this section, we will implement the basic interface and following/unfollowing functionality shown in those mockups. We will also make separate pages to show the user following and followers arrays. In Section 12.3, we'll complete our sample application by adding the user's status feed.

12.2.1 Sample Following Data

As in previous chapters, we will find it convenient to use the sample data Rake task to fill the database with sample relationships. This will allow us to design the look and feel of the web pages first, deferring the back-end functionality until later in this section.

When we last left the sample data populator in Listing 11.20, it was getting rather cluttered, so we begin by defining separate methods to make users and microposts, and then add sample relationship data using a new **make_relationships** method. The results are shown in Listing 12.18.

Listing 12.18 Adding following/follower relationships to the sample data.
lib/tasks/sample_data.rake

```
require 'faker'

namespace :db do
  desc "Fill database with sample data"
  task :populate => :environment do
    Rake::Task['db:reset'].invoke
    make_users
    make_microposts
    make_relationships
  end
end

def make_users
  admin = User.create!(:name => "Example User",
                       :email => "example@railstutorial.org",
                       :password => "foobar",
                       :password_confirmation => "foobar")
  admin.toggle!(:admin)
  99.times do |n|
    name  = Faker::Name.name
    email = "example-#{n+1}@railstutorial.org"
    password  = "password"
    User.create!(:name => name,
                 :email => email,
                 :password => password,
                 :password_confirmation => password)
  end
end

def make_microposts
  User.all(:limit => 6).each do |user|
    50.times do
      content = Faker::Lorem.sentence(5)
      user.microposts.create!(:content => content)
    end
  end
end

def make_relationships
  users = User.all
```

```
user    = users.first
following = users[1..50]
followers = users[3..40]
following.each { |followed| user.follow!(followed) }
followers.each { |follower| follower.follow!(user) }
end
```

Here the sample relationships are created using the code

```
def make_relationships
  users = User.all
  user  = users.first
  following = users[1..50]
  followers = users[3..40]
  following.each { |followed| user.follow!(followed) }
  followers.each { |follower| follower.follow!(user) }
end
```

We somewhat arbitrarily arrange for the first user to follow the next 50 users, and then have users with ids 4 through 41 follow that user back. The resulting relationships will be sufficient for developing the application interface.

To execute the code in Listing 12.18, populate the database as usual:

```
$ rake db:populate
```

12.2.2   Stats and a Follow Form

Now that our sample users have both following and followers arrays, we need to update the profile pages and home pages to reflect this. We'll start by making a partial to display the following and follower statistics on the profile and home pages, as mocked up in Figure 12.1 and Figure 12.5. The result will be displays of the number following and the number of followers, together with links to their dedicated display pages. We'll next add a follow/unfollow form, and then make dedicated pages for showing user following and followers.

A close-up of the stats area, taken from the mockup in Figure 12.1, appears in Figure 12.10. These stats consist of a count of the number of users the current user is following and that user's number of followers, each of which should be a link to its respective dedicated display page. In Chapter 5, we stubbed out such links with the

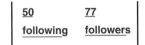

Figure 12.10   A mockup of the stats partial.

dummy text `'#'`, but that was before we had much experience with routes. This time, although we'll defer the actual pages to Section 12.2.3, we'll make the routes now, as seen in Listing 12.19. This code uses the **:member** method inside a **resources** *block*, which we haven't seen before, but see if you can guess what it does.

Listing 12.19   Adding **following** and **followers** actions to the Users controller.
config/routes.rb

```
SampleApp::Application.routes.draw do
  resources :users do
    member do
      get :following, :followers
    end
  end
  .
  .
  .
end
```

You might suspect that the URLs for user following and followers will look like /users/1/following and /users/1/followers, and that is exactly what the code in Listing 12.19 does. Since both pages will be showing data, we use **get** to arrange for the URLs to respond to GET requests (as required by the REST convention for such pages), and the **member** method means that the routes respond to URLs containing the user id. (The other possibility, **collection**, works without the id, so that

```
resources :users do
  collection do
    get :tigers
  end
end
```

would respond to the URL /users/tigers—presumably to display all the tigers in our application. For more details on such routing options, see the Rails Guides article on

Table 12.1 RESTful routes provided by the custom rules in resource in Listing 12.19

HTTP Request	URL	Action	Named route
GET	/users/1/following	**following**	**following_user_path(1)**
GET	/users/1/followers	**followers**	**followers_user_path(1)**

"Rails Routing from the Outside In".) A table of the routes generated by Listing 12.19 appears in Table 12.1; note the named routes for the following and followers pages, which we'll put to use momentarily.

   With the routes defined, we are now in a position to make tests for the stats partial. (We could have written the tests first, but the named routes would have been hard to motivate without the updated routes file.) We could write tests for the user profile page, since the stats partial will appear there, but it will also appear on the Home page, and this is a nice opportunity to refactor the Home page tests to take into account users signing in. The result appears in Listing 12.20.

Listing 12.20 Testing the following/follower statistics on the Home page.
spec/controllers/pages_controller_spec.rb

```
describe PagesController do
  render_views

  before(:each) do
    @base_title = "Ruby on Rails Tutorial Sample App"
  end
  .
  .
  .
  describe "GET 'home'" do

    describe "when not signed in" do

      before(:each) do
        get :home
      end

      it "should be successful" do
        response.should be_success
      end

      it "should have the right title" do
        response.should have_selector("title",
                                      :content => "#{@base_title} | Home")
```

```
      end
    end

  describe "when signed in" do

    before(:each) do
      @user = test_sign_in(Factory(:user))
      other_user = Factory(:user, :email => Factory.next(:email))
      other_user.follow!(@user)
    end

    it "should have the right follower/following counts" do
      get :home
      response.should have_selector("a", :href => following_user_path(@user),
                                         :content => "0 following")
      response.should have_selector("a", :href => followers_user_path(@user),
                                         :content => "1 follower")
    end
  end
 end
end
```

The core of this test is the expectation that the following and follower counts appear on the page, together with the right URLs:

```
response.should have_selector("a", :href => following_user_path(@user),
                                   :content => "0 following")
response.should have_selector("a", :href => followers_user_path(@user),
                                   :content => "1 follower")
```

Here we have used the named routes shown in Table 12.1 to verify that the links have the right URLs.

The application code for the stats partial is just a table inside a div, as shown in Listing 12.21.

Listing 12.21 A partial for displaying follower stats.
app/views/shared/_stats.html.erb

```erb
<% @user ||= current_user %>
<div class="stats">
  <table summary="User stats">
    <tr>
```

```
<td>
  <a href="<%= following_user_path(@user) %>">
    <span id="following" class="stat">
      <%= @user.following.count %> following
    </span>
  </a>
</td>
<td>
  <a href="<%= followers_user_path(@user) %>">
    <span id="followers" class="stat">
      <%= pluralize(@user.followers.count, "follower") %>
    </span>
  </a>
</td>
    </tr>
  </table>
</div>
```

Here the user following and follower counts are calculated through the associations using

```
@user.following.count
```

and

```
@user.followers.count
```

Compare these to the microposts count from Listing 11.16, where we wrote

```
@user.microposts.count
```

to count the microposts.

Since we will be including the stats on both the user show pages and the home page, the first line of Listing 12.21 picks the right one using

```
<% @user ||= current_user %>
```

As discussed in Box 9.4, this does nothing when **@user** is not **nil** (as on a profile page), but when it is (as on the Home page) it sets **@user** to the current user.

One final detail worth noting is the presence of CSS ids on some elements, as in

```
<span id="following" class="stat">
...
</span>
```

This is for the benefit of the Ajax implementation in Section 12.2.5, which accesses elements on the page using their unique ids.

With the partial in hand, including the stats on the Home page is easy, as shown in Listing 12.22. (This also gets the test in Listing 12.20 to pass.) The result appears in Figure 12.11.

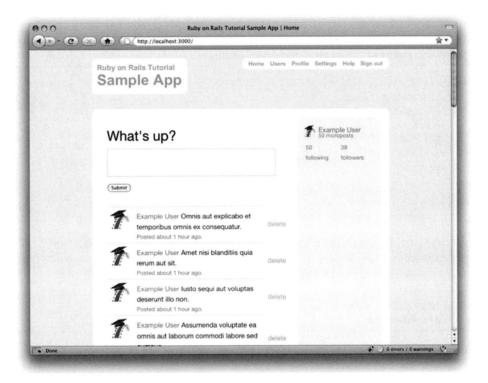

Figure 12.11 The Home page (/) with follow stats.

Listing 12.22 Adding follower stats to the Home page.
`app/views/pages/home.html.erb`

```
<% if signed_in? %>
      .
      .
      .
        <%= render 'shared/user_info' %>
        <%= render 'shared/stats' %>
      </td>
    </tr>
  </table>
<% else %>
  .
  .
  .
<% end %>
```

We'll render the stats partial on the profile page in a moment, but first let's make a partial for the follow/unfollow button, as shown in Listing 12.23.

Listing 12.23 A partial for a follow/unfollow form.
`app/views/users/_follow_form.html.erb`

```
<% unless current_user?(@user) %>
  <div id="follow_form">
  <% if current_user.following?(@user) %>
    <%= render 'unfollow' %>
  <% else %>
    <%= render 'follow' %>
  <% end %>
  </div>
<% end %>
```

This does nothing but defer the real work to **follow** and **unfollow** partials, which need a new routes file with rules for the Relationships resource, which follows the Microposts resource example (Listing 11.21), as seen in Listing 12.24.

Listing 12.24 Adding the routes for user relationships.
`config/routes.rb`

```
SampleApp::Application.routes.draw do
  .
  .
  .
```

```
resources :sessions,      :only => [:new, :create, :destroy]
resources :microposts,    :only => [:create, :destroy]
resources :relationships, :only => [:create, :destroy]
  .
  .
  .
```

end

The follow/unfollow partials themselves are shown in Listing 12.25 and Listing 12.26.

Listing 12.25 A form for following a user.
app/views/users/_follow.html.erb

```
<%= form_for current_user.relationships.
                          build(:followed_id => @user.id) do |f| %>
  <div><%= f.hidden_field :followed_id %></div>
  <div class="actions"><%= f.submit "Follow" %></div>
<% end %>
```

Listing 12.26 A form for unfollowing a user.
app/views/users/_unfollow.html.erb

```
<%= form_for current_user.relationships.find_by_followed_id(@user),
            :html => { :method => :delete } do |f| %>
  <div class="actions"><%= f.submit "Unfollow" %></div>
<% end %>
```

These two forms both use **form_for** to manipulate a Relationship model object; the main difference between the two is that Listing 12.25 builds a *new* relationship, whereas Listing 12.26 finds the existing relationship. Naturally, the former sends a POST request to the Relationships controller to **create** a relationship, while the latter sends a DELETE request to **destroy** a relationship. (We'll write these actions in Section 12.2.4.) Finally, you'll note that the follow/unfollow form doesn't have any content other than the button, but it still needs to send the **followed_id**, which we accomplish with **hidden_field**; this produces HTML of the form

```
<input id="relationship_followed_id" name="relationship[followed_id]"
type="hidden" value="3" />
```

which puts the relevant information on the page without displaying it in the browser.

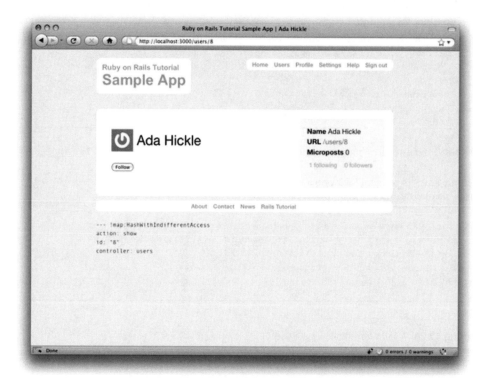

Figure 12.12   A user profile with a follow button (`/users/8`).

We can now include the follow form and the following statistics on the user profile page simply by rendering the partials, as shown in Listing 12.27. Profiles with follow and unfollow buttons, respectively, appear in Figure 12.12 and Figure 12.13.

Listing 12.27   Adding the follow form and follower stats to the user profile page.
`app/views/users/show.html.erb`

```
<table class="profile" summary="Profile information">
  <tr>
    <td class="main">
      <h1>
        <%= gravatar_for @user %>
        <%= @user.name %>
      </h1>
      <%= render 'follow_form' if signed_in? %>
      .
      .
```

```
    .
  </td>
  <td class="sidebar round">
    <strong>Name</strong> <%= @user.name %><br />
    <strong>URL</strong> <%= link_to user_path(@user), @user %><br />
    <strong>Microposts</strong> <%= @user.microposts.count %>
    <%= render 'shared/stats' %>
  </td>
 </tr>
</table>
```

We'll get these buttons working soon enough—in fact, we'll do it two ways, the standard way (Section 12.2.4) and using Ajax (Section 12.2.5)—but first we'll finish the HTML interface by making the following and followers pages.

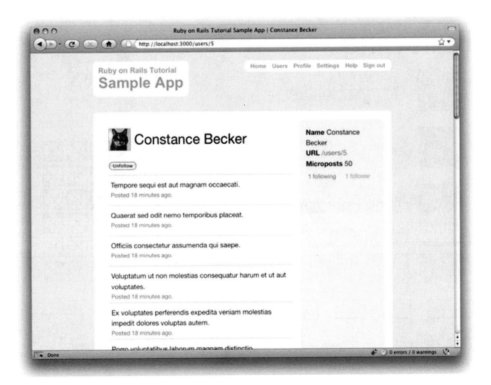

Figure 12.13   A user profile with an unfollow button (`/users/6`).

12.2.3 Following and Followers Pages

Pages to display user following and followers will resemble a hybrid of the user profile page and the user index page (Section 10.3.1), with a sidebar of user information (including the following stats) and a table of users. In addition, we'll include a raster of user profile image links in the sidebar. Mockups matching these requirements appear in Figure 12.14 (following) and Figure 12.15 (followers).

Our first step is to get the following and followers links to work. We'll follow Twitter's lead and have both pages to require user signin. For signed-in users, the pages

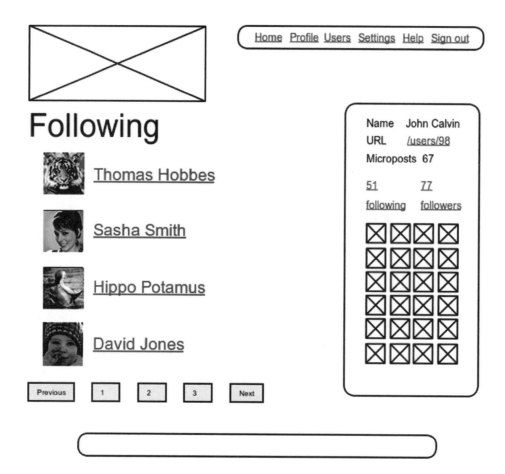

Figure 12.14 A mockup of the user following page.

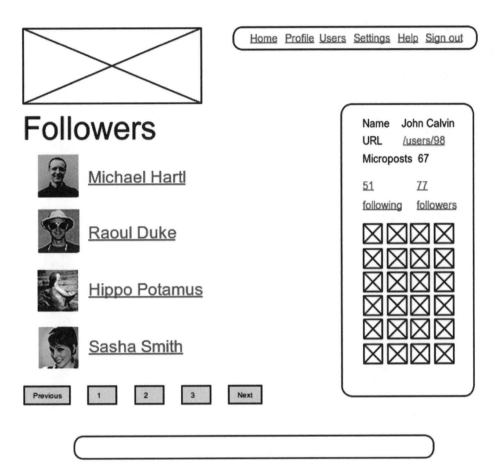

Figure 12.15   A mockup of the user followers page.

should have links for following and followers, respectively. Listing 12.28 expresses these expectations in code.[12]

Listing 12.28   Test for the **following** and **followers** actions.
spec/controllers/users_controller_spec.rb

```
describe UsersController do
  .
  .
```

---

12. Everything in Listing 12.28 has been covered elsewhere in this tutorial, so this is a good exercise in reading code.

```ruby
describe "follow pages" do

  describe "when not signed in" do

    it "should protect 'following'" do
      get :following, :id => 1
      response.should redirect_to(signin_path)
    end

    it "should protect 'followers'" do
      get :followers, :id => 1
      response.should redirect_to(signin_path)
    end
  end

  describe "when signed in" do

    before(:each) do
      @user = test_sign_in(Factory(:user))
      @other_user = Factory(:user, :email => Factory.next(:email))
      @user.follow!(@other_user)
    end

    it "should show user following" do
      get :following, :id => @user
      response.should have_selector("a", :href => user_path(@other_user),
                                         :content => @other_user.name)
    end

    it "should show user followers" do
      get :followers, :id => @other_user
      response.should have_selector("a", :href => user_path(@user),
                                         :content => @user.name)
    end
  end
 end
end
```

The only tricky part of the implementation is realizing that we need to add two new actions to the Users controller; based on the routes defined in Listing 12.19, we need to call them **following** and **followers**. Each action needs to set a title, find the user, retrieve either **@user.following** or **@user.followers** (in paginated form), and then render the page. The result appears in Listing 12.29.

Listing 12.29 The **following** and **followers** actions.
`app/controllers/users_controller.rb`

```ruby
class UsersController < ApplicationController
  before_filter :authenticate, :except => [:show, :new, :create]
    .
    .
    .
  def following
    @title = "Following"
    @user = User.find(params[:id])
    @users = @user.following.paginate(:page => params[:page])
    render 'show_follow'
  end

  def followers
    @title = "Followers"
    @user = User.find(params[:id])
    @users = @user.followers.paginate(:page => params[:page])
    render 'show_follow'
  end
    .
    .
    .
end
```

Note here that both actions make an *explicit* call to **render**, in this case rendering a view called **show_follow**, which we must create. The reason for the common view is that the ERb is nearly identical for the two cases, and Listing 12.30 covers them both.

Listing 12.30 The **show_follow** view used to render following and followers.
`app/views/users/show_follow.html.erb`

```erb
<table summary="Information about following/followers">
  <tr>
    <td class="main">
      <h1><%= @title %></h1>

      <% unless @users.empty? %>
        <ul class="users">
          <%= render @users %>
        </ul>
        <%= will_paginate @users %>
      <% end %>
    </td>
```

```
<td class="sidebar round">
  <strong>Name</strong> <%= @user.name %><br />
  <strong>URL</strong> <%= link_to user_path(@user), @user %><br />
  <strong>Microposts</strong> <%= @user.microposts.count %>
  <%= render 'shared/stats' %>
  <% unless @users.empty? %>
    <% @users.each do |user| %>
      <%= link_to gravatar_for(user, :size => 30), user %>
    <% end %>
  <% end %>
</td>
</tr>
</table>
```

There's a second detail in Listing 12.29 worth noting: in order to protect the pages for following and followers from unauthorized access, we have changed the authentication before filter to use :except instead of :only. So far in this tutorial, we have used :only to indicate which actions the filter gets applied to; with the addition of the new protected actions, the balance has shifted, and it is simpler to indicate which actions *shouldn't* be filtered. We do this with the :except option to the authenticate before filter:

```
before_filter :authenticate, :except => [:show, :new, :create]
```

With that, the tests should now be passing, and the pages should render as shown in Figure 12.16 (following) and Figure 12.17 (followers).

You might note that, even with the common show_followers partial, the following and followers actions still have a lot of duplication. Moreover, the show_followers partial itself shares common features with the user show page. Section 12.5 includes exercises to eliminate these sources of duplication.

12.2.4 A Working Follow Button the Standard Way

Now that our views are in order, it's time to get the follow/unfollow buttons working. Since following a user creates a relationship, and unfollowing a user destroys a relationship, this involves writing the create and destroy actions for the Relationships controller. Naturally, both actions should be protected; for signed-in users, we will use the follow! and unfollow! utility methods defined in Section 12.1.4 to create and destroy the relevant relationships. These requirements lead to the tests in Listing 12.31.

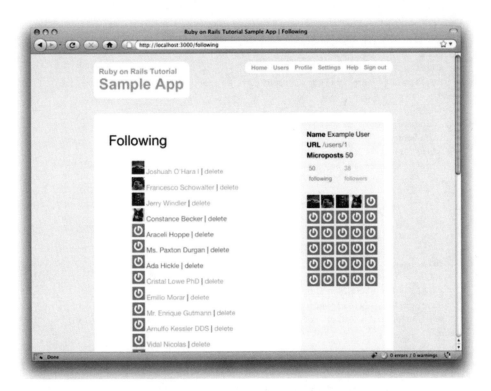

Figure 12.16   Showing the users being followed by the current user.

Listing 12.31   Tests for the Relationships controller actions.
`spec/controllers/relationships_controller_spec.rb`

```ruby
require 'spec_helper'

describe RelationshipsController do

  describe "access control" do

    it "should require signin for create" do
      post :create
      response.should redirect_to(signin_path)
    end

    it "should require signin for destroy" do
      delete :destroy, :id => 1
      response.should redirect_to(signin_path)
    end
  end
end
```

```
describe "POST 'create'" do

  before(:each) do
    @user = test_sign_in(Factory(:user))
    @followed = Factory(:user, :email => Factory.next(:email))
  end

  it "should create a relationship" do
    lambda do
      post :create, :relationship => { :followed_id => @followed }
      response.should be_redirect
    end.should change(Relationship, :count).by(1)
  end
end

describe "DELETE 'destroy'" do

  before(:each) do
    @user = test_sign_in(Factory(:user))
    @followed = Factory(:user, :email => Factory.next(:email))
    @user.follow!(@followed)
    @relationship = @user.relationships.find_by_followed_id(@followed)
  end

  it "should destroy a relationship" do
    lambda do
      delete :destroy, :id => @relationship
      response.should be_redirect
    end.should change(Relationship, :count).by(-1)
  end
end
end
```

Note here how

```
:relationship => { :followed_id => @followed }
```

simulates the submission of the form with hidden field given by

```
<%= f.hidden_field :followed_id %>
```

The controller code needed to get these tests to pass is remarkably concise: we just retrieve the user followed or to be followed, and then follow or unfollow the user using the relevant utility method. The full implementation appears in Listing 12.32.

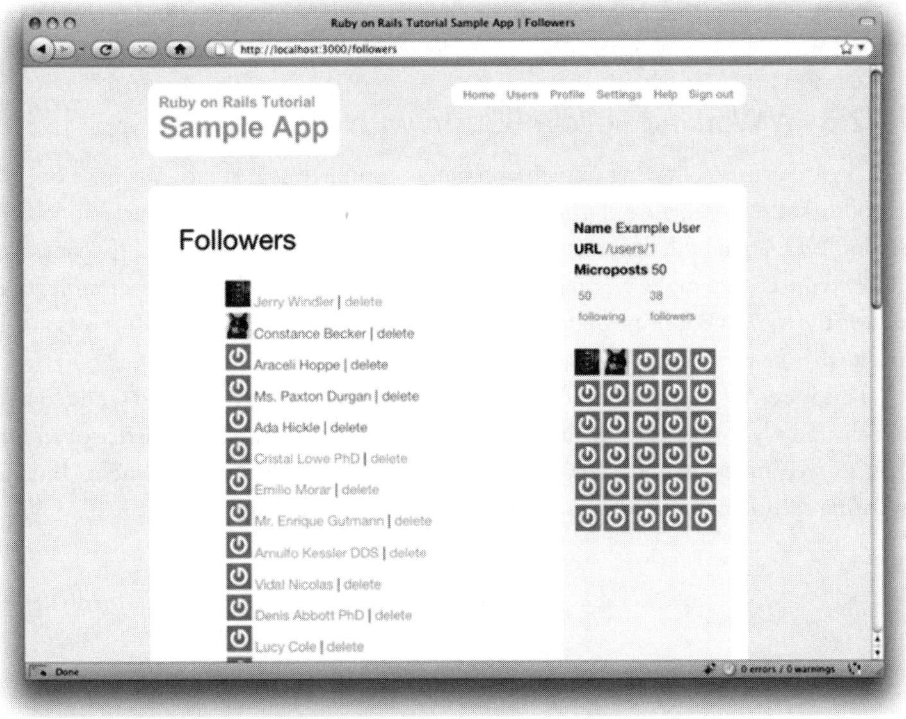

Figure 12.17   Showing the current user's followers.

Listing 12.32   The Relationships controller.
app/controllers/relationships_controller.rb

```ruby
class RelationshipsController < ApplicationController
  before_filter :authenticate

  def create
    @user = User.find(params[:relationship][:followed_id])
    current_user.follow!(@user)
    redirect_to @user
  end

  def destroy
    @user = Relationship.find(params[:id]).followed
    current_user.unfollow!(@user)
    redirect_to @user
  end
end
```

With that, the core follow/unfollow functionality is complete, and any user can follow (or unfollow) any other user.

12.2.5 A Working Follow Button with Ajax

Although our user following implementation is complete as it stands, we have one bit of polish left to add before starting work on the status feed. You may have noticed in Section 12.2.4 that both the **create** and **destroy** actions in the Relationships controller simply redirect *back* to the original profile. In other words, a user starts on a profile page, follows the user, and is immediately redirected back to the original page. It is reasonable to ask why the user needs to leave that page at all.

This is exactly the problem solved by *Ajax*, which allows web pages to send requests asynchronously to the server without leaving the page.[13] Because the practice of adding Ajax to web forms is quite common, Rails makes Ajax easy to implement. Indeed, updating the follow/unfollow form partials is trivial: just change

```
form_for
```

to

```
form_for ..., :remote => true
```

and Rails automagically uses Ajax.[14] The updated partials appear in Listing 12.33 and Listing 12.34.

Listing 12.33 A form for following a user using Ajax.
app/views/users/_follow.html.erb

```erb
<%= form_for current_user.relationships.build(:followed_id => @user.id),
              :remote => true do |f| %>
  <div><%= f.hidden_field :followed_id %></div>
  <div class="actions"><%= f.submit "Follow" %></div>
<% end %>
```

---

13. Because it is nominally an acronym for *asynchronous JavaScript and XML*, Ajax is sometimes misspelled "AJAX", even though the original Ajax article spells it as "Ajax" throughout.

14. This only works if JavaScript is enabled in the browser, but it degrades gracefully, working exactly as in Section 12.2.4 if JavaScript is disabled.

Listing 12.34   A form for unfollowing a user using Ajax.
`app/views/users/_unfollow.html.erb`

```erb
<%= form_for current_user.relationships.find_by_followed_id(@user),
              :html => { :method => :delete },
              :remote => true do |f| %>
  <div class="actions"><%= f.submit "Unfollow" %></div>
<% end %>
```

The actual HTML generated by this ERb isn't particularly relevant, but you might be curious, so here's a peek:

```html
<form action="/relationships/117" class="edit_relationship" data-remote="true"
    id="edit_relationship_117" method="post">
    .
    .
    .
</form>
```

This sets the variable **`data-remote="true"`** inside the form tag, which tells Rails to allow the form to be handled by JavaScript. By using a simple HTML property instead of inserting the full JavaScript code (as in previous versions of Rails), Rails 3 follows the philosophy of *unobtrusive JavaScript.*

Having updated the form, we now need to arrange for the Relationships controller to respond to Ajax requests. We'll start with a couple simple tests. Testing Ajax is quite tricky, and doing it thoroughly is a large subject in its own right, but we can get started with the code in Listing 12.35. This uses the **`xhr`** method (for "XmlHttpRequest") to issue an Ajax request; compare to the **`get`**, **`post`**, **`put`**, and **`delete`** methods used in previous tests. We then verify that the **`create`** and **`destroy`** actions do the correct things when hit with an Ajax request. (To write more thorough test suites for Ajax-heavy applications, take a look at Selenium and Watir.)

Listing 12.35   Tests for the Relationships controller responses to Ajax requests.
`spec/controllers/relationships_controller_spec.rb`

```ruby
describe RelationshipsController do
  .
  .
  .
  describe "POST 'create'" do
```

```
      .
      .
      .
    it "should create a relationship using Ajax" do
      lambda do
        xhr :post, :create, :relationship => { :followed_id => @followed }
        response.should be_success
      end.should change(Relationship, :count).by(1)
    end
  end

  describe "DELETE 'destroy'" do
      .
      .
      .
    it "should destroy a relationship using Ajax" do
      lambda do
        xhr :delete, :destroy, :id => @relationship
        response.should be_success
      end.should change(Relationship, :count).by(-1)
    end
  end
end
```

As implied by the tests, the application code uses the same **create** and **delete** actions to respond to the Ajax requests that it uses to respond to ordinary POST and DELETE HTTP requests. All we need to do is respond to a normal HTTP request with a redirect (as in Section 12.2.4) and respond to an Ajax request with JavaScript.[15] The controller code appears as in Listing 12.36. (See Section 12.5 for an exercise showing an even more compact way to accomplish the same thing.)

Listing 12.36 Responding to Ajax requests in the Relationships controller.
app/controllers/relationships_controller.rb

```
class RelationshipsController < ApplicationController
  before_filter :authenticate

  def create
    @user = User.find(params[:relationship][:followed_id])
    current_user.follow!(@user)
    respond_to do |format|
```

---

15. At this point you will have to include the default Prototype JavaScript Library into your Rails application as in Listing 10.39 if you have not done so already.

```
      format.html { redirect_to @user }
      format.js
    end
  end

  def destroy
    @user = Relationship.find(params[:id]).followed
    current_user.unfollow!(@user)
    respond_to do |format|
      format.html { redirect_to @user }
      format.js
    end
  end
end
```

This code uses **respond_to** to take the appropriate action depending on the kind of request.[16] The syntax is potentially confusing, and it's important to understand that in

```
respond_to do |format|
  format.html { redirect_to @user }
  format.js
end
```

only *one* of the lines gets executed (based on the nature of the request).

In the case of an Ajax request, Rails automatically calls a *JavaScript Embedded Ruby* (**.js.erb**) file with the same name as the action, i.e., **create.js.erb** or **destroy.js.erb**. As you might guess, the files allow us to mix JavaScript and Embedded Ruby to perform actions on the current page. It is these files that we need to create and edit in order to update the user profile page upon being followed or unfollowed.

Inside a JS-ERb file, Rails automatically provides the Prototype JavaScript helpers to manipulate the page using the Document Object Model (DOM). Prototype provides a large number of methods for manipulating the DOM, but here we will need only two. First, we will need to know about the Prototype dollar-sign syntax to access a DOM element based in its unique CSS id. For example, to manipulate the **follow_form** element, we will use the syntax

```
$("follow_form")
```

16. There is no relationship between this **respond_to** and the **respond_to** used in the RSpec examples.

(Recall from Listing 12.23 that this is a **div** that wraps the form, not the form itself.) The second method we'll need is **update**, which updates the HTML inside the relevant element with the contents of its argument. For example, to replace the entire follow form with the string **"foobar"**, we would write

```
$("follow_form").update("foobar")
```

Unlike plain JavaScript files, JS-ERb files also allow the use of Embedded Ruby, which we apply in the **create.js.erb** file to update the follow form with the **unfollow** partial (which is what should show after a successful following) and update the follower count. The result is shown in Listing 12.37.

Listing 12.37 The JavaScript Embedded Ruby to create a following relationship.
app/views/relationships/create.js.erb

```
$("follow_form").update("<%= escape_javascript(render('users/unfollow')) %>")
$("followers").update('<%= "#{@user.followers.count} followers" %>')
```

The **destroy.js.erb** file is analogous (Listing 12.38). Note that, as in Listing 12.37, we must use the **escape_javascript** to escape out the result when inserting HTML.

Listing 12.38 The Ruby JavaScript (RJS) to destroy a following relationship.
app/views/relationships/destroy.js.erb

```
$("follow_form").update("<%= escape_javascript(render('users/follow')) %>")
$("followers").update('<%= "#{@user.followers.count} followers" %>')
```

With that, you should navigate to a user profile page and verify that you can follow and unfollow without a page refresh.

Using Ajax in Rails is a large and fast-moving subject, so we've only been able to scratch the surface here, but (as with the rest of the material in this tutorial) our treatment gives you a good foundation for more advanced resources. It's especially worth noting that, in addition to Prototype, the JavaScript framework jQuery has gotten a lot of traction in the Rails community. Implementing the Ajax functions from this section using jQuery is left as an exercise; see Section 12.5.

12.3 The Status Feed

We come now to the pinnacle of our sample application: the status feed. Appropriately, this section contains some of the most advanced material in the entire tutorial. Making the status feed involves assembling an array of the microposts from the users being followed by the current user, along with the current user's own microposts. To accomplish this feat, we will need some fairly advanced Rails, Ruby, and even SQL programming techniques.

Because of the heavy lifting ahead, it's especially important to have a sense of where we're going. A mockup of the final user status feed, which builds on the proto-feed from Section 11.3.3, appears in Figure 12.18.

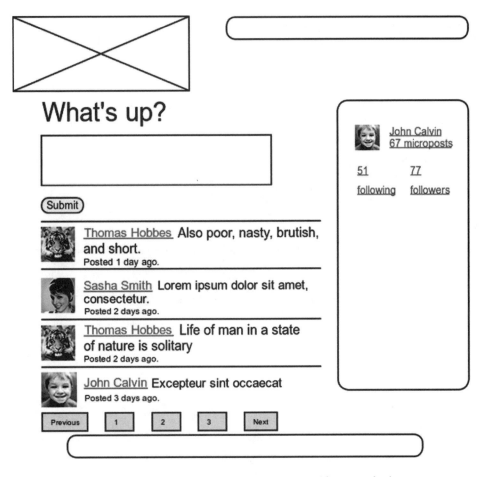

Figure 12.18 A mockup of a user's Home page with a status feed.

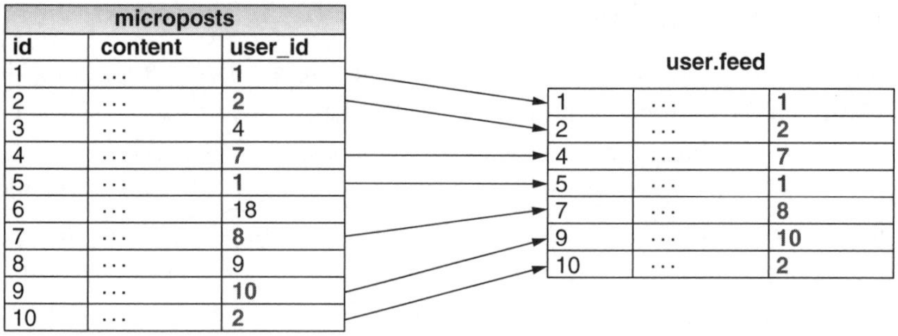

Figure 12.19   The feed for a user (id 1) following users 2, 7, 8, and 10.

12.3.1 Motivation and Strategy

The basic idea behind the feed is simple. Figure 12.19 shows a sample **microposts** database table and the resulting feed. The purpose of a feed is to pull out the microposts whose user ids correspond to the users being followed by the current user (and the current user itself), as indicated by the arrows in the diagram.

Since we need a way to find all the microposts from users followed by a given user, we'll plan on implementing a method called **from_users_followed_by**, which we will use as follows:

```
Micropost.from_users_followed_by(user)
```

Although we don't yet know how to implement it, we can already write tests for **from_users_followed_by**, as seen in Listing 12.39.

Listing 12.39   Tests for **Micropost.from_users_followed_by**.
spec/models/micropost_spec.rb

```
describe Micropost do
  .
  .
  .
  describe "from_users_followed_by" do

    before(:each) do
      @other_user = Factory(:user, :email => Factory.next(:email))
      @third_user = Factory(:user, :email => Factory.next(:email))

      @user_post  = @user.microposts.create!(:content => "foo")
```

```
      @other_post = @other_user.microposts.create!(:content => "bar")
      @third_post = @third_user.microposts.create!(:content => "baz")

      @user.follow!(@other_user)
    end

    it "should have a from_users_followed_by class method" do
      Micropost.should respond_to(:from_users_followed_by)
    end

    it "should include the followed user's microposts" do
      Micropost.from_users_followed_by(@user).should include(@other_post)
    end

    it "should include the user's own microposts" do
      Micropost.from_users_followed_by(@user).should include(@user_post)
    end

    it "should not include an unfollowed user's microposts" do
      Micropost.from_users_followed_by(@user).should_not include(@third_post)
    end
  end
end
```

The key here is building the associations in the **before(:each)** block and then checking all three requirements: microposts for followed users and the user itself are included, but a post from an *unfollowed* user is not.

The feed itself lives in the User model (Section 11.3.3), so we should add an additional test to the User model specs from Listing 11.31, as shown in Listing 12.40. (Note that we've switched here from using **include?**, as seen in Listing 11.31, to the more compact **include** convention introduced in Listing 12.12.)

Listing 12.40 The final tests for the status feed.
spec/models/user_spec.rb

```
describe User do
  .
  .
  .
  describe "micropost associations" do
    .
    .
    .
    describe "status feed" do
```

```
    it "should have a feed" do
      @user.should respond_to(:feed)
    end

    it "should include the user's microposts" do
      @user.feed.should include(@mp1)
      @user.feed.should include(@mp2)
    end

    it "should not include a different user's microposts" do
      mp3 = Factory(:micropost,
                    :user => Factory(:user, :email => Factory.next(:email)))
      @user.feed.should_not include(mp3)
    end

    it "should include the microposts of followed users" do
      followed = Factory(:user, :email => Factory.next(:email))
      mp3 = Factory(:micropost, :user => followed)
      @user.follow!(followed)
      @user.feed.should include(mp3)
    end
  end
    .
    .
    .

  end
end
```

Implementing the feed will be easy; we will simply defer to **Micropost.from_-users_followed_by**, as shown in Listing 12.41.

Listing 12.41 Adding the completed feed to the User model.
app/models/user.rb

```
class User < ActiveRecord::Base
  .
  .
  .
  def feed
    Micropost.from_users_followed_by(self)
  end
  .
  .
  .
end
```

12.3.2 A First Feed Implementation

Now it's time to implement **Micropost.from_users_followed_by**, which for simplicity we'll just refer to as "the feed". Since the final result is rather intricate, we'll build up to the final feed implementation by introducing one piece at a time.

The first step is to think of the kind of query we'll need. What we want to do is select from the **microposts** table all the microposts with ids corresponding to the users being followed by a given user (or the user itself). We might write this schematically as follows:

```
SELECT * FROM microposts
WHERE user_id IN (<list of ids>) OR user_id = <user id>
```

In writing this code, we've guessed that SQL supports an **IN** keyword that allows us to test for set inclusion. (Happily, it does.)

Recall from the proto-feed in Section 11.3.3 that Active Record uses the **where** method to accomplish the kind of select shown above, as illustrated in Listing 11.32. There, our select was very simple; we just picked out all the microposts with user id corresponding to the current user:

```
Micropost.where("user_id = ?", id)
```

Here, we expect it to be more complicated, something like

```
where("user_id in (#{followed_ids}) OR user_id = ?", user)
```

(Here we've used the Rails convention of **user** instead of **user.id** in the condition; Rails automatically uses the **id**. We've also omitted the leading **Micropost.** since we expect this method to live in the Micropost model itself.)

We see from these conditions that we'll need an array of ids that a given user is following (or something equivalent). One way to do this is to use Ruby's **map** method, available on any "enumerable" object, i.e., any object (such as an Array or a Hash) that consists of a collection of elements.[17] We saw an example of this method in Section 4.3.2; it works like this:

---

17. The main requirement is that enumerable objects must implement an **each** method to iterate through the collection.

```
$ rails console
>> [1, 2, 3, 4].map { |i| i.to_s }
=> ["1", "2", "3", "4"]
```

Situations like the one illustrated above, where the same method (e.g., `to_s`) gets called on each element, are common enough that there's a shorthand notation using an *ampersand* `&` and a symbol corresponding to the method:[18]

```
>> [1, 2, 3, 4].map(&:to_s)
=> ["1", "2", "3", "4"]
```

We can use this notation to construct the necessary array of followed user ids by calling `id` on each element in `user.following`. For example, for the first user in the database this array appears as follows:

```
>> User.first.following.map(&:id)
=> [4, 5, 6, 7, 8, 9, 10, 11, 12, 13, 14, 15, 16, 17, 18, 19, 20, 21, 22, 23,
24, 25, 26, 27, 28, 29, 30, 31, 32, 33, 34, 35, 36, 37, 38, 39, 40, 41, 42,
43, 44, 45, 46, 47, 48, 49, 50, 51]
```

At this point, you might guess that code like

```
Micropost.from_users_followed_by(user)
```

will involve a class method in the `Micropost` class (a construction last seen in the `User` class in Section 7.12). A proposed implementation along these lines appears in Listing 12.42.

---

18. This notation actually started as an extension Rails made to the core Ruby language; it was so useful that it has now been incorporated into Ruby itself. How cool is that?

Listing 12.42 A first cut at the **from_users_followed_by** method.
app/models/micropost.rb

```ruby
class Micropost < ActiveRecord::Base
  .
  .
  .
  def self.from_users_followed_by(user)
    followed_ids = user.following.map(&:id).join(", ")
    where("user_id IN (#{followed_ids}) OR user_id = ?", user)
  end
end
```

Although the discussion leading up to Listing 12.42 was couched in hypothetical terms, it actually works! In fact, it might be good enough for most practical purposes. But it's not the final implementation; see if you can make a guess about why not before moving on to the next section. (*Hint:* What if a user is following 5000 other users?)

12.3.3   Scopes, Subselects, and a Lambda

As hinted at in the last section, the feed implementation in Section 12.3.2 doesn't scale well when the number of microposts in the feed is large, as would likely happen if a user were following, say, 5000 other users. In this section, we'll reimplement the status feed in a way that scales better with the number of followed users.

There are a couple of problems with the code in Section 12.3.2. First, the expression

```ruby
followed_ids = user.following.map(&:id).join(", ")
```

pulls *all* the followed users into memory, and creates an array the full length of the following list. Since the condition in Listing 12.42 actually just checks inclusion in a set, there must be a more efficient way to do this, and indeed SQL is optimized for just such set operations. Second, the method in Listing 12.42 always pulls out *all* the microposts and sticks them into a Ruby array. Although these microposts are paginated in the view (Listing 11.33), the array is still full-sized.[19] What we really want is honest pagination that only pulls out 30 elements at a time.

---

19. Calling **paginate** on an **Array** object converts it into a **WillPaginate::Collection** object, but that doesn't help us much since the entire array has already been created in memory.

The solution to both problems involves converting the feed from a class method to a *scope*, which is a Rails method for restricting database selects based on certain conditions. For example, to arrange for a method to select all the administrative users in our application, we could add a scope to the User model as follows:

```
class User < ActiveRecord::Base
  .
  .
  .
  scope :admin, where(:admin => true)
  .
  .
  .
end
```

As a result of this scope, the code

```
User.admin
```

would return an array of all the site admins.

The main reason scopes are better than plain class methods is that they can be *chained* with other methods, so that, for example,

```
User.admin.paginate(:page => 1)
```

actually paginates the admins in the database; if (for some odd reason) the site has 100 administrators, the code above will still only pull out the first 30.

The scope for the feed is a bit more complex than the one illustrated above: it needs an *argument*, namely, the user whose feed we need to generate. We can do this with an *anonymous function*, or **lambda** (discussed in Section 8.4.2), as shown in Listing 12.43.[20]

---

20. A function bundled with a piece of data (a user, in this case) is known as a *closure*, which we encountered briefly in the discussion of blocks in Section 4.3.2.

Listing 12.43 Improving **`from_users_followed_by`**.
`app/models/micropost.rb`

```ruby
class Micropost < ActiveRecord::Base
  .
  .
  .
  default_scope :order => 'microposts.created_at DESC'

  # Return microposts from the users being followed by the given user.
  scope :from_users_followed_by, lambda { |user| followed_by(user) }

  private

    # Return an SQL condition for users followed by the given user.
    # We include the user's own id as well.
    def self.followed_by(user)
      followed_ids = user.following.map(&:id).join(", ")
      where("user_id IN (#{followed_ids}) OR user_id = :user_id",
            { :user_id => user })
    end
end
```

Since the conditions on the **`from_users_followed_by`** scope are rather long, we have
defined an auxiliary function to handle it:

```ruby
def self.followed_by(user)
  followed_ids = user.following.map(&:id).join(", ")
  where("user_id IN (#{followed_ids}) OR user_id = :user_id",
        { :user_id => user })
end
```

As preparation for the next step, we have replaced

```ruby
where("... OR user_id = ?", user)
```

with the equivalent

```ruby
where("... OR user_id = :user_id", { :user_id => user })
```

The question mark syntax is fine, but when we want the *same* variable inserted in more than one place, the second syntax, using a hash, is more convenient.

> ### Box 12.1 Percent paren
>
> The code in this section uses the Ruby percent-parentheses construction, as in
>
> ```
> %(SELECT followed_id FROM relationships
>   WHERE follower_id = :user_id)
> ```
>
> You can think of `%()` as equivalent to double quotes, but capable of making multiline strings. (If you need a way to produce a multiline string without leading whitespace, do a Google search for "ruby here document".) Since `%()` supports string interpolation, it is particularly useful when you need to put double quotes in a string and interpolate at the same time. For example, the code
>
> ```
> >> foo = "bar"
> >> puts %(The variable "foo" is equal to "#{foo}".)
> ```
>
> produces
>
> ```
> The variable "foo" is equal to "bar".
> ```
>
> To get the same output with double-quoted strings, you would need to escape the internal double quotes with backslashes, as in
>
> ```
> >> "The variable \"foo\" is equal to \"#{foo}\"."
> ```
>
> In this case, the `%()` syntax is more convenient since is gets you the same result without the explicit escaping.

The above discussion implies that we will be adding a *second* occurrence of **user_id** in the SQL query, and indeed this is the case. We can replace the Ruby code

```
followed_ids = user.following.map(&:id).join(", ")
```

with the SQL snippet

```
followed_ids = %(SELECT followed_id FROM relationships
                 WHERE follower_id = :user_id)
```

(See Box 12.1 for an explanation of the `%()` syntax.) This code contains an SQL *subselect*, and internally the entire select for user 1 would look something like this:

```
SELECT * FROM microposts
WHERE user_id IN (SELECT followed_id FROM relationships
                  WHERE follower_id = 1)
    OR user_id = 1
```

This subselect arranges for all the set logic to be pushed into the database, which is more efficient.[21]

With this foundation, we are ready for the final feed implementation, as seen in Listing 12.44.

Listing 12.44 The final implementation of **`from_users_followed_by`**. **`app/models/micropost.rb`**

```
class Micropost < ActiveRecord::Base
  .
  .
  .
  default_scope :order => 'microposts.created_at DESC'

  # Return microposts from the users being followed by the given user.
  scope :from_users_followed_by, lambda { |user| followed_by(user) }

  private

    # Return an SQL condition for users followed by the given user.
    # We include the user's own id as well.
    def self.followed_by(user)
      followed_ids = %(SELECT followed_id FROM relationships
                       WHERE follower_id = :user_id)
      where("user_id IN (#{followed_ids}) OR user_id = :user_id",
            { :user_id => user })
    end
end
```

21. For a more advanced way to create the necessary subselect, see the blog post "Hacking a subselect in ActiveRecord".

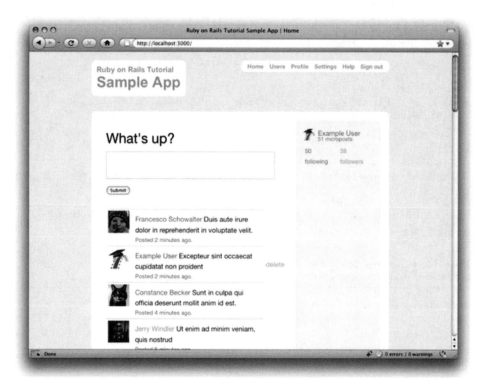

Figure 12.20   The Home page with a working status feed.

This code has a formidable combination of Rails, Ruby, and SQL, but it does the job, and does it well.[22]

12.3.4   The New Status Feed

With the code in Listing 12.44, our status feed is complete. As a reminder, the code for the Home page appears in Listing 12.45; this code creates a paginated feed of the relevant microposts for use in the view, as seen in Figure 12.20.[23] Note that the **paginate**

---

22. Of course, even the subselect won't scale forever. For bigger sites, you would probably need to generate the feed asynchronously using a background job. Such scaling subtleties are beyond the scope of this tutorial, but the Scaling Rails screencasts are a good place to start.

23. In order make a prettier feed for Figure 12.20, I've added a few extra microposts by hand using the Rails console.

method actually reaches all the way into the Micropost model method in Listing 12.44, arranging to pull out only 30 microposts at a time from the database.[24]

Listing 12.45   The **home** action with a paginated feed.
app/controllers/pages_controller.rb

```ruby
class PagesController < ApplicationController

  def home
    @title = "Home"
    if signed_in?
      @micropost = Micropost.new
      @feed_items = current_user.feed.paginate(:page => params[:page])
    end
  end
  .
  .
  .
end
```

12.4   Conclusion

With the addition of the status feed, we've finished the core sample application for *Ruby on Rails Tutorial*. This application includes examples of all the major features of Rails, including models, views, controllers, templates, partials, filters, validations, callbacks, **has_many**/**belongs_to** and **has_many :through** associations, security, testing, and deployment. Despite this impressive list, there is still much to learn about Rails. As a first step in this process, this section contains some suggested extensions to the core application, as well as suggestions for further learning.

Before moving on to tackle any of the application extensions, it's a good idea to merge in your changes and deploy the application:

```
$ git add .
$ git commit -am "Added user following"
$ git checkout master
$ git merge following-users
$ git push heroku
$ heroku rake db:migrate
```

---

24. You can verify this by examining the SQL statements in the development server log file. (The Rails Tutorial screencasts will cover such subtleties in more depth.)

12.4.1   Extensions to the Sample Application

The proposed extensions in this section are mostly inspired either by general features common to web applications, such as password reminders and email confirmation, or features specific to our type of sample application, such as search, replies, and messaging. Implementing one or more of these application extensions will help you make the transition from following a tutorial to writing original applications of your own.

Don't be surprised if it's tough going at first; the blank slate of a new feature can be quite intimidating. To help get you started, I can give two pieces of general advice. First, before adding any feature to a Rails application, take a look at the Railscasts archive to see if Ryan Bates has already covered the subject.[25] If he has, watching the relevant Railscast first will often save you a ton of time. Second, always do extensive Google searches on your proposed feature to find relevant blog posts and tutorials. Web application development is hard, and it helps to learn from the experience (and mistakes) of others.

Many of the following features are quite challenging, and I have given some hints about the tools you might need to implement them. Even with hints, they are *much* more difficult than the book's end-of-chapter exercises, so don't be discouraged if you can't solve them without considerable effort. Due to time constraints, I am not available for one-on-one assistance, but if there is sufficient interest I might release standalone article/screencast bundles on some of these extensions in the future; go to the main Rails Tutorial website at http://www.railstutorial.org/ and subscribe to the news feed to get the latest updates.

Replies

Twitter allows users to make "@replies", which are microposts whose first characters are the user's login preceded by the @ sign. These posts only appear in the feed of the user in question or users following that user. Implement a simplified version of this, restricting @replies to appear only in the feeds of the recipient and the sender. This might involve adding an **in_reply_to** column in the **microposts** table and an extra **including_replies** scope to the Micropost model.

Since our application lacks unique user logins, you will also have to decide on a way to represent users. One option is to use a combination of the id and the name, such as

---

25. My only reservation about Railscasts is that they often omit the tests. This is probably necessary to keep the episodes nice and short, but you could get the wrong idea about the importance of tests. Once you've watched the relevant Railscast to get a basic idea of how to proceed, I suggest writing the new feature using test-driven development.

@1-michael-hartl. Another is to *add* a unique username to the signup process and then use it in @replies.

Messaging

Twitter supports direct (private) messaging by prefixing a micropost with the letter "d". Implement this feature for the sample application. The solution will probably involve a Message model and a regular expression match on new microposts.

Follower Notifications

Implement a feature to send each user an email notification when they gain a new follower. Then make the notification optional, so that users can opt out if desired.

Among other things, adding this feature requires learning how to send mail with Rails. There is a Railscast on sending email to get you started. Beware that the main Rails library for sending email, Action Mailer, has gotten a major overhaul in Rails 3, as seen in the Railscast on Action Mailer in Rails 3.

Password Reminders

Currently, if our application's users forget their passwords, they have no way to retrieve them. Because of the one-way secure password hashing in Chapter 7, our application can't email the user's password, but it can send a link to a reset form. Introduce a **PasswordReminders** resource to implement this feature. For each reset, you should create a unique token and email it to the user. Visiting a URL with the token should then allow them to reset their password to a value of their choice.

Signup Confirmation

Apart from an email regular expression, the sample application currently has no way to verify the validity of a user's email address. Add an email address verification step to confirm a user's signup. The new feature should create users in an inactive state, email the user an activation URL, and then change the user to an active state when the URL gets hit. You might want to read up on state machines in Rails to help you with the inactive/active transition.

RSS Feed

For each user, implement an RSS feed for their microposts. Then implement an RSS feed for their status feed, optionally restricting access to that feed using an authentication scheme. The Railscast on generating RSS feeds will help get you started.

REST API

Many web sites expose an Application Programmer Interface (API) so that third-party applications can get, post, put, and delete the application's resources. Implement such a REST API for the sample application. The solution will involve adding `respond_to` blocks (Section 12.2.5) to many of the application's controller actions; these should respond to requests for XML. Be careful about security; the API should only be accessible to authorized users.

Search

Currently, there is no way for users to find each other than paging through the user index or viewing the feeds of other users. Implement a search feature to remedy this. Then add another search feature for microposts. The Railscast on simple search forms will help get you started. If you deploy using a shared host or a dedicated server, I suggest using Thinking Sphinx (following the Railscast on Thinking Sphinx). If you deploy on Heroku, you should follow the Heroku full text search instructions.

12.4.2 Guide to Further Resources

There are a wealth of Rails resources in stores and on the web—indeed, the supply is so rich that it can be overwhelming, and it can be hard to know where to start. By now you *know* where to start—with this book, of course. And if you've gotten this far, you're ready for almost anything else out there. Here are some suggestions:

- *Ruby on Rails Tutorial* screencasts: I will be preparing a full-length screencast course based on this book. In addition to covering all the material in the book, the screencasts will be filled with tips, tricks, and the kind of see-how-it's-done demos that are hard to capture in print. They will be available on the Ruby on Rails Tutorial website, through Safari Books Online, and through InformIT. Visit the Rails Tutorial website at http://www.railstutorial.org/ and sign up for the news feed to find out when the screencasts will be released.[26]

- Railscasts: It's hard to overemphasize what a great resource the Railscasts are. I suggest starting by visiting the Railscasts episode archive and clicking on subjects that catch your eye.

---

26. Of course, by the time you read this, they might already be out! In that case, you should definitely buy them.

- Scaling Rails: One topic we've hardly covered in the *Ruby on Rails Tutorial* book is performance, optimization, and scaling. Luckily, most sites will never run into serious scaling issues, and using anything beyond plain Rails is probably premature optimization. If you do run into performance issues, the Scaling Rails series from Gregg Pollack of Envy Labs is a great place to start. I also recommend investigating the site monitoring applications Scout and New Relic.[27] And, as you might suspect by now, there are Railscasts on many scaling subjects, including profiling, caching, and background jobs.

- Ruby and Rails books: As mentioned in Chapter 1, I recommend *Beginning Ruby* by Peter Cooper, *The Well-Grounded Rubyist* by David A. Black, and *The Ruby Way* by Hal Fulton for further Ruby learning, and *The Rails 3 Way* by Obie Fernandez for more about Rails.

- PeepCode: I mentioned several commercial screencasters in Chapter 1, but the only one I have extensive experience with is PeepCode. The screencasts at PeepCode are consistently high-quality, and I warmly recommend them.

12.5 Exercises

1. Add tests for `dependent :destroy` in the Relationship model (Listing 12.5 and Listing 12.17) by following the example in Listing 11.11.
2. The `respond_to` method seen in Listing 12.36 can actually be hoisted out of the actions into the Relationships controller itself, and the `respond_to` blocks can be replaced with a Rails method called `respond_with`. Prove that the resulting code, shown in Listing 12.46, is correct by verifying that the test suite still passes. (For details on this method, do a Google search on "rails respond_with".)
3. The `following` and `followers` actions in Listing 12.29 still have considerable duplication. Verify that the `show_follow` method in Listing 12.47 eliminates this duplication. (See if you can infer what the `send` method does, as in, e.g., `@user.send(:following)`.)
4. Refactor Listing 12.30 by adding partials for the code common to the following/followers pages, the Home page, and the user show page.
5. Following the model in Listing 12.20, write tests for the stats on the profile page.

---

27. In addition to being a clever phrase—*new relic* being a contradiction in terms—New Relic is also an anagram for the name of the company's founder, Lew Cirne.

6. Write an integration test for following and unfollowing a user.
7. Rewrite the Ajax methods from Section 12.2.5 using jQuery in place of Prototype. *Hint:* You might want to read the jQuery section of Mikel Lindsaar's blog post about jQuery, RSpec, and Rails 3.

Listing 12.46   A compact refactoring of Listing 12.36.

```ruby
class RelationshipsController < ApplicationController
  before_filter :authenticate

  respond_to :html, :js

  def create
    @user = User.find(params[:relationship][:followed_id])
    current_user.follow!(@user)
    respond_with @user
  end

  def destroy
    @user = Relationship.find(params[:id]).followed
    current_user.unfollow!(@user)
    respond_with @user
  end
end
```

Listing 12.47   Refactored **following** and **followers** actions.
app/controllers/users_controller.rb

```ruby
class UsersController < ApplicationController
  .
  .
  .
  def following
    show_follow(:following)
  end

  def followers
    show_follow(:followers)
  end

  def show_follow(action)
    @title = action.to_s.capitalize
    @user = User.find(params[:id])
```

```
  @users = @user.send(action).paginate(:page => params[:page])
  render 'show_follow'
end
  .
  .
  .
end
```

Index

References to figures are in italics.
References to footnotes are indicated with an " n" followed by the number of the footnote.

Addison Wesley

REGISTER

THIS PRODUCT

informit.com/register

Register the Addison-Wesley, Exam Cram, Prentice Hall, Que, and Sams products you own to unlock great benefits.

To begin the registration process, simply go to **informit.com/register** to sign in or create an account. You will then be prompted to enter the 10- or 13-digit ISBN that appears on the back cover of your product.

Registering your products can unlock the following benefits:

- Access to supplemental content, including bonus chapters, source code, or project files.
- A coupon to be used on your next purchase.

Registration benefits vary by product. Benefits will be listed on your Account page under Registered Products.

About InformIT — **THE TRUSTED TECHNOLOGY LEARNING SOURCE**

INFORMIT IS HOME TO THE LEADING TECHNOLOGY PUBLISHING IMPRINTS Addison-Wesley Professional, Cisco Press, Exam Cram, IBM Press, Prentice Hall Professional, Que, and Sams. Here you will gain access to quality and trusted content and resources from the authors, creators, innovators, and leaders of technology. Whether you're looking for a book on a new technology, a helpful article, timely newsletters, or access to the Safari Books Online digital library, InformIT has a solution for you.

informIT.com

THE TRUSTED TECHNOLOGY LEARNING SOURCE

Addison-Wesley | Cisco Press | Exam Cram
IBM Press | Que | Prentice Hall | Sams

SAFARI BOOKS ONLINE